T0367680

MONEY AND THE ECONOMY

MONEY AND THE ECONOMY

Apostolos Serletis
University of Calgary, Canada

World Scientific

NEW JERSEY · LONDON · SINGAPORE · BEIJING · SHANGHAI · HONG KONG · TAIPEI · CHENNAI

Published by

World Scientific Publishing Co. Pte. Ltd.

5 Toh Tuck Link, Singapore 596224

USA office: 27 Warren Street, Suite 401-402, Hackensack, NJ 07601

UK office: 57 Shelton Street, Covent Garden, London WC2H 9HE

Library of Congress Cataloging-in-Publication Data
Serletis, Apostolos.
 Money and the economy / Apostolos Serletis.
  p. cm.
 Includes bibliographical references and index.
 ISBN-13 978-981-256-818-2
 ISBN-10 981-256-818-2
 1. Demand for money. 2. Money supply. 3. Monetary policy. I. Title.

 HG226.5.S473 2006
 332.4--dc22

                                            2006045700

British Library Cataloguing-in-Publication Data
A catalogue record for this book is available from the British Library.

Printed in Singapore

Contents

Foreword   xi

Editor's Introduction   xvii

Part 1: The Theory of Monetary Aggregation   1

1 Consumer Theory and the Demand for Money   3
   1.1 Introduction 3
   1.2 The Definition of Money 6
   1.3 The Microeconomic Theory of a Monetary Economy 11
      1.3.1 The Aggregation-Theoretic Approach 14
      1.3.2 Index Number Theory 16
      1.3.3 The Links Between Aggregation and Index Number
             Theory 18
      1.3.4 Understanding the Divisia Aggregates 23
      1.3.5 The Optimal Level of Subaggregation 24
   1.4 Econometric Considerations 26
      1.4.1 Approximating the Subutility Function 28
      1.4.2 An Example 30
   1.5 Empirical Dimensions 31
      1.5.1 Empirical Comparisons of Index Numbers 31
      1.5.2 Results for the Demand System Approach 34
   1.6 Extensions 37
   1.7 Conclusions 42

Part 2: Money, Prices and Income   44

2 Nominal Stylized Facts of U.S. Business Cycles   47
   2.1 Introduction 47

2.2 Methodology 49
2.3 Hodrick-Prescott Stylized Facts 50
2.4 Robustness 53
2.5 Conclusion 54

3 Money, Prices, and Income 57
3.1 Introduction 57
3.2 The Money-Measurement Theme 59
3.3 Granger-Sims Causality Tests 61
3.4 Statistical Issues 62
3.5 Money, Prices, and Income 66
3.6 Conclusion 70

4 Monetary Aggregation and the Neutrality of Money 72
4.1 Introduction 72
4.2 The Many Kinds of Money 73
4.3 Univariate Time-Series Properties 75
4.4 Long-run Neutrality and Superneutrality 78
4.5 Stability Analysis 90
4.6 Conclusion 91

Part 3: Aggregation, Inflation and Welfare 96

5 Monetary Aggregation, Inflation, and Welfare 98
5.1 Introduction 98
5.2 Theoretical Foundations 99
5.2.1 The Consumer Surplus Approach 100
5.2.2 The Compensating Variation Approach 101
5.3 The Demand for Money 103
5.4 The Empirical Evidence 107
5.5 Conclusion 108

Part 4: Chaotic Monetary Dynamics 117

6 Random Walks, Breaking Trend Functions, and Chaos 119
6.1 Searching for a Unit Root 121
6.2 Detecting Chaotic Dynamics 124
6.2.1 The Nychka et al. (1992) Estimator 125
6.2.2 Empirical Results 127
6.3 Conclusion 128

7 Chaotic Analysis of U.S. Money and Velocity Measures 131
  7.1   Introduction 131
  7.2   The Many Kinds of Money 132
  7.3   Chaos Tests 135
  7.4   Conclusion 140

Part 5: Monetary Asset Demand Systems   144

8 Monetary Asset Substitutability   147
  8.1   Introduction 147
  8.2   Theoretical Foundations 149
  8.3   Demand System Specification 152
  8.4   Stochastic Specification and Estimation 153
  8.5   Elasticities 154
  8.6   Data 154
        8.6.1   Near-Bank Liabilities 155
        8.6.2   Aggregation 155
        8.6.3   Aggregation of Components 159
        8.6.4   Data Sources and Adjustments 159
  8.7   Empirical Results Interpretation 160
  8.8   Conclusions 165

9 The Demand for Divisia M1, M2, and M3   167
  9.1   Introduction 167
  9.2   Model Specification 169
        9.2.1   The Consumer's Problem 169
        9.2.2   Preference Structure Over Monetary Assets 170
        9.2.3   Aggregator Function Specifications 171
        9.2.4   Recursive Multistage Decentralization 172
        9.2.5   Duality 174
  9.3   Demand System Specification and Data 175
        9.3.1   Functional Form 175
        9.3.2   Data 176
  9.4   Econometric Results 177
        9.4.1   Some Econometric Considerations 177
        9.4.2   Results 177
        9.4.3   The Separability Tests 182
  9.5   Summary and Concluding Remarks 184
  9.6   Appendix 187

10 Translog Flexible Functional Forms   **189**
   10.1 Introduction 189
   10.2 The Theoretical Background 191
   10.3 Demand System Specification and Data 192
      10.3.1 Functional Forms 192
      10.3.2 Data 194
   10.4 Econometric Results 194
      10.4.1 The Functional-Form Tests 196
      10.4.2 The Regularity Tests 196
      10.4.3 The Elasticities 200
   10.5 Conclusion 204

Part 6: Dynamic Asset Demand Systems   **206**

11 A Dynamic Flexible Demand System   **208**
   11.1 Introduction 208
   11.2 Theoretical Foundations 210
   11.3 Dynamic Demand System Specification 213
   11.4 Econometric Results 215
   11.5 Conclusion 226

12 Consumption Goods and Liquid Assets   **227**
   12.1 Introduction 227
   12.2 Aggregation and Subutility Functions 229
   12.3 Supernumerary Quantities 230
   12.4 Demand System Specification 232
   12.5 Estimation and Testing 233
   12.6 Empirical Results 234
   12.7 Conclusion 240

Part 7: Empirical Comparisons   **245**

13 Empirical Comparisons of Functional Forms   **247**
   13.1 Introduction 247
   13.2 The Demand Systems Approach 248
   13.3 Eight Flexible Functional Forms 250
      13.3.1 Locally Flexible Functional Forms 250
      13.3.2 Effectively Globally Regular Functional Forms . . . 252
      13.3.3 Globally Flexible Functional Forms 254
   13.4 The U.S. Consumption Data 255
   13.5 Econometric Results 257

13.6 Morishima Elasticities of Substitution 266
13.7 Forecast Results 272
13.8 Conclusions 276

14 A Semi-Nonparametric Approach   **278**
14.1 Introduction 278
14.2 The Demand for Monetary Services 280
14.3 The Data 281
14.4 The Fourier and AIM Models 282
       14.4.1 The Fourier 283
       14.4.2 The AIM 285
14.5 Computational Considerations 287
14.6 Imposing Curvature Restrictions 291
14.7 Income and Price Elasticities 293
14.8 Elasticities of Substitution 294
14.9 On Confidence Intervals 295
14.10 Conclusions 296

Consolidated References   **299**
Subject Index 321
Author Index 327

Foreword

Is Macroeconomics a Science?

In his Foreword to Barnett and Samuelson (2006), Paul Samuelson (2006) wrote:

> "I conclude with an unworthy hypothesis regarding past and present directions of economic research. Sherlock Holmes said, 'Cherchez la femme.' When asked why he robbed banks, Willie Sutton replied, 'That's where the money is.' We economists do primarily work for our peers' esteem, which figures in our own self-esteem. When post-depression Roosevelt's New Deal provided exciting job opportunities, first the junior academic faculties moved leftward. To get back ahead of their followers, subsequently the senior academic faculties shoved ahead of them. As post-Reagan, post-Thatcher electorate turned rightward, follow the money pointed, alas, in only one direction. So to speak, we eat our own cooking.

> We economists love to quote Keynes's final lines in his 1936 General Theory — for the reason that they cater so well to our vanity and self-importance. But to admit the truth, madmen in authority can self-generate their own frenzies without needing help from either defunct or avant garde economists. What establishment economists brew up is as often what the Prince and the Public are already wanting to imbibe. We guys don't stay in the best club by proffering the views of some past academic crank or academic sage."

For the benefit of those who do not meet Paul's high standards of erudition, I here provide Keynes (1936, pp. 383-384) statement, to which Paul alludes in his Foreword:

"Practical men, who believe themselves to be quite exempt from any intellectual influences, are usually the slaves of some defunct economist. Madmen in authority, who hear voices in the air, are distilling their frenzy from some academic scribbler of a few years back. I am sure that the power of vested interests is vastly exaggerated compared with the gradual encroachment of ideas ... Sooner or later, it is ideas, not vested interests, which are dangerous for good or evil."

When I showed the first draft of Paul's Foreword to some eminent economists, many reacted with shock and dismay. One replied that Paul was accusing us all of being "a bunch of whores." But the more that I thought about it, the clearer it became to me that Paul's insights in his Foreword merit serious consideration. As a result, I resisted pressures to request that his Foreword be toned down. In fact, what Paul is saying in that Foreword has relevancy to what I have experienced in my own professional experiences, and is valuable in putting this important book by Apostolos Serletis into proper context.

When I founded the Cambridge University Press journal, *Macroeconomic Dynamics*, which I edit, I needed to write a statement of purpose to appear in the first issue. The statement needed to include a definition of macroeconomics that could be used to motivate the intended focus of the journal. I defined "macroeconomics" to be "dimension reduction." The reason is clear. Macroeconomic policy cannot be implemented by reference to high dimensional models, in which there is no aggregation over goods or economic agents, or separability of structure into sectors that can be modeled independently. Indeed, dimension reduction can be accomplished in a rigorous manner using aggregation theory, separability tests, and nonlinear dynamics. But is such rigorous formalism in dimension reduction typical of most macroeconomics? I don't think so, and many microeconomists and political scientists do not think so. The dimension reduction typifying much macroeconomics is characterized by the use of untested, atheoretical oversimplifications. If the oversimplifications are contradicted by empirical evidence, then an alternative to statistical hypothesis testing is sought to avoid the embarrassment. As observed by Thomas Sargent, in his interview by Evans and Honkapohja (2005, pp. 567-568):

"Calibration is less optimistic about what your theory can accomplish, because you'd only use it, if you didn't fully trust your entire model, meaning that you think your model is partly misspecified or incompletely specified, or if you trusted someone else's model and data set more than your own. My recollection is that Bob Lucas and Ed Prescott were initially very enthusiastic about rational expectations econometrics. After all, it simply involved imposing on ourselves the same high standards we had criticized the Keynesians for failing to live up to. But after about five years of doing likelihood ratio tests on rational expectations models, I recall Bob Lucas and Ed Prescott both telling me that those tests were rejecting too many good models. The idea of calibration is to ignore some of the probabilistic implications of your model, but to retain others. Somehow, calibration was intended as a balanced response to professing that your model, though not correct, is still worthy as a vehicle for quantitative policy analysis."

As Paul Samuelson (2006) has observed, the direction that the profession takes has a strong correlation with the existing direction of thought in other academic fields and in government. The direction of causation is not always clear, but I agree with Paul that the causation often comes from outside the field of economics. This direction of causation often is particularly evident in its effects on macroeconomics, which depends for its very existence upon its policy relevance. Anyone who has worked for many decades in macroeconomics, monetary economics, and policy, has observed the frequent changes in direction, and the nontrivial correlation with the political winds that are blowing in the background. For example, when I resigned from the Federal Reserve Board staff to accept a position at the University of Texas, after 8 years in the Board's Special Studies Section, two high ranking officers of the Board's staff entered my office and threatened me with harassment by the Board's attorneys, if I ever were to become known in the press as a critic of Board policy. Having always been dedicated to high tech scientific research, rather than to visible criticism of Board policy, I could not imagine the reason for that threat, but it is not irrelevant to understanding the nature of the connection between government policy and macroeconomic research.

During the years I was at the Board, Karl Brunner and Allan Meltzer were very visible critics of Board policy through their Shadow Open Market Committee. But there was a difference in their degree of willingness to be cooperative with the Board. Allan, who got along well with the Board, was often included among the semiannual meeting of the Academic Advisors to the Board. On the other hand, Karl, who tended to be uncompromising in the nature of his policy advocacy, was banned from the Board building. In fact, the security guards at the entrances were instructed never to permit Karl to enter the building. Karl once confided to me that the rumors about the ban had done wonders for his career.

Prior to the three years of the "monetarist experiment" in the United States, the research staff of the Philadelphia Federal Reserve Bank produced a large document containing research supporting a change in policy direction — the same change in direction that subsequently was adopted by Paul Volcker during the "monetarist experiment" years. But that research at the Philadelphia Federal Reserve Bank was prior to the arrival of Paul Volcker as Chairman of the Federal Research Board. As a result, the Board Staff at the time was instructed to crush the research at the Philadelphia Federal Reserve Bank and discredit its staff. The Board Staff succeeded to the degree that almost the entire research staff of the Philadelphia Federal Reserve Bank resigned. Prior to their resignation, I was invited to the Philadelphia Federal Reserve Bank as a possible new hire, who might be able to help hold the staff together. Although I had said nothing about this to the Federal Reserve Board, on the morning that I returned from Philadelphia to the Board Staff in Washington, D.C., I was called into the office of the Director of Personnel and given an immediate raise along with instructions not to help "those bad people" in Philadelphia.

Not long thereafter, when inflation was becoming intolerable to the Carter administration in Washington, Paul Volcker was moved from the New York Federal Reserve Bank to become Board Chairman in Washington, D.C. He then instituted precisely the policies that had been advocated by the former staff at the Philadelphia Federal Reserve Bank. Chairman Volcker, knowing that his staff had been geared up to oppose precisely that approach, did not confer with his large staff before his announced policy change. Reputedly only about three staff members at the top were informed of the impending change. The rest of us learned from the newspaper the next morning. In fact the next morning, I had breakfast at the Board's cafeteria and observed the stunned looks on the faces of the staff and bewildered conversations among us over our eggs and coffee. In contrast, Carl Christ was visiting from Johns Hopkins University that day and joined us at that breakfast. He was clearly amused and pleased by what had just happened.

Over the past 50 years, the frequency of changes in the choice of policy instruments and policy designs by the world's central banks have been astonishing. There has not been a clear trend in any one direction, with reversions to some of the oldest approaches being common and frequent. Is this science, or is this politics? If unanticipated shocks to the economy were to cause unemployment to rise dramatically, would the currently spreading fashion of targeting solely inflation continue? If unanticipated shocks were to cause a return of double digit inflation, would the current emphasis on interest rates rather than on monetary service flows continue? Is it really true that monetary quantity is harder to measure than the "natural" or "neutral" interest rate needed in Taylor rules? Is the economy so simple that all that is needed to conduct monetary policy is an interest rate feedback rule, a Phillips curve, and perhaps one or two other equations? With all economic theory being nonlinear, is it reasonable to believe that estimated or calibrated models should be linear? Is it reasonable to believe that macroeconomic policy has no distribution effects, as is commonly assumed in macroeconomic models, despite the fact that most politicians advocate macroeconomic policies based precisely upon their distribution effects? If there are no such distribution effects, why is there such a strong correlation between macroeconomic policy advocacy and political party affiliation? Is it reasonable to continue to assume that monetary assets yield no own-rate of return, as assumed in many demand for money functions, despite the fact that currency and non-interest-bearing demand deposit accounts have not dominated the money supply for over a half century?

In short, as has been pointed out by Paul Samuelson (2006), we macroeconomists work within an environment of pressure and influence from our governments and societies. While few are willing to recognize or admit the existence of those pressures or the influence of those pressures on our own work, a clear understanding of trends in macroeconomic research is not possible without recognition of the influence of the intellectual, societal, and political environment within which the research is conducted.

I started out as a rocket scientist (yes, a real one), after receiving my engineering degree from MIT in 1963. I worked on the development of the F-1 booster rocket engine that got the Apollo Saturn vehicle off the ground. I worked for a firm called Rocketdyne, which had that rocket engine contract from NASA. Although I changed professional directions, when I went back for my Ph.D., I have never forgotten what real science is. The more that I think about what Paul Samuelson has written in his Foreword to Barnett and Samuelson (2006) and my experience as an economist for over 30 years, the more I recognize the depth of the insights provided by Paul in his short Foreword. A not unrelated comment is Jim Heckman's (2005) in his Minneapolis Federal Reserve Bank interview:

"In economics there's a trend now to come up with cute papers in an effort to be cited as many times as possible. All the incentives point that way, especially for young professors who seem risk-averse rather than risk-taking after they get tenure. In some quarters of our profession, the level of discussion has sunk to the level of a New Yorker article: coffee-table articles about "cute" topics, papers using "clever" instruments. The authors of these papers are usually unclear about the economic questions they address, the data used to support their conclusions and the econometrics used to justify their estimates. This is a sad development that I hope is a passing fad. Most of this work is without substance, but it makes a short-lived splash and it's easy to do. Many young economists are going for the cute and the clever at the expense of working on hard and important foundational problems."

This might all sound like "bad news" in its implications for macroeconomics as a science, and sadly is consistent with the views of many microeconomists (some of whom oppose the inclusion of macroeconomics in their academic departments). But there also is "good news." There are some hard-core scientists who work in macroeconomics and monetary economics. They do not respond to political pressures, they resist oversimplification, and they seek to advance macroeconomics in the uncompromising manner that characterizes real science. They are willing to take on the difficult problems that often are assumed away solely for the convenience of economists.

That "good news" is what this book is about. That is what Apostolos Serletis is about. This is an important book for anyone who has a serious interest in what science has to say about modern macroeconomics and monetary economics. This book emphasizes what real progress is being made to advance our entirely inadequate knowledge of the macroeconomy. For an overview of the contents, see Serletis's own introduction.

William A. Barnett
University of Kansas
January 2006

Editor's Introduction

This book contains a collection of my most important contributions in the area of monetary aggregation and flexible demand systems. It is organized and discussed in a systematic way, providing a unified perspective on the state of play in this important literature. It is a follow up to the following books:

- William A. Barnett and Apostolos Serletis (ed.). *The Theory of Monetary Aggregation*. Contributions to Economic Analysis, Amsterdam: North-Holland (2000),

- Apostolos Serletis. *The Demand for Money: Theoretical and Empirical Approaches*. Kluwer Academic (2001), 2nd edition, Springer Science (2007), and

- William A. Barnett and Jane M. Binner (ed.). *Functional Structure and Approximation in Econometrics*. Contributions to Economic Analysis, Amsterdam: North-Holland (2004).

In particular, the book focuses on the demand for money and liquid assets, building on a large body of recent literature, which Barnett (1997) calls the 'high road' literature, that takes a microeconomic- and aggregation-theoretic approach. This literature follows the innovative works by Chetty (1969), Donovan (1978), and Barnett (1980, 1983) and utilizes the flexible functional forms and demand systems approach to investigating the interrelated problems of monetary aggregation and estimation of monetary asset demand functions.

This new literature is actually an ongoing one that has only just begun to produce empirical results worthy of the effort required to understand it. The main research lies in the following areas:

- the use of microeconomic- and aggregation-theoretic foundations in the construction of monetary aggregates,

- the investigation of the cyclical behavior of money and velocity measures, the long-run neutrality and superneutrality of money, and the welfare cost of inflation,

- the use of tools from dynamical systems theory to test for nonlinear chaotic dynamics in money and velocity measures, and

- the estimation of systems of liquid asset-demand equations consistent with the theoretical regularity conditions of neoclassical microeconomic theory (positivity, monotonicity, and curvature).

In particular, the book addresses the problem of the definition (aggregation) of money and shows how the successful use in recent years of the simple representative consumer paradigm in monetary economics has opened the door to the succeeding introduction into monetary economics of the entire microfoundations, aggregation theory, and micro-econometrics literatures. It illustrates how a simultaneous-equations monetary assets structure both fits neatly into the new microeconomic- and aggregation-theoretic approach to the definition of money and also how it provides a structure that can be used to measure income and interest rate elasticities as well as the important elasticities of substitution among financial entities.

The book also contrasts the random walk behavior of money and velocity measures to nonlinear chaotic dynamics. Chaos represents a radical change of perspective in the explanation of fluctuations observed in economic time series. In this view, the fluctuations and irregularities observed in economic time series receive an endogenous explanation and are traced back to the strong nonlinear deterministic structure that can pervade the economic system. Chaos is important since evidence of chaos implies that (nonlinearity-based) prediction is possible, at least in the short run and provided that the actual generating mechanism is known exactly. Prediction, of monetary variables, of course, is valuable to monetary policy, insofar as it is short-run policy.

Finally, the book investigates the welfare cost of inflation, building on Lucas (2000) and using Bailey's (1956) consumer surplus approach as well as the compensating variation approach.

Even though this is an evolving literature, the research presented in this book supports the following conclusions:

- the simple-sum approach to monetary aggregation and log-linear money demand functions, currently used by central banks, are inappropriate for monetary policy purposes,

- the choice of monetary aggregation procedure is crucial in evaluating the welfare cost of inflation,

- most of the older monetary demand systems literature ignores the theoretical regularity conditions and hence has to be disregarded, and

- the inter-related problems of monetary aggregation and money demand will be successfully investigated in the context of flexible functional forms that satisfy theoretical regularity globally.

Of course, many unsolved problems exist in this literature. The investigation of those problems, however, is likely to be significantly useful and productive.

Apostolos Serletis

Part 1

The Theory of
Monetary Aggregation

Overview of Part 1

Apostolos Serletis

The following table contains a brief summary of the contents of the chapter in Part 1 of this book. This chapter of the book contains the economic theory, aggregation theory, and index number theory that are fundamental to the rest of the book.

The Theory of Monetary Aggregation

Chapter Number	Chapter Title	Contents
1	The Theory of Monetary Aggregation	A *Journal of Economic Literature* survey of the state of the art, with particular emphasis on the empirical results internationally.

Chapter 1:

Chapter 1 is a survey paper of the subject matter of this book. The chapter consists of a paper originally published in the *Journal of Economic Literature*. Of interest is the emphasis upon the vast accumulated quantity of international research using the approach advocated by this book. References to published sources of those results are contained in the chapter. The international research has been produced both by academic researchers and central bank economists from throughout the world.

Chapter 1

Consumer Theory and the Demand for Money

William A. Barnett, Douglas Fisher, and Apostolos Serletis[*]

1.1 Introduction

The demand for money has been at the center of the macro-policy debate ever since Keynes's *General Theory* set down the initial version of what has become the standard macroeconomic version of the theory. Over the years it has become almost a dictum that a necessary condition for money to exert a predictable influence on the economy is a stable demand function for money, as often emphasized by Milton Friedman. While 'stability' hardly means 'simplicity,' it has also become believed, rather optimistically in our view, that this self-same demand function should be linear (or linear in the logs) and should have as arguments a *small* number of variables, themselves representing significant links to spending and economic activity in the other sectors of the economy. This complete argument appears in numerous places in the literature, from basic textbooks to research monographs (see, for example, the statement in John Judd and John Scadding (1982, p. 993)).

The theoretical literature on money demand does not contain the result that a linear function of a few key variables would be expected to serve as the demand for money. In particular, there exist a large number of potential alternatives to money, the prices of which might reasonably be expected to

---
[*]Originally published in the *Journal of Economic Literature* 30 (1992), 2086–2119. Reprinted with permission.

influence the decision to hold money. Furthermore, microeconomic theory rarely produces linear demand functions for rational economic agents. Even so, linear single-equation estimates of money demand with only a few variables continue to be produced, in spite of serious doubts in the literature about their predictive performance. Stephen Goldfeld (1976) brought wide attention to the poor predictive performance of the standard function. The result was a large literature that introduced new variables and/or transformations of the old; this largely inconclusive literature is surveyed in Judd and Scadding.[1]

There is another problem with this literature, and this is that the studies of the demand for money — and the many studies of the influence of money on the economy — are based on official monetary aggregates (currently M1, M2, M3, and L) constructed by a method (simple-sum aggregation over arbitrary financial components) that does not take advantage of the results either of existing aggregation theory or of recent developments in the application of demand theory to the study of financial institutions. Part of the problem is certainly perceived in the literature: the possible influences of financial innovation and regulatory changes. How this is usually handled is that money is frequently redefined — in the sense of composing new arrangements of the component assets — in order to capture the appearance of changing characteristics of the representative monetary product. This largely unstructured approach appears not to have produced an agreed-upon monetary measure. Instead, what we have seen over time is a considerable array of what actually turn out to be temporary monetary aggregates whose existence creates both unnecessary baggage in empirical studies as well as obvious problems for monetary-policy decision makers.

More central to the objectives of this survey are problems arising from the simple-sum method of aggregation itself. There are conditions under which this approach is appropriate, as we will explain, but if the relative prices of the monetary components fluctuate over time, then neither this method nor the Hicksian approach to aggregation will produce theoretically satisfactory definitions of money. The problem is the incorrect accounting for substitution effects that these methods entail, and the result is a set of monetary aggregates that do not accurately measure the actual quantities of the monetary services that optimizing economic agents select (in the aggregate). To underscore this issue we note that the empirical work discussed and illustrated below suggests that actual fluctuations in the relative prices of the monetary products of the U.S. financial system definitely

---

[1] Separately, Thomas Cooley and Stephen LeRoy (1981) question the econometric methodology common in the literature. A key concern is whether classical statistical properties can be attributed to estimators obtained by the "grid search" approach common to many of these studies.

are sufficient to generate concern about the method of aggregation.

Until recently the existing attempts to structure the search for a stable money demand — and a satisfactory measure of moneyness — using traditional macroeconomic paradigms (e.g., Keynesian, monetarist) do not seem to have provided any very firm assistance for empirical purposes. In contrast, as this survey will make clear, there is in place a steadily growing literature that does offer a solution; this is the integrated literature on monetary aggregation and the demand-systems approach to money demand. What we propose to do here is to lay out the theory and main empirical results of this important 'microfoundations' approach to money demand. Microfoundations approaches to macro topics usually imply either disaggregated general equilibrium modelling or the use of simple forms of aggregation over goods and over economic agents, but the literature we have in mind uses aggregation theory in a way that enables the researcher to test for the existence of both the postulated aggregate good and the aggregate economic agent while estimating the demand for (aggregate) financial services. Success here could well provide significant gains in both the study of monetary phenomena and in the application of monetary policy.

This new literature is actually an ongoing one that has only just begun to produce empirical results worthy of the effort required to understand it. The main research lies in two areas: the construction of *monetary aggregates* that conform to the specifications of demand theory and the estimation of systems of financial asset-demand equations in which the restrictions of demand theory are incorporated in such a manner as to assure consistency with the optimizing behavior of economic agents. Of course, there are useful paradigms in existence that employ a simultaneous-equations structure — notably the asset and transactions approaches to money demand — as typified by the mean-variance model of James Tobin (1958) or the transactions model as explained by Jürg Niehans (1978). But these approaches do not integrate the choice of monetary aggregate with the consumer choice problem and, depending on the version, often do not take full advantage of the simultaneous-equations structure inherent in the choice of a portfolio of monetary assets.[2]

We have four tasks before us. First, we discuss the problem of the definition (aggregation) of money; after a consideration of the theoretical problems, we will propose the use of the Divisia method of aggregation for the construction of monetary aggregates. Second, we show how a simultaneous-equations financial assets structure both fits neatly into the

---

[2]The two general approaches mentioned can be shown to be special cases of the approach we are surveying once risk is introduced into decisions; see James Poterba and Julio Rotemberg (1987); Barnett, Melvin Hinich, and Piyu Yue (1991a); Barnett and Apostolos Serletis (1990); and Barnett, Hinich, and Yue (2000).

definitional approach we are recommending and also provides a structure that can be used to measure income and interest rate elasticities as well as the important elasticities of substitution among financial entities. An econometric digression here will emphasize the contribution that can be made by employing one of the flexible functional forms at the estimation stage. Third, in our discussion of the empirical literature, we will emphasize how the theory might be implemented (and briefly show some of the results); the purpose of this discussion will be to illustrate the theory rather than to survey what is a rapidly changing empirical record. Finally, we briefly discuss ongoing research and extensions of the literature. The work discussed here includes the use of formal methods of aggregating over economic agents as well as the incorporation into the general framework of risk aversion and rational expectations (both for consumers and firms).

1.2   The Definition of Money

The natural place to begin is with the definition of money. Currently, the common practice among central banks is to construct monetary aggregates from a list of entities by adding together those that are considered to be the likely sources of monetary services. That is, commercial banks and other financial intermediaries provide demand deposits, certificates of deposit and the like, and it is from this list that the (usually simple-sum) monetary aggregates are composed. At the Federal Reserve, for example, there are currently 27 components in the entire collection of liquid financial assets — as shown in Table 1.1 — and, as also shown, the four popular aggregates of M1, M2, M3, and L are constructed directly from this list by means of a recursive form of accounting that starts with M1 (the inside block) and adds blocks of items to M1 until all 27 entities are included (in L, for 'liquid assets').

What is important about these components for what follows in this chapter is that the quantities of each vary at different rates over time (and so do their 'prices').[3] To see the behavior of the quantities, consider the collection in Figure 1.1 of monthly Federal Reserve data.[4]

Here Figure 1.1a shows the behavior of the components of M1 in recent years, while Figures 1.1b and 1.1c show that behavior for the items added

---

[3]As we will describe below, from the point of view of this survey, the appropriate price for each entity in Table 1.1 is the *user cost* of the asset. These are based partly on the nominal interest rate just mentioned. Some of the more liquid items (such as currency) do not possess an "own" interest rate and so a zero rate is usually assumed. We illustrate the behavior of user costs in Figure 1.3, below.

[4]These numbers were supplied by the Federal Reserve and are available from the authors.

to M1 to construct M2. Not only are the fluctuations of the quantities different for different assets, especially since 1979, but also new assets appear in the list from time to time. These sorts of changes potentially complicate the calculation of a unique measure of moneyness, although broader measures might well perform better than narrower ones simply because the new assets, e.g., are likely to draw funds from other entities within the broader collection of potential substitutes.

As noted, the monetary aggregates currently in use by the Federal Reserve are simple-sum indices in which all monetary components are assigned a constant and equal (unitary) weight. This index is M in

$$M = \sum_{i=1}^{n} x_i, \tag{1.1}$$

where x_i is the ith monetary component of, say, the subaggregate M1; it clearly implies that all monetary components are weighted linearly and equally in the final total. This sort of index has some use as an accounting measure of the stock of nominal monetary wealth, of course, and this is an important advantage. More tellingly, this form of aggregation implies that all components are dollar-for-dollar perfect substitutes, since all indifference curves and isoquants over those components must be linear with slopes of minus 1.0 if this aggregate is to represent the monetary service flow selected by the economic agents. This is the source of its potential weakness.

The main problem with the simple-sum index arises from the fact that in aggregation theory a quantity index should measure the income effects (i.e., welfare or service flow changes) of a relative price change but should be unresponsive to pure substitution effects (at constant utility), which the index should internalize. The simple-sum index cannot untangle income from substitution effects if its components are not perfect substitutes.[5] In the face of what appear to be significant changes in the relative prices of financial assets and with increasing numbers of apparently imperfect substitutes among the relevant short-term financial assets, it is not surprising that attempts are now common to arrive at a definitional procedure that will accommodate this volatility. Milton Friedman and Anna Schwartz, in their monumental survey of the literature on the definition of money, when discussing the simple-sum approach, discuss the basic issue in the following terms:

---

[5]What is required for a consistent aggregation is an *aggregator function*, which the simple sum is. The problem is that the natural choice for an aggregator function is a utility or production function; only if the components are perfect substitutes is the simple-sum the appropriate utility or production function.

TABLE 1.1

OFFICIAL MONETARY AGGREGATES/COMPONENTS
U.S. FEDERAL RESERVE

```
┌─ L ──────────────────────────────────────────────────┐
│ ┌─ M 3 ───────────────────────────────────────────┐  │
│ │ ┌─ M 2 ─────────────────────────────────────┐    │  │
│ │ │ ┌─ M 1 ───────────────────────────────┐    │    │  │
│ │ │ │                                     │    │    │  │
```

M 1
- Currency and travelers' checks
- Demand deposits held by consumers
- Demand deposits held by businesses
- Other checkable deposits
- Super NOW accounts held at commercial banks
- Super NOW accounts held at thrifts

M 2
- Overnight RPs
- Overnight Eurodollars
- Money market mutual fund shares
- Money market deposit accounts at commercial banks
- Money market deposit accounts at thrifts
- Savings deposits at commercial banks
- Savings deposits at savings and loans (S&Ls)
- Savings deposits at mutual savings banks (MSBs)
- Savings deposits at credit unions
- Small time deposits and retail RPs at commercial banks
- Small time deposits at S&Ls and MSBs and retail RPs at thrifts
- Small time deposits at credit unions

M 3
- Large time deposits at commercial banks
- Large time deposits at thrifts
- Institutional money market funds
- Term RPs at commercial banks and thrifts
- Term Eurodollars

L
- Savings bonds
- Short-term Treasury securities
- Bankers' acceptances
- Commercial paper

Figure 1.1a: Components of M1 in the United States.

"This (summation) procedure is a very special case of the
more general approach. In brief, the general approach consists
of regarding each asset as a joint product having different degrees of 'moneyness,' and defining the quantity of money as the
weighted sum of the aggregate value of all assets, the weights
for individual assets varying from zero to unity with a weight
of unity assigned to that asset or assets regarded as having the
largest quantity of 'moneyness' per dollar of aggregate value.
The procedure we have followed implies that all weights are
either zero or unity. The more general approach has been suggested frequently but experimented with only occasionally. We
conjecture that this approach deserves and will get much more
attention than it has so far received." (Friedman and Schwartz
1970, pp. 151-152)

Their observation is deficient only in failing to point out that even
weighted aggregation implies perfect (but not dollar-for-dollar) substitutability unless the aggregation procedure is nonlinear.[6]

---

[6]For example, introduction of estimated multiplicative coefficients into Equation (1.1)
would retain the linearity of the aggregation and hence the implication of perfect substitutability.

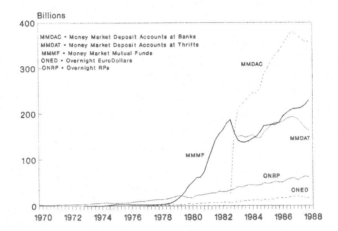

Figure 1.1b: Liquid instruments in the United States.

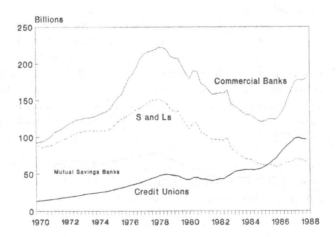

Figure 1.1c: Savings deposits in the United States.

Over the years, there have been a series of attempts to achieve a rule for aggregating monetary components without abandoning the simple-sum structure. There is, indeed, a theory that might seem to back this up: that of Hicksian aggregation (John Hicks 1946; Don Patinkin 1965). The main difficulty is that for Hicksian aggregation to be possible it is required that the relative prices (user costs) of the financial commodities not change over the sample period. Even if that assumption were true, Hicksian aggregation alone is not sufficient for simple-sum aggregation; it also is necessary that the constant user cost between any two assets be equal to 1.0. Once again, this condition can be expected to hold only if the component assets are indistinguishable perfect substitutes; this is unlikely if only because all financial assets one can think of provide different services and hence have different 'own rates' of return — and these change over time. The user costs depend upon those yields.

An attractive alternative to the simple-sum approach is to use microeconomic aggregation theory to define money. This theory has two branches, one leading to the construction of index numbers using methods derived from economic theory and one leading to the construction of money-demand functions in the context of a system of equations modelling the wealth-holder's allocation of funds among money and non-money assets. The two branches are supported by the same structure, in that the supporting theory in both cases is that of the constrained maximization of the aggregate consumer's intertemporal utility function. The following section, in spelling out the theory, emphasizes this theoretical coherence.

1.3 The Microeconomic Theory of a Monetary Economy

Consider an economy with identical individuals, having three types of goods: consumption goods, leisure, and the services of monetary assets. Assuming that the services of these three entities enter as arguments in the individual's utility function, the utility function can be written as[7]

$$u = U(c, L, x) \tag{1.2}$$

where c is a vector of the services of consumption goods, L is leisure time, and x is a vector of the services of monetary assets. For money, the services

---

[7]Putting money into the utility function, for some utility functions, is observationally equivalent to putting money (solely) into the constraints. This result is established by Robert Feenstra whose demonstration applies for a broad class of utility functions and a broad class of transactions cost models (including the inventory-theoretic model and the Robert Clower (1967) cash-in-advance constraint formulation). Much of this is also discussed in Patinkin (1965). Feenstra notes...

could be convenience, liquidity, and information (as in Karl Brunner and Allan Meltzer 1971).

The utility function in Equation (1.2) can be assumed to be maximized subject to the full income constraint

$$q'c + \pi'x + wL = y \tag{1.3}$$

where y is full income (i.e., income reflecting expenditures on time as well as on goods and services); q is a vector of the prices of c; π is a vector of monetary asset *user costs* (or rental prices); and w is the shadow price of leisure (see Barnett 1981b). The ith component of π is given by (see Barnett 1978 and Donal Donovan 1978),

$$\pi_i = p^* \left(\frac{R - r_i}{1 + R} \right) \tag{1.4}$$

This formula measures the opportunity cost — at the margin — of the monetary services provided by asset i. It is calculated as the discounted value of the interest foregone by holding a dollar's worth of that asset. Here r_i is the expected nominal holding-period yield on the ith asset, R is the maximum expected holding-period yield available on an alternative asset (the 'benchmark' asset) and p^* is the true cost-of-living index.[8] Note, especially, that this formula is not arbitrary but can be derived from an in-

---

"We demonstrate a functional equivalent between using real balances as an argument of the utility function and entering money into liquidity costs which appear in the budget constraints." (p. 271)

This should dispose of the issue for purposes of this survey, since the utility-maximizing models discussed here are of the very general sort that Feenstra discusses. In a general equilibrium context, the same result also has been proved by Kenneth Arrow and Frank Hahn (1971); a parallel proof in a production context is due to Stanley Fischer (1974). See also Louis Philips and Frank Spinnewyn (1982) and Poterba and Rotemberg (1987). Once money has been put into the utility function, the inverse mapping to the motivating transactions constraint is not unique, so that the reason for holding money is lost. But we do not seek to explain the reason for holding money. We simply observe that money does have a positive value in equilibrium so that we can appeal to the Arrow and Hahn proof.

[8]The benchmark asset is specifically assumed to provide no liquidity or other monetary services and is held solely to transfer wealth intertemporally. In theory, R is the maximum expected holding period yield in the economy. It is usually defined in practice in such a way that the user costs for the monetary assets are positive. The true cost of living index, p^*, is defined for the consumer goods, c; we use the term "true" merely to warn the reader that this is an *exact* price index, as this concept is described below. Note that if p^* is deleted from the user cost formula, the formula produces real rather than nominal user cost. The interest rates are nominal so that inflationary expectations appear here (in the denominator, since the effects in the two rates in the numerator of the formula may well cancel out).

tertemporal optimization problem of a standard sort (see Barnett 1981b).[9]

In order to focus on the details of the demand for monetary services, a good starting point is the theory of two-stage optimization investigated initially in the context of consumer theory by Robert Strotz (1957, 1959) and William Gorman (1959). The theory describes a sequential expenditure allocation in which in the first stage (that of budgeting or 'price aggregation') the consumer allocates his expenditure *among* broad categories (consumption goods, leisure, and monetary services in the context of the model used here) and then in the second stage (that of 'decentralization') allocates expenditures *within* each category. In the first stage his decision is guided by price indices among the three categories, while in the monetary part of the decentralized decision, he responds to changes in the relative prices of the monetary assets (π_i/π_j as defined above).

Decomposition of the consumer choice problem along these lines is possible only if the individual's utility function (1.2) is *weakly separable* in the services of monetary assets. That is, it must be possible to write the utility function as

$$u = U[c, L, f(x)] \tag{1.5}$$

in which f defines the monetary subutility function. As laid out originally by Masaza Sono (1961) and Wassily Leontief (1947a), the condition of weak separability described in (1.5) is equivalent to

$$\frac{\partial}{\partial \phi}\left(\frac{\partial U/\partial x_i}{\partial U/\partial x_j}\right) = 0 \tag{1.6}$$

---

[9]For example, suppose that the representative consumer (under continuous replanning) maximizes utility over three periods $(1, 2, 3)$, subject to a budget constraint. For simplicity, we can fix the time path of leisure and consider only one monetary asset and one consumption good. The one-period budget constraint for period 2 is

$$p_2^* c_2 = (1 + r_1)p_1^* x_1 - p_2^* x_2 + [(1 + R_1)A_1 - A_2]$$

where A denotes per capita holdings of an alternative asset (say, a bond), while R is the expected nominal yield on A and r is that on x. The other variables are defined the same way as in the text, above.

Solve the period 2 budget constraint for A_2 and write the resulting equation for each of the three periods. Then by back substituting for A, starting from A_3 and working down to A_1, we obtain (after some manipulation) the consumer's budget constraint in present value form:

$$(1 + R_0)A_0 + (1 + r_0)p_0^* m_0 = \frac{A_3}{\rho_3} + \sum_{s=1}^{3}\frac{p_s^*}{\rho_s}c_s + \sum_{s=1}^{3}\left[\frac{p_s^*}{\rho_s} - p_s^*\frac{(1 + r_s)}{\rho_{s+1}}\right]x_s + \frac{p_3^*(1 + r_3)}{\rho_4}x_3$$

where the discount factor, ρ_s, equals 1 for $s = 1$, $(1 + R_1)$ for $s = 2$, etc. ..... In the equation just given, the term in the bracket is the user cost of x. Writing the user cost for $s = 1$ (the current period), we obtain equation (1.4).

for $i \neq j$, where ϕ is any component of $\{c, L\}$. This condition asserts that under weak separability the marginal rate of substitution between any two monetary assets is independent of the values of c and L.[10]

If we have established a separable subset of assets, whether by separability test or by assumption, we then can continue in the framework of the following neoclassical consumer problem,

$$\max f(\boldsymbol{x}) \qquad \text{subject to } \boldsymbol{\pi}'\boldsymbol{x} = m \qquad (1.7)$$

where m is the total expenditures on monetary services, a total that is determined in the first stage of the two-level optimizing problem. It is this simple structure that we will need to recall in the work in the following sections.

Whether or not the utility function (1.2) is weakly separable in monetary services is, ultimately, an empirical question. Ideally, instead of treating equation (1.5) as a maintained (and therefore untested) hypothesis as so much of the money-demand literature implicitly does, one could test whether the utility function (1.2) is appropriately separable in monetary services — the assumption implicit in the traditional 'money-nonmoney' dichotomization. The existing methods of conducting such tests are not, however, very effective tools of analysis, as discussed below.

1.3.1 The Aggregation-Theoretic Approach to Money Demand

In the preceding discussion we have shown the steps that are normally taken to reduce a very general consumer choice problem to an asset choice problem. At this point, we are prepared to proceed to results in the 'aggregation-theoretic' literature on money demand. This literature ties up the theory just sketched with that on the macroeconomic demand for money in an obvious and logical way. What we are after here are monetary aggregates that are consistent with the optimizing behavior of rational economic agents.

We begin with the *aggregator function*. In the aggregation-theoretic literature for the consumer choice problem, the quantity aggregator function has been shown to be the subutility function defined solely over the individual monetary components (as listed in Table 1.1). This function, for the

---

[10]Note that the separability structure is asymmetric. That is, c is not separable from x and L in U unless there exists a function $g(c)$ such that $u = U(c, L, x) = U[g(c), L, f(x)]$. For an extensive discussion of separability, see Charles Blackorby, Daniel Primont, and Robert Russell (1978).

monetary services problem defined in equation (1.7), is $f(\boldsymbol{x})$.[11] Using a specific and differentiable form for the monetary services aggregator function $f(\boldsymbol{x})$, and solving decision (1.7), we can derive the inverse and/or the direct demand-function system. Using these derived solution functions and specific monetary data, we then could estimate the parameters and replace the unknown parameters of $f(\boldsymbol{x})$ by their estimates. The resulting estimated function is called an *economic* (or functional) monetary *index*, and its calculated value at any point is an economic monetary-quantity index number.

We have noted that the researcher would choose a specific and differentiable functional form if he were to follow this approach. The problem is that the use of a specific function necessarily implies a set of implicit assumptions about the underlying preference structure of the economic agent. For example, as we have already emphasized, the use of a weighted-linear function for $f(\boldsymbol{x})$ implies perfect substitutability among the monetary assets. If the weights are all unity so that we get the widely used simple-summation functions, the consumer will specialize in the consumption of the highest yielding asset. The use of the more general Cobb-Douglas function imposes an elasticity of substitution equal to unity between every pair of assets. To continue, the constant elasticity of substitution function, although relaxing the unitary elasticity of substitution restriction imposed by the Cobb-Douglas, nevertheless imposes the restriction that the elasticity of substitution is the same between any pair of assets. The list of specific functional forms is, of course, boundless, but the defining property of the more popular of these entities is that they imply strong limitations on the behavior of the consumer. While the issue of their usefulness is ultimately an empirical question — and we shall treat the issue that way below — we feel that most members of this class of functions should be rejected for estimation of money demand, partly in view of the restrictive nature of their implicit assumptions, and partly because of the existence of attractive alternatives.

Among the alternatives is a member of the class of quadratic utility functions. With a member of the quadratic class, we would be using a *flexible functional form* to approximate the unknown monetary-services aggregator function. Flexible functional forms — such as the translog — can locally approximate to the second order any unknown functional form for the monetary services aggregator function, and even higher quality approximations

---

[11]The argument just given requires that $f(\cdot)$ be homothetic. In the nonhomothetic utility case, the aggregator function is the distance function (see Barnett 1987). However, since the resulting index is the same in either case, the conclusions of this section are unaffected by this assumption. This topic is considered further, below.

are available.[12] We will consider the details of this method below.

If one is to do away with the simple-sum method of aggregating money and replace it with a nonlinear aggregator function as suggested, one will be able to deal with less than perfect substitutability and, for that matter, with variations over time in the elasticities of substitution among the components of the monetary aggregates. There is a problem, however, and this is that the functions must be estimated over specific data sets (and re-estimated periodically) with the attendant result that the index becomes dependent upon the specification. This dependence is particularly troublesome to government agencies that have to justify their procedures to persons untrained in econometrics. This is a reasonable concern — and it is exacerbated by the fact that there are many possible nonlinear models from which to choose. Under these circumstances, government agencies around the world have taken a more direct approach and use index number formulas from statistical index number theory for most of their calculations. We will explain how this approach can be implemented in a way that simultaneously deals with the theoretical and the practical issues. We will not, however, be able to explain why there is not more use of the approach by the monetary authorities of these same governments.

1.3.2   Index Number Theory

Statistical index-number theory provides a variety of quantity and price indices that treat prices and quantities as jointly independent variables. Indeed, whether they are price or quantity indices, they are widely used, since they can be computed from price and quantity data alone, thus eliminating the need to estimate an underlying structure. In fact, since the appearance of Irving Fisher's (1922) early and now classic study on statistical index number theory, nearly all national government data series have been based upon aggregation formulas from that literature. Well-known examples are the Consumer Price Index (a Laspeyres price index), the Implicit GNP Deflator (a Paasche price index), and real GNP (a Laspeyres quantity index). The simple-sum index often used for monetary quantities is a member of the broad class. But the simple sum is a degenerative measure, since it contains no prices.

Statistical indices are distinguished by their known statistical properties. These properties are described in detail by Irving Fisher (1922), and in that work he provides a set of tests (known as Fisher's System of Tests)

---

[12]Such as the Minflex Laurent (see Barnett 1983a, 1985; Barnett and Yul Lee 1985), the Fourier (see Ronald Gallant 1981), and the Asymptotically Ideal Models (see Barnett and Andrew Jonas 1983; Barnett and Yue 1988; Yue 1991; and Barnett, John Geweke , and Michael Wolfe 1991a).

useful for assessing the quality of a particular statistical index.[13] The index that he believes often to be the best in the sense of possessing the largest number of satisfactory statistical properties, has now become known as the Fisher Ideal Index. Another index found to possess a very large number of these properties is the Törnqvist discrete-time approximation to the Divisia Index.[14] We note that Fisher found the simple-sum index and to be the worst of the literally hundreds of possible indices that he studied.

Let x_{it} be the quantity of the ith asset during period t, and let π_{it} be the rental price (that is, user cost) for that good during period t. Then, the *Fisher ideal index* (Q_t^F) during period t is the geometric average of the Laspeyres and Paasche indices:

$$\frac{Q_t^F}{Q_{t-1}^F} = \left[\frac{\sum\limits_{i=1}^{n} s_{i,t-1} \left(\dfrac{x_{it}}{x_{i,t-1}} \right)}{\sum\limits_{i=1}^{n} s_{it} \left(\dfrac{x_{i,t-1}}{x_{it}} \right)} \right]^{1/2} \tag{1.8}$$

where

$$s_{it} = \frac{\pi_{it} x_{it}}{\sum\limits_{k=1}^{n} \pi_{kt} x_{kt}}.$$

On the other hand, the discrete time (Törnqvist) *Divisia index* during period t is Q_t^D, where

$$\frac{Q_t^D}{Q_{t-1}^D} = \prod_{i=1}^{n} \left(\frac{x_{it}}{x_{i,t-1}} \right)^{(1/2)(s_{it}+s_{i,t-1})} \tag{1.9}$$

It is informative to take the logarithms of each side of (1.9), so that

$$\log Q_t^D - \log Q_{t-1}^D = \sum_{i=1}^{n} s_{it}^* (\log x_{it} - \log x_{i,t-1}) \tag{1.10}$$

where $s_{it}^* = (1/2)(s_{it} + s_{i,t-1})$. In this form, it is easy to see that for the Divisia index the growth rate (log change) of the aggregate is the share-weighted average of the growth rates of the component quantities.

A characteristic of the Fisher Ideal Index is that the Fisher Index is 'self dual.' In such a case, if the quantity index is the Fisher *quantity* index, then the implied price index — defined by dividing total expenditure on

---

[13] Fisher's tests for statistical indices are proportionality, circularity, determinateness, commensurability, and factor reversal. For recent discussions, see Eichhorn (1976, 1978), Diewert (1992), and Balk (1995).

[14] The Divisia index was originated by the French economist Francois Divisia (1925).

the components by the quantity index — is the Fisher *price* index. Hence, the Fisher price and quantity indices comprise a dual pair in the sense that their product equals total expenditure on their components; this is known as Fisher's *factor reversal test*. In contrast, the price index that is dual to the Divisia quantity index is actually not a Divisia price index. Nevertheless, even if the Divisia price index were used to measure the price of the Divisia quantity index, the size of the error produced as a result of the violation of the factor reversal test would be very small (third order in the changes). Indeed, the failure to be self-dual is common among the most popular index numbers.[15] In view of the fact that the Divisia quantity index has the very considerable advantage of possessing an easily interpreted functional form, as in equation (1.10), it is now often employed in the emerging literature on monetary aggregation. It has another desirable property, as we shall see in a moment.

1.3.3   The Links Between Aggregation Theory, Index Number Theory, and Monetary Theory

Until relatively recently, the fields of aggregation theory and statistical index number theory developed independently. Erwin Diewert (1976, 1978), however, provided the link between aggregation theory and statistical index number theory by attaching economic properties to statistical indices. These properties are defined in terms of the statistical indices' effectiveness in tracking a particular functional form for the unknown aggregator function. Recall in thinking about this that the utility function is itself the appropriate aggregator function. What Diewert shows is that using a number of well-known statistical indices is equivalent to using a particular functional form to describe the unknown economic aggregator function. Such statistical indices are termed *exact* in this literature. Exactness, briefly, occurs when the specific aggregator function (e.g., the linear-homogeneous translog) is exactly tracked by a particular statistical index (e.g., the discrete-time Divisia); the parentheses illustrate one such case.[16]

Having the property of exactness for *some* aggregator function, however, is not sufficient for acceptability of a particular statistical index when the true functional form for the aggregator function is not known, *a priori*. What can be done in these circumstances is to choose a statistical index that is exact for a *flexible* functional form — a functional form that can

---

[15]For example, neither the Paasche nor the Laspeyres index is self-dual, although the Paasche and the Laspeyres are a dual pair. Hence it is common to use Laspeyres (not Paasche) quantity indexes with Paasche (not Laspeyres) price indexes.

[16]Diewert also shows that the Fisher-Ideal Index is exact for the square root of a homogeneous quadratic function.

provide a second-order approximation to any arbitrary unknown aggregator function. Taking this approach cuts through the problem of not knowing the underlying structure. Diewert terms such a statistical index *superlative*. As it turns out, the Divisia Index is exact for the linearly homogeneous (*and flexible*) translog and is, therefore, superlative; that is, it approximates an arbitrary unknown exact aggregator function up to a third-order remainder term.[17] What one gains from this is the ability to do precise work even when the form of the underlying function is not known.

With Diewert's successful merging of index number theory and economic aggregation theory and the rigorous derivation of the appropriate price of monetary services in the form of the user cost of these services (Donovan 1978; Barnett 1978), the loose link between monetary theory and economic aggregation theory has been turned into a firm one and the scene has been set for the construction of theoretically inspired monetary aggregates. In our discussion, we have pointed out that either the Divisia Index or the Fisher-Ideal Index of monetary services would be superlative. Actually, it has been demonstrated (Barnett 1980a) that the difference between the two is typically less than the roundoff error in the monetary data. The Federal Reserve, indeed, has employed both procedures as alternatives to the much more widely-known simple-sum aggregates [18]

There is one other aggregate in at least limited use in the monetary literature, and that is MQ, the monetary quantities index. In the particular form computed by Paul Spindt (1985a), MQ is measured as in equation (1.8), but with the user costs replaced by monetary-asset turnover rates. The problem with this procedure is that the MQ index, unlike the Divisia, is inconsistent both with existing aggregation and index number theories. The relevant foundations (both index-number theoretic and aggregation theoretic) for the Fisher-Ideal Index *require* the use of prices and quantities and not turnover rates and quantities.[19] An attempt to define money in yet another way is due to Don Roper and Stephen Turnovsky (1980). In their paper the object is to determine the optimal monetary aggregate for stabilization policy assuming a one-goal objective function — which is the minimization of the variance of income. This, too, is an atheoretical approach from the point of view of this survey. It has the added difficulty that there are significant theoretical and empirical problems associated with expanding the objective function to incorporate multiple goals (and with

---

[17]In fact, even if the aggregator is not homogenous, the Divisia Index remains exact — but for the distance function, which is the economic aggregator function in that case.

[18]However, the Federal Reserve does not publish these numbers.

[19]For a proof, see Barnett (1987, 1990). If nothing else, MQ can be said to be no less arbitrary than the official simple-sum aggregates. But the number of such atheoretical aggregates is infinite, as is the number of possible nonlinear functions of quantities and turnover rates.

dealing with a large number of monetary assets and other policy tools).

There has recently been some interest in measuring wealth effects produced from changes in expected monetary service flows. The formula for the monetary capital stock was derived by Barnett (1991, eq. 2.2), who proved that it equals the discounted present value of the expected future Divisia monetary service flow. Under the assumption of stationary expectations, this expected discounted present value simplifies to an index called the CE index (see Barnett 1991, theorem 1).[20] Rotemberg (1991) and Rotemberg, Driscoll, and Poterba (1995) present some interesting empirical results with the CE index. While the implicit stationary expectations assumption is troubling, the CE index, unlike the MQ and the Roper-Turnovsky indexes, is not atheoretical. We anticipate that future applications of Barnett's capital stock formula, with less restrictive assumptions on expectations than used in generating the CE special case, will produce further advances in measuring monetary wealth effects.

At this point we might pause to consider the composition of these new indices and what their recent behavior has been. The indices are constructed from the same components as the traditional measures (e.g., Divisia M1 is constructed from the components list used for M1, as described in Table 1.1); they employ user costs, as defined above, in their calculations. As the graphs in Figure 1.2 indicate, these numbers differ, sometimes considerably, from the summation indices. This difference is especially large for the broader measures and for the years since 1978.

The simple correlations that go with these figures are

	Level	Differenced
Sum/Divisia M1	.998	.964
Sum/Divisia M2	.986	.542
Sum/Divisia M3	.982	.407
Sum/Divisia L	.985	.487

While these correlations are quite high in the trend-dominated level figures, when differenced, the broader series show considerably smaller correlations. Because it is in differenced form that the monetary data are usually studied, there is sufficient reason in these figures to dig further into their relative performances. Note also that the user costs (of the components of these aggregates) are often not highly correlated (see Figure 1.3 below).

---

[20]There is also a considerably less attractive interpretation of the CE index as a flow index. See Barnett (1995, section 5) regarding the flow interpretation, which requires stronger assumptions than those needed to derive the Divisia flow index.

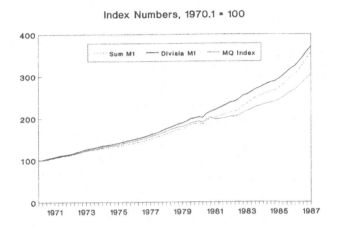

Figure 1.2a: Sum M1 versus Divisia M1 in the United States.

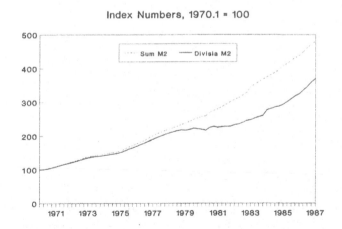

Figure 1.2b: Sum M2 versus Divisia M2 in the United States.

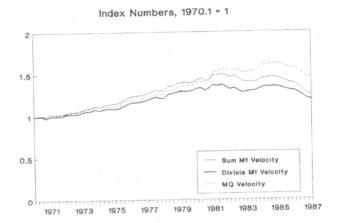

Figure 1.2c: Sum M3 versus Divisia M3 in the United States.

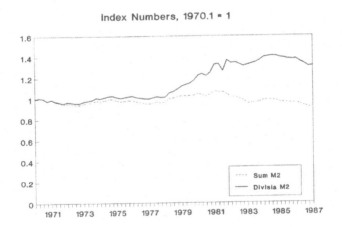

Figure 1.2d: Sum L versus Divisia L in the United States.

1.3.4 Understanding the New Divisia Aggregates

To understand the new Divisia aggregates, we must consider the underlying microeconomic theory behind the Divisia Index. Let us return to the consumer's utility function over monetary assets as defined above (this was $f(x)$). Writing out the total differential of $f(x)$, we obtain

$$df(x) = \sum_{i=1}^{n} \left(\frac{\partial f}{\partial x_i} \right) dx_i \tag{1.11}$$

where the partial derivatives are marginal utilities (which are functions themselves containing the unknown parameters of the function $f(x)$). From the first-order conditions for the expenditure-constrained maximization of $f(x)$, we can write the marginal utilities as

$$\lambda \pi_i = \frac{\partial f}{\partial x_i} \quad i = 1, \ldots, n \tag{1.12}$$

Here λ is the Lagrange multiplier, and π_i is the user-cost (i.e., the rental price) of asset i. This expression can then be substituted into equation (1.11) to yield

$$df(x) = \sum_{i=1}^{n} \lambda \pi_i \, dx_i \tag{1.13}$$

which is written not in unknown marginal utilities but in the unknown Lagrange multiplier, user costs, and changes in quantities.

In equation (1.13) the Lagrange multiplier is itself a function of unknown tastes and thereby a function of the parameters of the unknown utility function. Hence, we have one more step to go; we must eliminate the Lagrange multiplier. This involves the assumption that the economic quantity aggregate, $f(x)$, is linearly homogeneous in its components. This is, indeed, a reasonable assertion, since it would be very curious indeed if linear homogeneity of $f(x)$ failed. It is reasonable because if it does not hold, the growth rate of the aggregate differs from the growth rates of its components, even if all components are growing at the same rate.[21]

Let us now define $P(\pi)$ to be the dual price index satisfying Fisher's factor-reversal test as this was described above.

$$P(\pi)f(x) = \sum_{i=1}^{n} \pi_i x_i \quad [= m]. \tag{1.14}$$

---

[21] In fact, the linear homogeneity assumption not only is necessary, but also is harmless. In the general case of nonhomothetic tastes and technology, the aggregator function is the distance function — which *always* is linearly homogeneous.

It can then be shown that[22] $\lambda = 1/P(\pi)$, in which case equation (1.13) can be written as

$$df(\boldsymbol{x}) = \sum_{i=1}^{n} \frac{1}{P(\pi)} \pi_i \, dx_i. \qquad (1.15)$$

Manipulating equation (1.15) algebraically to convert to growth rate (log change) form, we find that

$$d \log f(\boldsymbol{x}) = \sum_{i=1}^{n} s_i \, d \log x_i \qquad (1.16)$$

where

$$s_i = \frac{\pi_i x_i}{\sum\limits_{k=1}^{n} \pi_k x_k}$$

is the ith asset's value share in the total expenditures on monetary services. The result is the Divisia index, as defined in equation (1.10), where the log change in the utility level (and therefore in the level of the aggregate) is the weighted average of the log changes of the component levels, with expenditure shares providing the weights. This exercise demonstrates the solid micro-foundations of the Divisia index. It is, indeed, the logical choice for an index from a theoretical point of view, being exactly the transformed first-order conditions for constrained optimization. In addition, the derivation just completed demonstrates that the prices appearing in index numbers cannot be replaced by any other variables, such as turnover rates, bid-ask spreads, brokerage fees, etc. To do so would be to violate the first-order conditions, (1.12). In particular, for the case of monetary assets, it is user costs that preserve (1.12) and therefore permit (1.13).

1.3.5   The Optimal Level of Monetary Subaggregation

Even if the utility function, $U(\cdot)$, is weakly separable in its monetary assets group, there remains the problem of selecting monetary asset subgroups for inclusion in monetary *subaggregates*. In particular, the use of any monetary sub-aggregate (such as M1, M2, M3, or L) implies that the components of

---

[22]Let $\boldsymbol{x} = D(m, \pi)$ to be the solution to the maximization of $f(\boldsymbol{x})$ subject to $\pi'\boldsymbol{x} = m$. The linear homogeneity of $f(\boldsymbol{x})$ implies that there must exist a vector of functions $\boldsymbol{h}(\pi)$ such that $\boldsymbol{x} = m\boldsymbol{h}(\pi)$. Substituting for $\boldsymbol{x}$ into $f(\boldsymbol{x})$, we find that

$$f(\boldsymbol{x}) = f[m\boldsymbol{h}(\pi)] = mf[\boldsymbol{h}(\pi)].$$

As $\lambda = \partial f/\partial m$, we have from the last equation that $\lambda = f[\boldsymbol{h}(\pi)]$. In addition, from Equation (1.14), $P(\pi)f(\boldsymbol{x}) = m$. Hence from $f(\boldsymbol{x}) = mf[\boldsymbol{h}(\pi)]$ we have that $f[\boldsymbol{h}(\pi)] = 1/P(\pi)$. Hence, $\lambda = 1/P(\pi)$.

the subaggregate are themselves weakly separable within x. This additional nested separability condition is required, regardless of the type of index used *within* the subaggregate. Weak separability over the component assets is both necessary and sufficient for the existence of stable preferences (or technology) over those components of the subaggregate. This implies that without separability such a subaggregate has no meaning in theory, since the subaggregate fails the existence condition.

Even so, weak separability establishes only a necessary condition for subaggregation in its simplest form. In particular, if we wish to measure the subaggregate using the most elementary method, we would require the additional assumption that the separable subfunction within f be homothetic. Then f is said to be homothetically weakly separable. Indeed, homothetic weak separability is necessary and sufficient for the simplified form of subaggregation.[23]

For illustration, let us describe the Federal Reserve Board's *a priori* assignment of assets to monetary subaggregates. As illustrated in Table 1.1, their method is based on the implicit assumption that the monetary services aggregator function, $f(x)$, has the recursive weakly separable form of

$$f(x) = f_4(x^4, f_3(x^3, f_2(x^2, f_1(x^1)))). \qquad (1.17)$$

This clearly implies that the marginal rate of substitution between, say, an asset in x^1 and an asset in x^2 is independent of the values of assets in x^3 and x^4.

In equation (1.17), the components of x^1 are those included in the Federal Reserve Board's M1 monetary aggregate, the components of $\{x^1, x^2\}$ are those of the M2 aggregate, the components of $\{x^1, x^2, x^3\}$ are those of the M3 aggregate, and the components of x are those of the L aggregate. The aggregator functions f_i, for $i = 1, \ldots, 4$, would rationalize the Federal Reserve's component groupings, M1, M2, M3, and L. Of course, the actual numbers produced for the official monetary aggregates further require the assumptions that f_1, f_2, f_3, f_4 (and hence f itself) are all simple summations.

---

[23] In its most general form, however, aggregation is possible without homotheticity but with only the minimal existence condition of weak separability. That generalization uses the distance function for the aggregator function and produces the Malmquist index (see Barnett 1987); see below for more on the distance function. Hence we currently are presenting a special case, to which the Malmquist index reduces if and only if f is linearly homogeneous.

1.4   Econometric Considerations

In recent years there have been a number of related developments that have increased the usefulness of the 'demand systems' modeling approach for monetary studies. The following discussion attempts to clarify just what these developments are and how they are tending to reorganize a very traditional literature on an important topic.

The first problem is involved with the definition of money: what assets should be selected and how should they be grouped? As a first pass, one might aggregate (by a Divisia index) those assets that have highly collinear rates of return; examples would be savings deposits held by consumers at various types of financial institutions or negotiable large-scale CDs and commercial paper. Similarly, small time deposits at various financial institutions would probably qualify for this sort of preaggregation. One is still left with a considerable number of other disaggregated assets when this is done, however. If a demand system is the object of the exercise, the problem becomes that of an excessive number of equations and thereby also of parameters to estimate (for the sample size available).

Instead of the *a priori* assignment of assets to monetary groups, the structure of preferences over monetary assets could be discovered by actually testing for weakly separable sub-groupings. There are problems, however, with the available tests for separability. For example, consider the most common separability pretest in this literature: Hal Varian's (1982, 1983) nonparametric (NONPAR) revealed preference procedure. This test examines the results of (what are assumed to be) actual consumer choices to see if there are any violations of consistency.[24] However, the NONPAR procedure possesses a number of undesirable features, possibly the most serious being its inherently nonstatistical nature.[25] Even so, there do exist studies in the monetary literature that employ this methodology, with a frequent result being that the traditional monetary subgroupings are not those that appear to be separable within wealth holders' choices.[26] This is

---

[24] A violation would occur if consumers actually choose new market baskets that make them worse off than their original choice (evaluated at the original prices).

[25] The NONPAR procedure produces a total rejection if there is a single violation; in this case, the data having been rejected, it is also impossible to test for separable groupings, even though the rejection could have been produced from purely white noise in the data. See Barnett and Seungmook Choi (1989a) for some rather pessimistic results drawn from Monte Carlo experiments on various methods used (including NONPAR) in testing for weak separability.

[26] James Swofford and Gerald Whitney (1988) *on annual data*, conclude that there exist relatively liquid sets of assets — one group being M1, other checkable deposits, and savings deposits at each institution type (taken separately) — that are separable from consumption expenditures and leisure. *On quarterly data*, they find that no interesting collection of financial assets passes both of Varian's necessary and sufficient conditions for

clearly a very preliminary observation, however.

There is a further problem, already discussed in a theoretical context, that concerns the separability of the monetary asset decision from the consumption/leisure decision. Most money-demand studies simply ignore the possible difficulties, but recent empirical tests, either utilizing the NONPAR procedure or embedding the hypothesis parametrically in a set of simultaneous equations, generally do not support this separability.[27] We should note, somewhat parenthetically, that tests that employ the wage rate in the money demand function — usually as a proxy for the 'value of time' — also could be interpreted as providing evidence of the lack of separability of the money-holding decision from the leisure (and hence consumption) decision.[28]

Moving on to the main issues of this section, the next topic concerns the relationship between the direct monetary services aggregator function and the indirect user cost aggregator function. Since the structural properties of the two are not necessarily the same, and since one generally theorizes about the direct function but estimates the indirect function, a correspondence between the two must be established. In the case at hand, the indirect utility function corresponding to the direct utility function in equation (1.2) would be weakly separable in expenditure-normalized monetary-asset user costs if there exists an indirect aggregator function $H(\mathbf{v})$ such that we can write

$$g = G(\mathbf{q}, w, H(\mathbf{v})) \tag{1.18}$$

where $\mathbf{q}$ and $\mathbf{v}$ are the expenditure-normalized price vectors for $\mathbf{c}$ and $\mathbf{x}$, respectively, and w is the expenditure-normalized wage rate.[29] The weak separability condition in equation (1.18) holds if and only if the marginal rate of substitution between any two user costs in the monetary index is

---

weak separability. This is discouraging, although the NONPAR procedure is definitely biased toward rejection (since one violation of consistency produces a rejection). Michael Belongia and James Chalfant (1989) also test for what they call "admissible" monetary groupings on quarterly U.S. data; the groupings that pass the necessary conditions are M1A (currency plus demand deposits, M1 (as currently defined), and M1+ (M1 plus interest-bearing checkable deposits currently included in M2.)

[27] The Swofford and Whitney paper just mentioned provides the nonparametric results as does Salam Fayyad (1986). For a system study that rejects the separability of consumption goods from monetary assets, also see Fayyad, who employs the Rotterdam model in his calculations.

[28] The rationale (see Edi Karni 1974; Thomas Saving 1971; or Dean Dutton and William Gramm 1973) is often that of saving time in transactions by employing money; time is then valued at the wage rate. A recent paper by Kevin Dowd (1990) continues this tradition. Note that the lack of separability between money holding and consumption is explicit in the Dutton and Gramm paper just referred to.

[29] In particular, if $(\mathbf{q}, w, \pi)$ are the corresponding nonnormalized prices and if y is total expenditure on $(\mathbf{c}, L, \mathbf{x})$, then the expenditure-normalized prices are $(\mathbf{q}, w, \pi)/y$.

independent of changes in prices outside the monetary group.[30]

1.4.1   Approximating the Monetary Services Subutility Function

In recent years a number of empirical studies have made use of the *flexible functional form* method to approximate unknown utility functions. The advantage of this method is that the corresponding demand system can approximate systems of demand equations (for liquid assets in this case) that arise from a broad class of utility functions. Flexible functional forms have the defining property that they can attain arbitrary level and both first- and second-order derivatives at a predetermined single point (see Diewert 1974); they are, in the terminology of the literature, 'locally' flexible, and they provide second-order local approximations to the desired function.

The two most commonly used flexible functional forms are the Generalized Leontief, introduced by Diewert (1971), and the translog, introduced by Laurits Christensen, Dale Jorgenson, and Lau (1975). These have been especially appealing in econometric work because they have close links to economic theory and because their strengths and weaknesses are generally understood. Below we will use the translog as an example that reveals the characteristics of this approach in modeling the demand for money.

The decision problem with which we are working is the maximization of 'second-stage' utility subject to the second-stage monetary expenditures constraint. That is, in the second stage of a two-stage maximization problem with weak separability between monetary assets and consumer goods, the consumer maximizes a direct utility function of the general form

$$f(x_{1t}, x_{2t}, \ldots, x_{nt})$$

subject to

$$\sum_{i=1}^{n} \pi_{it}^* x_{it} - m_t^* = 0$$

with $m^* = m/p^*$ being real expenditure on the services of monetary assets (determined in the first stage and hence given at this point), and where

---

[30]Lawrence Lau (1969, Theorem VI) shows that a homothetic direct aggregator function is weakly separable if and only if the indirect aggregator function is weakly separable in the same partition. Hence, if one wishes to test for homothetic separability of the direct aggregator function, one equivalently can test for homothetic separability of the more easily approached indirect aggregator function. This survey deals with the homothetic case, which has self-duality of separability between the direct and indirect utility function.

$\pi_{it}^* = \pi_{it}/p^*$ is the real user cost of asset i, so that,

$$\pi_{it}^* = \left(\frac{R_t - r_{it}}{1 + R_t}\right).$$

The user cost here would be calculated from the own rate of return and the return (R_t) on the benchmark asset. The latter would normally be the highest available rate in the set of monetary assets.[31]

Let the indirect utility function be

$$H(v_1, v_2, \ldots, v_n)$$

with v_i defining the expenditure-normalized user costs, as in

$$v_i = \frac{\pi_i}{m} \qquad i = 1, \ldots, n.$$

Then, by application of Roy's Theorem, we will be able to move directly from the estimates of the parameters of the indirect utility function to calculations of income and price elasticities and the elasticities of substitution among the various assets.[32]

The demand-systems approach provides the ability to impose, and for that matter to test, the set of neoclassical restrictions on individual behavior; here we are referring specifically to monotonicity and curvature restrictions.[33] In addition, the approach provides an infinite range of possible parametric functional forms, thereby affording a rich supply of alternative models for actual estimation. Indeed, in the monetary literature a number of such models have been employed in the attempt to represent consumer preferences. These alternative models transform the behavioral postulates of the theory into restrictions on parameters; they differ in the specific parameterization and approximation properties of the model.

In many studies of money demand, the restrictions of theory are *implicit* at best — as in the standard Goldfeld (1973) money-demand specification

---

[31]The role of the benchmark asset is to establish a nonmonetary alternative. It is acceptable for this to be a different asset in each period, since the maximization is repeated each period. In theory, any measurement of R_t could be viewed as a proxy for the unknown rate of return on human capital.

[32]Once the form of the indirect utility function is specified (and under the assumption that this function is differentiable), Roy's Theorem allows one to derive the system of ordinary demand functions by straightforward differentiation, as follows:

$$-x_i(\pi_1, \pi_2, \ldots, \pi_n, m) = \frac{\partial H}{\partial \pi_i}\bigg/ \frac{\partial H}{\partial m} \qquad (i = 1, \ldots, n).$$

[33]The monotonicity restriction requires that, given the estimated parameter values and given prices v_i, the values of fitted demand be nonnegative. It can easily be checked by direct computation of the values of the fitted budget shares. The curvature condition requires quasi-convexity of the indirect utility function.

— but because the connection with optimization theory is either unclear or nonexistent in such cases, we are often not in a position to test or impose those restrictions. A simultaneous-equations demand system is an effective alternative, because in this case the restrictions of theory become *explicit* in the context of a particular functional form. In addition, flexible functional forms, because they permit a wide range of interactions among the commodities being tested, are especially useful in this respect.[34]

1.4.2   An Example

Consider the popular basic translog model. The logarithm of the indirect utility function $\log h = H(\log v_1, \log v_2, \ldots, \log v_n)$ can be approximated by a function that is quadratic in the logarithms as in equation (1.19)

$$\log h = \log \alpha_0 + \sum_i \alpha_i \left(\log v_i\right) + \frac{1}{2} \sum_i \sum_j \gamma_{ij} \left(\log v_i\right)\left(\log v_j\right). \qquad (1.19)$$

In fact, the function just exhibited can be derived as a second-order Taylor-series expansion to an arbitrary indirect utility function at the point $v_i^* = 1$ $(i = 1, \ldots, n)$. The translog actually is likely to be an adequate approximation at that point, although away from the point its effectiveness decreases rapidly (see Barnett and Lee 1985).

One normally does not estimate the translog model in the form of equation (1.19). Rather, starting with the indirect utility function of

$$\log h = \log H(v_1, v_2, \ldots, v_n) \qquad (1.20)$$

and applying Roy's Theorem (see Varian 1984), the budget share for the jth asset for translog tastes becomes

$$S_j = \frac{\alpha_j + \sum\limits_i \delta_{ij} \log v_i}{\alpha + \sum\limits_i \delta_i \log v_i} \qquad (1.21)$$

with $j = 1, \ldots, n$ where, for simplicity, $S_j = \pi_j x_j / m$, $\alpha = \sum_j \alpha_j$ and $\delta_i = \sum_j \delta_{ij}$. The equation system given in (1.21) is what is typically estimated.

There is, however, a significant weakness to the translog model just described, in that as a *locally* flexible functional form it is capable of an effective approximation of an arbitrary function only at or near a single point

---

[34]But note that the application of a separability restriction in this context will generally alter the flexibility characteristics of a flexible functional form (toward less flexibility); see Blackorby, Primont, and Russell (1977).

(v^*). This has inspired research on approximating the unknown monetary services aggregator function based on the use of flexible functional forms possessing *global* properties (in the limit implying an approximation at *all* points). Three such forms in use with U.S. monetary data are the Fourier, the Minflex Laurent generalized Leontief, and the Minflex Laurent translog.

The Fourier form uses the Fourier series expansion as the approximating mechanism (see Gallant 1981, and footnote 40), while the Minflex Laurent models make use of the Laurent series expansion — a generalization of the Taylor series expansion — as the approximating mechanism (see Barnett 1985; Barnett and Lee 1985; and Barnett, Lee and Wolfe 1985, 1987).[35] We shall discuss their brief empirical record in the next section.

1.5 Empirical Dimensions

There are two major observations in what has gone before in this survey. These are (1) that ideal index numbers represent a theoretically attractive alternative to fixed weight or simple sum aggregation and (2) that a systems approach to studying the demand for money is consistent with the same theory that generates the ideal index numbers, and clearly provides a promising alternative strategy for locating the apparently elusive demand for money. These topics will be the theme of the following discussion.

1.5.1 Empirical Comparisons of Index Numbers

Divisia indices will be more effective — and simple-sum (and fixed weight) indices less, ceteris paribus — if user costs of the different component monetary assets are unequal and fluctuate to any degree over the sample period, whether one needs the aggregate for direct policy purposes or as an input into a money demand study. In Figures 1.3a and 1.3b, we graph the behavior of the user costs of some of the components of the monetary aggregates M1, M2, M3, as defined in Table 1.1. There are two collections, one with user costs picked from three simple-sum categories, and one with three user costs taken from among the components of M1.[36]

In Figure 1.3a, three series are graphed, one from M1, one from the additional set of assets that makes up M2, and one, similarly, from M3.

---

[35] An especially promising global approximation not yet applied to monetary data is the AIM ("asymptotically ideal model"), generated from the Müntz-Szatz series expansion (Barnett and Jonas 1983; Barnett and Yue 1988; and Barnett, Geweke, and Wolfe 1991a).

[36] These user costs were obtained from Gerald Whitney of the University of New Orleans; their method of construction is described by Swofford and Whitney (1987, 1988) but is, in any case, carried out by the method of calculation recommended in this survey.

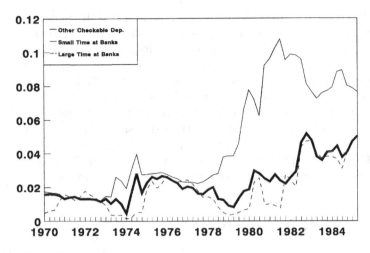

Quarterly Data, 1970.1 - 1985.2

Figure 1.3a: Sample user costs, items from M1, M2, M3.

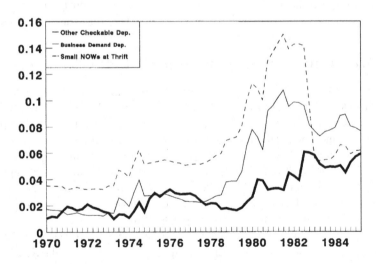

Quarterly Data, 1970.1 - 1985.2

Figure 1.3b: Sample user costs, items from M1.

They are not very highly correlated (a significant fact for the construction of M3) and, what is particularly noticeable, they often go in different directions during periods of general economic disturbance (1970, 1973-5, 1977-85). Similar results hold for the three items selected from the six that make up M1 in the official aggregates.[37]

Because the user costs (as estimated) are neither equal to each other nor constant, an interesting question is opened up about the relative performance of the monetary aggregates over this period. The safest generalization at which we could arrive at is that the different aggregates behave differently (as we illustrated in Figure 1.2) and, when compared for particular money demand models, often perform differently there, too. For example, the Divisia numbers usually provide a better fit than the simple-sum measures, but the nature of the differences among the aggregates appears to depend on the particular specification at hand and upon the choice of components over which the aggregation occurs. Under these circumstances it would be premature to assert that one component grouping is best for all purposes and, in fact, that simply may not be the case.

For example, Barnett, Edward Offenbacher, and Spindt (1984) provide a comparison in the context of a Granger-causality test of money on income (and prices) — where simple sums sometimes show up well — while Serletis (1988a) employs the Akaike Information Criterion (as defined in H. Akaike 1969b) to effect statistical comparisons. In another study, Belongia and Chalfant test the St. Louis Equation and find evidence in favor of Divisia M1A; this measure is currency plus demand deposits. Cagan (1982) finds the velocity of money series more stable when Divisia M1 is employed, while Douglas Fisher and Serletis (1989) find that Divisia measures built from short-term assets work better than those constructed from longer-term assets in a framework that attempts to explain recent velocity behavior in terms of monetary variability (see Friedman 1983). Finally, Lawrence Christiano (1986), attempting to explain the alleged structural shift in the U.S. monetary data in 1979, finds that a differenced Divisia measure does just that.

---

[37] The correlation matrix for the level figures of the three entities in Figure 1.3a is:

	OCD	STDCB	LTDCB
Other Checkable Deposits	1.00		
Small Time Deposits at Banks	.71	1.00	
Large Time Deposits at Banks	.50	.90	1.00

The matrix for the items in Figure 3b is:

	BUSDD	OCD	SNOWT
Business Demand Deposits	1.00		
Other Checkable Deposits	.78	1.00	
Small NOW Accounts at Thrifts	.44	.82	100

1.5.2   Empirical Results for the Demand System Approach

The second major issue raised above concerns the advantages one might gain by employing the demand-systems approach to the study of money demand (and monetary interaction). The fluctuations in the user costs just referred to provide one possible reason for taking this route, since the same economic theory that recommends using the Divisia technique also supports the use of the demand systems approach coupled with a flexible functional form. Before beginning, however, the reader should be warned that the best of the models put a lot of strain on the data in terms of their need for large sample size (generally, the more flexible models have more parameters to estimate).[38]

The demand-system approach produces interest-rate and income elasticities — as well as the elasticities of substitution among monetary assets. The underlying question for the income elasticities is whether they are less than 1.0, particularly for the narrowest measures. On the whole, across this entire literature, the answer is 'yes.' With respect to the elasticities of substitution, one of the most curious — *and consistent* — results in all of monetary economics is the evidence in such studies of very low substitution or even (sometimes) complementarity among the liquid financial assets; this is a general result that occurs in all but the very earliest studies.[39] These results are robust across definitions of the money stock and across *flexible* functional forms. We should note that the reason for referring to this as a 'curious result' is that there is a traditional view in the monetary literature that most of these assets are very close substitutes, as is, in fact, necessary for simple-sum aggregation. The policy importance of this result, should it continue to stand up, can hardly be exaggerated in view of the dependence of existing policies on aggregation procedures that require very high (really infinite) elasticities of substitution.

A second equally important finding concerns the temporal behavior of

---

[38] Most seriously, when the simple-sum aggregates are included, tests for model failure (e.g., symmetry, monotonicity, and quasi-convexity) generally show such failures (sometimes even quite a few failures); see Donovan (1978), Nabil Ewis and Douglas Fisher (1984, 1985), and Douglas Fisher (1989, 1992).

[39] The early study by Karuppan Chetty (1969), which employed a constant elasticity of substitution format, found relatively high elasticities of substitution. Since then, Donovan (1978), Ewis and Douglas Fisher (1984, 1985), Fayyad (1986), Serletis and Leslie Robb (1986), Serletis (1988b), and Douglas Fisher (1992), have found the lower elasticities. These studies have in common their employment of one or another of the popular flexible functional forms.

Another controversial finding is that in several studies it is suggested that currency might be a closer substitute for time deposits than it is for demand deposits (Offenbacher 1979, Ewis and Douglas Fisher 1984).

these same elasticities. We noted in Figure 1.3 that user costs appear to have fluctuated considerably in recent years; the next question concerns the behavior of the various elasticities over the same period. One can certainly generate a time series of elasticities of substitution for models such as the translog, but a far more attractive approach is to use a model like Gallant's (1981) Fourier flexible form because it provides a global approximation (at each data point) rather than a local one.[40] A few of these results have been published; we reproduce one set of these (Douglas Fisher 1989) for the same U.S. data that figured in the calculations in Figure 1.3. At stake is the reputation of single equation money demand studies that (implicitly) rely on linearity of the demand equation in its parameters. The results, which appear in Figure 1.4, are drawn from a four-equation system (three financial assets and one set of consumption expenditures) for quarterly U.S. data.[41] S12 refers to the elasticity of substitution between cash assets and savings deposits (and money market accounts), S13 refers to the elasticity of substitution between cash assets and small time deposits, while Y_i is the income elasticity of the ith category.[42]

---

[40]The Fourier model that is equivalent to Equation (1.19) for the translog is

$$h_k(v\}) = u_0 + b'v + \frac{1}{2}v'Cv + \sum_{\alpha=1}^{A} \left(u_{0\alpha} + 2\sum_{j=1}^{J} \left[u_{j\alpha}\cos(jk'_\alpha v) - w_{j\alpha}\sin(jvk'_\alpha v) \right] \right)$$

in which

$$C = -\sum_{\alpha=1}^{A} u'_{0\alpha}k_\alpha k'_a$$

This is a set of equations (which would be estimated in budget share form after application of Roy's identity) in which the parameters are the $b_i\}$, u_{ij}, and w_{ji}. The researcher picks the degree of the approximation (by picking j) and the particular form and number of the so-called multi-indices, (the k vectors). The latter are generally taken as $0, 1$ vectors of length $n - 1$ (n is the number of assets in the problem) whose purpose is to form simple indices of the normalized user costs. These decisions are made on goodness-of-fit criteria. See Gallant (1981) or Douglas Fisher (1989).

[41]The financial categores are:

Group 1: currency, consumer demand deposits, other checkable deposits
Group 2: small NOW accounts, money market deposit accounts, and savings deposits
Group 3: small time deposits

The fourth category, total consumption expenditures, was included in the system because of the failure to establish separability between financial asset holding and consumption for these data. See the discussion in Douglas Fisher (1989). There is another, similar, study by Douglas Fisher (1992).

[42]The model estimates a set of parameters employing the iterative seemingly unrelated equation approach. The elasticities and their standard errors are generated from these estimated parameters and the data at each point.

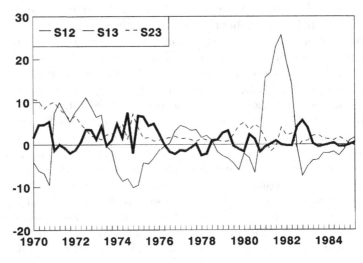

Quarterly Data, 1970.1 - 1985.2

Figure 1.4a: Substitution elasticities.

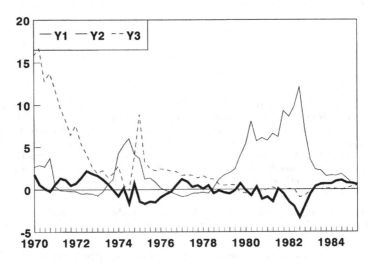

Quarterly Data, 1970.1 - 1985.2

Figure 1.4b: Income elasticities.

It is readily apparent that none of the elasticities are constant for the comparisons made, and that, in particular, the elasticities of substitution change considerably over approximately the same subperiods of the data as did the user costs. This is no coincidence, of course, since the elasticities often change in response to changes in relative prices for plausible *fixed* tastes. What it does provide — and the differences were often statistically significant in the study from which they were taken — is a possible explanation of why approaches involving simple-sum aggregation and single-equation linear money demand functions might not perform particularly well, as indeed they often have not.[43]

We should note that most of the early studies of demand systems — such as that in equation (1.19) — have tended to be cast in static terms, although the issue of dynamic adjustment has been addressed frequently in the traditional money-demand literature.[44] Recently, though, attention has been focused on the development of dynamic generalizations of the traditional static systems models in such a way as to enable tests of the model and its theoretical restrictions and simplifications. Gordon Anderson and Richard Blundell (1982), for instance, develop an unrestricted dynamic formulation in order to accommodate short-run disequilibrium; this is effected through the use of lagged endogenous and exogenous regressors. In the same spirit, Serletis (1991a) applies the Anderson and Blundell approach to various demand-systems models and demonstrates that the dynamic generalizations of the traditional static models (e.g., the dynamic translog) provide more convincing overall fits as well as empirically credible estimates of the various elasticities.

1.6 Extensions

The purpose of this chapter is to survey and assess the mainstream of the recent literature on neoclassical system-wide modeling and testing in monetary economics. Because of the complexity of that topic — and the limitations of space — the discussion to this point has been limited to the most central and fundamental of the research in this area. Extensions including such important topics as uncertainty, rational expectations, non-homotheticity, intertemporal optimization, and the possibility of extend-

---

[43]For similar results with other series expansion models, see Barnett (1983a) and Yue (1991). Briefly, the evidence of instability of money demand from the old linear models results from the fact that in general the slopes of local linear approximations to nonlinear functions vary over time as the tangency moves along the nonlinear function.

[44]For example, there is a "real adjustment" specification in Gregory Chow (1966), a "price adjustment" specification in Robert Gordon (1984), and the "nominal adjustment" specification in Goldfeld (1976). For a recent approach, see Choi and Sosin (1992).

ing the framework to study the supply of money function, have not been presented. Nevertheless, the reader should not thereby conclude that the literature has not in fact been extended in those directions.

In Section 1.3, we stated the consumer's decision problem to be the maximization of contemporaneous single-period utility, in equation (1.2), subject to the current period expenditures constraint, equation (1.3). In fact, it can be shown that this decision is consistent with rational *intertemporal optimization* by the consumer if the consumer's intertemporal utility function is intertemporally blockwise weakly separable, so that $U(c, L, x)$ is a weakly separable block within the intertemporal utility function. The current period decision that we use in Section 1.3 then can be shown to be the second-stage decision in the two-stage decision of maximizing intertemporal utility subject to a sequence of single-period constraints (Barnett 1980a, 1987). Hence, all of the results surveyed above are consistent with rational intertemporal optimization by the consumer if the relevant weak separability assumption holds. As nearly all intertemporal decision models currently in use in economics are in fact intertemporally *strongly* separable, the assumption of intertemporal *weak* separability does not seem excessive.

The first stage of the two-stage decomposition of the intertemporal decision allocates total wealth over periods. In the second stage, the total expenditure allocated in the first stage to the current period is then allocated over current period consumption of individual goods, asset services, and leisure. The two-stage decomposition can be produced under intertemporal weak separability of tastes, if there is perfect certainty or risk aversion. However, the two-stage solution, producing the current period conditional second-stage decision, is not possible under risk aversion. With risk aversion, the intertemporal decision becomes a problem in stochastic optimal control, which can be solved by dynamic programming methods.

This implies that another productive direction for future research in this area is likely to be the search for nonparametric statistical index numbers that will track the exact *rational expectations aggregator function* in the risk-averse case as effectively as the Divisia can track the exact aggregator function in the risk-neutral case.[45] The existing literature on index number

---

[45] In the work referred to in earlier sections, there is the assumption of risk neutrality, so that the decision can be stated in certainty-equivalent form, with random variables replaced by their expectations. A means for extending this literature to include risk aversion and rational expectations has been proposed by Poterba and Rotemberg (1987). Subsequent work by Barnett, Hinich, and Yue (1991) and Barnett, Hinich, and Yue (2000) has produced a solution to the intertemporal stochastic optimal control problem characterizing a rational consumer, when current period consumption of monetary services is weakly separable within the consumer's intertemporal expected utility function. Those papers also contain an empirical implementation that produces the "exact" rational expectations monetary aggregates for M1. This does not appear to differ materially

theory, which has never before been extended to the risk-averse case, provides no guidance here. This is in striking contrast to the risk-neutral case, in which the existing literature on index numbers and aggregation theory has provided all of the tools that have been found necessary.

In the discussion so far, we have assumed that the aggregator function is linearly homogeneous. We also have assumed that the aggregator function is a utility function. There is a paradox in this. On the one hand, it is clear that the aggregator function does indeed have to be linearly homogeneous. Otherwise the aggregate will grow at a different rate than the components in the case of identical growth rates for all components. That, of course, would make no sense. On the other hand, linear homogeneity of a utility function is a strong assumption empirically. The solution to the paradox is that the aggregator function is a utility function only if the utility function is linearly homogeneous. If the utility function over component quantities is not linearly homogeneous, then it is known from aggregation theory that the aggregator function is the distance function.

The quantity aggregate defined by the distance function is called the Malmquist index.[46] The distance function is always linearly homogeneous in x, regardless of whether or not the utility function, U, is itself linearly homogeneous. We concentrate above on the special case of linear homogeneous utility in this chapter for expositional reasons, but the generalization to the nonhomothetic utility case presents no problems at all. If we seek to estimate the aggregator function, then the literature described in the earlier sections is directly applicable to estimating the parameters of the utility function. Once the estimation is complete, the parameter estimates are substituted into the distance function rather than into the utility function to produce the estimated aggregator function. The situation is even simpler if we seek a nonparametric statistical index number. Diewert (1976, pp. 123-4) has proved that under an appropriate method for selecting the base level of utility, U_0, the Divisia index provides a superlative approximation to the distance function, just as it did to the utility function in the special case of linearly homogeneous utility. Hence, the second-order approximation property of the Divisia index to the exact aggregator holds true, regardless of whether or not utility is homothetic (Barnett 1987).

Since we see that homotheticity of utility is not needed at all — and was used in our earlier discussion only to simplify the presentation — we are left

---

from Divisia M1 (but does differ from the simple-sum version of M1.

[46]For the definition of the distance function, see Barnett (1987, Equations (7.1) and (7.2), pp. 146-47). For the Malmquist index, see Barnett (1987, Equation (7.7), p. 148). The distance function $d(u_0, x)$ relative to base utility level u_0 can be acquired by solving the equation $f(x/d(u_0, x)) = u_0$ for $d(u_0, x)$ where f is the utility function. Hence, the distance function measures the amount by which the monetary asset vector x must be deflated to reduce the utility vector to its base level u_0.

with the weak separability condition as the key indispensable assumption. Here it is important to observe that weak separability is not an additional assumption imposed to permit use of one particular approach to modeling or aggregation, but rather is the fundamental *existence* condition, without which aggregates and sectors do not exist. It should be observed that we do not require that weak separability hold for some particular prior clustering, but rather that there exists at least one clustering of goods or assets that satisfies weak separability. Empirically, when one is free in that way to consider all possible clusterings, weak separability is indeed a weak assumption.[47]

Another important extension that is just beginning to appear in this literature is the application of the available theorems on aggregation over economic agents. It should be observed that the theory of aggregation over economic agents is independent of the theory of aggregation over goods, and hence the theory discussed above on aggregation over goods for one economic agent remains valid for any means of aggregation over economic agents. However, the existing theory on aggregation over economic agents is much more complicated than that for aggregation over goods. While a unique solution exists to the problem of aggregation over goods, and the necessary and sufficient conditions are known, the same cannot be said for aggregation over economic agents. The solution to the latter problem is dependent upon the modeler's views regarding the importance of distribution effects.

In particular, an array of solutions exists to the problem of aggregation over economic agents, depending upon the model's dependence on distribution effects. At one extreme is Gorman's (1953) solution by means of the 'representative agent' who can be proved to exist if all Engel curves are linear and are parallel across economic agents. At the other extreme is Pareto's perfectly general stratification approach, which integrates utility functions over the distribution functions of all variables that can produce distribution effects; these would be such as the distribution of income or wealth and the distribution of demographic characteristics of the population. Between these two extremes are such approaches as John Muellbauer's, which introduces dependency upon the second moments as well as on the first moments of distributions but does so in a manner that preserves the existence of a representative consumer.[48] Somewhat closer to the general Pareto

---

[47]If the procedure is reversed, and a clustering is chosen by some other means prior to separability testing — and one clustering then is subjected to a test for weak separability — the assumption of weak separability becomes a strong one that is not likely to be satisfied empirically.

[48]In particular, Muellbauer preserves the representative consumer by retaining the dependence of the decision upon only one income index, although that income index, in turn, depends jointly upon the mean and variance of the income distribution.

approach is Barnett's (1981b, pp. 58-68) stochastic convergence method, which requires fewer assumptions than Muellbauer's method while, at the same time, not preserving the existence of the representative consumer.[49]

The importance of distribution effects is central to the choice between methods of aggregating over economic agents. The Gorman method assumes away all distribution effects and leaves only dependence upon means (i.e., per capita variables). The further away one moves from Gorman's assumptions, the further one must move along the route to the Pareto method, which requires estimation of all of the moments of the distribution functions.[50] At present, the empirical research on this subject seeks to test for the depth of dependence upon distribution effects. Barnett and Serletis (1990) have done so with monetary data by explicitly introducing Divisia second moments into models and testing for their statistical significance. The importance of the induced distribution effects was found to be low.[51]

In short, the empirical evidence does not yet suggest the need to move away from Gorman's representative consumer approach towards any of the generalizations. However, should the need arise, these generalizations do exist for any applications in which complex distribution effects might be suspected. There are surveys of many of these approaches in Barnett (1981b, pp. 306–07 and 1987, pp. 153–54) and Barnett and Serletis (1990).

Finally, we consider some results that come from the application of the neoclassical theory of the firm to the financial sector. For the supply of money problem there exists system-wide modeling that employs aggregation and index number theory that is analogous to that for the demand side. An especially interesting development from this literature is the proof that the exact supply-side monetary aggregate may not equal the exact demand-side monetary aggregate, even if all component markets are cleared. This situation is produced by the existence of a regulatory wedge created by the nonpayment of interest on the reserves required of financial intermediaries. The wedge is reflected in different user costs on each side of the market. The relevant theory is available in Diana Hancock (1985, 1991) and Barnett (1987), and the statistical significance of the wedge is investigated empirically by Barnett, Hinich, and Weber (1986). They find that the size of the

---

[49]In this case some of the properties of the Slutsky equation are retained after aggregation over consumers.

[50]Another highly general approach, requiring extensive data availability, is the Henri Theil (1967) and Barnett (1987, p. 154) approach to Divisia aggregation over economic agents. By this method, a single Divisia index can aggregate jointly over goods and economic agents, although detailed data on the distribution of asset holdings over economic agents is required.

[51]Similarly, Ernst Berndt, W. Erwin Diewert, and Masako Darrough (1977) use the Pareto appproach by integrating over the entire income distribution with Canadian consumption data and similarly find little significance to the distribution effects.

wedge is astonishingly large when measured in terms of the dollar value of the implicit tax on financial firms but nevertheless produces only insignificant divergence between the demand-side and supply-side exact monetary aggregates. In that study, the wedge was found to have potentially important effects in the dynamics of the monetary transmission mechanism only at very high frequency (i.e., in the very short run).

It is perhaps worth observing that analogous wedges are produced by differences in explicit marginal tax rates among demanders and suppliers of monetary services through differences in capital gains taxation, in local and federal income taxation, and in sales and corporate income taxation. The resulting divergence in user costs between the demand and supply side of the market can create the analogous paradox to the one produced by the implicit taxation of financial firms through the nonpayment of interest on required reserves. The empirical importance of these explicit wedges for the monetary transmission mechanism has not yet been investigated systematically.

1.7 Conclusions

In the history of economic thought, economic paradigms rise and fall based upon how well they actually work in the eyes of the public. The acid test usually is the connection between the paradigm and the performance of economies that adopt the paradigm for policy purposes. The approach that we survey in this chapter has been used in research in many countries, both in academia and in central banks [52] While these data along with some of the modeling principles described in this chapter are available and are being used internally within some central banks, the methods we have just surveyed have not yet, to our knowledge, been adopted publicly as formally announced targeting methods by any country's central bank or government. Hence, the ultimate acid test cannot yet be applied.

A way to visualize how this new work affects the traditional money-demand literature is to think — as we have occasionally done in this survey — in terms of the well-known 'missing money' puzzle (Goldfeld 1976). What is being suggested here is that a good part of the problem may be in the way money is measured — both in the choice of component groupings and in the method of aggregating over those groups — and in the way that the demand model's capabilities relate to the generally nonlinear optimizing behavior of economic agents. Unlike conventional linear money demand

---

[52]For example, Divisia monetary aggregates have been produced for Britain (Roy Batchelor 1989, Leigh Drake 1992, and Belongia and Alec Chrystal 1991), Japan (Kazuhiko Ishida 1984), Holland (Martin Fase 1985), Canada (Jon Cockerline and John Murray 1981b), Australia (Tran Van Hoa 1985), and Switzerland (Yue and Fluri 1991).

equations, a system of demand equations derived from a flexible functional form with data produced from the Divisia index can be expected to capture those movements in money holding that are due to changes in the relative prices among assets. In the increasingly unregulated and volatile financial markets that have followed the collapse of the Bretton-Woods system, this would seem to be useful. In addition, the approach offers a solution to the long-running money-demand puzzle: the observed variability of elasticities is actually consistent with the variability occurring naturally along stable, nonlinear, integrable demand systems. Linear approximations to nonlinear functions are useful only locally.

In sum, the successful use in recent years of the simple representative consumer paradigm in monetary economics has opened the door to the succeeding introduction into monetary economics of the entire microfoundations, aggregation theory, and microeconometrics literatures. The moral of the story is that the nonlinearity produced by economic theory is important.[53] We have surveyed a growing literature on the importance of the use of nonlinear economic theory in modeling the demand for money. We also have surveyed the recent literature on the use of aggregation theoretic nonlinear quantity aggregation in producing monetary data. Finally, we agree with Irving Fisher (1922) that the simple-sum index should be abandoned both as a source of research data and as an intermediate target or indicator for monetary policy.

---

[53] In fact there recently has been an explosion of interest in the dynamic implications of nonlinearity in economics, and the relationship with chaotic dynamics. It is possibly not surprising that the only successful detection of chaos with economic data has been with the Divisia monetary aggregates. See Barnett and Ping Chen (1988).

Part 2

Money, Prices and Income

Overview of Part 2

Apostolos Serletis

The following table contains a brief summary of the contents of each chapter in Part 2 of the book. This part of the book examines the cyclical behavior of money and velocity measures in the United States, investigates the role of monetary aggregates in monetary policy, and provides conclusive evidence regarding the long-run neutrality and superneutrality of money.

Money, Prices and Income

Chapter Number	Chapter Title	Contents
2	Nominal Stylized Facts of U.S. Business Cycles	Investigates the nominal stylized facts of business cycles in the United States.
3	The Empirical Relationship Between Money, Prices and Income Revisited	An investigation of the relation between money, prices and income using the notion of Granger causality.
4	Monetary Aggregation and the Neutrality of Money	Investigates the issue of whether money is neutral using recent advances in the field of applied econometrics.

Chapter 2:

This chapter investigates the basic nominal stylized facts of business cycles in the United States using the methodology suggested by Kydland and Prescott (1990). Comparisons are made among simple sum, Divisia, and currency equivalent monetary aggregates. The robustness of the results to alternative (relevant) nonstochastic stationarity-inducing transformations of the data are also investigated.

Chapter 3:

This chapter investigates the relationship between money, prices and income using the notion of Granger (1969) causality and United States data.

This is achieved by evaluating whether the macroeconomic time series are trend stationary or difference stationary and by conducting tests paying explicity attention on the lag structure of the models used. Comparisons are made among simple sum, Divisia, and currency equivalent monetary aggregates.

Chapter 4:

This chapter tests the long-run neutrality of money proposition using United States data and the methodology suggested by King and Watson (1997), paying particular attention to the integration and cointegration properties of the variables. Comparisons are made among simple sum, Divisia, and currency equivalent monetary aggregates.

Chapter 2

Nominal Stylized Facts of U.S. Business Cycles

*Apostolos Serletis and David Krause**

2.1 Introduction

This chapter investigates the basic nominal stylized facts of business cycles in the United States using monthly data from 1960:1 to 1993:4 and the methodology suggested by Kydland and Prescott (1990). Comparisons are made among simple-sum and Divisia aggregates using the Thornton and Yue (1992) series of Divisia monetary aggregates. The robustness of the results to (relevant) nonstochastic stationarity-inducing transformations is also investigated.

Kydland and Prescott (1990) argue that business cycle research took a wrong turn when researchers abandoned the effort to account for the cyclical behavior of aggregate data following Koopmans's (1947) criticism of the methodology developed by Burns and Mitchell (1946) as being "measurement without theory." Crediting Lucas (1977) with reviving interest in business cycle research, Kydland and Prescott initiated a line of research that builds on the growth theory literature. Part of it involves an effort to assemble business cycle facts. This boils down to investigating whether deviations of macroeconomic aggregates from their trends are correlated with the cycle, and if so, at what leads and lags.

*Originally published in the Federal Reserve Bank of St. Louis *Review* 78 (1996), 49–54. Reprinted with permission.

Kydland and Prescott (1990) report some original evidence of the U.S. economy and conclude that several accepted nominal facts, such as the procyclical movements of money and prices, appear to be business cycle myths. In contrast to conventional wisdom, they argue that the price level (whether measured by the implicit GNP deflator or by the consumer price index), is countercyclical. Although the monetary base and M1 are both procyclical, neither leads the cycle. This evidence counters Mankiw's (1989) criticism of real business cycle models on the grounds that they do not predict procyclical variation in prices. Moreover, the evidence of countercyclical price behavior has been confirmed by Cooley and Ohanian (1991), Backus and Kehoe (1992), Smith (1992), and Chadha and Prasad (1994).

The cyclical behavior of money and prices has important implications for the sources of business cycles and therefore for discriminating among competing models. Initially it was argued, for example, that procyclical prices will be consistent with demand-driven models of the cycle, whereas countercyclical prices would be consistent with predictions of supply-determined models, including real business cycle models. Subsequently, however, Hall (1995) has shown that adding more detail to traditional demand-driven models can produce countercyclical prices, whereas Gavin and Kydland (1995) have shown that alternative money supply rules can generate either procyclical or countercyclical prices in a real business cycle setting.

The objective of this chapter is to re-examine the cyclical behavior of money and prices using monthly U.S. data. For comparison purposes, the methodology used is mainly that of Kydland and Prescott (1990). Therefore in accordance with the real business cycle approach to economic fluctuations, we define the growth of a variable as its smoothed trend and the cycle components of a variable as the deviation of the actual values of the variable from the smoothed trend. However, we investigate robustness of the results to alternative (relevant) nonstochastic stationarity-inducing transformations.

To highlight the influence of money measurement on statistical inference [as in Belongia (1996)], comparisons are made among simple-sum and Divisia monetary aggregates (of M1A, M1, M2, M3, and L) — see Barnett, Fisher, and Serletis (1992) regarding the state of the art in monetary aggregation. The money measures employed are monthly simple-sum and Divisia indexes (from 1960:1 to 1993:4), as described in Thornton and Yue (1992), and were obtained from the Federal Reserve Economic Data (FRED) bulletin board of the Federal Reserve Bank of St. Louis.

The chapter is organized as follows. Section 2.1 briefly discusses the Hodrick Prescott (HP) filtering procedure for decomposing time series into long-run and business cycle components. Section 2.2 presents HP empirical correlations of money, prices, and nominal interest rates with industrial production. In section 2.3 we investigate the robustness of our results to alternative stationarity-inducing transformations, and in the last section we summarize the main results and conclude.

2.2 Methodology

For a description of the stylized facts, we follow the current practice of detrending the data with the HP filter — see Prescott (1986). For the logarithm of a time series X_t, for $t = 1, 2, \ldots, T$, this procedure defines the trend or growth component, denoted τ_t, for $t = 1, 2, \ldots, T$, as the solution to the following minimization problem

$$\min_{\tau_t} \sum_{t=1}^{T} (X_t - \tau_t)^{2+\mu} \sum_{t=2}^{T-1} \left[(\tau_{t+1} - \tau_t) - (\tau_t - \tau_{t-1}) \right]^2$$

so $X_t - \tau_t$ is the filtered series. The larger the μ, the smoother the trend path, and when $\mu = \infty$, a linear trend results. In our computations, we set $\mu = 129,600$, as it has been suggested for monthly data. Note that the monthly cyclical components defined by $\mu = 129,600$ approximately average to the quarterly components defined by $\mu = 1,600$ which is commonly used to define business cycle fluctuations in research literature.

We measure the degree of co-movement of a series with the pertinent cyclical variable by the magnitude of the correlation coefficient $\rho(j)$, $j \in \{0, \pm 1, \pm 2, \ldots\}$. The contemporaneous correlation coefficient — $\rho(0)$ — gives information on the degree of contemporaneous co-movement between the series and the pertinent cyclical variable. In particular, if $\rho(0)$ is positive, zero, or negative, we say that the series is procyclical, acyclical, or countercyclical, respectively. In fact, for $0.23 \leq |\rho(0)| < 1$, $0.10 \leq |\rho(0)| < 0.23$, and $0 \leq |\rho(0)| < 0.10$, we say that the series is strongly contemporaneously correlated, weakly contemporaneously correlated, and contemporaneously uncorrelated with the cycle, respectively. Following Fiorito and Kollintzas (1994) in our sample of 400 observations, the cutoff point 0.1 is close to the value 0.097 that is required to reject the null hypothesis, $H_0 : \rho(0) = 0$, at the 5 percent level in a two-sided test for bivariate normal random variables. Also, the cutoff point 0.23 is close to the value of 0.229 that is required to reject the null hypothesis $H_0 : |\rho(0)| \leq 0.5$, in the corresponding one-tailed test. Also, $\rho(j)$, $j \in \{\pm 1, \pm 2, \ldots\}$ — the cross correlation coefficient — gives information on the phase-shift of the series relative to the cycle. If $|\rho(j)|$ is maximum for a negative, zero, or positive j, we say that the series is leading the cycle by j periods, is synchronous, or is lagging the cycle by j periods, respectively.

2.3　Hodrick-Prescott Stylized Facts

In Table 2.1 we report contemporaneous correlations, as well as cross correlations (at lags and leads of one through six months) between the cyclical components of money and the cyclical component of industrial production. We see that all the monetary aggregates are strongly procyclical. With a minor exception for M1A, for both Divisia and simple-sum measures, the broader the aggregate the more procyclical it is. There is also evidence that M2 money, however defined, leads the cycle by more than the other aggregates and, if anything, Sum L is slightly lagging. These results suggest the only major differences among simple-sum and Divisia monetary aggregates occur in the stronger correlation at leads for the broad Divisia aggregates, M3 and L.

We interpret these results as being generally consistent with the cyclical money behavior in the United States reported (using quarterly data) by Kydland and Prescott (1990) and Belongia (1996). Unlike Belongia, who like Kydland and Prescott, uses quarterly data and only the simple-sum and Divisia measures of M1 and M2, we find no significant differences across narrow simple-sum and Divisia monetary aggregates. We find strong contemporaneous correlations between broad-sum and Divisia money and the cyclical indicator. Divisia L, however, is leading the cycle, and Sum L is slightly lagging the cycle. This result seems to be consistent with the evidence reported by Barnett, Offenbacher, and Spindt (1984), who found that Divisia L was the best aggregate in terms of causality tests, produced the most stable demand-for-money function, and provided the best reduced form results.

Next we turn to the statistical properties of the cyclical components of the price level (measured by the consumer price index) and two short-term nominal interest rates (to deal with anomalies that arise because of different ways of measuring financial market price information) — the Treasury bill rate and the commercial paper rate. The Treasury bill rate is the interest rate on short-term, unsecured borrowing by the U.S. government, whereas the commercial paper rate is the interest rate on short-term, unsecured borrowing by corporations. As Friedman and Kuttner (1993, p. 194) argue, the commercial paper rate is superior in capturing the information in financial prices because "the commercial paper rate more directly reflects the cost of finance corresponding to potentially interest-sensitive expenditure flows than does the Treasury bill rate."

TABLE 2.1

CORRELATIONS OF HP-FILTERED SUM AND DIVISIA MONETARY AGGREGATES
WITH INDUSTRIAL PRODUCTION*

Variable x	Volatility	\multicolumn{13}{c}{Correlation coefficients of industrial production with}
		x_{t-6}	x_{t-5}	x_{t-4}	x_{t-3}	x_{t-2}	x_{t-1}	x_t	x_{t+1}	x_{t+2}	x_{t+3}	x_{t+4}	x_{t+5}	x_{t+6}
Sum M1A	2.09	0.43	0.43	0.43	0.43	0.42	0.40	0.38	0.35	0.31	0.28	0.25	0.24	0.22
Sum M1	1.93	0.37	0.37	0.37	0.36	0.35	0.32	0.28	0.24	0.19	0.15	0.11	0.08	0.05
Sum M2	1.41	0.71	0.70	0.66	0.62	0.56	0.49	0.40	0.32	0.24	0.16	0.09	0.03	-0.03
Sum M3	1.48	0.50	0.52	0.53	0.53	0.52	0.50	0.47	0.44	0.41	0.38	0.35	0.32	0.29
Sum L	1.11	0.33	0.39	0.44	0.49	0.52	0.55	0.57	0.58	0.59	0.58	0.58	0.56	0.55
Divisia M1A	1.74	0.39	0.40	0.40	0.40	0.39	0.37	0.35	0.32	0.29	0.27	0.26	0.25	0.24
Divisia M1	1.50	0.28	0.28	0.29	0.28	0.27	0.24	0.21	0.18	0.14	0.10	0.08	0.05	0.03
Divisia M2	1.81	0.67	0.65	0.62	0.59	0.54	0.47	0.40	0.33	0.25	0.19	0.13	0.08	0.03
Divisia M3	1.78	0.68	0.67	0.66	0.64	0.60	0.56	0.50	0.45	0.39	0.34	0.29	0.25	0.21
Divisia L	1.58	0.62	0.63	0.64	0.64	0.62	0.60	0.57	0.53	0.49	0.45	0.41	0.37	0.33

* Monthly data from sample period 1960:1–1993:4.

TABLE 2.2

CORRELATIONS OF HP-FILTERED PRICES AND SHORT-TERM NOMINAL INTEREST RATES
WITH INDUSTRIAL PRODUCTION*

Variable x	Volatility	Correlation coefficients of industrial production with												
		x_{t-6}	x_{t-5}	x_{t-4}	x_{t-3}	x_{t-2}	x_{t-1}	x_t	x_{t+1}	x_{t+2}	x_{t+3}	x_{t+4}	x_{t+5}	x_{t+6}
Consumer price index	1.46	-0.73	-0.71	-0.68	-0.65	-0.60	-0.55	-0.48	-0.43	-0.37	-0.31	-0.25	-0.20	-0.15
Treasury bill rate	1.66	-0.17	-0.09	0.01	0.11	0.22	0.32	0.40	0.44	0.46	0.47	0.47	0.48	0.48
Commercial paper rate	1.44	-0.12	-0.03	0.05	0.15	0.25	0.33	0.39	0.42	0.43	0.43	0.43	0.43	0.43

* Monthly data from sample period 1960:1–1993:4.

Table 2.2 reports HP cyclical correlations of prices and short-term nominal interest rates with industrial production. We see that the price level is strongly countercyclical, whereas both the Treasury bill rate and the commercial paper rate are strongly procyclical and lag the cycle. These results provide strong confirmation for the countercyclical price behavior in the United States reported by Kydland and Prescott (1990), Cooley and Ohanian (1991), Backus and Kehoe (1992), Smith (1992), and Chadha and Prasad (1994). They clearly support the Kydland and Prescott (1990) claim that the perceived fact of procyclical prices is but a myth.

2.4 Robustness

We have characterized the key nominal features of U.S. business cycles using a modern counterpart of the methods developed by Burns and Mitchell (1946) — HP cyclical components. The HP filter is used almost universally in the real business cycle research program and extracts a long-run component from the data, rendering stationary series that are integrated up to the fourth order. HP filtering, however, has recently been questioned as a unique method of trend elimination. For example, King and Rebelo (1993) argue that HP filtering may seriously change measures of persistence, variability, and co-movement. They also give a number of examples that demonstrate that the dynamics of HP filtered data can differ significantly from the dynamics of differenced or detrended data.

Also, Cogley and Nason (1995), in analyzing the effect of HP filtering on trend- and difference-stationary time series, argue that the interpretation of HP stylized facts depends on assumptions about the time series properties of the original data. For example, when the original data are trend stationary, the HP filter operates like a high-pass filter. That is, it removes the low frequency components and allows the high frequency components to pass through. When the original data are difference stationary, however, the HP filter does not operate like a high-pass filter. In this case, HP stylized facts about periodicity and co-movement are determined primarily by the filter and reveal very little about the dynamic properties of the original data.

More recently, however, Baxter and King (1995) argue that HP filtering can produce reasonable approximations of an ideal business cycle filter. Though we believe that the results based on the HP filter are reasonably robust across business cycle filters, we believe it is useful to compare what we are doing with alternative popular methods of detrending the data. Once, however, we abstract from growth theory, we need to make some assumption about the trend. In particular, deterministic detrending will be the appropriate stationarity-inducing transformation under trend stationarity and differencing under difference stationarity.

Results reported in Koustas and Serletis (1996), based on augmented Dickey-Fuller-type regressions, indicate that the null hypothesis of a unit root in levels cannot be rejected for any of the series used here, whereas the null hypothesis of a second unit root is rejected except for Sum M3, Sum L, and the price level which appear to be integrated of order 2 [or I(2) in Engle and Granger (1987) terminology]. Based on this evidence, in Tables 2.3 and 2.4 we report correlations (in the same fashion as in Tables 2.1 and 2.2) based on differenced data, keeping in mind that although differencing yields stationary series, these stationary series do not in general correspond to cyclical components. See, for example, Baxter and King (1995). These results are generally supportive of the hypothesis of acyclical money and price behavior. Nominal interest rates appear to be strongly procyclical and lagging slightly.

2.5   Conclusion

In this chapter we investigated the cyclical behavior of U.S. money, prices, and short-term nominal interest rates, using monthly data from 1960:1 to 1993:4 and the methodology of Kydland and Prescott (1990). Based on stationary HP cyclical deviations, our results fully match recent evidence on the countercyclicality of the price level. We also found that short-term nominal interest rates are strongly procyclical and that money is in general procyclical. Furthermore, the evidence suggests that there are only slight differences across narrow simple-sum and Divisia money measures.

TABLE 2.3

CORRELATIONS OF FIRST DIFFERENCES OF SUM AND DIVISIA MONEY WITH FIRST DIFFERENCES OF INDUSTRIAL PRODUCTION*

Variable x	Volatility	Correlation coefficients of industrial production with												
		x_{t-6}	x_{t-5}	x_{t-4}	x_{t-3}	x_{t-2}	x_{t-1}	x_t	x_{t+1}	x_{t+2}	x_{t+3}	x_{t+4}	x_{t+5}	x_{t+6}
Sum M1A	0.005	0.09	0.06	0.05	0.17	0.14	0.12	0.10	0.06	−0.04	−0.08	−0.08	−0.03	−0.06
Sum M1	0.004	0.09	0.08	0.07	0.17	0.14	0.12	0.05	0.04	−0.05	−0.12	−0.08	−0.04	−0.05
Sum M2	0.003	0.25	0.23	0.21	0.27	0.23	0.16	0.11	0.04	−0.07	−0.07	−0.07	−0.05	−0.04
Sum M3	0.003	0.16	0.18	0.17	0.21	0.17	0.13	0.11	0.10	0.04	0.03	0.05	0.04	0.01
Sum L	0.003	0.10	0.11	0.07	0.12	0.10	0.14	0.15	0.17	0.11	0.11	0.11	0.08	0.09
Divisia M1A	0.005	0.04	0.03	0.01	0.14	0.11	0.09	0.04	0.02	−0.07	−0.08	−0.06	−0.02	−0.02
Divisia M1	0.004	0.04	0.05	0.03	0.14	0.10	0.08	−0.02	−0.01	−0.06	−0.10	−0.04	−0.01	−0.04
Divisia M2	0.004	0.18	0.20	0.17	0.28	0.25	0.20	0.07	0.02	−0.09	−0.10	−0.07	−0.05	−0.04
Divisia M3	0.003	0.17	0.20	0.18	0.27	0.24	0.19	0.08	0.06	−0.03	−0.04	0.00	0.01	0.02
Divisia L	0.003	0.14	0.16	0.13	0.24	0.21	0.21	0.12	0.12	0.02	0.02	0.04	0.05	0.07

* Monthly data from sample period 1960:1–1993:4.

TABLE 2.4

CORRELATIONS OF FIRST DIFFERENCES OF PRICES AND SHORT-TERM NOMINAL INTEREST RATES WITH FIRST DIFFERENCES OF INDUSTRIAL PRODUCTION*

Variable x	Volatility	Correlation coefficients of industrial production with												
		x_{t-6}	x_{t-5}	x_{t-4}	x_{t-3}	x_{t-2}	x_{t-1}	x_t	x_{t+1}	x_{t+2}	x_{t+3}	x_{t+4}	x_{t+5}	x_{t+6}
Consumer price pndex	0.003	−0.23	−0.22	−0.30	−0.23	−0.23	−0.16	−0.08	−0.07	−0.07	0.00	−0.01	−0.04	−0.07
Treasury bill rate	0.006	−0.10	−0.06	−0.06	−0.08	0.13	0.20	0.30	0.24	0.18	0.04	0.00	0.02	−0.00
Commercial paper rate	0.006	−0.03	−0.02	−0.08	−0.04	0.14	0.21	0.23	0.23	0.11	0.03	−0.03	0.02	0.02

* Monthly data from sample period 1960:1–1993:4.

Chapter 3

The Empirical Relationship Between Money, Prices, and Income Revisited

*Apostolos Serletis**

3.1 Introduction

The purpose of this chapter is to establish the relationship between money (on various definitions), real income, and prices using the notion of Granger (1959) causality. The chapter differs from previous work in that attention is focused on aggregation-theoretic monetary aggregates and the appropriate representation of the nature of nonstationarities apparent in the macroeconomic time series under consideration, as well as on the sensitivity of causality tests to detrending and lag-length specifications.

A rapidly growing line of research has begun to appear recently on the rigorous use of microeconomic and aggregation-theoretic foundations in the construction of monetary aggregates. An important reason for this interest is the fact that simple summation aggregation implies perfect substitutability among components — an assumption that does not hold for the component monetary assets and one that is especially distortive of high-level monetary aggregates.

Barnett (1980), in a challenging paper, voiced objections to simple-sum aggregation procedures and derived the theoretical linkage between monetary theory and index-number theory. He applied economic aggregation and index-number theory and constructed monetary aggregates based on Diewert's (1976) class of 'superlative' quantity index numbers. The new aggregates are Divisia quantity indexes and represent a practically viable and theoretically meaningful alternative to the flawed simple-summation aggregates.

Another example is the monetary velocity (MQ) aggregate, proposed by Spindt (1985), which uses the Fisher ideal index to produce a monetary aggregate and a velocity aggregate. This aggregate, however, is inconsistent with the existing aggregation and index-number theory, because it uses turnover rates, rather than the user cost prices, to calculate the weights appearing in the usual Fisher ideal index.

There is an extensive literature on causality tests between money, prices, and income. To mention only two (and, in fact, those on which I build), Barnett, Offenbacher, and Spindt (1984) reported results of applying several standard tests of the Granger causality relation between sum and Divisia money (on all definitions) and income. Moreover, Thornton and Batten (1985) systematically investigated the effects of using different statistical criteria for specifying the lag length for causal relationships between income and the sum monetary aggregates M1, M2, M2 net of M1, and the adjusted monetary base.

No one has yet systematically considered the nonstationary behavior of the time series under consideration, however, although the empirical evidence (see, e.g., Nelson and Plosser 1982; Wasserfallen 1986) clearly implies that most economic time series are nonstationary in the sense that they tend to depart from any given value as time goes on. Of course, failure to account for nonstationarities or choice of the wrong assumption concerning the form of nonstationarity has far-reaching consequences in Granger-causality test results as well as in applied work in general.

Nonstationary time series are frequently detrended in empirical investigations by regressing the series on time or a function of time (see, e.g., Thornton and Batten 1985). As Nelson and Plosser (1982) and Wasserfallen (1986) showed, however, most economic time series are better characterized as difference-stationary (DS) processes rather than trend-stationary (TS) processes. As a result, differencing rather than detrending is usually necessary to achieve stationarity.

In this chapter I investigate the relationship between sum, Divisia, and MQ money, prices, and income using the notion of Granger (1969) causality. This is achieved by evaluating empirically [using Dickey-Fuller unit root

tests similar to those in Nelson and Plosser (1982)] whether the variables
are TS or DS and by conducting tests using three different, ad hoc, lag
lengths — 8, 6, and 4 quarters — as well as a statistically determined —
using Akaike's (1969a,b) final prediction error criterion — lag structure.
As Thornton and Batten (1985), among others, found, the conclusions on
the causal relationships depend on model specification. In particular, ad
hoc approaches, such as considering arbitrary lag-length specifications or
employing rules of thumb, can provide misleading results.

The remainder of the chapter is organized as follows: Section 3.2 briefly
provides a qualitative assessment of the relative merits of the conventional
(summation) versus Barnett's Divisia and Spindt's Fisher money-stock indexes. Section 3.3 contains a brief presentation of Granger-Sims causality
testing with special emphasis given to the importance of the appropriate
transformation of the series to achieve stationarity. In Section 3.4, I test the
hypothesis that the time series are DS processes against the alternative that
they are TS processes. The evidence clearly implies that differencing is the
appropriate procedure to achieve stationarity. Section 3.5 shows the results
of causality tests between money, prices, and income. Tests are conducted
using three different, ad hoc, lag lengths — 8, 6, and 4 quarters — as well
as a statistically determined lag structure. Variables are transformed using
first-differencing, but I also try detrending along with differencing in order
to investigate the sensitivity of causality tests to detrending. Section 3.6
presents some brief concluding remarks.

3.2 The Money-Measurement Theme

The measurement of money is an important practical problem in monetary
theory, and it has been the focus of continuing controversy over the years.
Specifically, issues such as what serves as money, what are different degrees
of 'moneyness' and 'near-moneyness,' and what are the alternative money
substitutes play an important role in identifying a measure of money.

The official monetary aggregates are simple-sum indexes in which all
monetary components are assigned a constant and equal (unitary) weight.
This summation index,

$$Q = \sum_{i=1}^{n} x_i, \tag{3.1}$$

implies that all components (x_i) contribute equally to the money total (Q)
and it views all monetary assets as dollar-for-dollar perfect substitutes.
Under this convention, (3.1) represents an index of the stock of nominal
monetary wealth, but it cannot, in general, be assumed to represent a valid
structural economic variable for the services of the quantity of money.

That monetary assets are not perfect substitutes has long been recognized, and there has been a steady stream of attempts at weakening the perfect substitutability assumption and properly weighting monetary components within a simple-sum aggregate according to their degree of 'moneyness.' It is only recently, however, that Barnett (1980, 1982, 1987a,b; also Barnett, Offenbacher, and Spindt 1981, 1984) has voiced objections to simple-sum aggregation procedures and constructed monetary aggregates in a rigorous and unique manner derived directly from the theory of economic quantity aggregation. The new aggregates are Divisia quantity indexes, which are elements of the Diewert (1976) class of 'superlative' quantity-index numbers.

The application of aggregation theory and index-number theory to monetary aggregation requires information about the price of money. Although the meaning of the price of money is not obvious in monetary theory, in the recent literature monetary assets are viewed à la Friedman (1956) as durable goods that render to their holders a variety of nonobservable monetary services (either transaction services or store-of-wealth services). Under such assumptions the service flow of a given monetary asset is priced by the asset's user cost, as in Barnett (1978),

$$p_{it} = (R_t - r_{it})/(1 + R_t), \tag{3.2}$$

which is just the discounted interest foregone (and therefore opportunity cost) of holding a dollar's worth of that asset. Here r_{it} is the market yield on the ith asset, and R_t is the 'benchmark' rate (the highest available yield).

Having derived the user-cost prices of monetary assets, the Divisia index is defined as

$$\log Q_t - \log Q_{t-1} = \sum_{i=1}^{n} w_{it}^*(\log x_{it} - \log x_{i,t-1}), \tag{3.3}$$

where x_{it} represents (nominal or real, total or per capita) balances of monetary asset i at time t, $w_{it}^* = \frac{1}{2}(w_{it} + w_{i,t-1})$, and $w_{it} = p_{it}x_{it}/\sum_{k=1}^{n} p_{kt}x_{kt}$ is the expenditure share of monetary asset i during period t.

Clearly, the Divisia index, instead of adding up monetary assets on a dollar-for-dollar basis, weights each component's growth rate according to its degree of 'moneyness,' the weights being the asset's value shares in total expenditure on monetary-asset services. In addition, as I mentioned earlier, the Divisia index is an element of the 'superlative' class and, thus, provides second-order nonparametric approximations to any parameterized aggregator function (see Diewert 1976).

An alternative aggregate is that proposed by Spindt (1985). Based on the Fisher ideal index, it produces a monetary aggregate that, as Spindt argued, corresponds closely with the monetary aggregate contemplated in the equation of exchange. In the particular solution derived by Spindt (1985), money is measured as

$$Q_t/Q_{t-1} = \left[\sum_{i=1}^{n} w_{i,t-1}(x_{it}/x_{i,t-1}) / \sum_{i=1}^{n} w_{it}(x_{i,t-1}/x_{it}) \right]^{1/2}, \qquad (3.4)$$

where $w_{it} = v_{it}x_{it}/\sum_{k=1}^{n} v_{kt}, x_{kt}$, and v_{it} is the turnover rate of monetary asset i during period t.

Spindt's aggregate, however, unlike the aggregate in (3.3), seems to be arbitrary and inconsistent with the existing aggregation and index-number theory. The relevant aggregation and index-number theory producing the Fisher ideal index requires the use of prices and quantities, not turnover rates and quantities [see Barnett (1987a,b) for the current state of art in the theory of monetary aggregation].

3.3 Granger-Sims Causality Tests

To test the direction of causality between money, prices, and income, in the sense of Granger (1969) and Sims (1972), it must be assumed that the relevant information is entirely contained in the present and past values of these variables. A specification that suggests itself is

$$z_t = \alpha_0 + \sum_{i=1}^{r} \alpha_i z_{t-i} + \sum_{j=1}^{s} \beta_j m_{t-j} + u_t, \qquad (3.5)$$

where $z_t = \log y_t$ or $\log p_t$, $m_t = \log$ of a given monetary aggregate, $p_t =$ consumer price index (CPI), $y_t =$ real gross national product (GNP), and $u_t =$ a disturbance term. To test if m_t causes z_t in the Granger-Sims sense, equation (3.5) is first estimated by ordinary least squares (OLS) and the unrestricted sum of squared residuals (SSR_u) is obtained. Then, by running another regression equation under the restriction that all β_j's are 0, the restricted sum of squared residuals (SSR_r) is obtained. If u_t is a white noise, then the statistical computed as the ratio of ($SSR_r - SSR_u$)/s to $SSR_u/(n - r - s - 1)$ has an asymptotic F distribution with numerator degrees of freedom s and denominator degrees of freedom $n - r - s - 1$, where n is the number of observations and 1 is subtracted out to account for the constant term in equation (3.5). The roles of z_t and m_t are reversed in another F test to see whether there is a feedback relationship among these

variables. The lag lengths on the dependent variable and on the potential
causal variable are to be determined. I shall return to this matter in Section
3.4.

The disturbance u_t in equation (3.5) must be a white noise to make the
said test statistic an asymptotic F distribution. A white noise is a serially
uncorrelated process. Since many economic time series are nonstationary,
however, in the sense that they tend to depart from any given value as time
goes on, it is unlikely that the disturbance u_t in equation (3.5) will result
in a white-noise series. To remove apparent nonstationarity in economic
time series, the series are frequently detrended in empirical investigations
by regressing the series on time or a function of time. With a linear time
trend, equation (3.5) becomes

$$z_t = \alpha_0 + \sum_{i=1}^{r} \alpha_i z_{t-1} + \sum_{j=1}^{s} \beta_j m_{t-j} + dt + u_t. \tag{3.6}$$

As Kang (1985) argued, however, the causal relationships inferred from
the Granger-Sims tests depend very much on whether or not series are
detrended. In act, detrending tends to weaken causal relationships, and
conversely, failure to detrend tends to enhance causal relationships.

Many researchers have also transformed the series through prefilters,
perhaps to further satisfy the condition of a white noise for u_t. For instance,
most have used first-differencing of the natural logarithms of the data series
to reduce the serial correlation in the residuals. In particular, the $(1 - L)$
filter was used to transform the raw data, where L is the backward shift
operator, namely $L^j x_t = x_{t-j}$. Of course, once variables are transformed
using logarithms, a further transformation through the filter $(1 - L)$ yields
the growth rate of the series.

There is obviously an unlimited number of possibilities that can account
for nonstationary behavior, and, of course, failure to account for nonstationarities or choice of the wrong transformation has far-reaching consequences
in econometric work. Under these circumstances, it becomes important to
evaluate empirically what type of nonstationarity is present in the data. I
turn to this issue in Section 3.4.

3.4   Statistical Issues

The basic statistical issue is the appropriate representation of the nature
of nonstationarity in the series to satisfy the condition of white noise for
u_t. Nelson and Plosser (1982) showed that most economic series can be
viewed as DS processes — stationary in first differences — rather than TS

processes — deterministic functions of time. To determine whether the time series used here belong to the DS or TS class of models, one informal testing procedure was employed along with one formal test.

As an informal first step, I calculated the autocorrelation functions for each of the time series in both level and first-difference form (see Table 3.1). For the level form, sample autocorrelations are large and decay slowly with increasing lag. For the first-difference form, sample autocorrelations are positive and significant at large one for each of the series except for the Sum M1, the corresponding Divisia, and the MQ aggregates, but in most cases they are not significant at longer lags. These findings suggest that the series belong to the DS class of models.

My formal test for the hypothesis that the time series belong to the DS class against the alternative that they belong to the TS class involved Dickey-Fuller unit-root tests similar to those in Nelson and Plosser (1982) based on

$$w_t = \mu + \gamma t + \delta_1 w_{t-1} + \sum_{j=1}^{k} \delta_{j+1} \left(1 - L\right) w_{t-j} + e_t, \qquad (3.7)$$

where L is the lag operator and e_t is a stationary series with mean 0 and constant variance σ_e^2. Specifically, I tested the joint null hypothesis that $\delta_1 = 1$ and $\gamma = 0$ with univariate autoregressive models for each data series. Under this null hypothesis, Dickey and Fuller (1979) provided tabulations of the distribution of the t ratio for δ_1, denoted by τ, for testing the null hypothesis $\delta_1 = 1$. Note that they did not develop a statistic for the joint test or for γ alone. According to Nelson and Plosser (1982, p. 144, footnote 8), however, testing $\delta_1 = 1$ is sufficient for the model considered here.

These results are reported in Table 3.2 for the case in which an autoregressive process of order 2 is assumed. Using the distributions tabulated by Fuller (1976, Table 8.5.2) and based on a critical value for the test statistics $\tau(\hat{\delta}_1)$ of -3.50 corresponding to the 5% significance level for a sample size of 50, I fail to reject the hypothesis that the data have unit roots for all of the series except for Sum M3. Differencing, therefore, seems to be the appropriate transformation to achieve stationarity.

TABLE 3.1

SAMPLE AUTOCORRELATIONS OF THE NATURAL LOGS AND OF THE FIRST DIFFERENCES OF THE NATURAL LOGS

Series	Natural logs						First differences of natural logs					
	r_1	r_2	r_3	r_4	r_5	r_6	r_1	r_2	r_3	r_4	r_5	r_6
Sum M1	.950	.900	.849	.798	.747	.696	.068	.041	.113	−.188	.106	.051
Sum M2	.950	.900	.849	.798	.747	.698	.432	.181	.055	−.073	.030	−.134
Sum M3	.949	.898	.846	.796	.747	.698	.584	.385	.207	.141	.139	.014
Sum L	.952	.903	.853	.804	.755	.707	.543	.274	.015	−.080	−.100	−.054
Divisia M1	.951	.902	.853	.803	.754	.706	−.122	−.041	.129	−.290	.131	.136
Divisia M2	.948	.895	.842	.789	.737	.686	.507	.345	.404	.266	.346	.205
Divisia M3	.946	.890	.835	.781	.729	.679	.534	.391	.422	.290	.356	.243
Divisia L	.948	.895	.843	.790	.739	.689	.535	.393	.414	.254	.326	.199
MQ	.950	.901	.851	.800	.750	.701	−.087	−.180	.223	−.134	.200	−.069
CPI	.961	.921	.879	.836	.792	.747	.309	.393	.112	.364	.170	.157
Real GNP	.943	.881	.818	.750	.689	.633	.324	.223	.031	.005	−.089	−.082

NOTE: r_i is the ith-order autocorrelation coefficient.

TABLE 3.2

DICKEY-FULLER TESTS FOR AUTOREGRESSIVE UNIT ROOTS:

$$w_t = \mu + \gamma t + \delta_1 w_{t-1} + \delta_2(w_{t-1} - w_{t-2}) + u_t$$

Series	n	$\hat{\mu}$	$t(\hat{\mu})$	$\hat{\gamma}$	$t(\hat{\gamma})$	$\hat{\delta}_1$	$\tau(\hat{\delta}_1)$	SER	r_1
Sum M1	59	.348	1.423	.001	1.441	.926	−1.367	.007	.002
Sum M2	59	.695	3.349	.003	3.229	.850	−3.276	.006	−.086
Sum M3	59	.592	5.087	.003	4.841	.874	−4.954	.003	−.035
Sum L	59	.655	3.345	.003	3.271	.857	−3.283	.002	−.027
Divisia M1	59	.551	1.798	.002	1.739	.883	−1.732	.006	.004
Divisia M2	59	.201	2.107	.0005	1.434	.960	−1.943	.009	−.038
Divisia M3	59	.236	2.584	.0006	1.834	.953	−2.403	.008	−.042
Divisia L	59	.193	2.030	.0005	1.606	.960	−1.899	.007	−.074
MQ	59	.011	2.799	.003	2.428	.794	−2.456	.008	−.009
CPI	59	.315	1.694	.001	1.616	.934	−1.630	.010	−.130
Real GNP	59	.878	2.467	.0008	2.291	.875	−2.450	.010	−.093

NOTE: w_t represents the natural logs of the data. $t(\hat{\mu})$ and $t(\hat{\gamma})$ are the ratios of the OLS estimates of μ and γ to their respective standard errors. $\tau(\hat{\delta}_1)$ is the ratio of $\hat{\delta}_1 - 1$ to its standard error. SER is the standard error of the regression, and r_1 is the first-order auto-correlation coefficient of the residuals. For $n = 50$, the cutoff points from Fuller (1976, Table 8.5.2) for $\hat{\tau}_\tau$ at .01, .025, and .05 are $-4.15, -3.80,$ and -3.50, respectively.

On the basis of the preceding formal and informal statistical findings, I have used first differencing of the natural logarithms of the data series as a way of removing nonstationarities, but I have also tried detrending along with differencing in order to systematically investigate the sensitivity of causality tests to detrending. With the exception of Kang (1985), no one has yet systematically investigated the sensitivity of causality tests between money, prices, and income to detrending. Thus I have used both (3.5) and (3.6) with differenced series.

One preliminary matter also had to be dealt with before I could proceed to perform Granger-causality tests. It concerns the lengths of lags r and s. In the literature r and s are frequently chosen to have the same value, and lag lengths of 4, 6, or 8 are used most often with quarterly data. Such arbitrary lag specifications can produce misleading results, however, because they may imply misspecification of the order of the autoregressive process. For example, if either r or s (or both) is too large, the estimates will be unbiased but inefficient. If either r or s (or both) is too small, the estimates will be biased but have a smaller variance.

Here, I tried three different commonly chosen lag lengths — 8, 6, and 4 quarters — for both z_t and m_t in (3.5) and (3.6). In addition, following Hsiao (1979a,b), I used the data to determine the 'optimum' lag structure. In particular, the optimal r and s in each of equations (3.5) and (3.6) was determined using Akaike's (1969a,b) final prediction error (FPE) criterion. The FPE was calculated by Akaike (1969a) as the product of $(n + r + s + 1) / (n - r - s - 1)$ and SSR/n, where n is the number of observations and SSR is the sum of squared residuals. Note that the FPE balances the degrees of freedom used (as implied by the multiplicative factor) and the fit of the equation (as implied by SSR).

Of course, the FPE is only one of a number of possible statistical criteria that could be used to select the 'appropriate' lag length. [For a discussion of some of these and references to others, see Priestley (1981, pp. 370-376); see Thornton and Batten (1985) for an application to Granger causality between money and income.] Consequently, different causality test results could be obtained from the same data because of the use of different criteria for specifying the lag length. I chose the FPE criterion because, on the basis of experimentation by others (see, e.g., Hsiao 1981; Thornton and Batten 1985), it appears to perform well in selecting the model.

3.5   Money, Prices, and Income

The data that I used for the official summation aggregates, the corresponding Divisia aggregates, and the Fisher money-stock index were provided by official sources at the Federal Reserve Board. Note that the Divisia aggregate data were actually produced by the Fisher ideal index proposed by Barnett (1980). That index was shown by Barnett to be equal to the Divisia index to within three decimal places. Note also that the monetary aggregates are constructed from seasonally adjusted quantities and, in the case of the Divisia aggregates, from unadjusted interest rates. The data are at monthly frequency and, therefore, were converted to average quarterly data for the period 1970I-1985I. Seasonally adjusted series on real GNP and the CPI (all commodities) are taken from the CANSIM Databank — series B50301 and D134101, respectively.

I use the following notational conventions. At the four levels of aggregation, I use the notation M1, M2, M3, and L to designate the growth rates of the four simple sum aggregates. I designate the growth rates of the corresponding Divisia aggregates by DM1, DM2, DM3, and DL and that of the Fisher money-stock index by MQ. I also use p and y to designate growth rates of the CPI and the real GNP, respectively.

Since I am interested, among other things, in the sensitivity of causality test results to various lag-length specifications and to detrending, F tests for Granger causality were performed on the three different, ad hoc lag lengths — 8, 6, and 4 quarters — and on the FPE-lag structure. All of these were done with and without detrending. The F ratios and their p values are presented in Tables 3.3 and 3.4. Details on the lag-length selection procedures are of limited interest and are not reported here. In determining the optimal (in the minimum FPE sense) bivariate lag structures, however, I used the sequential procedure suggested by Hsiao (1979a). The lag-length selection results are summarized (in brackets) in the FPE lags columns of Tables 3.3 and 3.4.

I arrive at several stylized findings from Tables 3.3 and 3.4. First, for the detrending option, the F ratios (and therefore causality relationships) are not in general very different with and without detrending, as expected. Note, however, that causal relationships seem to become less significant with detrending and that there are four instances in which detrending produces contradictory results. In terms of these results, this chapter confirms the conclusion reached earlier by Nelson and Kang (1984) and Kang (1985) that detrending tends to remove or weaken causal relationships.

For the lag-length specification options, the results show that causal relationships between money, prices, and income are unquestionably sensitive to the lag specification. For example, there are many instances in which the ad hoc lag lengths of 4, 6, and 8 produce contradictory results. In other cases, the null hypothesis cannot be rejected for one or more of the arbitrarily chosen lag structures but is rejected for the FPE-lag structure. These results support the importance and sensitivity of lag-length specifications of Thornton and Batten (1985). I shall now look at the evidence based on the specification chosen by the FPE criterion.

With respect to the issue of money and real GNP causality, I find in Table 3.3, that the hypothesis that money does not 'Granger-cause' real GNP would be rejected at the 5% significance level with each of the monetary aggregates except for the MQ index. The causal relationships, however, are less significant for the sum aggregates than for the corresponding Divisia aggregates at each level of aggregation except at the lowest, M1, level and only in the case with time trend and with FPE lags (this latter result is reversed in every other column of the table). The hypothesis that real GNP does not Granger-cause money would be accepted at the 5% level with each of the monetary aggregates except for the Sum M2 aggregate and the corresponding Divisia aggregate, the latter only in the case of trended series.

TABLE 3.3

CAUSALITY TESTS BETWEEN MONEY AND INCOME WITH
AND WITHOUT TREND VARIABLES

F Ratio

Variable		Without time				With time			
Effect	Cause	8 lags	6 lags	4 lags	FPE lags	8 lags	6 lags	4 lag	FPE lags
y	M1	1.710	1.577	1.948	[1,2] 4.398*	1.733	1.836	1.961	[1,2] 5.058*
		(.131)	(.178)	(.118)	(0.17)	(.126)	(.116)	(.116)	(.009)
M1	y	.838	.982	.744	[1,1] .214	.911	.844	.588	[1,1] .138
		(.576)	(.450)	(.567)	(.645)	(.519)	(.544)	(.673)	(.712)
y	M2	1.794	2.617*	3.596*	[1,4] 3.947*	1.688	2.537*	3.602*	[1,4] 3.971*
		(.112)	(.031)	(.012)	(.007)	(.137)	(.036)	(.012)	(.007)
M2	y	.848	1.411	.683	[1,11] 2.254*	.831	1.386	.661	[1,11] 2.349*
		(.568)	(.234)	(.607)	(.033)	(.581)	(.244)	(.622)	(.027)
y	M3	2.228*	2.386*	3.702*	[1,4] 3.470*	2.096	2.303	3.666*	[1,4] 3.417*
		(0.49)	(.045)	(.011)	(.014)	(.064)	(.053)	(.011)	(.015)
M3	y	.439	.464	.213	[3,1] .130	.431	.455	.279	[3,1] .043
		(.890)	(.831)	(.930)	(.720)	(.894)	(.837)	(.890)	(.836)
y	L	.811	1.352	1.782	[1,3] 3.275*	.760	1.294	1.735	[1,3] 3.096*
		(.598)	(.257)	(.148)	(.028)	(.639)	(.282)	(.158)	(.035)
L	y	1.411	2.065	2.686*	[1,2] 2.383	1.349	2.026	2.592	[1,2] 2.304
		(.226)	(.079)	(.043)	(.101)	(.254)	(.085)	(.049)	(.109)
y	DM1	2.828*	2.932*	3.016*	[1,7] 2.805*	2.668*	2.960*	2.945*	[1,7] 2.722*
		(0.16)	(.018)	(.027)	(.017)	(.022)	(.017)	(.030)	(.020)
DM1	y	1.318	1.157	.836	[1,1] .083	1.344	1.106	.844	[1,1] .077
		(.267)	(.348)	(.059)	(.774)	(.256)	(.376)	(.504)	(.782)
y	DM2	1.726	2.770*	3.576*	[1,2] 8.888*	2.077	3.343*	5.030*	[1,2] 12.566*
		(.127)	(.024)	(.013)	(.000)	(.066)	(.009)	(.002)	(.000)
DM2	y	3.049*	2.946*	2.660*	[5,1] 11.677*	2.861*	3.072*	2.432	[1,1] 1.908
		(.010)	(.017)	(.044)	(.001)	(.015)	(.014)	(.061)	(.173)
y	DM3	1.451	2.263	2.483	[1,3] 4.618*	2.020	3.133*	3.414*	[1,2] 9.316*
		(.210)	(.056)	(.056)	(.006)	(.074)	(.013)	(.016)	(.000)
DM3	y	1.826	1.555	.730	[3,1] 3.153	1.695	1.491	.604	[1,1] .149
		(.105)	(.185)	(.575)	(.082)	(.136)	(.206)	(.661)	(.701)
y	DL	1.523	2.122	2.594*	[1,2] 6.293*	1.563	2.271	2.799*	[1,2] 6.962*
		(.185)	(.071)	(.048)	(.003)	(.173)	(.055)	(.037)	(.002)
DL	y	1.734	1.792	.823	[1,1] .108	1.628	1.738	.783	[1,1] .033
		(.125)	(.125)	(.517)	(.743)	(.153)	(.137)	(.542)	(.857)
y	MQ	1.601	1.232	1.450	[1,4] 1.615	1.534	1.173	1.417	[1,4] 1.582
		(.160)	(.310)	(.233)	(.185)	(.182)	(.340)	(.243)	(.194)
MQ	y	1.450	.532	.488	[7,1] .249	1.365	.518	.462	[1,1] .131
		(.2211)	(.781)	(.744)	(.620)	(.247)	(.791)	(.763)	(.719)

NOTE: Numbers in brackets indicate the optimal (in the minimum FPE sense) lag order of the bivariate autoregressive processes. p values of the F ratios are in parentheses.
*Significant at the 5% level.

TABLE 3.4

CAUSALITY TESTS BETWEEN MONEY AND PRICES WITH
AND WITHOUT TREND VARIABLES

F Ratio

Variable		Without time				With time			
Effect	Cause	8 lags	6 lags	4 lags	FPE lags	8 lags	6 lags	4 lag	FPE lags
p	M1	3.465*	3.347*	4.147*	[2,3] 6.793*	3.944*	4.468*	4.564*	[4,2] 9.393*
		(.005)	(.009)	(.006)	(.000)	(.002)	(.002)	(.003)	(.000)
M1	p	5.407*	5.966*	7.728*	[1,1] 9.791*	4.721*	5.980*	8.282*	[1,1] 10.593*
		(.000)	(.000)	(.000)	(.003)	(.000)	(.000)	(.000)	(.002)
p	M2	.897	.958	1.493	[2,3] 2.729	.869	1.062	1.562	[4,1] 2.803
		(.529)	(.465)	(.019)	(.053)	(.552)	(.401)	(.200)	(.100)
M2	p	4.152*	3.175*	3.618*	[1,9] 7.425*	5.019*	3.264*	3.550*	[1,9] 7.373*
		(.001)	(.012)	(.012)	(.000)	(.000)	(.010)	(.013)	(.000)
p	M3	3.400*	3.286*	3.838*	[2,5] 5.122*	3.204*	3.090*	3.686	[4,5] 3.812*
		(.005)	(.009)	(.009)	(.000)	(.008)	(.014)	(.011)	(.006)
M3	p	1.764	2.413*	3.406*	[3,1] 8.538*	1.870	2.468*	3.505*	[3,1] 9.172*
		(.118)	(.043)	(.016)	(.005)	(.098)	(.040)	(.014)	(.004)
p	L	1.933	2.409	2.957*	[2,2] 3.299*	2.082	2.581*	3.063*	[4,2] 6.156*
		(.086)	(.044)	(.029)	(.045)	(.066)	(.033)	(.026)	(.004)
L	p	1.075	2.075	2.068	[1,1] 10.236	1.090	2.052	2.008	[1,1] 9.955*
		(.403)	(.077)	(.101)	(.002)	(.394)	(.081)	(.109)	(.003)
p	DM1	2.928*	3.849*	5.084*	[2,2] 9.327*	3.196*	4.095*	5.220*	[4,2] 10.301*
		(.013)	(.004)	(.002)	(.000)	(.008)	(.003)	(.001)	(.000)
DM1	p	2.544*	2.358*	2.934*	[1,1] 4.302*	2.564*	2.273*	2.865*	[1,1] 4.275*
		(.027)	(.048)	(.031)	(.043)	(.026)	(.056)	(.034)	(.043)
p	DM2	4.424*	5.783*	4.579*	[2,6] 5.799*	4.268*	5.819*	4.709*	[4,3] 6.414*
		(.000)	(.000)	(.003)	(.000)	(.001)	(.000)	(.003)	(.000)
DM2	p	3.994*	5.449*	6.071*	[5,5] 6.692*	3.933	5.381*	6.376*	[1,1] 9.166*
		(.002)	(.000)	(.000)	(.000)	(.002)	(.000)	(.000)	(.004)
p	DM3	3.567*	4.421*	4.056*	[2,6] 5.033*	3.508*	4.189*	4.018	[4,3] 5.465*
		(.004)	(.002)	(.007)	(.000)	(.005)	(.002)	(.007)	(.003)
DM3	p	2.305*	2.992*	3.705*	[3,12] 3.918*	2.644*	3.272*	4.933*	[1,1] 11.310*
		(.042)	(.016)	(.011)	(.000)	(.023)	(.010)	(.002)	(.001)
p	DL	3.694*	4.816*	3.346*	[2,6] 5.509*	3.487*	4.583*	4.189*	[4,2] 8.024*
		(.003)	(.000)	(.017)	(.000)	(.005)	(.001)	(.006)	(.000)
DL	p	2.256*	3.121*	4.089*	[1,1] 8.001*	2.606*	3.382	4.595*	[1,1] 9.949*
		(.046)	(.013)	(.006)	(.006)	(.024)	(.009)	(.003)	(.003)
p	MQ	3.100*	2.949*	2.922*	[2,2] 6.678*	3.041*	2.964*	2.807*	[4,2] 5.165*
		(.009)	(.017)	(.031)	(.003)	(.000)	(.017)	(.036)	(.009)
MQ	p	6.318*	7.260*	9.896*	[7,8] 6.777*	6.045*	7.070*	9.598	[1,4] 4.645*
		(.000)	(.000)	(.000)	(.000)	(.000)	(.000)	(.000)	(.003)

NOTE: See note to Table 3.3.
*Significant at the 5% level.

Turning now to the issue of money and consumer prices causality, I find in Table 3.4 that the hypothesis that money does not Granger-cause consumer prices would be rejected at the 5% level with the summation aggregates at all levels of aggregation except M2. The same hypothesis would be rejected at the 5% significance level with the Divisia aggregates at all levels of aggregation and with the MQ aggregate. In addition, the causality relationship is more significant for Sum M1, Divisia M1, Divisia M2, and Divisia L. The hypothesis that consumer prices do not Granger-cause money would be rejected at the 5% level with each of the monetary aggregates. I find that Divisia M1 is the only case of marginally significant feedback from prices to money with all other aggregates producing significant feedback. The MQ index also did poorly in this test.

Tables 3.3 and 3.4 do not reveal a single uniformly best monetary aggregate. In terms of 5% significance-level tests, all monetary aggregates except for Sum M2 cause inflation, but only the summation and the Divisia aggregates cause real output fluctuations; the MQ index did badly in this regard. In terms of the p values, Sum M1, Divisia M1, Divisia M2, and Divisia L performed better in causing inflation, and Sum M2, Divisia M2, Divisia M3, and Divisia L performed better in causing real output fluctuations. Relative to these criteria, Divisia M2, Divisia M3, and Divisia L are most frequently best. These results support the findings of Barnett *et al.* (1984) on the causality relation between Divisia and sum money and GNP.

3.6 Conclusion

This chapter has employed Granger tests to provide updated results on the causality relationship between sum, Divisia, and MQ money, prices, and income. It has also investigated the sensitivity of causality test results to detrending and the lag structure. The central empirical finding is that, although aggregation theory and index-number theory favor the Divisia quantity index over the sum and the MQ index, the Granger causality test results do not reveal a single uniformly best monetary aggregate. The Divisia aggregates, however, generally performed better, especially Divisia M2 and Divisia L.

The results also suggest that researchers should be careful in their investigations of Granger causality using the Granger-Sims tests because of the sensitivity of the tests to detrending and the lag structure. In particular, either differencing or detrending, not both, should be used to remove apparent nonstationarity in economic time series. Unnecessary detrending of difference-stationary processes produces contradictory results. Moreover, arbitrary lag-length specifications may produce misleading results, because they may imply misspecification of the order of the autoregressive processes. The safest approach is to determine statistically the lag structures using model-specification criteria. On the basis of experimentation by others, Akaike's FPE criterion performs well in selecting the model relative to other criteria.

The empirical evidence offered in this chapter is not fully convincing because the equation-by-equation estimation procedure may be inappropriate for what is essentially a system of equations. A logical next step would, therefore, be to investigate simultaneously the causal relationships between money, prices, and income using a vector autoregressive moving average (VARMA) model. For a rigorous description of VARMA models, see Tiao and Box (1981).

Chapter 4

Monetary Aggregation and the Neutrality of Money

Apostolos Serletis and Zisimos Koustas[*]

4.1 Introduction

The aim of this chapter is to investigate a long-run question about the role of money in monetary policy — whether changes in the conduct of monetary policy influence the growth rate of output. As Lucas (1996, p. 661) puts it, "So much thought has been devoted to this question and so much evidence is available that one might reasonably assume that it had been solved long ago. But this is not the case." In fact, recently Fisher and Seater (1993) and King and Watson (1997) contribute to the literature on testing quantity-theoretic propositions (by developing tests using recent advances in the theory of nonstationary regressors) and show that meaningful long-run neutrality and superneutrality tests can only be constructed if both nominal and real variables satisfy certain nonstationarity conditions and that much of the older literature violates these requirements.

In this chapter, in the spirit of Serletis and Koustas (1998) and Koustas and Serletis (1999), we test the long-run neutrality and superneutrality

---

[*]Originally published in *Economic Inquiry* 39 (2001), 124-138. Reprinted with permission.

of money, using the King and Watson (1997) methodology, paying particular attention to the gains that can be achieved by rigorous use of microeconomic- and aggregation-theoretic foundations in the construction of money measures. This is accomplished by making comparisons among simple sum, Divisia, and currency equivalent (CE) monetary aggregates using the Anderson *et al.* (1997a, 1997b) data — see Anderson *et al.*, (1997a, 1997b) for more details. We also pay attention to the integration and cointegration properties of the variables, because meaningful neutrality and superneutrality tests critically depend on such properties.

The organization of the chapter is as follows. The next section briefly discusses the problem of the definition (aggregation) of money. In section 4.3, we investigate the univariate time-series properties of the variables, as these properties are relevant for some problems of potential importance in the practical conduct of monetary policy as well as for estimation and hypothesis testing. In section 4.4, we test the long-run neutrality and superneutrality of money propositions, using the King and Watson (1997) structural bivariate autoregressive methodology, paying particular attention to the integration and cointegration properties of the data. The final section concludes.

4.2   The Many Kinds of Money

The monetary aggregates currently in use by the Federal Reserve are simple-sum indices in which all monetary components are assigned a constant and equal (unitary) weight. This index is M in

$$M = \sum_{i=1}^{n} x_i \tag{4.1}$$

where x_i is one of the n monetary components of the monetary aggregate M. This summation index implies that all monetary components contribute equally to the money total, and it views all components as dollar-for-dollar perfect substitutes. There is no question that such an index represents an index of the stock of nominal monetary wealth but cannot, in general, represent a valid structural economic variable for the services of the quantity of money.

Over the years, there has been a steady stream of attempts at properly weighting monetary components within a simple-sum aggregate. With no theory, however, any weighting scheme is questionable. Barnett (1980) derived the theoretical linkage between monetary theory and aggregation and index number theory. He applied economic aggregation and index number theory and constructed monetary aggregates based on Diewert's

(1976) class of 'superlative' quantity index numbers. The new aggregates are Divisia quantity indices, which are elements of the superlative class. The Divisia index (in discrete time) is defined as

$$\log M_t^D - \log M_{t-1}^D = \sum_{i=1}^{n} s_{it}^* (\log x_{it} - \log x_{i,t-1}). \qquad (4.2)$$

According to equation (4.2) the growth rate of the aggregate is the weighted average of the growth rates of the component quantities, with the Divisia weights being defined as the expenditure shares averaged over the two periods of the change, $s_{it}^* = 1/2(s_{it} + s_{i,t-1})$ for $i = 1, \ldots, n$, where $s_{it} = \pi_{it} x_{it} / \sum \pi_{jt} x_{jt}$ is the expenditure share of asset i during period t, an π_{it} is the user cost of asset i, derived in Barnett (1978):

$$\pi_{it} = (R_t - r_{it})/(1 + R_t), \qquad (4.3)$$

which is just the opportunity cost of holding a dollar's worth of the ith asset. In equation (4.3), r_{it} is the market yield on the ith asset, and R_t is the yield available on a 'benchmark' asset that is held only to carry wealth between multiperiods — see Barnett *et al.* (1992) for more details regarding the Divisia approach to monetary aggregation.

More recently, Rotemberg *et al.* (1995) proposed the currency equivalent (CE) index:

$$CE = \sum_{i=1}^{n} [(R_t - r_{it})/R_t] x_{it}. \qquad (4.4)$$

In equation (4.4), as long as currency gives no interest, units of currency are added together with a weight of one. Other assets are added to currency but with a weight that declines toward zero as their return increases toward R_t.

The difference between Divisia and CE methods of monetary aggregation is that the former measures the flow of monetary services, whereas the latter, like simple summation aggregation, measures the stock of monetary assets. The CE aggregates, however, represent a major advance over the official simple-sum aggregates — see Rotemberg (1991) and Barnett (1991) for more details regarding Divisia and CE money measures.

In this chapter, we use the official simple-sum aggregates, Barnett's (1980) Divisia aggregates (also known as 'monetary services indices' [MSI]), and Rotemberg's (1991) CE indices to test the long-run neutrality of money proposition. The data are quarterly over the period from 1960:1 to 1996:2 and were obtained from the St. Louis MSI database, maintained by the Federal Reserve Bank of St. Louis as a part of the bank's Federal Reserve Economic Database (FRED) — see Anderson *et al.* (1997a, 1997b) for details regarding the construction of the Divisia and CE aggregates and related data issues.

4.3 Univariate Time-Series Properties

The long-run neutrality and superneutrality propositions have been investigated in a large number of studies. Recently, however, Fisher and Seater (1993) and King and Watson (1997) show that meaningful neutrality tests can only be constructed if both nominal and real variables satisfy certain nonstationarity conditions and that much of the older literature violates these requirements, and hence has to be disregarded. In particular, they show that neutrality tests are possible if both nominal and real variables are at least integrated of order one and superneutrality tests are possible if the order of integration of the nominal variables is equal to one plus the order of integration of the real variables.

To investigate the order of integration of the variables, we test for unit roots using two alternative testing procedures to deal with anomalies that arise when the data are not very informative about whether or not there is a unit root. In the first column of Table 4.1, we report p-values for the augmented Dickey-Fuller (ADF) test (see Dickey and Fuller [1981]).[1] These p-values (calculated using TSP 4.3) are based on the response surface estimates given by MacKinnon (1994). For the ADF test, the optimal lag length was taken to be the order selected by the Akaike information criterion (AIC) plus 2 — see Pantula *et al.* (1994) for details regarding the advantages of this rule for choosing the number of augmenting lags. Based on the p-values reported in Panel A of Table 4.1, the null hypothesis of a unit root in levels generally cannot be rejected.

---

[1]In particular, the null hypothesis of a unit root was tested using the following ADF unit root regression equation:

$$\Delta y_t = \alpha_0 + \alpha y_{t-1} + \beta t + \sum_{j=1}^{k} c_j \Delta y_{t-j} + e_t,$$

where e_t is white noise, k the optimal lag length, and t a time trend. In terms of this equation, testing the unit root null involves testing the null that $\alpha = 0$.

TABLE 4.1

UNIT ROOT TEST RESULTS IN THE MONEY VARIABLES

Money series	A. Log levels			B. First differences of log levels			
	ADF (p-values)	KPSS t-statistics $\hat{\eta}_\mu$	$\hat{\eta}_\tau$	ADF (p-values)	KPSS t-statistics $\hat{\eta}_\mu$	$\hat{\eta}_\tau$	Integration order
Sum M1	.317	1.914*	.375*	.016	.276	.147*	I(2)
Divisia M1	.283	1.917*	.373*	.040	.315	.174*	I(2)
CE M1	.112	1.905*	.314*	.000	.136	.045	I(1)
Sum M2	.996	1.924*	.304*	.217	.648*	.301*	I(2)
Divisia M2	.992	1.920*	.325*	.036	.458	.180*	I(2)
CE M2	.045	1.885*	.111	.000	.042	.041	I(1)
Sum M3	.994	1.919*	.318*	.035	.684*	.311*	I(2)
Divisia M3	.990	1.917*	.344*	.068	.535*	.176*	I(2)
CE M3	.034	1.883*	.093*	.000	.040	.039	I(1)
Sum L	.973	1.924*	.279*	.136	.548*	.354*	I(2)
Divisia L	.967	1.924*	.293*	.105	.399	.194*	I(2)
CE L	.016	1.880*	.058	.000	.037	.036	I(1)

Notes: Numbers in the ADF column are tail areas of unit root tests. An asterisk (next to a KPSS t-statistic) indicates significance at the 5% level. The 5% critical values for the KPSS $\hat{\eta}_\mu$ and $\hat{\eta}_\tau$ test statistics (given in Kwiatkowski et al. (1992)) are .463 and .146, respectively.

It is important to note that in the ADF unit root test, the unit root is the null hypothesis to be tested and that the way in which classical hypothesis testing is carried out ensures that the null hypothesis is accepted unless there is strong evidence against it. In fact, Kwiatkowski *et al.* (1992) argue that such unit root tests fail to reject a unit root because they have low power against relevant alternatives, and they propose tests (known as the KPSS [the initials of the authors in the Kwiatkowski *et al.* (1992) paper] tests) of the hypothesis of stationarity against the alternative of a unit root. They argue that such tests should complement unit root tests; by testing both the unit root hypothesis and the stationarity hypothesis, one can distinguish series that appear to be stationary, series that appear to be integrated, and series that are not very informative about whether or not they are stationary or have a unit root.

KPSS tests for level and trend stationarity are also presented in panel A of Table 4.1 under the KPSS columns.[2] As can be seen, the t-statistic $\hat{\eta}_\mu$ that tests the null hypothesis of level stationarity is large relative to the 5% critical value of .463 given in Kwiatkowski *et al.* (1992). Also, the statistic $\hat{\eta}_\tau$ that tests the null hypothesis of trend stationarity exceeds the 5% critical value of .146 (also given in Kwiatkowski *et al.* [1992]). Combining the results of the tests of the stationarity hypothesis with the results of the tests of the unit root hypothesis, it appears that all the series have at least one unit root.

To test the null hypothesis of a second unit root, in panel B of Table 4.1, we test the null hypothesis of a unit root (using the ADF test) as well as the null hypotheses of level and trend stationarity in the first differences of the series. Clearly, all series, except for CE money appear to have two unit roots, since the null hypothesis of a second unit root cannot be rejected and the null hypotheses of level and trend stationarity is rejected. For

---

[2]In particular, the null hypothesis of 'level stationarity' in y_t was tested by calculating the test statistic

$$\hat{\eta}_\mu = \frac{1}{T^2} \sum_{t=1}^{T} \frac{S_t^2}{\hat{\sigma}_k^2}$$

where $S_t = \sum_{i=1}^{t} e_i$, $t = 1, 2, \ldots, T$, e_t is the residuals from the regression of y_t on an intercept, and σ_k is a consistent estimate of the long-run variance of y_t calculated, using the Newey and West (1987) method, as

$$\hat{\sigma}_k = \frac{1}{T} \sum_{t=1}^{T} e_t^2 + \frac{2}{T} \sum_{s=1}^{T} b(s,k) \sum_{t=s+1}^{T} e_t e_{t-s}$$

where T is the number of observations, $b(s,k) = 1 + s/(1+k)$ is a weighting function and k is the lag truncation parameter.

The null hypothesis of 'trend stationarity' in y_t was tested by defining e_t as the residuals from the regression of y_t on an intercept and time trend (instead of as above) and calculating the $\hat{\eta}_\tau$ test statistic as above.

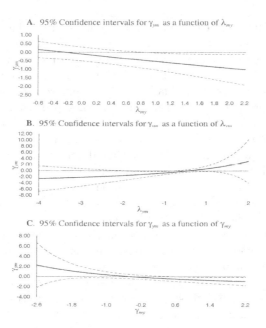

Figure 4.1: Neutrality Tests for CE M1.

CE money the second unit root hypothesis is rejected and the level and trend stationarity hypothesis cannot be rejected, suggesting that the CE monetary aggregates are I(1). The order of integration of the series is documented in the last column of Table 4.1.

4.4   Long-run Neutrality and Superneutrality

King and Watson (1997) argue that long-run neutrality tests are inefficient in the presence of cointegration, in the sense that if the output and money series are nonstationary and cointegrate, then a finite vector autoregressive process in first differences does not exist and this is typically sufficient for rejecting long-run neutrality. To present some evidence on this issue, in Table 4.2, we summarize the unit root test results (from Table 4.1) and report p-values of Engle and Granger (1987) cointegration tests. The cointegration tests are between logged real output (GDP), y, and logged money, m, in the case of the CE aggregates and between logged output and money growth rates, Δm, in the case of the sum and Divisia monetary aggregates.

The Engle-Granger cointegration tests are first done with y as the dependent variable in the cointegrating regression and then repeated with money as the dependent variable. These tests use a constant and a trend variable and the number of augmenting lags is chosen using the AIC+2 rule mentioned earlier. Asymptotic p-values for the Engle-Granger test are computed using the coefficients in MacKinnon (1994). These results suggest that the null hypothesis of no cointegration between output and money cannot be rejected (at the 5% level). Hence, the conditions necessary for meaningful neutrality and superneutrality tests hold and in what follows we use the King and Watson (1997) methodology to test the neutrality proposition in the case of the CE monetary aggregates (because these are of the same order of integration as the output series and do not cointegrate with output) and the superneutrality proposition in the case of the sum and Divisia monetary aggregates (because these series are I[2] and their I[1] growth rates do not cointegrate with output).

Following King and Watson (1997), we consider the following bivariate structural vector-autoregressive model of order p in m_t and y_t

$$m_t = \lambda_{my}\Delta y_t + \sum_{j=1}^{p} \alpha_{my}^j \Delta y_{t-j} + \sum_{j=1}^{p} \alpha_{mm}^j m_{t-j} + \varepsilon_t^m \qquad (4.5)$$

$$\Delta y_t = \lambda_{ym} m_t + \sum_{j=1}^{p} \alpha_{yy}^j \Delta y_{t-j} + \sum_{j=1}^{p} \alpha_{ym}^j m_{t-j} + \varepsilon_t^y \qquad (4.6)$$

where $m_t = \Delta m_t$ in the case of CE money and $m_t = \Delta^2 m_t$ in the case of simple-sum and Divisia money. ε_t^m and ε_t^y represent exogenous unexpected changes in money and output, respectively, and λ_{my} and λ_{ym} represent the contemporaneous effect of output on the money supply and the contemporaneous response of output to changes in the money supply, respectively. Our interest here will focus on the dynamic effects of the money shock, ε_t^m, on y_t.

The matrix representation of the model is

$$\alpha(L)X_t = \varepsilon_t \qquad (4.7)$$

where

$$\alpha(L) = \sum_{j=0}^{p} \alpha_j L^j$$

TABLE 4.2

COINTEGRATION TEST RESULTS

Monetary aggregate	Integration order $\langle y_t \rangle$	$\langle m_t \rangle$	Long-run neutrality Proposition to be tested	p-values of the Engle-Granger cointegration test, using $I(1)$ variables Dependent variables: y_t	m_t
Sum M1	1	2	Superneutrality	.215	.093
Divisia M1	1	2	Superneutrality	.042	.091
CE M1	1	1	Neutrality	.025	.061
Sum M2	1	2	Superneutrality	.159	.200
Divisia M2	1	2	Superneutrality	.273	.070
CE M2	1	1	Neutrality	.347	.112
Sum M3	1	2	Superneutrality	.054	.037
Divisia M3	1	2	Superneutrality	.205	.096
CE M3	1	1	Neutrality	.396	.072
Sum L	1	2	Superneutrality	.141	.185
Divisia L	1	2	Superneutrality	.155	.128
CE L	1	1	Neutrality	.698	.097

Notes: $\langle x_t \rangle$ represents the order of integration of x_t, based on the results reported in Table 4.1. All tests use a constant and trend variable. The cointegration tests are between y and m in the case of the simple-sum and Divisia aggregates and between y and m in the case of the CE aggregates. Asymptotic p-values for the Engle-Granger cointegration test are computed using the coefficients in MacKinnon (1994). The number of augmenting lags in the Engle-Granger test is determined using the AIC+2 rule.

TABLE 4.3

THE NEUTRALITY OF MONEY

Monetary Aggregate	X_t (in Equation 4.7)	$\gamma_{ym} = 0$ in 95% Confidence Interval			Estimates Imposing $\gamma_{ym} = 0$		
		λ_{my}	λ_{ym}	γ_{my}	λ_{my}	λ_{ym}	γ_{my}
CE M1	$(\Delta m_t, \Delta y_t)'$	≤ 0.85	$\geq -0.20, \leq -1.60$	≤ 0.70	$-0.25(0.15)$	$0.14(0.18)$	$-0.39(0.33)$
CE M2	$(\Delta m_t, \Delta y_t)'$	≤ 2.20	$\geq -0.10, \leq -0.60$	≤ 0.90	$-0.05(0.42)$	$0.01(0.04)$	$-0.40(0.59)$
CE M3	$(\Delta m_t, \Delta y_t)'$	≤ 2.20	$\geq -0.10, \leq -1.20$	≤ 0.65	$0.17(0.47)$	$-0.02(0.04)$	$-0.75(0.70)$
CE L	$(\Delta m_t, \Delta y_t)'$	≤ 2.50	$\geq -0.10, \leq -1.20$	≤ 0.55	$0.13(0.51)$	$-0.02(0.04)$	$-0.98(0.70)$

Note: All of the models include six lags of the relevant variables. Standard errors are shown in parentheses.

TABLE 4.4

THE SUPERNEUTRALITY OF MONEY

Monetary Aggregate	X_t (in Equation 4.7)	$\gamma_{y,\Delta m} = 0$ in 95% Confidence Interval			Estimates Imposing $\gamma_{y,\Delta m} = 0$		
		$\lambda_{\Delta m,y}$	$\lambda_{y,\Delta m}$	$\gamma_{\Delta m,y}$	$\lambda_{\Delta m,y}$	$\lambda_{y,\Delta m}$	$\gamma_{\Delta m,y}$
Sum M1	$(\Delta^2 m_t, \Delta y_t)'$	≤ 0.65	≥ -1.70	$\geq .20, \leq 0.05$	$0.25(0.06)$	$-0.70(0.40)$	$-0.03(0.04)$
Divisia M1	$(\Delta^2 m_t, \Delta y_t)'$	≤ 0.50	≥ -1.80	$\geq .40, \leq 0.05$	$0.19(0.05)$	$-0.70(0.44)$	$-0.03(0.04)$
Sum M2	$(\Delta^2 m_t, \Delta y_t)'$	≤ 0.40	≥ -2.00	≤ -0.05	$0.21(0.05)$	$-1.23(0.40)$	$-0.05(0.02)$
Divisia M2	$(\Delta^2 m_t, \Delta y_t)'$	≤ 0.60	≥ -2.50	≤ -0.10	$0.33(0.06)$	$-1.46(0.47)$	$-0.06(0.02)$
Sum M3	$(\Delta^2 m_t, \Delta y_t)'$	$\geq -.20, \leq 0.40$	$\geq -2.30, \leq -0.10$	≤ 0.20	$0.13(0.04)$	$-1.12(0.47)$	$0.00(0.03)$
Divisia M3	$(\Delta^2 m_t, \Delta y_t)'$	≤ 0.60	$\geq 0.20, \leq -0.30$	≤ 0.05	$0.30(0.06)$	$-1.61(0.52)$	$-0.03(0.03)$
Sum L	$(\Delta^2 m_t, \Delta y_t)'$	$\geq 0.05, \leq -0.50$	≥ -0.35	≤ -0.05	$0.15(0.03)$	$-1.48(0.66)$	$0.03(0.02)$
Divisia L	$(\Delta^2 m_t, \Delta y_t)'$	$\geq 0.10, \leq -0.10$	$\geq 0.90, \leq -0.70$	$\geq -0.10, \leq 0.05$	$0.33(0.05)$	$-2.00(0.66)$	$-0.01(0.02)$

Note: All of the models include six lags of the relevant variables. Standard errors are shown in parentheses.

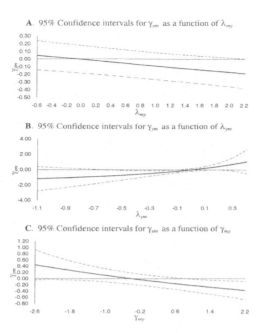

Figure 4.2: Neutrality Tests for CE M2.

and

$$X_t = \begin{bmatrix} m_t \\ \Delta y_t \end{bmatrix}, \quad \varepsilon_t = \begin{bmatrix} \varepsilon_t^m \\ \varepsilon_t^y \end{bmatrix},$$

$$\alpha_0 = \begin{bmatrix} 1 & -\lambda_{my} \\ -\lambda_{ym} & 1 \end{bmatrix},$$

$$\alpha_j = -\begin{bmatrix} \alpha_{mm}^j & \alpha_{my}^j \\ \alpha_{ym}^j & \alpha_{yy}^j \end{bmatrix}, \quad j = 1, 2, \ldots, p.$$

Thus, in this notation the long-run multipliers are $\gamma_{ym} = \alpha_{ym}(1)/\alpha_{yy}(1)$ and $\gamma_{my} = \alpha_{my}(1)/\alpha_{mm}(1)$, where γ_{ym} measures the long-run response of output to a permanent unit increase in m, and γ_{my} measures the long-run response to m to a permanent unit increase in output.

The endogeneity of the money supply, however, makes equation (4.7) econometrically unidentified, as noted by King and Watson (1997). To see

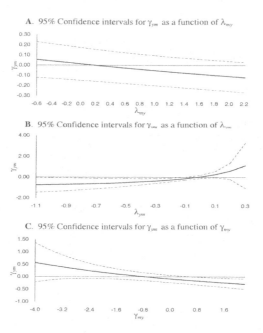

Figure 4.3: Neutrality Tests for CE M3.

this, write the primitive system (4.7) in standard form as

$$X_t = \sum_{j=1}^{p} \Phi_j X_{t-j} + e_t$$

where $\Phi_j = -\alpha_0^{-1}\alpha_j$ and $e_t = \alpha_0^{-1}\varepsilon_t$. The following equations determine the matrices α_j and $\sum_\varepsilon$:

$$\alpha_0^{-1}\alpha_j = -\Phi_j, \quad \text{where } j = 1,\ldots,p \qquad (4.8)$$

$$\alpha_0^{-1}\sum_\varepsilon \left(\alpha_0^{-1}\right)' = \sum_\varepsilon \qquad (4.9)$$

Equation (4.8) determines α_j as a function of α_0 and Φ_j. Equation (4.9) cannot determine both α_0 and $\sum_\varepsilon$, given that $\sum_\varepsilon$ is a 2×2 symmetric matrix with only three unique elements. Therefore, only three of the four unknown parameters — $\lambda_{my}, \lambda_{ym}, var(\varepsilon_t^y), var(\varepsilon_t^m)$ — can be identified, even under the assumption of independence of ε_t^m and ε_t^y. Clearly, one additional restriction is required to identify the model and test the long-run neutrality restrictions.

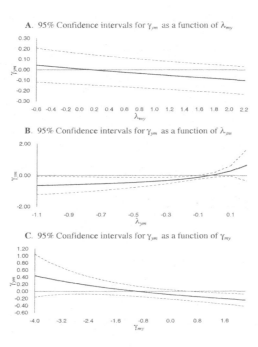

Figure 4.4: Neutrality Tests for CE L.

In this chapter, we follow King and Watson's (1997) eclectic approach, and instead of focusing on a single identifying restriction, we report results for a wide range of identifying restrictions. In particular, we iterate each of $\lambda_{my}, \lambda_{ym}, \gamma_{my}$, and γ_{ym} within a reasonable range, each time obtaining estimates of the remaining three parameters and their standard errors. This testing strategy is clearly more informative in terms of the robustness of inference about long-run neutrality to specific assumptions about $\lambda_{ym}, \lambda_{my}$, or γ_{my}. The model is estimated by simultaneous equations methods, as described in King and Watson (1997).

We follow the approach of King and Watson (1997) in reporting empirical results based on equation 4.7) for a wide range of plausible identifying parameter restrictions. We set $X_t = (\Delta m_t, \Delta y_t)$ to investigate long-run neutrality using the CE monetary aggregates, and $X_t = (\Delta^2 m_t, \Delta y_t)$ to investigate long-run superneutrality using the sum and Divisia monetary aggregates. All of the models include six lags of the relevant variables and the results are summarized in Tables 4.3 and 4.4 (with standard errors in

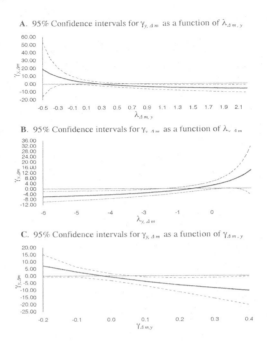

Figure 4.5: Superneutrality Tests for Sum M1.

parentheses) and Figures 4.1-4.12.[3]

To deal with the identification problem mentioned earlier, we estimate equation (4.7) under appropriate identification restrictions. Columns 3-5 of Table 4.3 provide ranges of values on the short-run impact of output on money, λ_{my} (in column 3); the short-run impact of money on output, λ_{ym} (in column 4); and the long-run impact of output on money, γ_{my} (in column 5), consistent with long-run neutrality ($\gamma_{ym} = 0$) at the 95% confidence level. The same information is summarized in Figures 4.1-4.4, which present point estimates and 95% confidence intervals for the long-run multiplier, γ_{ym}, for a wide range of values of λ_{my} (in panel A), λ_{ym} (in panel B), and γ_{my} (in panel C).

The results in column 3 of Table 4.3 and panel A of Figures 4.1-4.4 indicate that long-run neutrality cannot be rejected for a wide range of values of λ_{my}, including the frequently imposed identifying restriction of contemporaneous money exogeneity ($\lambda_{my} = 0$). Also, long-run neutrality cannot be rejected for a reasonable range of values of λ_{ym} (see column 4

---

[3] As King and Watson (1997) report, the results are not sensitive to the choice of the lag length in the VAR.

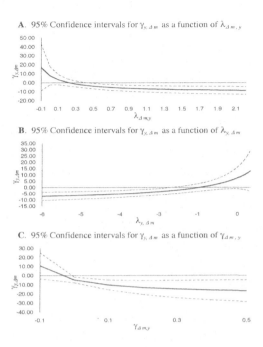

A. 95% Confidence intervals for $\gamma_{y, \Delta m}$ as a function of $\lambda_{\Delta m, y}$

B. 95% Confidence intervals for $\gamma_{y, \Delta m}$ as a function of $\lambda_{y, \Delta m}$

C. 95% Confidence intervals for $\gamma_{y, \Delta m}$ as a function of $\gamma_{\Delta m, y}$

Figure 4.6: Superneutrality Tests for Sum M2.

of Table 4.3 and panel B of Figures 4.1-4.4). This is consistent with both
traditional monetary models of the business cycle, which imply $\lambda_{ym} \geq 0$
(that is, output does not decline on impact in response to a monetary
expansion) as well as with Lucas's (1972) monetary misperceptions (due to
incomplete information concerning the state of the economy) theory, which
suggests that λ_{ym} could be negative. Finally, the results in column 5 of
Table 4.3 and panel C of the relevant figures indicate that the long-run
neutrality hypothesis cannot be rejected for a reasonable range of values of
γ_{my}, consistent with long-run deflationary policies $(\gamma_{my} \leq 1)$.

A second set of evidence is presented in the last three columns of Table
4.3. It concerns the estimates of $\lambda_{my}, \lambda_{ym}$, and γ_{my}, and their associated
standard errors, under long-run neutrality $(\gamma_{ym} = 0)$ as an identifying restriction. This is also shown in panels A-C of Figures 4.1-4.4, which present
95% confidence intervals for $\lambda_{my}, \lambda_{ym}$, and γ_{my} (containing [by definition]
the true values of $\lambda_{my}, \lambda_{ym}$, and γ_{my} 95% of the time), under the maintained
hypothesis of long-run neutrality. The confidence intervals are reasonably
wide in all cases. Under the frequently imposed identifying restriction of
contemporaneous exogeneity $(\lambda_{my} = 0)$, long-run neutrality cannot be re-

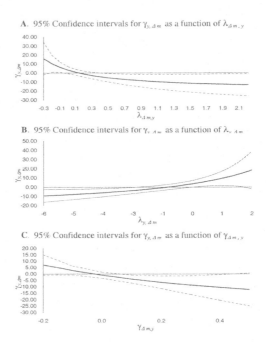

A. 95% Confidence intervals for $\gamma_{y,\Delta m}$ as a function of $\lambda_{\Delta m,y}$

B. 95% Confidence intervals for $\gamma_{y,\Delta m}$ as a function of $\lambda_{y,\Delta m}$

C. 95% Confidence intervals for $\gamma_{y,\Delta m}$ as a function of $\gamma_{\Delta m,y}$

Figure 4.7: Superneutrality Tests for Sum M3.

jected for all four CE monetary aggregates. The confidence intervals for λ_{my} are consistent with accommodative monetary policy and Goodfriend's (1987) argument that the monetary authority responds to changes in output to achieve interest rate smoothing. The confidence intervals for the contemporaneous effect of money on output (λ_{ym}) are reasonable. The point estimates of λ_{ym} under the restriction of long-run money neutrality are not statistically different from zero in all cases, suggesting long-run money neutrality is consistent with short-run money neutrality. The same is true in all cases for γ_{my}, suggesting that long-run money neutrality is consistent with long-run money exogeneity.

We now turn to the long-run superneutrality test results with the simple-sum and Divisia monetary aggregates. These results are presented in Table 4.4 and Figures 4.5-4.12, in the same fashion as the long-run neutrality test results with the CE money measures in Table 4.3 and Figures 4.1-4.4. There is evidence against the superneutrality of money. In particular, under the assumption of contemporaneous money growth exogeneity ($\lambda_{\Delta m,y} = 0$), long-run money superneutrality can be rejected at the 5% level in the case with the simple-sum and Divisia L monetary aggregates. Long-run money

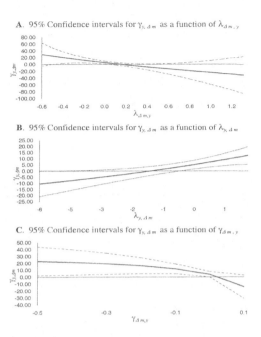

Figure 4.8: Superneutrality Tests for Sum L.

superneutrality can also be rejected in all cases, except with Sum L, for accommodative monetary policy involving values of $\lambda_{\Delta m,y} > 0.5$. For such values of $\lambda_{\Delta m,y}$ the point estimate of $\gamma_{y,\Delta m}$ is negative, consistent with cash-in-advance models, predicting that sustained inflation acts as a tax on investment. Further, long-run superneutrality can be rejected for a range of positive values of $\lambda_{y,\Delta m}$ with Sum M3, Sum L, Divisia M3, and Divisia L.

However, Figures 4.5-4.12 indicate that the estimates of the long-run multiplier are very sensitive to the identification assumption. For example, under the assumption of contemporaneous exogeneity $(\lambda_{\Delta m,y} = 0)$, the estimated effect of money growth on output is very large, ranging from 2.86 with Sum M1 to 14.02 with Divisia M2. Even if one believed that the Tobin effect is empirically important, such high estimates are extremely implausible, suggesting that these results should be regarded with great caution.

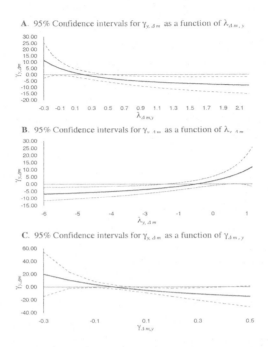

Figure 4.9: Superneutrality Tests for Divisia M1.

4.5 Stability Analysis

To provide some evidence on the stability of the structural estimates, we split the sample in October 1982 (because of the Fed's shift to a policy of smoothing interest rates at that time) and reestimate the model over pre- and post-October 1982 periods. in Tables 4.5 and 4.6 we present estimates of the long-run multiplier over the full sample as well as over each of the split samples for the cases where $\lambda_{my} = 0$, $\lambda_{ym} = 0$, $\gamma_{my} = 0$. Of course, splitting the sample reduces the degrees of freedom and the precision of our estimates over each of the split samples.

Regarding the neutrality results in Table 4.5, splitting the sample does not reverse any of the inferences obtained from the full sample analysis. That is, we are unable to reject long-run money neutrality for all the currency equivalent monetary aggregates and for all sample periods. The results for long-run money superneutrality are presented in Table 4.6, in the same fashion as those for long-run money neutrality in Table 4.5. Clearly, the precision of the estimated long-run multipliers has declined considerably, especially for the 1962:1-1982:4 subsample, as indicated by the re-

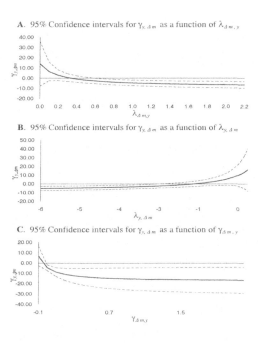

A. 95% Confidence intervals for $\gamma_{y,\Delta m}$ as a function of $\lambda_{\Delta m,y}$

B. 95% Confidence intervals for $\gamma_{y,\Delta m}$ as a function of $\lambda_{y,\Delta m}$

C. 95% Confidence intervals for $\gamma_{y,\Delta m}$ as a function of $\gamma_{\Delta m,y}$

Figure 4.10: Superneutrality Tests for Divisia M2.

ported standard errors. In fact, the large standard errors lead to inability to reject superneutrality for the 1962:1-1982:4 period, with some money measures. However, given the low quality of the estimates for the split samples, we base our conclusions on the full sample results.

4.6 Conclusion

We have looked at data consisting of the traditional simple-sum monetary aggregates, as published by the Federal Reserve Board, and Divisia and CE monetary aggregates, recently produced by the Federal Reserve Bank of St. Louis, to infer the long-run effect of money on economic activity and to address disputes about the relative merits of different monetary aggregation procedures. In doing so, we used the bivariate autoregressive methodology recently proposed by King and Watson (1997), paying explicit attention to the univariate time series properties of the variables.

One puzzling results is that the CE monetary aggregates are integrated of order one, whereas the corresponding simple sum and Divisia aggregates are integrated of order two. This difference, which probably stems from

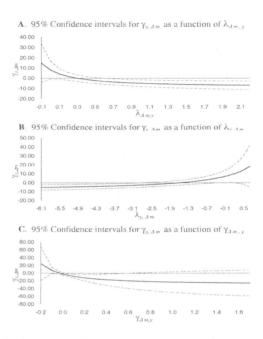

Figure 4.11: Superneutrality Tests for Divisia M3.

small sample problems, reflects the essentially complicated monetary aggregation issues and makes results hard to interpret. In particular, the stochastic properties of the regressors influence the type of tests that we perform. However, based on these properties, the hypothesis of long-run neutrality finds support in the CE money data, whereas the hypothesis of long-run superneutrality finds little support in the simple sum and Divisia data.

We think the results of this chapter suggest answers to a number of questions raised over previous studies of the role of money in the economy. Most important, we think, is the idea that a meaningful comparison of alternative monetary aggregation procedures requires the discovery of the structure of preferences over monetary assets by testing for weakly separable subgroupings. Leaving aside the method of aggregating over monetary assets (i.e., Divisia as opposed to other possibilities), the problem is the *a priori* assignment of monetary assets to monetary aggregates. The typical applied study, like this one, starts from a structure specified *a priori* and never exploits the sample to find other groupings consistent with the optimizing behavior of economic agents. We believe that separability-based

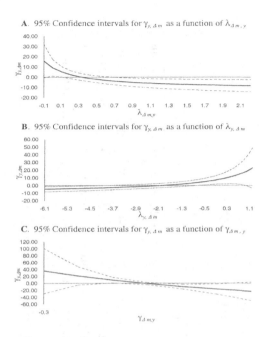

Figure 4.12: Superneutrality Tests for Divisia L.

definitions of money will improve our understanding of how money affects the economy — see Barnett (1982), Serletis (1987), Swofford and Whitney (1987, 1988, 1994), Fleissig and Swofford (1996), Fisher and Fleissig (1997), and Serletis (2001) for some work along these lines.

TABLE 4.5

SENSITIVITY OF THE NEUTRALITY RESULTS TO SAMPLE PERIOD

Estimates of γ_{ym} when

Monetary	$\lambda_{my}=0$			$\lambda_{ym}=0$			$\gamma_{my}=0$		
aggregate	Full sample	Pre-1982	Post-1982	Full sample	Pre-1982	Post-1982	Full sample	Pre-1982	Post-1982
CE M1	−0.11(0.21)	−0.86(0.56)	0.10(0.12)	−0.16(0.20)	−1.06(0.55)	0.17(0.12)	−0.19(0.21)	−0.82(0.55)	0.07(0.11)
CE M2	−0.01(0.09)	−0.26(0.23)	0.07(0.07)	−0.02(0.08)	−0.28(0.21)	0.07(0.07)	−0.07(0.09)	−0.22(0.22)	−0.04(0.05)
CE M3	0.01(0.08)	−0.16(0.19)	0.04(0.06)	0.03(0.08)	−0.12(0.18)	0.08(0.06)	−0.09(0.07)	−0.35(0.20)	−0.04(0.04)
CE L	0.01(0.08)	−0.14(0.17)	0.03(0.05)	0.03(0.07)	−0.10(0.17)	0.07(0.06)	−0.09(0.07)	−0.34(0.17)	−0.04(0.04)

Note: All of the models include six lags of the relevant variables. Standard errors are shown in parentheses.

TABLE 4.6

SENSITIVITY OF THE NEUTRALITY RESULTS TO SAMPLE PERIOD

Estimates of $\gamma_{y,\Delta m}$ when

Monetary aggregate	$\lambda_{\Delta m,y}=0$			$\lambda_{y,\Delta m}=0$			$\gamma_{\Delta m,y}=0$		
	Full sample	Pre-1982	Post-1982	Full sample	Pre-1982	Post-1982	Full sample	Pre-1982	Post-1982
Sum M1	2.86(1.84)	16.34(7.58)	−0.64(0.63)	2.53(1.58)	10.29(4.50)	−0.39(0.66)	−0.94(1.20)	3.55(4.02)	−1.25(0.51)
Divisia M1	2.90(2.01)	18.44(8.70)	−0.90(0.66)	2.52(1.72)	11.19(4.99)	−0.68(0.69)	−1.24(1.40)	3.45(4.53)	−1.56(0.58)
Sum M2	7.74(5.13)	37.33(74.37)	3.08(2.24)	8.56(5.01)	62.55(164.31)	2.47(1.64)	−4.79(1.59)	−7.55(2.08)	0.58(1.86)
Divisia M2	14.01(11.13)	275.00(32.41)	2.84(2.70)	11.38(7.60)	46.60(100.29)	2.69(2.17)	−4.66(1.39)	−6.35(1.90)	−1.59(1.46)
Sum M3	3.10(1.99)	6.97(5.49)	1.62(1.44)	4.02(1.95)	7.88(5.46)	2.44(1.31)	−0.31(1.65)	−3.02(2.71)	1.67(1.44)
Divisia M3	7.91(4.38)	20.57(23.85)	2.23(2.11)	7.97(3.96)	16.34(15.14)	3.61(2.27)	−2.43(1.47)	−4.33(2.05)	0.75(1.85)
Sum L	5.29(2.08)	11.32(5.76)	2.57(1.29)	4.46(1.77)	8.38(4.17)	2.34(1.16)	3.81(1.98)	3.12(3.96)	2.89(1.29)
Divisia L	9.23(4.14)	20.36(17.77)	3.69(2.19)	7.67(3.07)	14.62(9.71)	3.23(1.81)	−0.79(1.67)	−2.62(2.31)	3.00(2.08)

Note: All of the models include six lags of the relevant variables. Standard errors are shown in parentheses.

Part 3

Monetary Aggregation, Inflation and Welfare

Overview of Part 3

Apostolos Serletis

The following table contains a brief summary of the content of the chapter in Part 3 of this book. This part of the book investigates the welfare implications of alternative monetary aggregation procedures.

Monetary Aggregation, Inflation and Welfare

Chapter Number	Chapter Title	Contents
5	Monetary Aggregation, Inflation and Welfare	Explores the welfare cost of inflation using tools from public finance and applied microeconomics.

Chapter 5:

This chapter investigates the welfare implications of alternative monetary aggregation procedures by providing a comparison among simple sum, Divisia, and currency equivalent monetary aggregates at different levels of monetary aggregation. We find that the choice of monetary aggregation procedure is crucial in evaluating the welfare cost of inflation.

Chapter 5

Monetary Aggregation, Inflation, and Welfare

Apostolos Serletis and Jagat Jit Virk.[*]

5.1 Introduction

Lucas (2000) provides estimates of the welfare cost of inflation based on U.S. time series for 1900-1994. In doing so, he defines the money supply as simple-sum M1, assumes that money pays no interest, and estimates the welfare cost of inflation using Bailey's (1956) consumer surplus approach as well as the compensating variation approach. Lucas argues that money demand behavior at hyperinflation or at rates of interest close to zero is crucial for welfare cost calculations; in those cases the semi-log money demand function, used by Cagan (1956) and Bailey (1956), fits the data better and should be used for such calculations. However, the U.S. time series data includes only moderate inflation rates, and Lucas' calculations, based on the double log demand schedule, indicate that reducing the interest rate from 3% to zero yields a benefit equivalent to an increase in real output of about 0.009 (or 0.9%).

More recently, Serletis and Yavari (2004) calculate the welfare cost of inflation for Canada and the United States, in the post-World War II period, from 1948 to 2001. In doing so, they use the same double log money demand specification used by Lucas (2000), but pay particular attention to the integration and cointegration properties of the money demand variables

---

[*]Originally published in *Applied Financial Economics* (http:/www.tandf.co.uk) 16 (2006), 499-512. Reprinted with permission.

and use recent advances in the field of applied econometrics to estimate the interest elasticity of money demand. They conclude that the welfare cost of inflation is significantly lower than Lucas reported. In particular, for the United States, they find that reducing the interest rate from 3% to zero, would yield a benefit equivalent to 0.0018 (less than two tenths of one percent) of real income. This is much smaller than the 0.9% (nine tenths of one percent) figure obtained by Lucas under the assumption that the interest elasticity of money demand is −0.5. Similar welfare cost estimates are also reported by Serletis and Yavari (2005) for Italy, using the low frequency data from Muscatelli and Spinelli (2000) over the 1861 to 1996 period.

As Lucas (2000, p. 270) puts it in his conclusions, a direction for potentially productive research "is to replace M1 with an aggregate in which different monetary assets are given different weights." In this chapter, we take up Lucas on his suggestion and provide a comparison among the official simple-sum aggregates, Barnett's (1980) Divisia aggregates, and Rotemberg's (1991) currency equivalent (CE) aggregates, at four different levels of monetary aggregation, to investigate the welfare implications of alternative monetary aggregation procedures. We make the bold assumption that money is non-interest bearing and also assume that the different monetary aggregates face the same double log demand function, since our data does not include regions of hyperinflation or rates of interest approaching zero. However, following Serletis and Yavari (2004), we pay particular attention to the integration and cointegration properties of the money demand variables and use the Fisher and Seater (1993) long-horizon regression approach to obtain an estimate of the interest rate elasticity of money demand.

The organization of the chapter is as follows. The next section provides a brief summary of the theoretical issues regarding the estimation of the welfare cost of inflation. Section 3 discusses the data and presents empirical evidence regarding the interest elasticity of money demand, using recent advances in the field of applied econometrics (such as integration theory, cointegration theory, and long-horizon regression tests). Section 4 investigates the sensitivity of the welfare cost calculations to monetary aggregation procedures and Section 5 closes with a brief summary and conclusion.

5.2 Theoretical Foundations

Consider the following money demand function

$$\frac{M}{P} = L(i, y)$$

where M denotes nominal money balances, P the price level, y real income, and i the nominal rate of interest, all at time t. Assuming that the $L(i,y)$ function takes the form $L(i,y) = \Phi(i)y$, the money demand function can be written as $m = \Phi(i)y$, where m denotes real money balances, M/P. Equivalently, we can write

$$z = \frac{m}{y} = \Phi(i)$$

which gives the demand for real money balances per unit of income as a function of the nominal interest rate i.

The specification of the money demand function is crucial in the estimation of the welfare cost of inflation. Bailey (1956) and Friedman (1969) use a semi-log demand schedule whereas Lucas (2000) uses a double log (constant elasticity) schedule on the grounds that the double log performs better on the U.S. data that does not include regions of hyperinflation or rates of interest approaching zero.[1] We, like Lucas, use the double log functional form,

$$z = \Phi(i) = Ai^{\eta}, \tag{5.1}$$

where η is the interest elasticity.

5.2.1 The Consumer Surplus Approach

The traditional approach to estimating the welfare cost of inflation is the one developed by Bailey (1956). It uses tools from public finance and applied microeconomics and defines the welfare cost of inflation as the area under the inverse money demand schedule — the 'consumer surplus' that can be gained by reducing the nominal interest rate from a positive level of i to the lowest possible level (perhaps zero). In particular, based on Bailey's consumer surplus approach, we estimate the money demand function $z = \Phi(i)$, calculate its inverse $i = \Psi(z)$, and define

$$w(i) = \int_{\Phi(i)}^{\Phi(0)} \Psi(x)dx = \int_{0}^{i} \Phi(x)dx - i\Phi(i), \tag{5.2}$$

where $w(i)$ is the welfare cost of inflation, expressed as a fraction of income. With (5.1), equation (5.2) takes the form

---

[1] In this regard, Bali (2000) performs tests based on the Box-Cox transformation and confirms that the double log fits the U.S. data better than the semi-log function.

$$w(i) = \left[\frac{A}{\eta+1}i^{\eta+1}\right]_0^i - iAi^\eta = -A\frac{\eta}{\eta+1}i^{\eta+1}. \tag{5.3}$$

5.2.2 The Compensating Variation Approach

Lucas (2000) takes a 'compensating variation' approach to the problem of estimating the welfare cost of inflation. In doing so, he also provides theoretical, general equilibrium justifications for Bailey's consumer surplus approach.

Lucas starts with Brock's (1974) perfect foresight version of the Sidrauski (1967) model, and defines the welfare cost of a nominal interest rate i, $w(i)$, to be the income compensation needed to leave the household indifferent between living in a steady state with an interest rate constant at i and an otherwise identical steady state with an interest rate of zero. Thus, $w(i)$ is the solution to the following equality

$$\mathcal{U}\left[(1+w(i))\,y, \Phi(i)y\right] = \mathcal{U}\left[y, \Phi(0)y\right]. \tag{5.4}$$

Assuming a homothetic current period utility function

$$u(c,m) = \frac{1}{1-\sigma}\left[cf\left(\frac{m}{c}\right)\right]^{1-\sigma}, \quad \sigma \# 1, \tag{5.5}$$

where c and m are real consumption and money balances, and setting up the dynamic programming problem [see Lucas (2000) for details], Lucas obtains the differential equation

$$w'(i) = -\Psi\left(\frac{\Phi(i)}{1+w(i)}\right)\Phi'(i), \tag{5.6}$$

in the welfare cost function $w(i)$. For any given money demand function, (5.6) can be solved numerically for an exact welfare cost function $w(i)$. In fact, with (5.1), equation (5.6) can be written as

$$w'(i) = -\eta Ai^\eta\,(1+w(i))^{-1/\eta},$$

with solution

$$w(i) = \exp\left[-\frac{\eta \ln\left(-\frac{1}{A(i\exp(\eta \ln i)) - \frac{\eta}{A(\eta+1)} - \frac{1}{A(\eta+1)}}\right)}{\eta + 1}\right] - 1. \quad (5.7)$$

Thus the welfare cost of inflation is easily obtained using equation (5.7).

Lucas also investigates the robustness of his results to the non-existence of lump sum taxes and inelastic labor supply, by introducing theoretical modifications to the Sidrauski model. In particular, (5.5) is modified to include the consumption of leisure l

$$u(c,m,l) = \frac{1}{1-\sigma}\left[cf\left(\frac{m}{c}\right)\phi(l)\right]^{1-\sigma}, \quad \sigma \# 1, \quad (5.8)$$

the consumer's constraint to reflect income taxation, and the resource constraint to include government consumption. In this case the welfare cost function $w(i)$ is defined as the solution to the following equality

$$\mathcal{U}\left[(1+w(i))\,c(i), \Phi(i), l(i)\right] = \mathcal{U}\left[c(\delta), \Phi(\delta), l(\delta)\right], \quad (5.9)$$

where $i = \delta$ is used as a benchmark rather than $i = 0$, because depending on the assumed functions f and ϕ, the system may not have a solution at $i = 0$. With (5.8), (5.9) is equivalent to

$$(1+w(i))\,c(i)f\left(\frac{\Phi(i)}{(1+w(i))\,\omega(i)}\right)\phi(l(i)) = c(\delta)f\left(\frac{\Phi(\delta)}{\omega(\delta)}\right)\phi(l(\delta)), \quad (5.10)$$

where $\omega = c/y$. Moreover, with (5.1), equation (5.10) becomes [see Lucas (2000) for details]

$$(1+w(i))\,\omega(i)\left[\left(\frac{\Phi(i)}{(1+w(i))\,\omega(i)}\right)^{(b-1)/b}A^{1/b}+1\right]^{b/(b-1)}\phi(l(i)) = F(\delta),$$

with solution[2]

---

[2] In equation (5.11),

$$F(\delta) = \omega(\delta)\phi(l(\delta))\left[\left(\frac{\Phi(\delta)}{\omega(\delta)}\right)^{(b-1)/b}A^{1/b}+1\right]^{b/(b-1)}.$$

$$w(i) = \frac{\left[\left(\dfrac{F(\delta)}{\phi(l(i))}\right)^{(b-1)/b} - \left(\Phi(i)\right)^{(b-1)/b} A^{1/b}\right]^{b/(b-1)}}{\omega(i)} - 1. \qquad (5.11)$$

Equation (5.11) is used to calculate the welfare cost of inflation in the case of income taxation and elastic supply of labor.

Lucas (2000) also uses a version of the McCallum and Goodfriend (1987) variation of the Sidrauski model to provide another general equilibrium rationale for Bailey's consumer surplus approach. However, the relevant differential equation [equation (5.8) in Lucas (2000)] cannot be solved for interest rate elasticities different than -0.50 that Lucas assumes. As a result we are not exploring that approach in this chapter.

5.3   The Demand for Money

To investigate the welfare implications of alternative monetary aggregation procedures, we use the official simple-sum monetary aggregates, Barnett's (1980) Divisia aggregates (also known as "monetary services indices"), and Rotemberg's (1991) currency equivalent (CE) indices. The use of monetary aggregates (in various forms and at different levels of aggregation) is subject to a comment by Prescott (1996, p.114) that (in the case of M1)

> "[t]he theory has households holding non-interest bearing money, while the monetary aggregate used in the demand for money function is M1. Most of M1 is not non-interest bearing debt held by households. Only a third is currency and half of that is probably held abroad. Another third is demand deposits held by businesses, which often earn interest *de facto*. Households do not use these demand deposits to economize on shopping time. The final third is demand deposits held by households that, at least in recent years, can pay interest."

With Percott's comment in mind, we use quarterly data over the period from 1960:1 to 2001:4, obtained from the St. Louis MSI database, maintained by the Federal Reserve Bank of St. Louis as a part of the bank's Federal Reserve Economic Database (FRED) — see Anderson *et al.* (1997a, 1997b) for details regarding the construction of the Divisia and CE monetary aggregates and related data issues, and Serletis and Koustas (2001) for a brief discussion of the problem of the definition (aggregation) of money. Moreover, we use real GDP as the real output series, the GDP deflator as the price level series, and the 90-day Treasury bill rate as the relevant interest rate series.

Welfare cost calculations are also sensitive to the specification of the money demand function. As already noted, we follow Lucas (2000) and assume a double log schedule. However, to obtain an estimate of the interest elasticity, we first investigate the time series properties of the money demand variables to avoid what Granger and Newbold (1974) refer to as "spurious regression." In doing so, we first test for stochastic trends (unit roots) in the autoregressive representation of each individual logged series z_t and the logged interest rate series. In Table 5.1 we report p-values for the weighted symmetric (WS) unit root test [see Pantula, Gonzalez-Farias, and Fuller (1994)], the augmented Dickey-Fuller (ADF) test [see Dickey and Fuller (1981) for more details], and the nonparametric $Z(t_{\hat{\alpha}})$ test of Phillips and Perron (1987). As discussed in Pantula et al. (1994), the WS test dominates the ADF test in terms of power. Also the $Z(t_{\hat{\alpha}})$ test is robust to a wide variety of serial correlation and time-dependent heteroskedasticity. For the WS and ADF tests, the optimal lag length is taken to be the order selected by the Akaike Information Criterion (AIC) plus 2 - see Pantula et al. (1994) for details regarding the advantages of this rule for choosing the number of augmenting lags. The $Z(t_{\hat{\alpha}})$ is done with the same Dickey-Fuller regression variables, using no augmenting lags.

According to the p-values [based on the response surface estimates given by MacKinnon (1994)] for the WS, ADF, and $Z(t_{\hat{\alpha}})$ unit root tests reported in the first three columns of each panel of Table 5.1, the null hypothesis of a unit root in levels cannot in general be rejected, except for the CE M2 and CE M3 monetary aggregates.[3] Hence, we conclude that both the z_t and i_t series are integrated of order 1 [or I(1) in the terminology of Engle and Granger (1987)].[4] We also tested the null hypothesis of no cointegration (against the alternative of cointegration) between each I(1) money measure and i_t using the Engle and Granger (1987) two-step procedure, which is well suited for the bivariate case which can have at most one cointegrating vector.[5] The tests were first done with z_t as the dependent variable in the cointegrating regression and then repeated with the nominal interest rate i_t as the dependent variable. The results, under the "Cointegration" columns

---

[3]See Serletis (2001, Chapter 10) for similar results over a different sample period.

[4]It should also be noticed that time series data on nominal interest rates reflects time-series data on inflation, and the persistence of inflation episodes makes it difficult to reject I(1) behavior in interest rates.

[5]In cointegration tests using three or more variables the Engle and Granger (1987) approach does not distinguish between the existence of one or more cointegrating vectors. In those cases, the Johansen (1988) maximum likelihood extention of the Engle and Granger (1987) cointegration approach or the Pesaran et al. (2001) bounds testing approach should be used.

of Table 5.1, suggest that the null hypothesis of no cointegration between z_t and i_t cannot be rejected (at the 5% level) for all I(1) money measures.

Since we are not able to find evidence of cointegration, to avoid the spurious regression problem we use the long-horizon regression approach developed by Fisher and Seater (1993) to obtain an estimate of the interest rate elasticity of money demand. One important advantage to working with the long-horizon regression approach is that cointegration is neither necessary nor sufficient for tests on the interest rate elasticity of money demand. Long-horizon regressions have received a lot of attention in the recent economics and finance literature, because studies based on long-horizon variables seem to find significant results where short-horizon regressions commonly used in economics and finance have failed.

Following Fisher and Seater (1993), we consider the following bivariate autoregressive representation

$$\alpha_{zz}(L)\Delta^{\langle z \rangle} z_t = \alpha_{zi}(L)\Delta^{\langle i \rangle} i_t + \varepsilon_t^z$$
$$\alpha_{ii}(L)\Delta^{\langle i \rangle} i_t = \alpha_{iz}(L)\Delta^{\langle z \rangle} z_t + \varepsilon_t^i$$

where $\alpha_{zz}^0 = \alpha_{ii}^0 = 1$, $\Delta = 1 - L$, where L is the lag operator, z is the money-income ratio, i is the nominal interest rate, and $\langle \varkappa \rangle$ represents the order of integration of $\varkappa$, so that if $\varkappa$ is integrated of order γ, then $\langle \varkappa \rangle = \gamma$ and $\langle \Delta\varkappa \rangle = \langle \varkappa \rangle - 1$. The vector $(\varepsilon_t^z, \varepsilon_t^i)'$ is assumed to be independently and identically distributed normal with zero mean and covariance $\sum_\varepsilon$, the elements of which are $\mathrm{var}(\varepsilon_t^z)$, $\mathrm{var}(\varepsilon_t^i)$, $\mathrm{cov}(\varepsilon_t^z, \varepsilon_t^i)$.

According to this approach, the null hypothesis of $\eta = 0$ can be tested in terms of the long-run derivative of z with respect to a permanent change in i, $LRD_{z,i}$, which is defined as follows. If $\lim_{k \to \infty} \partial z_{t+k}/\partial \varepsilon_t^i \neq 0$, then

$$LRD_{z,i} = \lim_{k \to \infty} \frac{\partial z_{t+k}/\partial \varepsilon_t^i}{\partial i_{t+k}/\partial \varepsilon_t^i}$$

and expresses the ultimate effect of an exogenous interest rate disturbance on z, relative to that disturbance's ultimate effect on i. When $\lim_{k \to \infty} \partial i_{t+k}/\partial \varepsilon_t^i = 0$, there are no permanent changes in i and thus $LRD_{z,i}$ is undefined.

The above bivariate autoregressive system can be inverted to yield the following vector moving average representation

$$\Delta^{\langle z \rangle} z_t = \theta_{zi}(L)\varepsilon_t^i + \theta_{zz}(L)\varepsilon_t^z$$
$$\Delta^{\langle i \rangle} i_t = \theta_{ii}(L)\varepsilon_t^i + \theta_{iz}(L)\varepsilon_t^z$$

In terms of this moving average representation, Fisher and Seater (1993) show that $LRD_{z,i}$ depends on $\langle i \rangle - \langle z \rangle$, as follows

$$LRD_{z,i} = \frac{(1-L)^{\langle i \rangle - \langle z \rangle} \, \theta_{zi}(L)|_{L=1}}{\theta_{ii}(1)}$$

Hence, meaningful long-horizon regression tests can be conducted if both z_t and i_t satisfy certain nonstationarity conditions. In particular, long-horizon regression tests require that both z_t and i_t are at least I(1) and of the same order of integration. In fact, when $\langle z \rangle = \langle i \rangle = 1$, the long-run derivative becomes

$$LRD_{z,i} = \frac{\theta_{zi}(1)}{\theta_{ii}(1)}$$

where $\theta_{zi}(1) = \sum_{j=1}^{\infty} \theta_{zi}^j$ and $\theta_{ii}(1) = \sum_{j=1}^{\infty} \theta_{ii}^j$. The coefficient $\theta_{zi}(1)/\theta_{ii}(1)$ is the long-run value of the impulse-response of z with respect to i, suggesting that $LRD_{z,i}$ can be interpreted as the long-run elasticity of z with respect to i.

Under the assumptions that $\text{cov}(\varepsilon_t^z, \varepsilon_t^i) = 0$ and that i is exogenous in the long-run, the coefficient $\theta_{zi}(1)/\theta_{ii}(1)$ equals the zero-frequency regression coefficient in the regression of $\Delta^{\langle z \rangle} z$ on $\Delta^{\langle i \rangle} i$ — see Fisher and Seater (1993, note 11). This estimator is given by $\lim_{k \to 0} \eta_k$, where η_k is the coefficient from the regression

$$\left[\sum_{j=0}^{k} \Delta^{\langle z \rangle} z_{t-j} \right] = a_k + \eta_k \left[\sum_{j=0}^{k} \Delta^{\langle i \rangle} i_{t-j} \right] + e_{kt}$$

In fact, when $\langle z \rangle = \langle i \rangle = 1$, consistent estimates of η_k can be derived by applying ordinary least squares to the regression

$$z_t - z_{t-k-1} = a_k + \eta_k \left[i_t - i_{t-k-1} \right] + e_{kt}, \qquad k = 1, ..., K \qquad (5.12)$$

We estimate equation (5.12) and in Table 5.2 report ordinary least squares estimates of η_k, tests of the null hypothesis that $\eta_k = 0$, and Andrews (1989) IPFs at low type II error, $\eta_{k,0.05}$, and high type II error, $\eta_{k,0.50}$, at forecast horizons $k = 10, 15, 20, 25$, and 30, for each money measure that is I(1). An asterisk next to an η_k value indicates rejection of the null hypothesis that $\eta_k = 0$; the test statistic is the t-ratio of $\hat{\eta}_k$ with

T/k degrees of freedom, where T is the sample size and $\hat{\sigma}_{\eta_k}$ is computed following Newey and West (1994). Clearly, the null hypothesis that $\eta_k = 0$ is rejected (at the 5% level and for all values of k) only with the M1 and MZM monetary aggregates (irrespective of how they are measured).

As noted by Andrews (1989), when the null hypothesis is not rejected the IPF allows us to gauge which alternatives are consistent with the data. In particular, when $\eta_k = 0$ is not rejected at the 5% level, there are alternatives to the null that can be ruled out at the same level of significance. In this case, the IPF at the 95% level of power provides a lower bound, $\eta_{k,0.05}$, that is significantly different than the true value of η_k at the 0.05 level, $\{\eta_k : |\eta_k| > \eta_{k,0.05}\}$. Following Andrews (1989), we compute the asymptotic approximation to the IPF at the 0.95 level of power as $\eta_{k,0.05} = \lambda_{1,0.05}(0.95)\hat{\sigma}_{\eta_k}$, where $\hat{\sigma}_{\eta_k}$ is the standard error of $\hat{\eta}_k$ and the subscripts of $\lambda_{1,0.05}(0.95)$ indicate a test of one restriction at a 0.05 level. From Andrews (1989, Table 1), $\lambda_{1,0.05}(0.95) = 3.605$. Similarly, the IPF allows us to examine alternatives that possess a high type II error. At a 0.50 error probability that is suggested by Andrews (1989), the asymptotic approximation to the IPF is $\eta_{k,0.50} = \lambda_{1,0.05}(0.50)\hat{\sigma}_{\eta_k}$ for those alternatives to $\eta_k = 0$ that are consistent with the data, $\{\eta_k : 0 < |\eta_k| \le \eta_{k,0.50}\}$. From Andrews (1989, Table 1) $\lambda_{1,0.05}(0.50) = 1.960$.

Clearly, the IPFs at low and high power provide little evidence to doubt $\eta_k = 0$ for the simple-sum M2 and M3 and Divisia M2 and M3 monetary aggregates. This is consistent with Prescott's (1996) argument that, except for currency, few if any components of monetary aggregates are non-interest bearing. Currency is a much smaller fraction of these broad aggregates than of M1, so small a component that any welfare cost is difficult to detect.

For this reason, in the next section we use only the M1 and MZM money measures to calculate the welfare cost of inflation and provide a comparison among simple-sum, Divisia, and currency equivalent monetary aggregation procedures.

5.4 The Empirical Evidence

Figures 5.1 and 5.2 plot the welfare cost function $w(i)$, based on equation (5.3), for each of the M1 and MZM money measures at each of the three levels of monetary aggregation. In applying (5.3), we use the values of η given in Table 5.2 (under $k = 30$) and set A so that the welfare curve passes through the geometric means of i and the money-income ratio z.[6] Strong evidence exists of a positive relation between the welfare cost of inflation

---

[6]For example, if $\bar{z}$ is the geometric mean of z and $\bar{i}$ that of i, then A is set equal to $\bar{z}/\bar{i}^{\eta}$.

and the nominal rate of interest. Moreover, the results are substantially more favorable for the Divisia than for the simple-sum and currency equivalent monetary aggregates. In particular, the Divisia aggregates perform better than the other aggregates (in terms of producing a lower welfare cost) at both the lowest (M1) and highest (MZM) levels of aggregation, with that degree of superiority tending to increase at higher interest rates.

Next, we calculate the welfare cost of inflation using the Lucas (2000) compensating variation approach based on the simplified version of the Sidrauski (1967) model, discussed in Section 2. That is, we use equation (5.7) for our calculations. As in Lucas, the welfare cost estimates (not reported here) are very close to those in Figures 5.1 and 5.2; in fact, they are identical to four decimal places, so that the choice between these two approaches is of no importance.

In Figures 5.3-10 we plot welfare cost functions using equation (5.11). Here, we follow Lucas (2000) and investigate the welfare cost of inflation at very low interest rates. In particular, we let the nominal interest rate i range from zero to 2% (instead of using the actual interest rate values as we do in Figures 5.1 and 5.2), set the benchmark interest rate δ equal to 2% (thereby calculating the welfare cost relative to a 2% interest rate), set $g = 0.35$ (the approximate share of government expenditure in total income in the United States today), and assume that $\phi(l) = l^\theta$. We plot the welfare cost function for each of the M1 and MZM money measures, at each of the three levels of monetary aggregation, and for four different values of θ — 0.0001, 0.3, 0.6, and 0.9.

With almost inelastic labor supply ($\theta = 0.0001$), economic agents receive little utility from leisure and the welfare cost functions in Figures 5.3 and 5.7 indicate a positive relationship between the welfare cost of inflation and the nominal rate of interest, for nominal interest rates in the range between zero and 2%. Moreover, the Divisia aggregates show a smaller welfare cost than the simple-sum and currency equivalent aggregates, at both the M1 and MZM levels of aggregation. For $\theta = 0.3$, $\theta = 0.6$, and $\theta = 0.9$, the welfare cost functions in Figures 5.4-6 (for M1) and Figures 5.8-10 (for MZM) also indicate that the Divisia series show a lower welfare cost for each θ value and for each interest rate value.

5.5 Conclusion

We have investigated the welfare cost of inflation using tools from public finance and applied microeconomics and quarterly U.S. data from 1960:1 to 2001:4. We have used simple-sum, Divisia, and currency equivalent

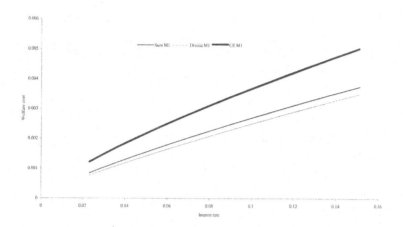

Figure 5.1: Welfare Cost Functions for M1 Money.

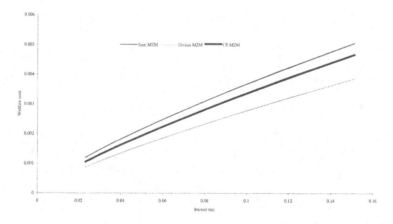

Figure 5.2: Welfare Cost Functions for MZM Money.

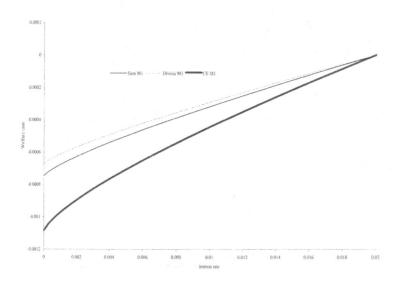

Figure 5.3: Welfare Cost Functions for M1, Based on Equation (5.11) with $\theta = 0.0001$.

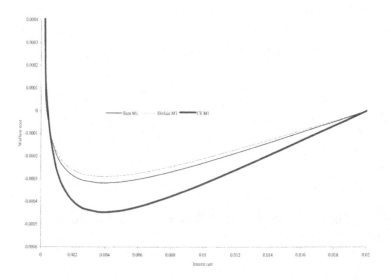

Figure 5.4: Welfare Cost Functions for M1, Based on Equation (5.11) with $\theta = 0.3$.

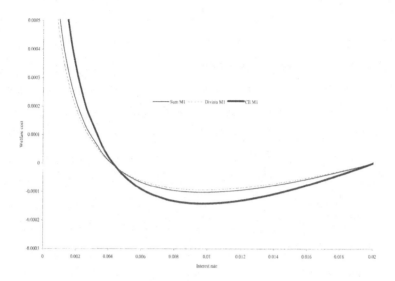

Figure 5.5: Welfare Cost Functions for M1, Based on Equation (5.11) with $\theta = 0.6$.

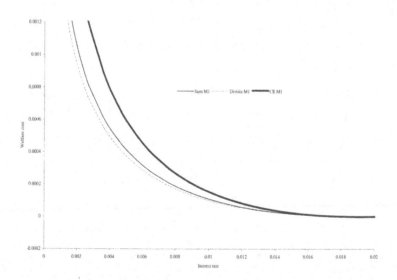

Figure 5.6: Welfare Cost Functions for M1, Based on Equation (5.11) with $\theta = 0.9$.

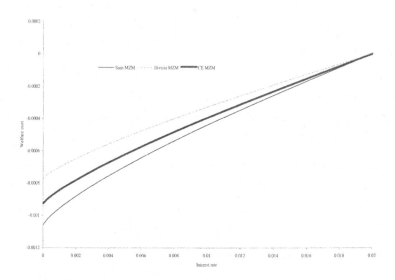

Figure 5.7: Welfare Cost Functions for MZM, Based on Equation (5.11) with $\theta = 0.0001$.

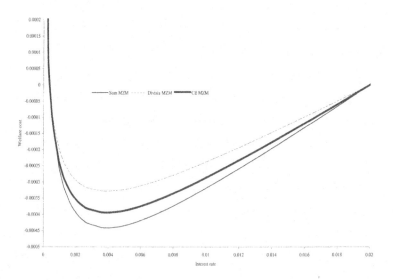

Figure 5.8: Welfare Cost Functions for MZM, Based on Equation (5.11) with $\theta = 0.3$.

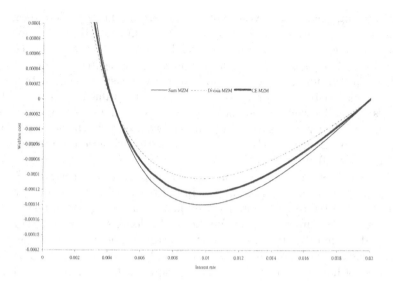

Figure 5.9: Welfare Cost Functions for MZM, Based on Equation (5.11) with $\theta = 0.6$.

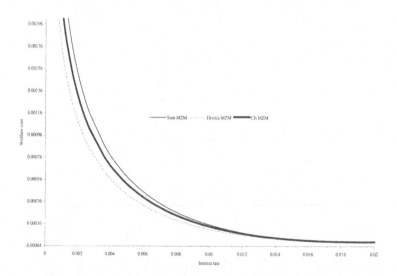

Figure 5.10: Welfare Cost Functions for MZM, Based on Equation (5.11) with $\theta = 0.9$.

monetary aggregates to investigate the welfare implications of alternative monetary aggregation procedures. Our results indicate that the choice of monetary aggregation procedure is crucial in evaluating the welfare cost of inflation. In particular, the Divisia monetary aggregates, which embody differentials in opportunity costs and correctly measure the monetary services furnished by the non-currency components (valued by households), suggest a smaller welfare cost than the simple-sum and currency equivalent aggregates. This result is robust to whether we use the traditional approach developed by Bailey (1956) or the compensating variation approach used by Lucas (2000).

We have used the long-horizon regression approach of Fisher and Seater (1993) to obtain an estimate of the interest elasticity of money demand and also investigated the power of the long-horizon regression tests using Andrews' (1989) inverse power functions. In doing so, however, we made the bold assumption (mentioned in the introduction) that money is non-interesting bearing and used the 90-day T-bill rate to capture the opportunity cost of holding money. Investigating how much this matters, and also dealing with the issues raised in the last section of Marty (1999), is an area for potentially productive future research.

TABLE 5.1

MARGINAL SIGNIFICANCE LEVELS OF UNIT ROOT AND COINTEGRATION TESTS

Level of aggregation	Simple sum Unit root WS	ADF	$Z(t_{\hat\alpha})$	Cointegration z	i	Divisia Unit root WS	ADF	$Z(t_{\hat\alpha})$	Cointegration z	i	Currency equivalent Unit root WS	ADF	$Z(t_{\hat\alpha})$	Cointegration z	i
M1	.751	.395	.837	.525	.357	.810	.448	.835	.400	.223	.668	.550	.844	.124	.051
M2	.769	.407	.389	.420	.226	.937	.560	.452	.530	.249	.005	.013	.019	n/a	n/a
M3	.814	.568	.693	.582	.157	.965	.750	.613	.776	.323	.002	.005	.017	n/a	n/a
MZM	.923	.912	.964	.383	.064	.965	.946	.983	.466	.055	.689	.609	.482	.284	.129
i	.796	.673	.536												

Note: Sample period, logged quarterly U.S. data: 1960:1-2001:4. Numbers are tail areas of tests.
All tests use a constant and trend. n/a = not applicable.

TABLE 5.2

ESTIMATES OF η_k, TESTS OF $\eta_k = 0$, AND IPF BOUNDS

Level of aggregation		Simple sum					Divisia					Currency equivalent				
		$k=10$	$k=15$	$k=20$	$k=25$	$k=30$	$k=10$	$k=15$	$k=20$	$k=25$	$k=30$	$k=10$	$k=15$	$k=20$	$k=25$	$k=30$
M1	$\hat{\eta}_k$	-0.10^*	-0.14^*	-0.18^*	-0.19^*	-0.20^*	-0.09^*	-0.13^*	-0.16^*	-0.18^*	-0.18^*	-0.13^*	-0.18^*	-0.22^*	-0.23^*	-0.24^*
	$\eta_{k,0.05}$	—	—	—	—	—	—	—	—	—	—	—	—	—	—	—
	$\eta_{k,0.50}$	—	—	—	—	—	—	—	—	—	—	—	—	—	—	—
M2	$\hat{\eta}_k$	-0.04^*	-0.03	-0.01	-0.00	-0.00	-0.03	-0.02	-0.01	-0.00	0.00					
	$\eta_{k,0.05}$	—	0.08	0.09	0.09	0.07	0.07	0.08	0.07	0.06	0.05					
	$\eta_{k,0.50}$	—	0.04	0.05	0.04	0.04	0.03	0.04	0.04	0.03	0.03					
M3	$\hat{\eta}_k$	-0.00	0.01	0.03	0.04	0.05	-0.01	-0.00	0.00	0.00	0.02					
	$\eta_{k,0.05}$	0.09	0.11	0.13	0.12	0.09	0.08	0.10	0.10	0.08	0.06					
	$\eta_{k,0.50}$	0.05	0.06	0.07	0.06	0.05	0.04	0.05	0.05	0.04	0.03					
MZM	$\hat{\eta}_k$	-0.17^*	-0.21^*	-0.23^*	-0.22^*	-0.22^*	-0.16^*	-0.19^*	-0.21^*	-0.20^*	-0.20^*	-0.19^*	-0.23^*	-0.22^*	-0.20^*	-0.20^*
	$\eta_{k,0.05}$	—	—	—	—	—	—	—	—	—	—	—	—	—	—	—
	$\eta_{k,0.50}$	—	—	—	—	—	—	—	—	—	—	—	—	—	—	—

Note: Sample period, logged quarterly U.S. data: 1960:1-2001:4. An asterisk indicates rejection (of the null that $\eta_k = 0$) at the 5% asymptotic level.

Part 4

Chaotic Monetary Dynamics

Overview of Part 4

Apostolos Serletis

The following table contains a brief summary of the contents of each chapter in Part 4 of the book. This part of the book uses tools from dynamical systems theory to investigate the properties of U.S. money and velocity series.

Chaotic Monetary Dynamics

Chapter Number	Chapter Title	Contents
6	Random Walks, Breaking Trend Functions, and the Chaotic Structure of the Velocity of Money	Tests for deterministic noisy chaos and contrasts the random walk hypothesis of the velocity of money to chaotic dynamics.
7	Chaotic Analysis of U.S. Money and Velocity Measures	Investigates the properties of money and velocity measures to further address disputes about their chaoticity.

Chapter 6:

This chapter examines the time series properties of U.S. velocity series and tests for deterministic noisy chaos using the Nychka, Ellner, Gallant, and McCaffrey nonparametric test for positivity of the maximum Lyapunov exponent. Comparisons are made among simple-sum and Divisia aggregates. The conclusion is that the unit root model cannot be rejected and that there is tentative evidence that some velocity measures are chaotic.

Chapter 7:

This chapter uses tools from dynamical systems theory to further investigate the properties of U.S. money and velocity series. Comparisons are made between simple-sum, Divisia and currency equivalent money and velocity aggregates.

Chapter 6

Random Walks, Breaking Trend Functions, and the Chaotic Structure of the Velocity of Money

*Apostolos Serletis**

Recently, a substantial amount of attention has been focused on the behavior of the velocity of money in the United States (primarily as the result of a relatively sudden and unanticipated decline in the velocity series, beginning in 1981 and continuing since then), and quite a few specific hypotheses have evolved. Among the propositions advanced, those most often cited involve the influence of structural changes in the financial sector, tax cuts, inflation (or expected inflation), changes in government expenditures, changes in energy prices, and money growth; see especially, Hall and Noble (1987), Judd and Motley (1984), Tatom (1983), Taylor (1986), Santoni (1987), and Fisher and Serletis (1989) for more on these and other suggested (and sometimes empirically supported) influences.

The most powerful element of this statistically unusual decline in velocity is the collapse of the longer-run relationship connecting money to both income and prices; see Friedman (1988). In fact, whether velocity is stable or at least predictable is essential to any empirical interpretation of the monetarist position and especially relevant for some problems of potential

---

*Reprinted with permission from the *Journal of Business and Economic Statistics*. Copyright [1995] by the American Statistical Association. All rights reserved.

importance in the practical conduct of monetary policy such as the 'base drift' problem. Regarding base drift, Walsh (1986) showed that zero drift will be optimal only if the shocks to velocity are transitory and full drift will be optimal only if the shocks to velocity are permanent.

Therefore, empirically evaluating the univariate time series properties of velocity is essential. Nelson and Plosser (1982) argued that most macroeconomic time series have a unit root (a stochastic trend) and described this property as one of being 'difference stationary' so that the first-difference of a time series is stationary. In fact, Gould and Nelson (1974), Nelson and Plosser (1982), and Haraf (1986) concluded that velocity is a difference-stationary process, suggesting that the recent change in velocity might have been produced by an unusually large shock that caused velocity to wander off in a new direction, with the probability of wandering back being very small.

In this chapter, I examine the time series properties of U.S. velocity by testing for the presence of a unit root in the univariate time series representation of the series. A test of the null hypothesis of difference stationarity against the trend-stationary alternative can be performed by estimating by ordinary least squares augmented Dickey-Fuller (see Dickey and Fuller 1981) type regressions, as done by Nelson and Plosser (1982). Such tests do not in general reject the null, but they were challenged by Perron (1989), who argued that most macroeconomic time series are trend stationary if one allows for structural changes in the trend function. Here, unit-root tests are conducted using Zivot and Andrews's (1992) variation of Perron's (1989) test in which the point of structural change is estimated rather than fixed. This test is more appropriate than Perron's because it circumvents the problem of data-mining; see Christiano (1992).

I also contrast the random-walk behavior of the velocity of money to chaotic dynamics. This is motivated by the notion that velocity follows a deterministic, dynamic, and nonlinear process, which generates output that mimics the output of stochastic systems. In other words, I address this question: Is it possible for velocity to appear to be random but not to be really random? In doing so, I test for chaos using the Lyapunov exponent estimator of Nychka, Ellner, Gallant, and McCaffrey (1992). This test is explicitly derived for use with noisy data and is currently [as Barnett *et al.* (1994a,b) put it] a well-established candidate for a test for the null hypothesis of chaos in small samples.

Chaos represents a radical change of perspective in the explanation of fluctuations observed in economic time series. In this view, the fluctuations and irregularities observed in economic time series receive an endogenous explanation and are traced back to the strong nonlinear deterministic structure that can pervade the economic system. Moreover, if chaos can be shown to exist, the implication would be that (nonlinearity-based) prediction is possible (at least in the short run and provided that the actual generating mechanism is known exactly). Prediction, however, over long periods is all but impossible due to the sensitive dependence on the initial conditions property of chaos.

Comparisons are made in all tests among simple-sum and Divisia velocities (of M1A, M1, M2, M3, and L) to deal with anomalies that arise because of different definitions of money [see Barnett, Fisher, and Serletis (1992) regarding the state of the art in monetary aggregation]. The money measures employed are monthly simple-sum and Divisia indexes (from 1960:1 to 1992:12) for the United States, as described by Thornton and Yue (1992), and were obtained from the Federal Reserve Economic Data (FRED) bulletin board of the Federal Reserve Bank of St. Louis. In calculating velocity, I followed a procedure for generating monthly gross national product (GNP) data developed by Christiano (1986). This involves the construction of a synthetic monthly GNP series by multiplying the industrial production index by the price level.

The chapter is organized as follows. Section 6.1 briefly describes the Zivot and Andrews (1992) unit-root testing procedure and reports the results. Section 6.2 provides a description of the key features of the Nychka *et al.* (1992) test for chaos, focusing explicit attention on the test's ability to detect chaos. The results are also presented in this section. Section 6.3 concludes the chapter with a discussion of the implications of the results.

6.1 Searching for a Unit Root

As was argued in the introduction, Nelson and Plosser's (1982) argument is that most macroeconomic time series have a unit root (a stochastic trend), meaning that movements in these variables result from the accumulation of shocks, each of which has large permanent effects. In view of the serious implications of unit roots, however, for both empirical and theoretical work, as well as the stakes in this line of research, the Nelson and Plosser unit-root testing approach was recently challenged by Perron (1989), who argued that most macroeconomic time series [and in particular those used by Nelson and Plosser (1982)] are trend stationary if one allows for structural changes in the trend function.

In particular, Perron's argument was that only certain 'big shocks' have had permanent effects on the various macroeconomic time series and that these shocks were exogenous — that is, not a realization of the underlying data-generation mechanism of the various series. Modeling such shocks as exogenous removes the influence of these shocks from the noise function and, in general, leads to a rejection of the null hypothesis of a unit root. Perron's assumption, however, that the dating of the breakpoint is known *a priori*, has been criticized, most notably by Christiano (1992), who argued that problems associated with 'pre-testing' are applicable to Perron's methodology and that the structural break should instead be treated as being correlated with the data.

More recently, Zivot and Andrews (1992), in the spirit of Christiano (1992), treated the selection of the breakpoint as the outcome of an estimation procedure and transformed Perron's (1989) conditional (on structural change at a known point in time) unit-root test into an unconditional unit-root test. In particular their null hypothesis is an integrated process with drift, and the relevant alternative hypothesis is a trend-stationary process with a one-time break in the trend at an unknown point in time.

Following Zivot and Andrews (1992), I test the null hypothesis of an integrated process with drift against the alternative hypothesis of trend stationarity with a one-time break in the intercept and slope of the trend function at an unknown point in time (denoting it throughout this chapter by T_B), using the following augmented regression equation [see Zivot and Andrews (1992) for more details]:

$$ y_t = \hat{\mu} + \hat{\theta} DU_t\left(\hat{\lambda}\right) + \hat{\beta} t + \hat{\gamma} DT_t(\hat{\lambda}) + \hat{\alpha} y_{t-1} + \sum_{i=1}^{k} \hat{c}_i \Delta y_{t-i} + \hat{e}_t, \quad (6.1) $$

where Δ is the difference operator, $DU_t = 1$, and $DT_t = t$ if $t > T_B$ and 0 otherwise.

In (6.1), testing the null hypothesis of a unit root amounts to estimating the break fraction λ — the ratio of pre-break sample size to total sample size — to minimize the one-sided t statistic for testing $\alpha = 1$. In particular, reject the null hypothesis of a unit root if $t_{\hat{\alpha}}(\hat{\lambda}) < t(\hat{\lambda})$, where $t(\hat{\lambda})$ denotes the 'estimated breakpoint' critical value reported by Zivot and Andrews (1992). For each tentative choice of λ, the choice of the truncation lag parameter, k, is correlated with the data. In particular, working backward from $k = 12$, I chose k such that the t statistic on the last included lag in the autoregression was greater than 1.6 in absolute value and that the t statistic on the last lag in higher-order autoregressions was less than 1.6.

Table 6.1 presents the results (for the logged levels of the velocity series) using regression (6.1) with λ chosen so as to minimize the one-sided t statistic for testing $\alpha = 1$ over all $T - 2$ regressions (where T is the number of observations). The t statistics on the parameters for the following respective hypothesis are also presented (in parentheses): $\mu = 0$, $\theta = 0$, $\beta = 0$,

TABLE 6.1

TESTS FOR A UNIT ROOT USING ZIVOT AND ANDREWS'S (1992) VARIATION OF PERRON'S (1989) TEST

Velocity series	T	$\hat{T}_B$	k	$\hat{\mu}$	$t(\hat{\mu})$	$\hat{\theta}$	$t(\hat{\theta})$	$\hat{\beta}$	$t(\hat{\beta})$	$\hat{\gamma}$	$t(\hat{\gamma})$	$\hat{\alpha}$	$t(\hat{\alpha})$	$S(\hat{e})$
Sum M1A	395	1980:5	11	−.220	−3.4	.008	2.9	.000	3.3	−.000	−3.7	.966	−3.4	.009
Sum M1	395	1977:12	11	−.260	−4.3	.008	3.2	.000	3.6	−.000	−4.3	.960	−4.3	.009
Sum M2	395	1977:12	9	−.290	−4.1	.005	2.5	.000	.4	−.000	−3.0	.956	−4.1	.008
Sum M3	395	1983:12	9	−.260	−3.7	−.007	−3.3	−.000	−1.4	.000	1.8	.961	−3.7	.008
Sum L	395	1982:1	2	−.256	−3.7	−.008	−3.7	.000	1.2	−.000	−.1	.962	−3.7	.008
Divisia M1A	395	1980:5	11	−.230	−3.4	.009	3.0	.000	3.3	−.000	−3.9	.965	−3.4	.009
Divisia M1	395	1977:12	11	−.301	−4.5	.010	3.7	.000	3.8	−.000	−4.6	.954	−4.6	.009
Divisia M2	395	1977:12	11	−.251	−4.6	.010	4.4	.000	2.7	−.000	−2.3	.962	−4.6	.008
Divisia M3	395	1978:1	11	−.257	−4.5	.010	4.1	.000	2.5	−.000	−1.9	.961	−4.5	.008
Divisia L	395	1977:12	11	−.258	−4.5	.010	4.2	.000	2.9	−.000	−2.9	.961	−4.6	.008

Note: All the series are in logs. $\hat{T}_B$ is the estimated breakpoint. The t-statistic for $\hat{\alpha}$ is the minimum t statistic over all $T-2$ regressions for testing $\alpha = 1$. $t(\hat{\alpha})$ is significant at the **1%, *5%, and +10% level. Critical values at the **1%, *5%, and +10% levels are -5.57, -5.08, and -4.82, respectively; see Zivot and Andrews (1992, table 4).

Regression $y_t = \hat{\mu} + \hat{\theta}DU_t(\hat{\lambda}) + \hat{\beta}t + \hat{\gamma}DT_t(\hat{\lambda}) + \hat{\alpha}y_{t-1} + \sum_{i=1}^{k}\hat{c}_i\Delta y_{t-i} + \hat{e}_t.$

$\gamma = 0$, and $\alpha = 1$. Moreover, the values of $\hat{T}_B \left(= T\hat{\lambda} \right)$ (i.e., the estimated break year) that minimize the one-sided t statistic for testing $\alpha = 1$ over all $T - 2$ regressions are reported.

The breakpoint that minimizes the one-sided t statistic for testing $\alpha = 1$ is 1980:5 for the Sum M1A and Divisia M1A series; 1977:12 for the Sum M1, Sum M2, Divisia M1, Divisia M2, and Divisia L; 1983:12 for Sum M3; 1982:1 for Sum L; and 1978:1 for Divisia M3. To evaluate the significance of $t_{\hat{\alpha}}(\hat{\lambda})$, the asymptotic estimated breakpoint critical values reported by Zivot and Andrews (1992, table 4) are used. Clearly, the null hypothesis of a unit root cannot be rejected even after allowance for a break in the level and slope of the trend function. Moreover, nonrejection of the unit root implies that the significance of the various other coefficients in the regression cannot be assessed.

6.2   Detecting Chaotic Dynamics

In recent years several attempts have been made to test for chaotic dynamics in economic time series. Although the analysis of macroeconomic time series (e.g., see Barnett and Hinich 1993; Brock and Sayers 1988; Frank and Stengos 1988; Scheinkman and LeBaron 1989a) has not yet led to particularly encouraging results, the analysis of financial series (e.g., Frank and Stengos 1989; Hsieh 1991; Scheinkman and LeBaron 1989b) has led to results that are as a whole more interesting and more reliable than that of macroeconomic series. This is primarily for two reasons, the low sample sizes (relative to the calculations to be performed) that are available with macroeconomic data and the high noise level that exists in most macroeconomic series because they are usually aggregated time series.

A particularly interesting study was performed by Barnett and Chen (1988), who reported evidence of chaoticity in the (demand-side) Divisia monetary aggregates and whose conclusion was further confirmed with the same data by DeCoster and Mitchell (1991, 1994). That published claim of successful detection of chaos has generated considerable controversy, as shown by Ramsey, Sayers, and Rothman (1990) and Ramsey and Rothman (1994), who, by reexamining the data set used by Barnett and Chen (1988), showed that there is no evidence for the presence of chaos. In fact, they raised similar questions regarding virtually all of the other published tests of chaos. More recently, however, Barnett et al. (1994a), using three of the most reputable inference methods to test for nonlinearity and chaos — the BDS (Brock, Dechert, and Scheinkman 1987) test for stochastic dependence, the Hinich (1982) bispectrum-based test for nonlinearity, and the dominant Lyapunov exponent estimator of Nychka   et al. (1992) —

found rather strong indications of nonlinearity, which is necessary (but not sufficient) for chaos, but rather slim evidence of the presence of chaos. They also found little consistency in inferences across inference methods.

In what follows, I test for chaos in the velocity of money using the Lyapunov exponent estimator of Nychka *et al.* (1992). This is a well-established non parametric test for positivity of the maximum Lyapunov exponent; see, for example, Barnett *et al.* (1994a,b) for more details. It is explicitly derived for use with noisy data and is a regression (or Jacobian) method, unlike the Wolf, Swift, Swinney, and Vastano (1985) direct method, which is the first method for calculating the largest Lyapunov exponent and which [as Brock and Sayers (1988) found] requires long data series and is sensitive to dynamic noise, so inflated estimates of the dominant Lyapunov exponent are obtained. Another very promising test was also recently proposed by Gencay and Dechert (1992). Their algorithm estimates (using multivariate feedforward networks) not only the largest but all Lyapunov exponents of the unknown system.

6.2.1   The Nychka *et al.* (1992) Estimator

The distinctive feature of chaotic systems is sensitive dependence on initial conditions (e.g., see Eckmann and Ruelle 1985) — that is, exponential divergence of trajectories with similar initial conditions. The most important tool for diagnosing the presence of sensitive dependence on initial conditions (and thereby of chaoticity) in a dynamical system is provided by the dominant Lyapunov exponent, λ. This exponent measures average exponential divergence of convergence between trajectories that differ only in having an 'infinitesimally small' difference in their initial conditions and remains well defined for noisy systems; see Kifer (1986). A bounded system with a positive Lyapunov exponent is one operational definition of chaotic behavior.

Consider the time series $\{x_t\}$. We can create the trajectory

$$X_t = F(X_{t-1}), \qquad F : R^m \to R^n, \tag{6.2}$$

where $X_t = (x_t, x_{t-1}, \ldots, x_{t-m+1})^T$ and $F(X_{t-1}) = (f(x_{t-1}, \ldots, x_{t-m}),$ $x_{t-1}, \ldots, x_{t-m+1})^T$. Gencay and Dechert (1992) showed that the dynamical system (6.2) is topologically equivalent to the true (but unknown) system $Y_t = G(Y_{t-1})$, $G : R^n \to R^n$, where $m \geq 2n + 1$ and x is seen through an observation function $x_t = h(Y_t)$, $h : R^n \to R$. Equation (6.2) may be written more generally as

$$
\begin{pmatrix} x_t \\ x_{t-L} \\ \vdots \\ x_{t-mL+L} \end{pmatrix} = \begin{pmatrix} f(x_{t-L}, \ldots, x_{t-mL}) \\ x_{t-L} \\ \vdots \\ x_{t-mL+L} \end{pmatrix} + \begin{pmatrix} e_t \\ 0 \\ \vdots \\ 0 \end{pmatrix}, \tag{6.3}
$$

which reduces to $x_t = f(x_{t-L}, \ldots, x_{t-mL}) + e_t$, where m is the length of the embedding, L is the number of lags between observations, and $\{e_t\}$ is a sequence of zero mean (and unknown constant variance) independent random perturbations.

The definition of the dominant Lyapunov exponent, λ, can be formulated more precisely as follows. Let X_0, $X_0' \in R^m$, denote two 'nearby' initial state vectors. After M iterations of model (6.3) with the same random shock, we have (using a truncated Taylor approximation)

$$
\|X_M - X_M'\| = \left\| F^M(X_0) - F^M(X_0') \right\|
$$
$$
\cong \left\| (DF^M)_{X_0}(X_0 - X_0') \right\|,
$$

where F^M is the Mth iterate of F and $(DF^M)_{X_0}$ is the Jacobian matrix of F evaluated at X_0. By application of the chain rule for differentiation, it is possible to show that

$$
\|X_M - X_M'\| \cong \|T_M(X_0 - X_0')\|
$$

where $T_M = J_M J_{M-1} \ldots J_1$ and $J_1 = (DF)_{X_t}$. Letting $v_1(M)$ denote the largest eigenvalue of $T_M^T T_M$, the formal definition of the dominant Lyapunov exponent, λ, is

$$
\lambda = \lim_{M \to \infty} \frac{1}{2M} \ln |v_1(M)|.
$$

In this setting, λ gives the long-term rate of divergence or convergence between trajectories. A positive λ measures exponential divergence of two nearby trajectories [and is often used as a definition of chaos; see, for example, Deneckere and Pelikan (1986)], whereas a negative λ measures exponential convergence of two nearby trajectories.

In what follows we use the Nychka et al. (1992) Jacobian-based method and the LENNS program (see Ellner, Nychka, and Gallant 1992) to estimate the dominant Lyapunov exponent. In particular we use a neural network (or equivalently neural net) model to estimate f by nonlinear least squares and used the estimated map $\hat{f}$ and the data $\{x_t\}$ to produce an estimate of the dominant Lyapunov exponent. In doing so, we follow the protocol described by Nychka et al. (1992).

The predominant model in statistical research on neural nets is the single (hidden) layer feedforward network with a single output. In the present context it can be written as

$$\hat{f}(X_t, \theta) = \alpha \sum_{j=1}^{k} \beta_j \psi(\omega_j + \gamma_j^T X_t),$$

where $X \in R^m$ is the input, ψ is known (hidden) univariate nonlinear 'activation function' [usually the logistic distribution function $\psi(u) = 1/(1 + \exp(-u))$; see, for example, Nychka et $al.$ (1992) and Gencay and Dechert (1992)], $\theta = (\alpha, \beta, \omega, \gamma)$ is the parameter vector, and $\gamma_j = (\gamma_{1j}, \gamma_{2j}, \ldots, \gamma_{mj})^T$. $\beta \in R^k$ represents hidden unit weights, and $\omega \in R^k$, $\gamma \in R^{k \times m}$ represent input weights to the hidden units. k is the number of units in the hidden layer of the neural net. Notice that there are $[k(m + 2) + 1]$ free parameters in this model.

Given a data set of inputs and their associated outputs, the network parameter vector, θ, is fit by nonlinear least squares to formulate accurate map estimates. Because appropriate values of L, m, and k are unknown, LENNS selects the value of the triple (L, m, k) that minimizes the Bayesian information criterion (BIC); see Schwartz (1978). Gallant and White (1992) showed that we can then use $\hat{J}_t$, the estimate of the Jacobian matrix J_t obtained from the approximate map $\hat{f}$, as a nonparametric estimator of J_t. The estimate of the dominant Lyapunov exponent then is

$$\hat{\lambda} = \frac{1}{2N} \ln |\hat{v}_1(N)|,$$

where $\hat{v}_1(N)$ is the largest eigenvalue of $T_N^T T_N$ and where $\hat{T}_N = \hat{J}_N \hat{J}_{N-1} \ldots \hat{J}_1$.

6.2.2 Empirical Results

Before conducting nonlinear analysis, the data must be rendered stationary, delinearized (by replacing the stationary data with residuals from an autoregression of the data), and transformed (if necessary) as described by Hsieh (1991). Because a stochastic trend has been confirmed for each of the series, the data are rendered stationary by taking first differences of logarithms. Moreover, because I am interested in nonlinear dependence, I remove any linear dependence in the stationary data by fitting the best possible linear model. In particular, I prefilter the logarithmic differences by the following autoregression:

$$\Delta \log z_t = b_0 + \sum_{j=1}^{q} b_j \Delta \log z_{t-j} + \varepsilon_t, \quad \varepsilon_t \mid I_{t-1} \sim N(0, w_0),$$

using for each series the number of lags, q, for which the Ljung-Box (1978) $Q(12)$ statistic is not significant at the 5% level.

Finally, because I am interested in deterministic nonlinear dependence, I remove any stochastic nonlinear dependence by fitting a (generalized autoregressive conditional heteroscedasticity) GARCH (1,1) model with the same AR structure as the one determined previously, using the $Q(12)$ statistic. In particular, I estimate the following GARCH (1,1) model:

$$\Delta \log z_t = b_0 + \sum_{j=1}^{q} b_j \Delta \log z_{t-j} + \varepsilon \quad \varepsilon_t \mid I_{t-1} \sim N(0, h_t)$$

$$h_t = w_0 + \alpha_1 \varepsilon_{t-1}^2 + \beta_1 h_{t-1},$$

where $N(0, h_t)$ represents the normal distribution with mean 0 and variance, h_t. Lyapunov exponent estimates are next calculated for the standardized GARCH (1,1) residuals, $\varepsilon_t / \hat{h}_t^{1/2}$, where ε_t is the residual of the mean equation and $\hat{h}_t$ its estimated (time-varying) variance.

Using the Nychka *et al.* (1992) Lyapunov exponent test, the BIC point estimates of the dominant Lyapunov exponent for each velocity series and for each parameter triple (L, m, κ) are displayed in Table 6.2 along with the respective optimized values of the BIC. Clearly, all but the Lyapunov exponent point estimate for Divisia L velocity are negative. Because the standard errors of the estimated dominant Lyapunov exponents are not known, however [there has not yet been any published research on the computation of a standard error for the Nychka *et al.* (1992) Lyapunov-exponent estimate], it is difficult to tell whether the positive Lyapunov exponent is statistically larger than 0. It is possible, however, to produce sensitivity plots that are informative about precision. For example, Figure 6.1 indicates the dominant Lyapunov-exponent estimate for Divisia L velocity to variations in the parameters by plotting the estimated dominant Lyapunov exponent for each setting of (L, m, κ), where $L = 1, 2, 3$, $m = 1, \ldots, 10$, and $\kappa = 1, 2, 3$.

6.3   Conclusion

This chapter tests for unit roots in the univariate time series representation of 10 U.S. simple-sum and Divisia velocity series, using monthly data from 1960:1 to 1992:12. The results show that the random-walk hypothesis cannot be rejected even if allowance is made for the possibility of a one-time break in the intercept and the slope of the trend function at an unknown point in time. This is consistent with the Nelson and Plosser (1982) argument that most macroeconomic time series have a stochastic trend, meaning that movements in these variables result from the accumulation of shocks, each of which has large permanent effects.

I have also contrasted the random-walk behavior of velocity to chaotic dynamics by providing results of nonlinear dynamical analysis of the velocity series using the Nychka *et al.* (1992) test for positivity of the dominant Lyapunov exponent. Before conducting such a nonlinear analysis, the data were rendered stationary (by first-differencing) and then GARCH filtered to remove any linear, as well as nonlinear, stochastic dependence. I have found tentative evidence for a positive Lyapunov exponent for Divisia L velocity. Clearly then, an important area for potentially productive future research is to check whether the inference is robust to alternative methods of testing for chaos [on this issue, see Barnett *et al.* (1994a,b)] and to identify more precisely the nature of nonlinearity in the data.

TABLE 6.2

THE BIC SELECTION OF THE PARAMETER TRIPLE (L, m, k),
THE VALUE OF THE MINIMIZED BIC, AND THE DOMINANT
LYAPUNOV EXPONENT POINT ESTIMATE

Velocity series	(L, m, k) triple that minimizes the BIC	Value of the minimized BIC	Dominant Lyapunov exponent point estimate
Sum M1A	(3,3,2)	1.4449	−0.247
Sum M1	(2,5,1)	1.4470	−0.396
Sum M2	(1,1,1)	1.4468	−4.329
Sum M3	(3,4,2)	1.4443	−0.129
Sum L	(1,4,2)	1.4405	−0.547
Divisia M1A	(3,3,2)	1.4344	−0.245
Divisia M1	(2,1,1)	1.4480	−4.427
Divisia M2	(1,1,1)	1.4483	−6.091
Divisia M3	(1,1,1)	1.4476	−4.840
Divisia L	(3,6,2)	1.4456	0.100

NOTE: Numbers in parentheses represent the BIC selection of the parameter triple, (L, m, k), where L is the time delay parameter, m is the number of lags in the autoregression, and k is the number of units in the hidden layer of the neural net.

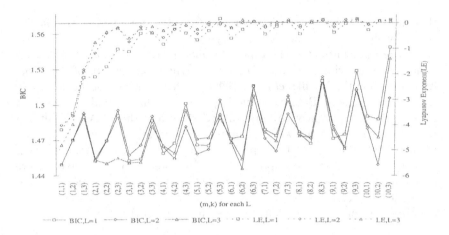

Figure 6.1: Estimated Largest Lyapunov Exponent for Each Triple (L, m, k) for the Divisia L Velocity.

Chapter 7

Chaotic Analysis of U.S. Money and Velocity Measures

*Apostolos Serletis and Ioannis Andreadis**

7.1 Introduction

Recently, attention has been focused on the gains that can be achieved by a rigorous use of microeconomic- and aggregation-theoretic foundations in the construction of monetary aggregates. This new approach to monetary aggregation was advocated by Barnett (1980) and has led to the construction of monetary aggregates based on Diewert's (1976) class of superlative quantity index numbers — the most recent example is Anderson, Jones, and Nesmith (1997a,b). The new aggregates are Barnett's monetary services indices (also known as Divisia aggregates), and Rotemberg's (1991) — see also Rotemberg, Driscoll, and Poterba (1995) — currency equivalent (CE) indices. These aggregates represent a viable and theoretically appropriate alternative to the simple-sum aggregates still in use both by central banks and researchers in the field.

Barnett and Chen (1988), claimed successful detection of chaos in the (demand-side) United States (U.S.) Divisia monetary aggregates. Their conclusion was further confirmed by DeCoster and Mitchell (1991, 1994).

*Originally published in the *International Journal of Systems Science* (http:/www.tandf.co.uk) 31 (2000), 161–169. Reprinted with permission.

This published claim of successful detection of chaos has generated considerable controversy, as in Ramsey, Sayers, and Rothman (1988) and Ramsey and Rothman (1994), who by re-examining the data utilized in Barnett and Chen (1988) show that there is no evidence for the presence of chaos. In fact, they raised similar questions regarding virtually all of the other published tests of chaos. Further results relevant to this controversy have recently been provided by Serletis (1995) who reports evidence of chaos only in the Divisia L velocity series.

Our objective in this chapter is to use nonlinear chaotic systems analysis to re-examine the properties of U.S. simple-sum, Divisia, and (for the first time) CE money and velocity series, using the new Anderson, Jones, and Nesmith (1997a,b) data. If chaos can be shown to exist, the implication would be that (nonlinearity-based) prediction is possible (at least in the short run and provided the actual generating mechanism is known exactly). Prediction of monetary variables, of course, is valuable to monetary policy, insofar as it is short-run policy. Of course, prediction over long periods is all but impossible, due to the sensitive dependence on initial conditions property of chaos.

The organization of the chapter is as follows. The next section briefly discusses the problem of the definition (aggregation) of money. In section 3, we investigate the chaotic properties of the money and velocity series, using the Nychka et al. (1992) dominant Lyapunov exponent estimator. The final section concludes.

7.2   The Many Kinds of Money

The monetary aggregates currently in use by the Federal Reserve are simple-sum indices in which all monetary components are assigned a constant and equal (unitary) weight. This index is M_t in

$$M_t = \sum_{j=1}^{n} x_{jt} \tag{7.1}$$

where x_{jt} is one of the n monetary components of the monetary aggregate M_t. This summation index implies that all monetary components contribute equally to the money total and it views all components as dollar for dollar perfect substitutes. Such an index, there is no question, represents an index of the stock of nominal monetary wealth, but cannot, in general, represent a valid structural economic variable for the services of the quantity of money.

Over the years, there has been a steady stream of attempts at properly weighting monetary components within a simple-sum aggregate. With no theory, however, any weighting scheme is questionable. It is Barnett (1980) that derived the theoretical linkage between monetary theory and aggregation and index number theory. He applied economic aggregation and index number theory and constructed monetary aggregates based upon Diewert's (1976) class of superlative quantity index numbers. The new aggregates are Divisia quantity indices which are elements of the superlative class. The Divisia index (in discrete time) is defined as

$$\log M_t^D - \log M_{t-1}^D = \sum_{j=1}^{n} s_{jt}^* (\log x_{jt} - \log x_{j,t-1}) \qquad (7.2)$$

According to equation (7.2) the growth rate of the aggregate is the weighted average of the growth rates of the component quantities, with the Divisia weights being defined as the expenditure shares averaged over the two periods of the change, $s_{jt}^* = (1/2)(s_{jt} + s_{j,t-1})$ for $j = 1, ..., n$, where $s_{jt} = \pi_{jt} x_{jt} / \sum \pi_{kt} x_{kt}$ is the expenditure share of asset j during period t, and π_{jt} is the user cost of asset j, derived in Barnett (1978),

$$\pi_{jt} = \frac{(R_t - r_{jt})}{(1 + R_t)} \qquad (7.3)$$

which is just the opportunity cost of holding a dollar's worth of the jth asset. In equation (7.3), r_{jt} is the market yield on the jth asset, and R_t is the yield available on a 'benchmark' asset that is held only to carry wealth between multiperiods — see Barnett, Fisher, and Serletis (1992) for more details regarding the Divisia approach to monetary aggregation.

More recently, Rotemberg (1991) and Rotemberg, Driscoll, and Poterba (1995) proposed the currency equivalent (CE) index

$$CE = \sum_{j=1}^{n} \frac{R_t - r_{jt}}{R_t} x_{jt}. \qquad (7.4)$$

In (7.4), as long as currency gives no interest, units of currency are added together with a weight of one. Other assets are added to currency but with a weight that declines toward zero as their return increases toward R_t.

The difference between Divisia and CE methods of monetary aggregation is that the former measures the flow of monetary services whereas the latter, like simple summation aggregation, measures the stock of monetary assets. The CE aggregates, however, represent a major advance over the official simple-sum aggregates — see Rotemberg (1991) and Barnett (1991) for more details regarding Divisia and CE money measures.

In this chapter, we use the official simple-sum aggregates, Barnett's (1980) Divisia aggregates (also known as 'monetary services indices'), and Rotemberg's (1991) currency equivalent indices. The data (over the period from 1960:1 to 1996:6) were obtained from the St. Louis MSI database, maintained by the Federal Reserve Bank of St. Louis as a part of the Bank's Federal Reserve Economic Database (FRED) — see Anderson, Jones, and Nesmith (1997a, b) for details regarding the construction of the Divisia and currency equivalent aggregates and related data issues.

To see the behavior of the money and velocity measures, consider Figures 7.1-4 and Figures 7.5-8, respectively, which provide graphical representations of sum, Divisia, and CE series at four levels of monetary aggregation — M1, M2, M3, and L.[1] Notice that the fluctuations of the money and velocity series in Figures 7.1-8 are different at different levels of aggregation and also across aggregation methods, reflecting the essentially complicated monetary aggregation issues — something to be kept in mind in interpreting the results later on.

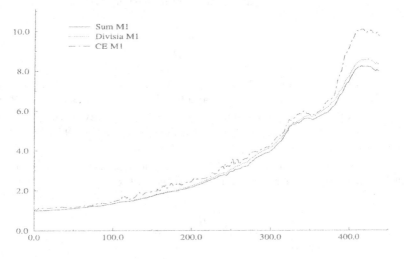

Figure 7.1: Sum M1, Divisia M1 and CE M1 monetary aggregates.

---

[1]In calculating velocity, we followed a procedure for generating monthly GNP data developed by Christiano (1986) and also used by Serletis (1995). This involves the construction of a synthetic monthly GNP series by multiplying the industrial production index by the consumer price index.

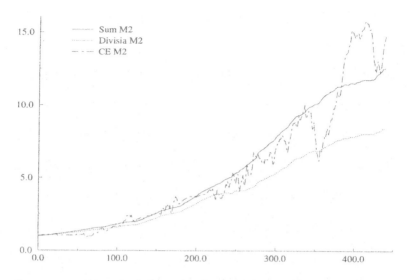

Figure 7.2: Sum M2, Divisia M2 and CE M2 monetary aggregates.

7.3 Chaos Tests

Sensitive dependence on initial conditions is the most relevant property of
chaos to economics and finance and its characterization in terms of Lyapunov exponents is the most satisfactory from a computable (i.e. possible
to estimate) perspective. Lyapunov exponents measure average exponential
divergence or convergence between trajectories that differ only in having an
'infinitesimally small' difference in their initial conditions and remain well-
defined for noisy systems. A bounded system with a positive Lyapunov
exponent is one operational definition of chaotic behavior.

One early method for calculating the dominant Lyapunov exponent is
the one proposed by Wolf *et al.* (1985). This method, however, requires
long data series and is sensitive to dynamic noise, so inflated estimates
of the dominant Lyapunov exponent are obtained. Recently, Nychka *et
al.* (1992) have proposed a new method, involving the use of neural network models, to test for positivity of the dominant Lyapunov exponent.
The Nychka *et al.* (1992) Lyapunov exponent estimator is a regression (or
Jacobian) method, unlike the Wolf *et al.* (1985) direct method which [as
Brock and Sayers (1988) have found] requires long data series and is sensitive to dynamic noise.[2] In what follows, we discuss the key features of the

---

[2] Another very promising approach to the estimation of Lyapunov exponents [that is
similar in some respects to the Nychka *et al.* (1992) approach] has also been recently

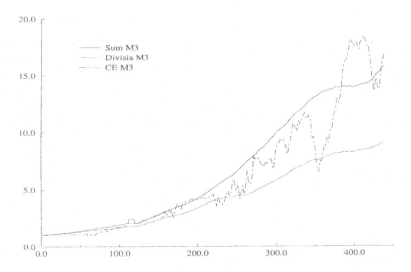

Figure 7.3: Sum M3, Divisia M3 and CE M3 monetary aggregates.

Nychka *et al.* (1992) dominant Lyapunov exponent estimator and present the results of the chaos tests.

Assume that the data $\{x_t\}$ are real-valued and are generated by a non-linear autoregressive model of the form

$$x_t = f(x_{t-L}, x_{t-2L}, ..., x_{t-mL}) + e_t \qquad (7.5)$$

for $1 \leq t \leq N$, where L is the time-delay parameter and m is the length of the autoregression. Here f is a smooth unknown function, and $\{e_t\}$ is a sequence of independent random variables with zero mean and unknown constant variance. The Nychka *et al.* (1992) approach to estimation of the maximum Lyapunov exponent involves producing a state-space representation of (7.5)

$$X_t = F(X_{t-L}) + E_t, \quad F : \mathbb{R}^m \to \mathbb{R}^m$$

where $X_t = (x_t, x_{t-L}, ..., x_{t-mL+L})'$, $F(X_{t-L}) = (f(x_{t-L}, ..., x_{t-mL}), x_{t-L}, ..., x_{t-mL+L})'$, and $E_t = (e_t, 0, ..., 0)'$, and using a Jacobian-based method to

---

proposed by Gencay and Dechert (1992). This involves estimating all Lyapunov exponents of an unknown dynamical system. The estimation is carried out, as in Nychka *et al.* (1992), by a multivariate feedforward network estimation technique — see Gencay and Dechert (1992) for more details.

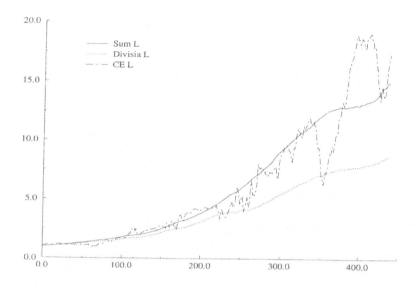

Figure 7.4: Sum L, Divisia L and CE L monetary aggregates.

estimate λ through the intermediate step of estimating the individual Jacobian matrices

$$J_t = \frac{\partial F(X_t)}{\partial X'}.$$

After using several nonparametric methods, McCaffrey *et al.* (1992) recommend using either thin plate splines or neural nets to estimate J_t. Estimation based on neural nets involves the use of the a neural net with q units in the hidden layer

$$f(X_{t-L}, \theta) = \beta_0 + \sum_{j=1}^{q} \beta_j \psi\left(\gamma_{0j} + \sum_{i=1}^{m} \gamma_{ij} x_{t-iL}\right)$$

where ψ is a known (hidden) nonlinear 'activation function' [usually the logistic distribution function $\psi(u) = 1/(1 + \exp(-u))$]. The parameter vector θ is then fit to the data by nonlinear least squares. That is, one computes the estimate $\widehat{\theta}$ to minimize the sum of squares $S(\theta) = \sum_{t=1}^{N} [x_t - f(X_{t-1}, \theta)]^2$, and uses $\widehat{F}(X_t) = (f(x_{t-L}, ..., x_{t-mL}, \widehat{\theta}), x_{t-L}, ..., x_{t-mL+L})'$ to approximate $F(X_t)$.

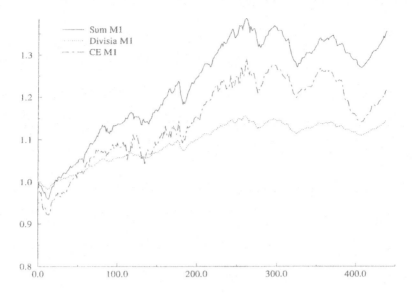

Figure 7.5: Sum M1, Divisia M1 and CE M1 velocity series.

As appropriate values of L, m, and q, are unknown, Nychka et al. (1992) recommend selecting that value of the triple (L, m, q) that minimizes the Bayesian Information Criterion (BIC) — see Schwartz (1978). As shown by Gallant and White (1992), we can use $\widehat{J}_t = \partial \widehat{F}(X_t)/\partial X'$ as a nonparametric estimator of J_t when (L, m, q) are selected to minimize BIC. The estimate of the dominant Lyapunov exponent then is

$$\widehat{\lambda} = \frac{1}{2N} \log |\widehat{v}_1(N)|$$

where $\widehat{v}_1(N)$ is the largest eigenvalue of the matrix $\widehat{T}'_N \widehat{T}_N$ and where $\widehat{T}_N = \widehat{J}_N \widehat{J}_{N-1}, ..., \widehat{J}_1$.

Before conducting nonlinear analysis the data must be rendered stationary, delinearized (by replacing the stationary data with residuals from an autoregression of the data) and transformed (if necessary).[3] Also, since we

---

[3]Results, not reported here but available upon request, indicate that the sum and Divisia monetary aggregates are integrated of order 2 [or I(2) in the terminology of Engle and Granger (1987)] and are therefore rendered stationary by taking logarithmic second differences. The CE monetary aggregates are I(1) and are rendered stationary by taking first logged differences. All the velocity series, except for CE M3 and CE L are stationary.

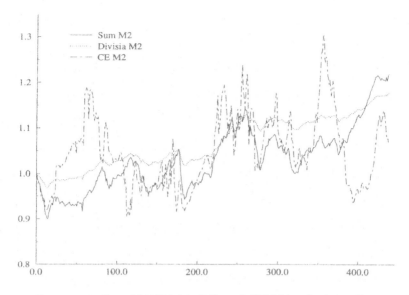

Figure 7.6: Sum M2, Divisia M2 and CE M2 velocity series.

are interested in nonlinear dependence, we remove any linear dependence in the stationary data by fitting the best possible linear model. In particular, we prefilter the stationary series by the following autoregression

$$z_t = b_0 + \sum_{j=1}^{q} b_j z_{t-j} + \varepsilon_t, \quad \varepsilon_t | I_{t-1} \sim N(0, w_0)$$

using for each series the number of lags, q, for which the Ljung-Box (1978) $Q(36)$ statistic is not significant at the 5% level.

Finally, since we are interested in deterministic nonlinear dependence, we remove any stochastic nonlinear dependence by fitting a GARCH (1,1) model with the same AR structure as the one determined above, using the $Q(36)$ statistic. In particular, we estimate the following GARCH (1,1) model

$$z_t = b_0 + \sum_{j=1}^{q} b_j z_{t-j} + \varepsilon_t, \quad \varepsilon_t | I_{t-1} \sim N(0, \sigma_t^2)$$
$$\sigma_t^2 = w_0 + \alpha_1 \varepsilon_{t-1}^2 + \beta_1 \sigma_{t-1}^2$$

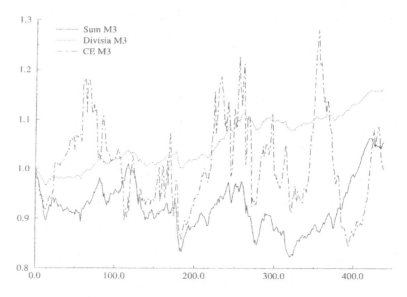

Figure 7.7: Sum M3, Divisia M3 and CE M3 velocity series.

where $N(0, \sigma_t^2)$ represents the normal distribution with mean zero and variance σ_t^2. Lyapunov exponent estimates are next calculated for the standardized GARCH (1,1) residuals, $\widehat{\varepsilon}_t/\widehat{\sigma}_t$.

Using the Nychka *et al.* (1992) Lyapunov exponent test, the Bayesian Information Criterion (BIC) point estimates of the dominant Lyapunov exponent for each parameter triple (L, m, k), are displayed in Table 7.1 for the money series and in Table 7.2 for the velocity series, along with the respective optimized values of the BIC criterion. Clearly, all but the Lyapunov exponent point estimate for CE M3 and CE L money and CE M2 and CE M3 velocity are negative. Of course, since the standard errors of the estimated dominant Lyapunov exponents are not known [there has not yet been any published research on the computation of a standard error for the Nychka et al. (1992) Lyapunov exponent estimate], it is difficult to tell whether the positive Lyapunov exponents are statistically larger than zero.

7.4   Conclusion

We have looked at data consisting of the traditional simple-sum monetary aggregates, as published by the Federal Reserve Board, and Divisia and

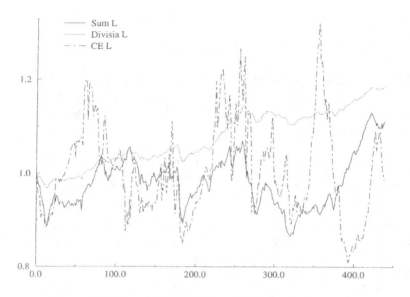

Figure 7.8: Sum L, Divisia L and CE L velocity series.

currency equivalent monetary aggregates, recently produced by the Federal Reserve Bank of St. Louis, to investigate the properties of money and velocity measures and to address disputes about their chaoticity. We have found tentative evidence for a positive Lyapunov exponent in the CE M2 and CE M3 monetary aggregates and in the CE M3 and CE L velocity series, but we haven't been able to confirm the results of Barnett and Chen (1988) and Serletis (1995).

In a sense, our results support the explanation provided in Barnett *et al.* (1995, p. 301) " ... that the inferences vary across tests for the same data, and within tests for varying sample sizes and various methods of aggregation of the data. Robustness of inferences in this area of research seems to be low and may account for the controversies surrounding empirical claims of nonlinearity and chaos in economics." See also Barnett *et al.* (1997) regarding similar conclusions.

TABLE 7.1

THE BIC SELECTION OF THE PARAMETER TRIPLE (L, m, k), THE
VALUE OF THE MINIMIZED BIC, AND THE DOMINANT LYAPUNOV
EXPONENT POINT ESTIMATE FOR GARCH $(1, 1)$ STANDARDIZED
RESIDUALS FOR MONEY MEASURES.

Series	(L, m, k) triple that minimizes the BIC	Value of the minimized BIC	Dominant Lyapunov exponent point estimate
Sum M1	$(3, 1, 1)$	1.437	-4.017
Divisia M1	$(1, 1, 1)$	1.437	-4.128
CE M1	$(2, 3, 2)$	1.435	-0.383
Sum M2	$(2, 6, 1)$	1.401	-0.304
Divisia M2	$(1, 2, 1)$	1.436	-2.267
CE M2	$(1, 8, 2)$	1.351	0.015
Sum M3	$(3, 2, 1)$	1.438	-0.706
Divisia M3	$(3, 1, 1)$	1.447	-3.922
CE M3	$(2, 7, 2)$	1.383	0.052
Sum L	$(3, 1, 1)$	1.447	-4.424
Divisia L	$(2, 1, 1)$	1.446	-4.911
CE L	$(1, 7, 2)$	1.393	-0.189

Note: The numbers in parentheses represent the BIC selection of the
parameter triple (L, m, k), where L is the time delay parameter,
m is the number of lags in the autoregression and k is the number
of units in the hidden layer of the neural net.

TABLE 7.2

THE BIC SELECTION OF THE PARAMETER TRIPLE (L, m, k), THE
VALUE OF THE MINIMIZED BIC, AND THE DOMINANT LYAPUNOV
EXPONENT POINT ESTIMATE FOR GARCH $(1, 1)$ STANDARDIZED
RESIDUALS FOR VELOCITY MEASURES.

Series	(L, m, k)triple that minimizes the BIC	Value of the minimized BIC	Dominant Lyapunov exponent point estimate
Sum M1	$(2, 1, 1)$	1.446	-4.498
Divisia M1	$(2, 1, 1)$	1.445	-4.541
CE M1	$(2, 1, 1)$	1.440	-4.036
Sum M2	$(1, 1, 1)$	1.445	-4.230
Divisia M2	$(3, 1, 1)$	1.445	-4.355
CE M2	$(3, 8, 2)$	1.385	-0.003
Sum M3	$(2, 1, 1)$	1.444	-4.223
Divisia M3	$(3, 1, 1)$	1.442	-5.246
CE M3	$(2.9.2)$	1.357	0.041
Sum L	$(3, 1, 1)$	1.445	-4.365
Divisia L	$(1, 1, 1)$	1.446	-4.651
CE L	$(1, 10, 2)$	1.386	0.068

Note: The numbers in parentheses represent the BIC selection of the
parameter triple (L, m, k), where L is the time delay parameter, m
is the number of lags in the autoregression and k is the number of
units in the hidden layer of the neural net.

Part 5

Monetary Asset Demand Systems

Overview of Part 5

Apostolos Serletis

The following table contains a brief summary of the contents of each chapter in Part 5 of the book. This part of the book is concerned with locally flexible functional forms and monetary asset demand systems used to estimate the substitutability/complementarity relationship among liquid assets. These forms provide the capability to approximate systems resulting from a broad class of generating functions and also to attain arbitrary elasticities of substitution among monetary assets (although only at a point). They have, however, very small regions of theoretical regularity.

Monetary Asset Demand Systems

Chapter Number	Chapter Title	Contents
8	Divisia Aggregation and Substitutability Among Monetary Assets	Compares the use of simple-sum and Divisia monetary aggregates as data in empirical demand systems.
9	The Demand for Divisia M1, M2, and M3 in the United States	Estimates the degree of substitution between Divisia money and the 'nested like assets' at different aggregation levels.
10	Translog Flexible Functional Forms and Substitutability of Monetary Assets	Estimates a sequence of four nested locally flexible demand systems.

Chapter 8:

This chapter estimates the degree of substitution between Canadian monetary assets and compares the use of Divisia and simple-sum monetary aggregates as data in empirical demand systems. The analysis in this chapter (as well as in Chapters 9 and 10) is conducted within a microtheoretical framework and makes use of the Strotz-Gorman multistage optimization framework. The most interesting finding is the low degree of substitution among the monetary assets and the evidence against simple-sum monetary aggregation procedures.

Chapter 9:

This chapter analyzes the demand for broad U.S. money measures and estimates the degree of substitution between Divisia money, defined from narrow to broad, and the 'nested like assets' at different levels of aggregation. A pleasing feature of our approach is the systematic testing for the appropriateness of the weak separability (aggregation) conditions at the various levels of aggregation.

Chapter 10:

This chapter attempts to establish the nature of the relationship between monetary assets by estimating a sequence of four nested (locally flexible) demand systems: the *generalized translog*, the *basic translog*, the *linear translog*, and the *homothetic translog*. The principal attraction of the empirical work is that we are able to test separately for both homothetic and quasi-homothetic preferences over monetary assets. The tests reject both homotheticity and quasi-homotheticity and thus consistency of the Strotz-Gorman two-stage optimization.

Chapter 8

Divisia Aggregation and Substitutability Among Monetary Assets

*Apostolos Serletis and A. Leslie Robb**

8.1 Introduction

We have two objectives in this chapter: (1) to estimate the degree of substitution between Canadian monetary assets; and (2) to compare the use of Divisia and simple-sum monetary aggregates as data in empirical demand systems.

The issue of monetary asset substitutability has attracted a great deal of attention and has been explored extensively in the literature during the past two decades. However, despite the volume of research undertaken, the results are still inconclusive, and suggestive of a need for further empirical exploration. As Feige and Pearce (1977, p. 465) put it, "... the issue of substitutability between money and near-monies is likely to continue to be an important question for monetary economics just as it has been since the days of the currency-banking school controversy."

Knowledge of the substitutability between monetary assets is essential in order to understand the potential effects of monetary policy actions. In particular, the appropriate definition of money, the stability of a narrowly

*Originally published in the *Journal of Money, Credit, and Banking* 18 (1986), 430-446. Reprinted with permission.

defined demand for money function, and the effect of the growth of financial intermediation are closely linked with the degree of substitutability that exists between monetary assets.

The issue of monetary asset aggregation has attracted a great deal of attention recently in the literature. Barnett (1980), in a challenging paper, voiced objections to the use of simple-sum aggregation procedures and drew on the literature on aggregation and statistical index number theory to construct alternative indices. As he and co-authors argued in a later paper,[1] "... if one wished to obtain an aggregate of transportation vehicles, one would never aggregate by simple summation over the physical units, of say, subway trains and roller skates. Instead, one could construct a quantity index using weights based upon the *values* of the different modes of transportation."

Simple-sum aggregation (the usual procedure) is justified, when viewed in this framework, only if the component assets are perfect substitutes (implying linear indifference surfaces) one for one. If this condition of perfect substitutability is violated, it is inappropriate to form a quantity index by giving an equal weight to each asset component. The fact that monetary assets are not perfect substitutes has long been recognized and there has been a steady stream of attempts at relaxing the perfect substitutability assumption. However, only Barnett (1980) has applied methods entirely consistent with aggregation and index number theory in constructing monetary aggregates. He has shown that the aggregation problem can be solved if aggregation is performed using any index from Diewert's (1976) superlative class. In particular, he has advocated use of the Divisia index.

Motivated by these considerations, and in order to investigate consumer monetary expenditure decisions in a utility-maximizing framework, we develop a demand system that is capable of generating some new results and is also theoretically more satisfactory than the monetary asset demand systems now in use.

The approach adopted makes use of the Strotz-Gorman two-stage optimization framework. This approach can be rationalized by certain assumptions regarding consumers' preferences. We make these assumptions and their analytical consequences explicit in the present chapter, in the belief that this will help to make clear the restrictive nature of these approaches which do not build upon a choice theoretic model.

A pleasing feature of our approach is that we are able to replace the assumption of homotheticity with the more general one of quasi-homotheticity, i.e., homotheticity with respect to a point which is not necessarily the origin. The specification of quasi-homothetic preferences makes the Engel

---

[1] Barnett, Offenbacher and Spindt (1984, p. 1051).

curves (income-consumption paths for fixed prices) linear, but does not require them to pass through the origin; in contrast, ordinary homotheticity
requires the Engel curves to pass through the origin.

Another important feature of our approach is the use of a flexible second-
order approximation to an arbitrary indirect utility function. We use the
translog functional form as proposed originally by Christensen, Jorgenson,
and Lau (1975). This form is relatively attractive in that it does not restrict
the values of the elasticities of substitution and does not impose undesirable
a priori restrictions.

In section 8.2, a general theoretical model is presented, the conditions
which allow two-level optimization are discussed, and the trade-off in choosing between homothetic and quasi-homothetic forms of utility functions is
indicated. In section 8.3, a flexible functional form for the monetary services indirect utility function is specified and the budget share system to
be used in the subsequent analysis is determined. Section 8.4 spells out the
stochastic specification of the equations to be estimated and the method
of estimation. Section 8.5 presents the formulas required for calculating
the expenditure, price and elasticities of substitution. The basic data and
adjustment to the data are described in section 8.6. Section 8.7 presents
and interprets the empirical results, and section 8.8 provides a summary
and statement of conclusions.

8.2   Theoretical Foundations

Consider an economy with identical individuals, having three types of
goods: consumption goods, leisure, and the services of monetary assets. It
is assumed that the services of consumption goods, as well as the services
of monetary assets and leisure, enter as arguments in the representative
individual's utility function:

$$u = u(c, l, m) \tag{8.1}$$

where c = a vector of the services of consumption goods,
       l = leisure time, and
       m = a vector of the services of monetary assets
             (assumed to be proportional to the stocks).

In order to focus on the details of demand for services of monetary
assets, ignoring other types of goods, a good starting point is a model consistent with the theory of two-stage optimization. The notion of two-stage
optimization was investigated in the context of consumer theory by Strotz
(1957, 1959) and Gorman (1959). It refers to a sequential expenditure allocation, where in the first stage the consumer allocates his expenditure

among broad categories (consumption goods, leisure, and monetary services in our context), and then in the second stage he allocates expenditure within each category. The particular two-level structure we would wish to utilize can be expressed by the following classical consumer problem:

$$\max_{m} f(m) \quad \text{subject to } p'm = y \tag{8.2}$$

in which $f(m)$, the monetary services aggregator function (quantity index), is continuous and twice differentiable. In addition, $f(m)$ satisfies a number of economically motivated conditions which will be mentioned later. The expenditure on the services of monetary assets is denoted by y, and p is a vector (with the prime indicating a row vector) of monetary asset user costs (or rental prices), with the ith component given by[2]

$$p_i = (R - r_i)/(1 + R) \tag{8.3}$$

where R = the highest rate of interest (benchmark rate), and
       r_i = own rate of return on the ith component.

The solution to (8.2) is a set of Marshallian demand functions which express the demands for monetary assets as functions of user costs and expenditure.

Decomposition of the consumer choice problem along these lines is possible if, and only if, the representative individual's utility function (8.1) is weakly separable (implying a utility tree) in the monetary assets group.[3] That is, it must be possible to write the utility function as

$$u = \hat{u}(c, l, f(m)). \tag{8.4}$$

This separability condition, which implies that asset demands are independent of relative prices outside the monetary group, is treated as a maintained (untested) hypothesis in this chapter. Such treatment, although not entirely satisfactory, appears necessary for the type of empirical demand analysis with which we are concerned.

Weak separability rationalizes the estimation of a monetary asset's demand system. However, the utility tree structure specified by (8.4) rests also on the assumption that the consumer is able to make a rational first-stage allocation of his full income[4] among consumption goods, leisure, and

---

[2] The user cost of a monetary asset is the price of the quantity of services provided by a unit of its stock during a finite holding period. The user cost formula was first derived by Donovan (1978) through general economic reasoning and later by Barnett (1978) through an intertemporal consumption allocation model.

[3] The utility function $u(.)$ is said to be weakly separable in the assets i and j from consumption goods, c, and leisure l, if: $\partial \left[(\partial u/\partial m_i) / (\partial u/\partial m_j) \right] / \partial x = 0$, $x = c, l$.

[4] Full income is the amount of income that would be available if all leisure were given up for work.

monetary assets. There must be a set of consistent group price indices (which depend only upon prices within the group) for this to be possible. Gorman (1959) took up this problem and showed that only a very restricted class of utility functions allow this kind of price aggregation. He has shown that, given a weakly separable utility function with more than two categories, price aggregation is possible if, and only if, the utility function is structured either as homothetically separable or as strongly separable with generalized Gorman polar forms, or is a mixture of the two structures, such as

$$u(x) = \sum_{s=1s}^{d} u_s(x^s) + F\left[u_{d+1}(x^{d+1}), \ldots, u_R(x^R)\right] \qquad (8.5)$$

where each $u_r(x^r)$ is homothetic in x^r for $r > d$ and each $u_s(x^s)$, $s = 1, \ldots, d$ can be written indirectly as

$$V_s(p^s, y_s) = G_s[y_s/h_s(p^s)] + H_s(p^s) \qquad (8.6)$$

where G_s is a strictly increasing function of a single variable, $h_s(p^s)$ is a linear homogeneous function of p^s, and $H_s(p^s)$ is homogeneous of degree zero (see Anderson 1979 or Gorman 1959). The indirect utility function (8.6) is known as "generalized Gorman polar form."

It is apparent that a demand system over monetary assets will meet the conditions for price aggregation if the monetary assets are placed in either a homothetic or a generalized Gorman polar form subfunction. Homotheticity, however, has very strong implications for demand behavior, since it imposes unitary expenditure elasticities. As a consequence, the assumption of a homothetic structure over monetary assets does not seem very attractive for purposes of empirical analysis. The generalized Gorman polar form is a good deal more flexible than the homothetic structure, because it allows for more complicated interdependencies among monetary assets and is restrictive only in the "monetary assets" versus "other types of goods" allocation (see Anderson 1979).

We choose a specification for the monetary services utility function on the basis of a compromise between the conflicting criteria of a homothetic structure, which is not empirically interesting but simplified the estimation considerably, and a generalized Gorman polar form, which is empirically more interesting but makes the estimated demand system deeply nonlinear. We assigned the monetary services a Gorman polar form — the best known subclass of the generalized Gorman polar form — for which G_s is the identity function. Preferences represented by a Gorman polar form are said to be quasi-homothetic, i.e., homothetic to a point other than the origin.[5]

---

[5]Quasi-homotheticity is exploited extensively by Gorman (1961). (A well-known ex-

All that remains in order to obtain an expenditure system for empirical work is to choose a specific functional form for the indirect utility function. We have chosen to approximate this function by the translog flexible form.[6]

8.3   Demand System Specification

The demand system used for estimation is the quasi-homothetic version of the translog, known as the linear translog (LTL).[7] This system is derived by assuming that the asset services indirect utility function with "subsistence expenditure" is the translog function

$$
\ln V = \alpha_0 + \sum_i \alpha_i \ln \left[p_i / \left(y - \sum_k p_k \gamma_k \right) \right]
$$
$$
+ \frac{1}{2} \sum_i \sum_j \beta_{ij} \ln \left[p_i / \left(y - \sum_k p_k \gamma_k \right) \right] \ln \left[p_j / \left(y - \sum_k p_k \gamma_k \right) \right]
$$

$$(8.7)$$

with the restrictions, $\beta_{ij} = \beta_{ji}$ and $\sum_i \beta_{ij} = 0$ for all j, imposed. Applying Roy's identity we can generate the corresponding budget shares as

$$
s_i = p_i \gamma_i / y + \left[1 - \left(\sum_k p_k \gamma_k \right) / y \right] \left(\alpha_i + \sum_j \beta_{ij} \ln p_j \right), \qquad (8.8)
$$

for $i = 1, 2, \ldots$ where the normalization $\sum_i \alpha_i = 1$ has been imposed. In equation (8.8), the α's, β's and γ's are parameters to be estimated. This equation is nonlinear in parameters and variables and has linear Engel curves which need not pass through the origin. If $\gamma_i = 0$, all i, the linear translog reduces to the homothetic translog, which is linear in the parameters and is given by

$$
s_i = \alpha_i + \sum_j \beta_{ij} \ln p_j, \quad i = 1, 2, \ldots \qquad (8.9)
$$

We are interested in estimating equations of the more general form (8.8) though we will compare the results to the version given in (8.9).

---

ample of quasi-homothetic utility function is the Stone-Geary utility function which is the quasi-homothetic version of the Cobb-Douglas.)

[6]We use the translog function and we interpret it to be a second-order apporoximation to the underlying "true" indirect utility function.

[7]The LTL has been estimated by Manser (1976).

8.4 Stochastic Specification and Estimation

In order to estimate the share equation system given by equations (8.8), a stochastic version must be specified. Since equations (8.8) are in share form and only exogenous variable appear on the right hand sides it seemed reasonable to assume that the observed share in the ith equation deviates from the true share by an additive disturbance term u_i. Furthermore, it was assumed, at least initially, that u_t is a "classical disturbance" term with the following properties

$$E(u_t) = 0 \quad E(u_t, u_s') = \begin{array}{l} \sum \quad \text{for } s = t \\ 0 \quad \text{for } s \neq t \end{array} \quad \text{all } s, t \quad (8.10)$$

where $\sum$ is a symmetric and positive semidefinite covariance matrix, and 0 is a null matrix. Thus, we can write the stochastic version of the model as:

$$s_t = f_t(x_t, \theta) = u_t. \quad (8.11)$$

Assumption (8.10) permits correlation among the disturbances at time t but rules out the possibility of autocorrelated disturbances. This assumption and the fact that the s_t (and therefore the u_t) satisfy an adding up condition (because this is a singular system) imply that the disturbance covariance matrix is also singular. If autocorrelation in the disturbances is absent (as assumed here), Barten (1969) has shown that full information maximum likelihood estimates of the parameters can be obtained by arbitrarily deleting one equation in such a system, and that the resulting estimates are invariant with respect to the equation deleted. The parameter estimates from the deleted equation can be recovered from the restrictions.

We initially estimated the model in (8.11). However, early results led us to believe that the disturbances were serially correlated.[8] We, therefore, assumed a first-order autoregressive process, such that

$$u_t = R u_{t-1} + v_t \quad (8.12)$$

where $R = [R_{ij}]$ is a matrix of unknown parameters and v_t is a non-autocorrelated vector disturbance term with constant covariance matrix. For parsimony, we restricted R to be diagonal which requires that, following Berndt and Savin (1975), the diagonal elements be equal.

Writing equation (8.11) for period $t - 1$, multiplying by R, and substituting, we obtain

$$s_t = f_t(x_t, \theta) - R f_{t-1}(x_{t-1}, \theta) + R s_{t-1} + v_t \quad (8.13)$$

which, with the aforementioned restrictions on R, is what we have estimated.

---

[8] The computed equation-by-equation Durbin-Watson statistics were very low.

8.5   Elasticities

The system of equations in (8.8) provided a complete characterization of consumer preferences over the services of monetary assets and can be used to estimate the price and income elasticities as well as the Allen partial elasticities of substitution. As will be shown below, these elasticities are particularly useful in judging the validity of the parameter estimates.

The income elasticities can be calculated as[9]

$$\eta_i = 1 - p_i\gamma_i/s_iy + \sum_k p_k\gamma_k \left(\alpha_i + \sum_j \beta_{ij} \ln p_j \right) /s_iy_i, \qquad (8.14)$$

for $i = 1, 2, \dots$. Similarly, the own-price elasticities are given as

$$\eta_{ii} = -1 + \beta_{ii} \left(1 - \sum_k p_k\gamma_k/y \right) /s_i$$

$$+ p_i\gamma_i \left(1 - \alpha_i - \sum_j \beta_{ij} \ln p_j \right) /s_iy \qquad (8.15)$$

and the cross-price elasticities are

$$\eta_{ij} = \beta_{ij} \left(1 - \sum_k p_k\gamma_k/y \right) /s_i - p_j\gamma_j \left(\alpha_i + \sum_j \beta_{ij} \ln p_j \right) /s_iy, \qquad (8.16)$$

for $i = 1, 2, \dots$. If $\eta_{ij} > 0$ $(i \neq j)$ the assets are substitutes, if $\eta_{ij} < 0$ they are complements, and if $\eta_{ij} = 0$ they are independent.

Finally, the elasticities of substitution can be calculated from the income elasticities and the price elasticities using the Slutsky equation, $\sigma_{ij} = \eta_{ij}/s_j + \eta_i$.

8.6   Data

Our data consist of quarterly Canadian observations for the period 1968.I-1982.IV on four types of monetary assets. The four (henceforth referred to as monetary subaggregates) are narrow money (C), other checkable deposits (D), savings deposits (S), and time deposits (T). The details about the

---

[9]The incoe elasticities as well as the own- and cross-price elasticities are derived from (8.8) by rewriting it as $\ln x_i = \ln s_i - \ln p_i + \ln y$ and using the following general formulas (see, for example, Ewis and Fisher 1984): $\eta_i = 1 + \partial \ln s_i/\partial \ln y$ $(i = 1, \dots)$, $\eta_{ii} = -1 + \partial \ln s_i/\partial \ln p_i$ $(i = 1, \dots)$, and $\eta_{ij} = \partial \ln s_i/\partial \ln p_j$ $(i \neq j : i, j = 1, \dots)$.

data used to generate these monetary subaggregates are presented in Table 8.1.

Three main issues relating to the components listed in Table 8.1 are: (1) the inclusion of near-bank liabilities, (2) the aggregation of the components, and (3) data sources and adjustments.[10]

8.6.1 Near-Bank Liabilities

In the empirical approach to defining money, the definition may change as the economic structure changes. In the last decade important changes took place that have eroded the distinction between banks and near banks. This suggests that conventional money measures, independent of the method of aggregation, have lost their significance, and that we should extend monetary definitions to include near-bank liabilities and money market instruments that function like bank liabilities. In order to reflect the declining differentiation between banks and near banks, we have chosen to include certain near-bank liabilities in the definition used here. Specifically, we include the liabilities of Trust and Mortgage Loan (TML) Companies,[11] the liabilities of Credit Unions and Caisses Populaires,[12] the liabilities of Quebec Savings Banks and Canada Savings Bonds. The last two types of near-bank liabilities have not been considered in previous studies on the substitutability of monetary assets, owing to the unavailability of information on the interest rates offered. However, here, following Cockerline and Murray (1981), we assume that Credit Unions and Caisses Populaires, and Quebec Savings Banks offer the same interest as TML companies.

8.6.2 Aggregation

We assume the mapping of monetary assets to monetary subaggregates provided in Table 8.1 is given. This *a priori* categorization of the assets is subjective and can be thought of as being based either on a separability assumption or on Hicks' price aggregation condition (relative prices remain in fixed proportions). We are forced to appeal to such maintained hypotheses because the estimation of a highly disaggregated demand system,

---

[10]No attempt has been made in the present chapter to disaggregate by sector. This would require construction of two sets of monetary asset holdings — one for consumers and another for business — and also, computation of sector-specific monetary aggregates. See Barnett (1987) for work along these lines.

[11]These liabilities fall into three categories: checkable demand deposits, noncheckable demand deposits, and term deposits of various maturities.

[12]These liabilities fall into three categories: demand deposits, term deposits, and credit union shares, with the first group further divided into checkable and noncheckable components.

TABLE 8.1

A Taxonomy of Monetary Assets and Data Sources of Deposit and Interest Rate Series

Group Number	Group Name	Variable Number	Monetary Asset	Source	Own Rate	Source
1	Money (C)	1	Currency outside banks	BCR; B2001	Zero	
		2	Demand deposits at banks	BCR; B478	Zero	
2	Checkable deposits (D)	3	Checkable personal savings deposits at banks	BCR; B452 to Dec. 1981 & BCR; B485 to Dec. 1982	Interest rate on checkable personal savings deposits(adjusted for minimum monthly balance)[d]	B14035
		4	Daily interest checking accounts at banks	BCR; B484	Average of rates paid to banks on balances above a certain level (usually $2,000)	DBFA
		5	Checkable nonpersonal deposits at banks	BCR; B472	Interest rate on 90-day personal fixed term deposits	B14043
		6	Checkable demand deposits at TML companies	BCR; T40	Interest rate on checkable demand deposits at TML companies (adjusted for minimum monthly balance)[e]	DBFA
		7	Checkable demand deposits at credit unions.[a]	FI (catalogue 61-006)	Same as for checkable demand deposits at TMLs	

(cont'd)

TABLE 8.1 CONT'D

A TAXONOMY OF MONETARY ASSETS AND DATA SOURCES OF DEPOSIT AND INTEREST RATE SERIES

Group Number	Group Name	Variable Number	Monetary Asset	Source	Own Rate	Source
3	Savings deposits (S)	8	Noncheckable personal savings excluding daily interest deposits at banks	BCR; B453 to Sept. 1979 & BCR; B479 to Dec 1982	Interest rate on noncheckable personal savings deposits (adjusted for minimum monthly balance)[f]	B14019
		9	Noncheckable personal daily interest savings deposits	BCR; B480	Interest rate on noncheckable personal daily interest savings deposits	DBFA
		10	Noncheckable nonpersonal deposits at banks	BCR; B473	Same as for checkable nonpersonal deposits at banks	
		11	Noncheckable demand deposits at TML companies	BCR; T40	Interest rate on noncheckable demand deposits at TML companies	DBFA
		12	Noncheckable demand deposits FI (catalogue 61-006) at credit unions[b]		Same as for noncheckable demand deposits at TMLS	
4	Time deposits (T)	13	Deposits at Quebec Savings Banks other than those of the Federal Government	BCR; B2255	Same as for noncheckable demand deposits at TMLs	
		14	Personal fixed term deposits at banks	BCR; B454	Same as for checkable non-personal deposits at banks	
		15	Less than one year term deposits at TML companies	BCR; T40	Interest rate on 1-2 years Trust Company GICs	DBFA
		16	Greater than one year term deposits at TML companies[c]	BCR; T40	Interest rate on 5 years Trust Company GICs	B14023

(cont'd)

TABLE 8.1 CONT'D

A TAXONOMY OF MONETARY ASSETS AND DATA SOURCES OF DEPOSIT AND INTEREST RATE SERIES

Group Number	Group Name	Variable Number	Monetary Asset	Source	Own Rate	Source
		17	Credit union shares	FI (catalogue 61-006)	Interest rate on 90-179 day Trust Company GICs	DBFA
		18	Credit union term deposits	BCR; B3919	Same as for Credit Union Shares	
		19	Canada Savings Bonds	BCR; B2406	First year coupon rate on Canada Savings Bonds	B14040

Notes: DBFA = Department of Banking and Financial Analysis of the Bank of Canada, which provided these data on request. FI = Statistics Canada Publication, Financial Institutions (catalogue 61-006). BCR = Bank of Canada Review. Series with a B prefix are taken from the BCR with the letter B and number following representing the series code therein. Series with a T prefix are also taken from the BCR with the letter T and the number following representing the table number therein.

[a] No data are available prior to 1975. However, we do not have data on the aggregate volume of demand deposits at Credit Unions and Caisses Populaires.

The amount of checkable deposits as of 1975.I was \$2,522 million amounting to 51.638 percent of aggregate deposits at that date. In order to obtain data on checkable deposits for 1968.I-1974.IV we multiplied the aggregate series by the factor 0.51638 for the earlier period.

[b] We constructed the series prior to 1975 by subtracting checkable demand deposits from demand deposits at Credit Unions and Caisses Populaires.

[c] This series was constructed by adding two separate series. TML 1 to 5-year term deposits and TML over 5-year term deposits. Figures for these series are available in BCR; T40.

[d] The adjustment was made as follows: adjusted rate = quoted rate $\times$[checkable, personal savings deposits (monthly, minimum of Wednesdays)/checkable, personal savings deposits (monthly, average of Wednesdays)].

[e] The adjustment was made as follows: adjusted rate = quoted rate - checkable personal savings deposit rate + adjusted rate checkable personal savings deposits.

[f] The adjustment was similar to the adjustment on the interest rate on checkable personal savings deposits.

encompassing the full range of assets, is not possible in practice, since the number of parameters to be estimated would be extremely large and many of the user costs would be highly, if not perfectly, collinear.

8.6.3 Aggregation of Components

We construct the monetary subaggregates using both a simple-sum and a Divisia aggregation procedure.[13] These subaggregates are then used as data in estimating the demand system specified above. Following Barnett (1983), when those monetary subaggregates are computed as Divisia indices we make use of Fisher's (1922) weak factor reversal test to compute the corresponding price indices. On the other hand, when the monetary subaggregates are computed as simple-sum indices, the price indices we use are Laspeyres indices.[14]

8.6.4 Data Sources and Adjustments

The basic data were obtained from a variety of statistical sources (see Table 8.1) including the Department of Monetary and Financial Analysis of the Bank of Canada. Missing data posed a problem for certain asset components and we were forced to construct reasonable proxies. Also, in an attempt to preserve consistency, the following adjustments were made to our disaggregated data.

The first adjustment is concerned with the conversion to real per capita balances. Given that the theoretical model is based on an individual decision-making problem, each asset stock was divided by the population of Canada to get per capita quantity series. Also, we have divided each asset stock by the Consumer Price Index (all commodities) to convert nominal quantities to real terms.

The second adjustment concerns the holding periods. Following Cockerline and Murray (1981), all the own rates with a maturity greater than one year were "yield-curve adjusted" to a 91-day Treasury bill rate.[15]

---

[13]We prefer the Divisia index from the Diewert superlative class of index numbers, because this index has been widely used in the literature, and has been recently advocated by Barnett as the most attractive quantity index for measuring money. In any event, as Diewert (1978) has shown, selection between index numbers from the superlative class is of little empirical importance, since these indices move very closely together.

[14]Barnett, instead, used the Leontief indices (the smallest element of the vector of component user costs), arguing that "simple sum quantity aggregation implies perfect substitutability of components and hence consumption only of the least expensive good" (Barnett, 1983, p. 18). While we agree with this argument, we note that the Leontief index ovccasionally leads to zero values which are inadmissible in the translog formulation. Our choice seemed to be a reasonable compromise.

[15]The adjustment was made as follows: $r_i^a = r_i^u - (r_G - r_{TB})$, where r_i^a is the yield

Finally, in order to apply the user-cost formula (8.3), we require data on the benchmark rate, R. Here, R was determined in each period as the maximum among all own rates. This procedure, while not ideal, was required because it is extremely difficult to find a single rate series that exceeds all other rates on monetary assets in every time period.

Prior to estimation, the price indices were all scaled to equal 1.0 in 1968.II. To ensure that the products of price and quantity indices remained unchanged by the rescaling, the quantity series were adjusted accordingly.

8.7 Empirical Results Interpretation

First, the use of simple-sum and Divisia monetary quantity indices as data in empirical demand systems will be compared, and second, the empirical results will be examined to shed light on the controversy of whether monetary assets are substitutes or complements.

Parameter estimates, based on FIML regressions for the quasi-homothetic translog model, are presented in Table 8.2.[16] The first two columns display the symmetry-restricted quasi-homothetic translog estimates (thirteen free parameters), and the last two, the symmetry-restricted homothetic translog estimates (nine free parameters). These results are discussed in two stages. First, we consider whether they are consistent with optimization by looking at the integrability conditions. Second, we present income elasticities, price elasticities and partial elasticities of substitution based on the parameter estimates.

When Divisia indices are used, positivity and monotonicity are satisfied at each observation point by the symmetry-restricted quasi-homothetic model but at no observation points by the homothetic model. However, the appropriate curvature conditions on the indirect utility function (i.e., the matrix of elasticities of substitution should be negative semidefinite) are satisfied for only about 80 percent of the observations by the quasi-homothetic model and at no observation points by the homothetic model. On the other hand, with simple-sum monetary quantity indices the quasi-homothetic model satisfied positivity and monotonicity for about 93 percent of the observations and the curvature conditions for about 75 percent of the observations. Again, these conditions are satisfied for no observation points by the homothetic form. These results clearly favor Divisia monetary quantity aggregation over simple-sum aggregation and the quasi-homothetic model over the homothetic one.

---

curve adjusted rate, r_i^u is the unadjusted rate, r_G is the ordinate on the yield curve of Canada bonds with the same maturity as i and r_{TB} is the 91-day Treasury bill rate.

[16]The results were checked for global convergence by estimating the model more than once, deleting a different equation each time.

TABLE 8.2

PARAMETER ESTIMATES, TRANSLOG FORMS, 1968.I-1982.IV

Parameter	Quasi-Homothetic Version		Homothetic Version	
	With Divisia Monetary Aggregation	With Simple-Sum Monetary Aggregation	With Divisia Monetary Aggregation	With Simple-Sum Monetary Aggregation
γ_C	0.200 (0.105)	11.209 (0.300)		
γ_D	0.007 (0.048)	5.644 (0.222)		
γ_S	0.033 (0.056)	17.882 (2.160)		
γ_T	0.164 (0.011)	25.019 (1.456)		
a_C	0.522 (0.061)	0.039 (0.061)	0.484 (0.040)	0.223 (0.014)
a_D	0.139 (0.028)	0.129 (0.036)	0.085 (0.040)	0.135 (0.012)
a_S	0.301 (0.063)	0.314 (0.063)	0.283 (0.046)	0.257 (0.014)
a_T	0.036 (0.030)	0.517 (0.056)	0.146 (0.042)	0.383 (0.015)
β_{CC}	0.237 (0.017)	−0.016 (0.019)	0.240 (0.010)	0.147 (0.007)
β_{CD}	−0.135 (0.027)	0.057 (0.020)	−0.094 (0.008)	−0.042 (0.008)
β_{CS}	−0.105 (0.017)	−0.031 (0.012)	−0.068 (0.004)	−0.035 (0.002)
β_{CT}	0.003 (0.011)	−0.010 (0.016)	−0.076 (0.003)	−0.070 (0.002)
β_{DD}	0.186 (0.030)	−0.054 (0.025)	0.147 (0.008)	0.108 (0.010)
β_{DS}	−0.035 (0.009)	−0.010 (0.012)	−0.022 (0.003)	−0.018 (0.004)
β_{DT}	−0.014 (0.006)	0.007 (0.007)	−0.030 (0.004)	−0.047 (0.002)
β_{SS}	0.123 (0.023)	0.259 (0.026)	0.102 (0.003)	0.171 (0.005)
β_{ST}	0.017 (0.006)	−0.217 (0.021)	−0.011 (0.003)	−0.117 (0.003)
β_{TT}	−0.005 (0.013)	0.220 (0.016)	0.119 (0.004)	0.234 (0.004)
R	0.952 (0.013)	0.943 (0.009)	0.961 (0.013)	0.774 (0.025)

SUMMARY STATISTICS				
L_n L	643.10	642.21	607.34	518.46
D-W$_C$	1.92	1.94	2.12	2.61
D-W$_D$	2.24	2.06	2.25	2.41
D-W$_S$	1.59	2.04	1.88	2.52
D-W$_T$	2.07	1.97	2.31	2.38

Notes: For (C) money, (D) checkable deposits, (S) savings deposits, (T) time deposits; symmetry imposed; standard errors in parentheses. In $L_n L$ refers to the log of the likelihood function. The estimates shown incorporate the correction for autocorrelation discussed above. Standard errors (asymptotic) are taken from more than one 'run' since restrictions eliminate some parameters in each run. D-W$_C$, D-W$_D$, D-W$_S$, and D-W$_T$ refer to Durbin-Watson statistics equations C, D, S and T, respectively.

To test the validity of the restrictions implied by the hypotheses of first-order autocorrelation and homotheticity, the likelihood ratio method was employed and the level of significance set at 0.01. The results are presented in Table 8.3.

TABLE 8.3

LIKELIHOOD RATIO TEST RESULTS
FOR THE QUASI-HOMOTHETIC TRANSLOG

Test	Restricted Log Likelihood	Test Statistic $2(U - R)$	D.F.	Critical Value (0.01)
H_0 :No autocorrelation $(H_1 :\text{Not } H_0)^a$				
Divisia Aggregation	475.1	335.8	1	6.6
Simple-Sum Aggregation	529.1	226.5	1	6.6
H_0 :Homotheticity $(H_1 :\text{Quasi Homotheticity})$				
Divisia Aggregation	607.3	71.3	4	13.3
Simple-Sum Aggregation	518.5	247.7	4	13.3

Note: ^{a}The exact form of H_1 is discussed in the text. It involves first-order autocorrelation in each share equation with the same coefficient of autocorrelation.

The null hypothesis of no autocorrelation clearly cannot be accepted. The likelihood ratio test statistics are 335.8 (Divisia) and 226.5 (simple-sum), while the 0.01 chi-square critical value is only 6.6. Next the hypothesis of homotheticity was tested, conditional on first-order autocorrelation. The likelihood ratio test statistics are 71.3 (Divisia) and 247.7 (simple-sum), while the 0.01 chi-square critical value is 13.3. We conclude that conditional on first-order autocorrelation, the homotheticity restrictions should be rejected.

The implications for consumer behavior of the estimated budget share equations are now examined, and monetary asset substitution possibilities are measured. The estimated expenditure elasticities (η_i), the price elasticities (η_{ij}), and the partial elasticities of substitution (σ_{ij}) are reported in Table 8.4 along with the standard errors in parentheses.[17]

---

[17]The elasticities are nonlinear functions of the parameters and we computed the

The estimated expenditure elasticities in Table 8.4 reveal a clear-cut pattern. All assets are "normal goods" $(\eta_i > 0)$. With Divisia monetary quantity indices, money (C), checkable deposits (D) and savings deposits (S) are clearly "luxury goods" $(\eta_i > 1)$ with money being more so; the other asset — time deposits — is expenditure inelastic. For the simple-sum monetary quantity indices, money and savings deposits are expenditure inelastic, while checkable and time deposits are expenditure elastic.

The own- and cross-price elasticities in Table 8.4 reveal a pattern consistent with demand theory. All own-price elasticities are negative, and the cross-price elasticities vary between positive and negative. Under Divisia monetary aggregation, all assets are own-price inelastic $(|\eta_{ii}| < 1)$; with the demand for checkable deposits being much more so than the demand for money, savings deposits and time deposits. All monetary assets are found to be (gross) complements $(\eta_{ij} < 0)$ with the exception of η_{ST}, η_{TS}, and η_{TC}; the sizes of these elasticities, however, are less than 0.1. The use of simple-sum monetary quantity indices, on the other hand, does not reveal such a complementarity pattern. Some of the assets that appear (by the cross-price elasticities) to be gross complements with Divisia aggregation are gross substitutes with simple-sum aggregation. This is not surprising given the big differences in income effects reported above.

The estimated partial elasticities of substitution show a quite different pattern of substitution. All own elasticities of substitution are negative, while the assets appear to be net substitutes for both types of aggregation. However, the estimated substitutability relationships among the monetary assets are not well determined and are inconsistent with the view that the substitutability between money (C) and the nested "similar assets" group (checkable deposits) should be stronger than the substitutability between money and other "less similar assets" groups (time deposits in this case).[18]

This raises a serious question about the aggregation of monetary assets which, itself, is linked with the problem of the definition of money. The problem is that the degree of substitutability among monetary assets has been used to provide — explicitly or implicitly — a rationale for the choice of assets to be included in the monetary aggregate. The argument was that, if different monetary assets are close substitutes, then there might be a summary measure of money which could be obtained simply by adding together in some way the different monetary assets in a functional group. Our

---

standard errors by linearizing them around the estimated parameter values and then using the standard formulas for the variance of linear functions of random variables. This was carried out by using the ANALYZ command in TSP.

[18]This result is consistent with the within-M1 low substitutability findings by Offenbacher (1979) and Ewis and Fisher (1984) in the US data.

TABLE 8.4

Estimated Expenditure Elasticities, Own- and
Cross-Price Elasticities and Elasticities of Substitution;
Quasi-Homothetic Translog with Symmetry Imposed

| | Estimate | |
Elasticity	Divisia Aggregation	Simple-Sum Aggregation
η_C	1.020 (0.024)	0.980 (0.012)
η_D	1.011 (0.007)	1.010 (0.004)
η_S	1.010 (0.007)	0.992 (0.015)
η_T	0.974 (0.001)	1.029 (0.010)
η_{CC}	−0.647 (0.037)	−0.948 (0.034)
η_{DD}	−0.357 (0.133)	−0.855 (0.048)
η_{SS}	−0.429 (0.095)	−1.289 (0.105)
η_{TT}	−0.999 (0.003)	−0.998 (0.285)
η_{CD}	−0.185 (0.039)	−0.099 (0.027)
η_{CS}	−0.146 (0.015)	0.052 (0.017)
η_{CT}	−0.040 (0.006)	0.014 (0.010)
η_{DC}	−0.472 (0.124)	−0.146 (0.039)
η_{DS}	−0.122 (0.030)	0.020 (0.034)
η_{DT}	−0.058 (0.007)	−0.028 (0.005)
η_{SC}	−0.489 (0.071)	0.034 (0.015)
η_{SD}	−0.163 (0.040)	0.009 (0.018)
η_{ST}	0.072 (0.011)	0.252 (0.068)
η_{TC}	0.014 (0.002)	−0.035 (0.001)
η_{TD}	−0.066 (0.008)	−0.026 (0.001)
η_{TS}	0.076 (0.010)	0.031 (0.024)
σ_{CC}	−0.270 (0.068)	−4.610 (0.196)
σ_{DD}	−0.799 (0.683)	−6.330 (0.414)
σ_{SS}	−1.895 (0.646)	−4.912 (0.474)
σ_{TT}	−5.557 (0.024)	−1.057 (0.054)
σ_{CD}	0.078 (0.197)	0.125 (0.230)
σ_{CS}	0.027 (0.108)	1.222 (0.082)
σ_{CT}	0.757 (0.025)	1.011 (0.010)
σ_{DS}	0.179 (0.201)	1.105 (0.160)
σ_{DT}	0.630 (0.044)	0.950 (0.009)
σ_{ST}	1.486 (0.069)	1.520 (0.149)

Notes: All elasticities are calculated at the mean. Standard errors in parentheses.

results concerning the low degree of substitutability among the monetary assets — a finding that corroborates previous results using other consumer demand models — suggest that this conventional *a priori* wisdom regarding the definition of money requires reexamination. The two major approaches to defining money — the *a priori* approach, which defines money in a theoretical sense by pointing to its functions, and the policy-oriented *empirical* approach, which defines money as that collection of monetary assets that has the most predictable effects on nominal income — implicitly make the assumption that aggregation over monetary assets is feasible. The final complication is that a number of different definitions of money are now available. While this may be encouraging for the econometrician who is unsure which definition of money to assume, and therefore can choose on the basis of best fit, it is not encouraging for someone interested in designing optimal economic policies, for whom different definitions of money have very different implications.

Regardless of the choice, however, Barnett (1982) has argued that when monetary aggregates are used as economic variables the aggregate should be computed using appropriate methods from aggregation theory. In particular the use of any aggregate implies that the aggregator function is weakly separable in the components of the aggregate. If this weak separability condition is violated, stable preferences cannot exist over the components of the aggregate and such an aggregate cannot be a useful theoretical tool. Of course, perfect substitutability is sufficient (but not necessary) for weak separability. Therefore, the weak substitutability finding of our study certainly warrants further empirical research into this important issue.[19]

8.8 Conclusions

The most interesting finding is the low degree of substitution among the monetary assets. Furthermore, money and checkable deposits have among the lowest partial elasticities of substitution. These results provide no justification for broad money measures and suggest that we can only identify the true monetary aggregate by testing for the necessary and sufficient separability conditions in the underlying utility function. Our results also favor Divisia monetary aggregation and are consistent with empirical evidence accumulated over the last five years in the United States in the debate on the aggregation of money. For example, Barnett, Offenbacher and Spindt (1981, 1984) compared the empirical performance of Divisia and simple-sum monetary aggregates in terms of policy criteria, such as causality, information content of an aggregate, and stability of money demand equations, and

---

[19]See Serletis (1987) for work along these lines.

found no basis for preferring the simple-sum aggregates. Similarly, Barnett (1983), comparing the simple-sum and Divisia aggregates in terms of the fit of a joint sector-wide demand system, concluded in favor of the Divisia aggregates.

Finally, in exploring the quasi-homothetic version of the translog we have found it a very attractive functional form. Furthermore, the hypothesis of homotheticity of the translog form is decisively rejected by the statistical tests. Our results highlight the important role that could be played by the quasi-homotheticity assumption in multistage budgeting and aggregation theory. Unfortunately, much recent work on the specification of utility-tree structures rests on the assumption that preferences are homothetically separable with implied unitary expenditure elasticities at all price and expenditure configurations. The quasi-homotheticity assumption provides a generalization that allows for more complicated interdependencies among monetary assets and allows a simple parametric test of the homotheticity restriction. In addition, quasi-homotheticity, like homotheticity, is a sufficient condition in the theory of consistent multistage optimization. As a consequence, quasi-homotheticity is clearly an attractive feature on which to build.

Chapter 9

The Demand for Divisia M1, M2, and M3 in the United States

*Apostolos Serletis**

9.1 Introduction

We have three objectives in this chapter: to analyze the demand for money, in the context of Divisia monetary quantity aggregation, in the U.S. economy; to estimate the degree of substitution between money, defined from narrow to broad, and near-money at different levels of aggregation; and to discover the structure of preferences over monetary assets by empirically testing for the appropriateness of the weak separability (aggregation) assumptions that underlie various money measures.

In recent years the issue of summation versus Divisia monetary quantity aggregation has attracted a great deal of attention in the literature. An important reason for this interest is the fact that simple summation aggregation implies perfect substitutability among components — an assumption which does not hold for the component monetary assets, and one which is especially distortive of high-level monetary aggregates. In a series of papers, Barnett (1980, 1982, 1983, 1987) and Barnett, Offenbacher and Spindt (1981, 1984) voice objections to simple-sum aggregation proce-

---

*Originally published in the *Journal of Macroeconomics* 9 (1987), 567-591. Reprinted with permission.

dures and derive the theoretical linkage between monetary theory and index number theory. They apply economic aggregation and index number theory and construct monetary aggregates based upon Diewert's (1976) class of "superlative" quantity index numbers. The new aggregates are Divisia quantity indices, which are elements of the superlative class and which represent a practically viable — and theoretically meaningful — alternative to the flawed simple-summation aggregates.

The question of money and near-money substitutability/complementarity has also attracted a great deal of attention in the literature (see, for example, Donovan 1978; Offenbacher 1979; Barnett 1980; Ewis and Fisher 1984, 1985; and Serletis and Robb 1986).[1] One reason for this concern is that the degree of substitutability among monetary assets has been used — explicitly or implicitly — to provide a rationale for the appropriate definition of money, which is itself an important problem in monetary theory and it has been the focus of continuing controversy over the years. However, in most of the research undertaken, investigators adopt the approach of estimating the degree of substitution between money, defined narrowly, and various arrangements of assets.[2]

In this chapter we contribute to the literature by analyzing the demand for broad money measures and by estimating the degree of substitution between Divisia money, defined from narrow to broad, and the "nested like assets" at different levels of aggregation. The analysis is conducted within a microtheoretical framework — utilizing the demand-system approach — that views money as a durable good (or monetary assets as durable goods) yielding a flow of nonobservable services, which enter as arguments in aggregator functions, and that makes use of the Strotz (1957, 1959) — Gorman (1959) multistage optimization framework. The theoretical foundations underlying this framework are also highlighted, in the belief that this will help to make clear the restrictive nature of those approaches which do not build upon a choice theoretic model.

Another important contribution is the systematic testing for the appropriateness of the weak separability (aggregation) conditions at successive levels of aggregation, using a flexible functional form interpretation of the homothetic translog functional form. As Barnett (1982) and Serletis (1987) argue, when monetary aggregates are used as economic variables, the aggregate should be constructed using appropriate methods from aggregation theory. In particular, the use of any aggregate implies that the aggregator function is weakly separable in the components of the aggregate whether

---

[1] Feige and Pearce (1977) review the early literature on the substitutability between money and near money.

[2] Noteworthy exceptions are Donovan (1978), Barnett (1980), and Serletis and Robb (1986), who model the demand for aggregate monetary assets.

or not the aggregate is generated via Diewert-superlative or any other respectable quantity index. If this weak separability condition is violated, stable preferences cannot exist over the components of the aggregate, and such an aggregate cannot be a useful theoretical tool. Here, assuming existence of (Divisia) M1, M2, and M3 as exact economic monetary aggregates — in the sense that each is assumed to behave as if it were one elementary asset — we follow Barnett (1982) and Serletis (1987) and test for the appropriateness of the weak separability conditions, at the various aggregation levels, utilizing the apparatus developed by Denny and Fuss (1977).

The chapter is organized as follows. Section 9.2 presents a general theoretical model, elaborates on the specification of monetary-services aggregator functions, and outlines the theory of recursive, multistage optimization as well as the correspondence between direct and indirect separable preference structures. Section 9.3 is concerned with the specification of a translog indirect utility function and the derivation of monetary-asset demand equations. Details of data considerations are also provided. In Section 9.4, the method of estimation is described, the hypothesis tests are outlined, and the empirical results are presented and discussed. Section 9.5 provides a summary and statement of conclusions.

9.2   Model Specification

9.2.1   The Consumer's Problem

We suppose an economy with identical individuals, whose direct utility function is weakly separable (a direct tree) of the form

$$u = u\left[c, l, f(x)\right], \tag{9.1}$$

where c is a vector of the services of consumption goods, l is leisure time, and x is a vector of the services of monetary assets (assumed to be proportional to the stocks).[3]

In order to focus on the details of demand for services of monetary assets, ignoring other types of goods, a good starting point is a model consistent with the theory of two-stage optimization.[4] In the first stage, consumers

---

[3]The utility-tree structure (9.1) is treated as a maintained (untested) hypothesis in this chapter, although it implies the assumption that the demand for monetary services is independent of relative prices outside the monetary group.

[4]The notion of two-stage optimization is investigated in the context of consumer theory by Strotz (1957, 1959) and Gorman (1959). It refers to a sequential expenditure allocation, where, in the first stage, consumers allocate their expenditures among broad categories (relying on price indices for these categories) and, in the second stage, within each category.

allocate their expenditures among broad categories (consumption goods, leisure, and monetary services in our context); in the second stage, they allocate expenditures within each category. The particular two-level structure we would wish to utilize can be expressed by the following classical consumer problem:

$$\max_{x} f(x), \quad \text{subject to } p'x = y, \tag{9.2}$$

in which $f(x)$, the monetary services aggregator function[5] (quantity index), is assumed to satisfy the usual regularity conditions. The expenditure on the services of monetary assets is denoted by y, and p is a vector of monetary-asset user costs, with the ith component given by[6]

$$p_i = (R - r_i) / (1 + R), \tag{9.3}$$

which denotes the discounted interest foregone by holding a dollar's worth of that asset. Here, R is the "benchmark" rate (the highest available yield) and r_i is the yield on the ith asset.

9.2.2   Preference Structure Over Monetary Assets[7]

Consider a partition of the n monetary assets into four groups, and let x^r be the subvector of assets in the rth group so that $x = (x^1, x^2, x^3, x^4)$. Similarly, $p = (p^1, p^2, p^3, p^4)$. The components of x^1 are those that are included in the Federal Reserve Board's M1 monetary aggregate. The components of x^2 are those of the board's M2 aggregate net of x^1. Similarly, the components of x^3 are those of the board's M3 aggregate net of x^1 and x^2, and the components of x^4 are those of the board's L aggregate net of x^1, x^2, and x^3.

We assume that the monetary-services aggregator function, $f(x)$, has the homothetically strongly recursive separable form[8]

$$f(x) = f_4(x^4, f_3\left\{x^3, f_2\left[x^2,, f_1(x^1)\right]\right\}), \tag{9.4}$$

---

[5] The term *aggregator function* is used to represente purchases by all economic agents. Here we are concerned with the problem of monetary asset aggregation and the application of empirical demand analysis. Questions of aggregation over economic agents are beyond the scope of this chapter, although we recognize that the data used are observations of expenditure on monetary assets made by a group of economic agents (both households and firms).

[6] The theoretical derivation of the user cost formula is by Barnett (1978).

[7] This section derives from Barnett, Offenbacher, and Spindt (1981, section 3.4).

[8] According to the original definition of separability by Sono (1961) and Leontief (1947), the algebraic requirement of strong recursive separability is that

$$\partial\left[(\partial f / \partial x_i) / (\partial f / \partial x_j)\right] / \partial x_k = 0, \quad \forall i \in I_r, j \in I_s, k \in I_t, t > r, s.$$

where the x^i's are vectors and where the (monotonically increasing and strictly quasi-concave) aggregator functions, f_i $(i = 1, \ldots, 4)$, are the board's functional monetary aggregates M1, M2, M3 and L, respectively. It is to be noted that only the component groupings are selected in accordance with the board's conventions, but not the aggregates. In particular, if Q_1 is the monetary aggregate for the components of M1, Q_2 for M2, Q_3 for M3, and Q_4 for L, then it follows that

$$Q_1 = f_1(x^1); \tag{9.5}$$

$$Q_2 = f_2\left[x^2, f_1(x^1)\right] = f_2\left(x^2, Q_1\right); \tag{9.6}$$

$$Q_3 = f_3\left\{x^3, f_2\left[x^2, f_1(x^1)\right]\right\} = f_3(x^3, Q_2); \quad \text{and} \tag{9.7}$$

$$Q_4 = f_4\left(x^4, f_3\left\{x^3, f_2\left[x^2, f_1(x^1)\right]\right\}\right) = f_4(x^4, Q_3). \tag{9.8}$$

Each aggregator function, f_i $(i = 1, \ldots, 4)$, is thought of as a specific utility function as well as a subaggregate measure of monetary services. These functions are very important in aggregation theory and in hypothesis testing, since the relationship that monetary assets bear to one another is ultimately determined by their role in these functions. In the next subsection, we elaborate on the specification of these aggregator functions.

9.2.3 Aggregator Function Specifications

Users of simple-sum monetary aggregates generally assume that the monetary quantity functions, f_i $(i = 1, \ldots, 4)$, are unit-weighted linear functions or, equivalently, that monetary assets within the same group are dollar-for-dollar perfect substitutes. However, Barnett, Offenbacher, and Spindt (1981, 497) clearly describe the monetary asset aggregation problem:

> "Whenever monetary aggregates are used in the context of economic theory (rather than as simple accounting identities), the theory of economic quantity aggregation is specifically applicable."

For example, the appropriate form of aggregation (simple-sum, as opposed to other possibilities) must involve consideration of the aggregator function underlying the demand for monetary assets. The use of any functional form for the aggregator function would reflect our assumptions about the underlying preference structure over monetary assets, and to fail to adopt the appropriate functional form is to commit a specification error.[9]

---

[9] For example, the use of the Cobb-Douglas functional form imposes an elasticity of substitution equal to unity between every pair of assets. Similarly, a constant elasticity of substitution (C.E.S.) functional form, although it relaxes the unitary elasticity

This problem might be partially overcome by using a flexible functional form — an aggregator function specification able to provide a second-order approximation to an arbitrary, twice-differentiable aggregator function (see Barnett 1983, appendix, for formal definitions of the flexibility property).

However, although the existence of an aggregator function that contains monetary assets as arguments is important for both aggregation theory and hypothesis testing, this function is not frequently used for data-construction purposes. Instead, parameter-free statistical indices are used, thus eliminating the need to estimate the parameters of a parameterized econometric specification for the aggregator function. Still, the choice of the appropriate statistical index is not arbitrary. Diewert (1976) provides a link between the economic and statistical approach to indexing numbers by attaching economic properties to statistical indices. These properties are defined in terms of the statistical indices' ability to approximate a particular functional form for the aggregator function. For example, Diewert shows that a number of well-known statistical indices are equivalent to the use of a particular functional form. Such statistical indices are called "exact." Exactness, however, is not sufficient for acceptability of a particular statistical index when the functional form for the aggregator function is not known. In this case, it seems desirable to choose a statistical index which is exact for a flexible functional form. Diewert terms such statistical indices "superlative." He also showed that the Divisia index is exact for the homogeneous translog and is, therefore, a superlative index (provides nonparametric, second-order approximations to parameterized aggregator functions).[10]

9.2.4   Recursive Multistage Decentralization[11]

In order to focus on the details of demand for services of monetary assets at different levels of aggregation, we assume a multistage decentralization procedure, analogous to the two-stage budgeting procedure discussed ear-

---

of substitution restriction imposed by the Cobb-Douglas, imposes the restriction that the elasticity of substitution between any pair of assets is always constant. If these propositions are at odds with the facts, the use of these functional forms seems inappropriate, since they all imply serious limitations on behavior if they are used as aggregator functions.

[10]The Divisia index is defined as follows:

$$\log Q_t - \log Q_{t-1} = \sum_i w_{it}^* (\log x_{it} - \log x_{i,t-1}),$$

where x_{it} represents (nominal or real, total or per capita) balances of monetary asset i during period t, $w_{it}^* = (1/2)\,(w_{it} + w_{i,t-1})$, and $w_{it} = p_{it}x_{it}/\sum_k p_{kt}x_{kt}$ is the expenditure share of monetary asset i during period t.

[11]By *decentralization* we mean the allocation of category budget shares among the assets in a group.

lier. Although the consumers are viewed as making their decentralization decisions from the top of the tree down, we will elaborate on the multistage decentralization properties of decision (9.4) — and we will later estimate conditional money demand models at successive levels of aggregation — recursively, from the bottom up.[12]

The first-stage decision is to select x_1 to solve

$$\max_{(x^1)} f_1(x^1), \quad \text{subject to } p^1 x^1 = y_1. \tag{9.9}$$

From the solution of problem (9.9), estimates of detailed parameters are available which permit the construction of an economic quantity index for the components of M1. However, as we argued in the previous subsection, indices so constructed would depend on the specification and parameter estimation of aggregator functions. That dependence would in turn render a (parameter-free) superlative statistical index more desirable. In this chapter, for purposes of investigating the demand for Divisia money, the Divisia index will be used. Hence, the monetary aggregates, Q_1, Q_2, and Q_3 in equations (9.6), (9.7), and (9.8), respectively, would be thought of as Divisia quantity indices, which correspond to Divisia price indices.

The second stage of the multistage decision is to select x^2 and Q_1 to solve

$$\max_{(x^2, Q_1)} f_2(x^2, Q_1), \quad \text{subject to } p^2 x^2 + P_1 Q_1 = y_2, \tag{9.10}$$

where P_1 is the (dual to Q_1) user cost aggregate[13] over p^1. From the solution of problem (9.10), the demand for Divisia M1 will be determined, and the substitutability/complementarity relationship between Divisia M1 and a number of "near-monies" will be investigated.

---

[12]This approach to the recursive estimation of utility trees is developed by Barnett (1977), Fuss (1977), and Anderson (1979).

[13]Following Barnett (1983), in computing user cost aggregates we make use of Fisher's (1922) weak factor reversal test. The test states that the product of the values of the price and quantity indices should be equal to the ratio of total expenditures in the two periods.

In the third stage, the consumer selects x^3 and Q_2 to solve[14]

$$\max_{(x^2,Q_2)} f_3(x^3, Q_2), \quad \text{subject to } p^3 x^3 + P_2 Q_2 = y_3, \qquad (9.11)$$

where P_2 is the user cost aggregate corresponding to Q_2. From the solution of problem (9.11), the consumer determines Divisia M2.

Finally in the fourth stage, the consumer selects x^4 and Q_3 to solve

$$\max_{(x^4,Q_3)} f_4(x^4, Q_3), \quad \text{subject to } p^4 x^4 + P_3 Q_3 = y_4, \qquad (9.12)$$

where P_3 is the user cost aggregate corresponding to Divisia Q_3. From the solution of problem (9.12), the consumer determines the demand for Divisia M3.

We could move farther up the utility tree by imbedding the results from the last stage in equation (9.1) and perhaps could test whether the utility function (9.1) is appropriately separable in money, consumption goods, and leisure — an assumption implicit in the traditional "money-nonmoney" dichotomization — as well as investigate the substitutability/complementarity relationship between these goods. Although these issues are relatively unexplored, our objective in this chapter is to estimate the degree of substitution between money, defined from narrow to broad, and the "nested like assets" at different levels of aggregation. As a result we only concentrate on the second, third, and fourth stages of the multistage decision.

9.2.5 Duality

Thus far, speaking about separable preference structures we have referred to the direct utility function. However, the structure of preferences can be represented by either a direct or an indirect utility function. The indirect utility function is more appealing because it simplifies the estimation considerably, since it has prices that are exogenous in explaining consumer behavior. However, a structural property of the direct utility function does not imply the same property on the indirect utility function. In order to

---

[14]Q_2 is a Divisia index over the components of M2, rather than being a Divisia index over x^2 and Q_1. This is so because (as Diewert 1978 has shown) the Divisia index is not consistent (but is only approximately consistent) in aggregation. Consistency in aggregation refers to a situation where the set of assets is partitioned into subsets and subindices for these subsets are calculated. Then the total index is calculated using these subindices and the same index formula. If this two-stage aggregation procedure gives the same results as a single-stage aggregation procedure, then we say that the index formula is consistent in aggregation. Only the Laspeyres and Vartia (1974) indices are consistent in aggregation, while all superlative indices are approximately consistent in aggregation.

implement a model of demand based on the indirect function that satisfies properties of the direct function, a correspondence between direct and indirect properties is needed. Although nonhomothetic direct and indirect strongly recursive functions are independent structures, Blackorby *et al.* (1974) show that if the direct utility function is strongly recursive separable with homothetic aggregator functions (as assumed here), then the indirect utility function will also be homothetically strongly recursive separable in normalized prices.[15] The choice of the homothetic indirect translog function, in the following subsection, is primarily motivated by these considerations.

9.3 Demand System Specification and Data

9.3.1 Functional Form

The demand system used for estimation is derived by approximating the indirect monetary-services aggregator functions, dual to the direct monetary-services utility functions, f_i $(i = 2, 3, 4)$, with the homothetic, transcendental logarithmic (translog) function:

$$\ln V = \alpha_0 + \sum_i \alpha_i \ln v_i + \frac{1}{2} \sum_i \sum_j \beta_{ij} \ln v_i \ln v_j, \qquad (9.13)$$

where $v_i = p_i/y$; p_i is the user cost price of asset i; y is expenditure on monetary services; $\beta_{ij} = \beta_{ji}$ for all i, j; and $\sum_i \beta_{ij} = 0$ for all j.

Applying Roy's Identity allows us to derive the demand system that is actually estimated here:

$$s_i = \alpha_i + \sum_j \beta_{ij} \ln v_j, \quad i = 1, 2, \dots, n, \qquad (9.14)$$

where the normalization $\sum_k \alpha_k = 1$ is imposed.

Finally, the estimated parameters are used to calculate the own- and cross-price elasticities,[16] $\eta_{ii} = -1 + \beta_{ii}/s_i$ and $\eta_{ij} = \beta_{ij}/s_i$, as well as the cross-elasticities of substitution, using the Slutsky equation, $\sigma_{ij} = 1 + \beta_{ij}/s_i s_j$.

---

[15] "Unfortunately, homotheticity does not generate a dual equivalence relation between direct and indirect weak recursivity" (Blackorby, Primont, and Russell 1975, 29). The algebraic requirement of weak recursive separability is that

$$\partial \left[(\partial f/\partial x_i) / (\partial f/\partial x_j) \right] / \partial x_k = 0, \quad \forall i, j \in I_r, \; k \in I_t, \; t < r.$$

[16] These elasticities are derived from (9.14) by rewriting it as $\ln x_i = \ln s_i - \ln p_i + \ln y$ and using the following general formulas (see, for example, Ewis and Fisher 1984): $n_{ii} = -1 + \partial \ln s_i / \partial \ln p_i$ and $n_{ij} = \partial \ln s_i / \partial \ln p_j$.

9.3.2 Data

Time-series data on the quantities of and the rates of return to the component monetary-asset stocks employed in this chapter derive entirely from official sources at the Federal Reserve Board. It is to be noted that the data reflect the revisions introduced by Farr and Johnson (1985). A brief description of each of the 27 component assets that the Fed currently recognizes as sources of monetary services in the U.S. economy is provided in the Appendix, Table 9A.1. Also observe that, according to the Fed's latest classification scheme, the narrow money measure, M1, consists of assets 1-6; M2 consists of assets 1-18; M3 consists of assets 1-23; and the broad money measure, L, consists of assets 1-27.

The data are monthly and, therefore, are converted to average quarterly data for the period 1970i-1985i. User costs for the various monetary assets are computed according to the user-cost formula (9.3). All quantities are deflated by the Consumer Price Index (all commodities) and population (including overseas) to give per capita real monetary assets.[17]

In constructing monetary aggregates consistent with those computed by the Federal Reserve Board, we take account of the five consolidation factors used to avoid double counting. Specifically, in constructing M1, vault cash at thrifts, demand deposits at thrifts, and other checkable deposits at corporate centrals are added to currency and traveler checks, demand deposits held by business firms, and other checkable deposits, respectively. M2 needed no consolidation adjustment, and in constructing M3, institutional overnight repurchase agreements are subtracted from overnight repurchase agreements.

In order to deal with the "new assets problem," the Fisher quantity index is computed for every time period during which a new asset is introduced (see Diewert 1980, 498-503, for a discussion of this problem). For all other time periods, the Divisia index is computed.

Prior to estimation, the prices are all scaled to equal 1.0 in 1974iii. To ensure that the products of prices and quantities remained unchanged by the rescaling, the quantity series are adjusted accordingly by multiplying each one by the original base-period value of the corresponding price series.

---

[17]A quarterly Consumer Price Index (all commodities) is highly correlated with the implicit GNP deflator.

9.4 Econometric Results

9.4.1 Some Econometric Considerations

Following conventional practice, we specify an additive error term in each share equation and assume that it is normally distributed with zero mean and constant covariance. This assumption and the fact that the dependent variables satisfy an adding-up condition (because this is a singular system) imply that the covariance matrix is also singular. To overcome this problem, we follow Barten (1969), drop one of the equations, and use a full-information maximum-likelihood procedure. In this case, any one equation may be deleted from the system and no additional parametric restrictions are implied.

Given the above assumptions and parametric restrictions, we drop the last equation at each stage of the multistage decision. Initial results, however, lead us to believe that the disturbances are serially correlated. As a result, first-order autocorrelation is assumed, and a result developed by Berndt and Savin (1975) is used. They show that if one assumes no autocorrelation across equations (that is, R is diagonal), the autocorrelation coefficients for each equation must be identical. Consequently, this is what we assume; we estimate, using the same procedure as described above, stochastic budget share equations given by

$$s_t = f_t(v_t, \theta) - R f_{t-1}(v_{t-1}, \theta) + R s_{t-1} + u_t. \qquad (9.15)$$

9.4.2 Results

Maximum-likelihood estimates of the parameters of the homothetic translog model are presented in Tables 9.1-9.3.[18] Table 9.1 pertains to the second stage of the multistage decision, where the demand for Divisia M1 is modelled; Table 9.2 pertains to the third stage, where the demand for Divisia M2 is modelled; and, finally, Table 9.3 pertains to the fourth stage, where the demand for Divisia M3 is modelled. For all three stages, the estimates shown incorporate the correction for autocorrelation discussed above. Numbers in parenthesis are standard errors and appear only in the first relevant place for only the free parameters (that is, parameters that are estimated directly). The own- and cross-price elasticities and diagonal and upper off-diagonal Allen elasticities of substitution (the matrix of the Allen elasticities of substitution is symmetric) calculated at the mean of the data are also presented in these tables, along with their standard errors.

---

[18]These estimates are obtained by using the TSP (version 4.0) econometric package on a Honeywell DPS 7/80 Multics system at the University of Calgary.

TABLE 9.1

The Demand for Divisia M1:
Parameter Estimates, 1970:i-1984:i

Asset i	α_i	β_{i1}	β_{i2}	β_{i3}	β_{i4}	R
(1)	0.333	0.231	−0.084	−0.084	−0.062	0.982
	(0.085)	(0.014)	(0.011)	(0.006)	(—)	(0.013)
(2)	−0.020	−0.084	0.133	−0.019	−0.029	
	(0.144)	(—)	(0.009)	(0.006)	(—)	
(3)	0.317	−0.084	−0.019	0.137	−0.033	
	(0.074)	(—)	(—)	(0.008)	(—)	
(4)	0.369	−0.062	−0.029	−0.033	0.125	
	(—)	(—)	(—)	(—)	(—)	

$DW_1 = 1.541$　　$DW_2 = 1.519$　　$DW_3 = 1.481$
Log of likelihood function $= 683.203$

	Elasticity and Substitution Terms						
	Price Elasticities				Elasticities of Substitution		
Asset i	η_{i1}	η_{i2}	η_{i3}	η_{i4}	σ_{i1}	σ_{i2}	σ_{i3}	σ_{i4}
(1)	−0.502	−0.520	−0.438	−0.347	−0.080	−2.191	−1.286	−0.927
	(0.030)	(0.070)	(0.034)	(0.026)	(0.065)	(0.430)	(0.178)	(0.149)
(2)	−0.182	−0.179	−0.100	−0.163		−0.104	0.473	0.091
	(0.024)	(0.055)	(0.034)	(0.027)		(0.339)	(0.180)	(0.154)
(3)	−0.180	−0.118	−0.284	−0.187			−0.483	−0.040
	(0.014)	(0.040)	(0.043)	(0.047)			(0.229)	(0.261)
(4)	−0.134	−0.181	−0.176	−0.301				−0.671
	(0.010)	(0.030)	(0.044)	(0.039)				(0.218)

Notes:　Standard errors are in parentheses.
Subscripts:　(1) Divisia M1;
　　　　　　(2) savings deposits at savings and loans;
　　　　　　(3) small time deposits at commercial banks; and
　　　　　　(4) small time deposits at thrifts.

These standard errors are computed by linearizing the elasticities around the estimated parameter values and then using the standard formulas for the variance of linear functions of random variables. (This is carried out in a somewhat automatic fashion, using the ANALYZ command in TSP.)

For the case involving the demand for Divisia M1, it can be seen from Table 9.1 that the own- and cross-price elasticities reveal a pattern consistent with demand theory. All own-price elasticities are negative with the own-price elasticity for Divisia M1 being particularly high $\eta_{11} = -0.502$). Looking now at the cross-price elasticities, we see that all are negative, suggesting that the assets are gross complements. The estimated elasticities of substitution, however, show quite different patterns of substitution from the uncompensated price elasticities. All own elasticities of substitution are negative and Divisia M1 is revealed to be an Allen complement of each of the three other assets. Also observe that savings deposits at savings and loans is a net substitute to small time deposits at commercial banks and to small time deposits at thrifts.

For the case involving the demand for Divisia M2, it can be seen from Table 9.2 that all own-price elasticities are negative and the cross-price elasticities, apart from η_{23}, all are negative. All assets are own-price inelastic with the demand for Divisia M2 being much more own-price inelastic than the demand for large time deposits at commercial banks, large time deposits at thrifts, and term repurchase agreements (RP's). All monetary assets are found to be (gross) complements ($\eta_{ij} < 0$) with the exception of η_{23}. Also observe that, in the Divisia M2 equation, the most important price elasticity was Divisia M2's own elasticity. Regarding the Allen elasticities of substitution, it can be seen from Table 9.2 that all own-elasticities of substitution are negative, with the own-elasticity for large time deposits at commercial banks being particularly high ($\sigma_{22} = -5.686$). The assets appear to be net substitutes — with large time deposits at commercial banks and at thrifts, as well as Divisia M2 and large time deposits at commercial banks, being more so.

Finally, for the case involving the demand for Divisia M3, it can be seen from Table 9.3 that the own-price elasticities are all negative, with the own-price elasticity for Divisia M3 being particularly high; short-term Treasury securities seems less sensitive to a change in its own-price. Looking now at the cross-price elasticities, we see that all are negative, suggesting that the assets are gross complements. Finally, regarding the diagonal and upper off-diagonal Allen elasticities of substitution, it can be seen that the own-elasticities of substitution are all negative and that the cross elasticities of substitution, with the exception of σ_{13} and σ_{14}, are all positive.

TABLE 9.2

The Demand for Divisia M2:
Parameter Estimates, 1970:iv-1985:i

Asset i	α_i	β_{i1}	β_{i2}	β_{i3}	β_{i4}	R
(1)	0.068	0.118	−0.004	−0.074	−0.039	0.968
	(0.211)	(0.008)	(0.009)	(0.010)	(—)	(0.020)
(2)	0.068	−0.004	0.008	0.037	−0.042	
	(0.165)	(—)	(0.014)	(0.011)	(—)	
(3)	0.705	−0.074	0.037	0.101	−0.064	
	(0.237)	(—)	(—)	(0.008)	(—)	
(4)	0.157	−0.039	−0.042	−0.064	−0.146	
	(—)	(—)	(—)	(—)	(—)	

$DW_1 = 1.661$ $DW_2= 1.119$ $DW_3= 1.717$
Log of likelihood function $= 430.844$

	Elasticity and Substitution Terms							
	Price Elasticities				Elasticities of Substitution			
Asset i	η_{i1}	η_{i2}	η_{i3}	η_{i4}	σ_{i1}	σ_{i2}	σ_{i3}	σ_{i4}
(1)	−0.272	−0.032	−0.182	−0.137	−0.670	0.769	0.553	0.521
	(0.060)	(0.070)	(0.026)	(0.034)	(0.315)	(0.506)	(0.064)	(0.119)
(2)	−0.027	−0.935	0.092	−0.146		−5.686	1.226	0.491
	(0.060)	(0.105)	(0.029)	(0.019)		(0.752)	(0.072)	(0.066)
(3)	−0.456	0.270	−0.752	−0.223			−0.842	0.225
	(0.066)	(0.085)	(0.021)	(0.023)			(0.051)	(0.080)
(4)	−0.243	−0.301	−0.157	−0.492				−0.707
	(0.060)	(0.039)	(0.016)	(0.036)				(0.124)

Notes: Standard errors are in parentheses.
Subscripts: (1) Divisia M2;
(2) large time deposits at commercial banks;
(3) large time deposits at thrifts; and
(4) term RP's.

TABLE 9.3

THE DEMAND FOR DIVISIA M3:
PARAMETER ESTIMATES, 1970:i-1985:i

Asset i	α_i	β_{i1}	β_{i2}	β_{i3}	β_{i4}	R
(1)	0.364	0.168	−0.009	−0.083	−0.076	0.976
	(0.063)	(0.011)	(0.006)	(0.008)	(—)	(0.022)
(2)	0.111	−0.009	0.071	−0.019	−0.042	
	(0.060)	(—)	(0.003)	(0.006)	(—)	
(3)	0.275	−0.083	−0.019	0.134	−0.032	
	(0.072)	(—)	(—)	(0.014)	(—)	
(4)	0.248	−0.076	−0.042	−0.032	0.152	
	(—)	(—)	(—)	(—)	(—)	

$DW_1 = 1.217$ $DW_2 = 1.624$ $DW_3 = 1.304$
Log of likelihood function $= 598.234$

	Elasticity and Substitution Terms						
	Price Elasticities				Elasticities of Substitution		
Asset i	η_{i1}	η_{i2}	η_{i3}	η_{i4}	σ_{i1}	σ_{i2}	σ_{i3}	σ_{i4}
(1)	−0.560	−0.071	−0.356	−0.296	−0.462	−0.432	−0.531	−0.148
	(0.030)	(0.049)	(0.034)	(0.026)	(0.080)	(0.391)	(0.148)	(0.102)
(2)	−0.023	−0.436	−0.081	−0.166		−2.461	0.648	0.353
	(0.016)	(0.031)	(0.028)	(0.020)		(0.251)	(0.123)	(0.079)
(3)	−0.216	−0.151	−0.421	−0.126			−0.808	0.508
	(0.020)	(0.053)	(0.060)	(0.031)			(0.261)	(0.123)
(4)	−0.199	−0.340	−0.140	−0.410				−0.591
	(0.017)	(0.041)	(0.035)	(0.018)				(0.071)

Notes: Standard errors are in parentheses.

Subscripts: (1) Divisia M3;

(2) savings bonds;

(3) short-term treasury securities; and

(4) a Divisia index over bankers acceptances and commercial paper.

9.4.3   The Separability Tests

One of the most important objectives of this chapter is to discover the structure of preferences over Divisia money and "near money" at successive levels of aggregation. In light of this objective, we will now test for the appropriateness of the aggregation assumptions that underlie the various money measures. For example, a necessary condition for an aggregate to exist is that the aggregator function, defined over the items of the aggregate and other items as well, be weakly separable in the components of the aggregate. Here, maintaining the assumption that the monetary-services utility function (9.4) is strongly recursive separable with homothetic aggregator functions, we test for the appropriateness of the weak-separability conditions at each stage of the multistage decision. This is equivalent to testing for weak homothetic separability, which Barnett (1982, 696) calls the "Consistency Condition."

Here, weak homothetic separability is obtained by combining weak separability with the homotheticity of the aggregation function. This permits the separability hypothesis to be interpreted in terms of direct (rather than solely in terms of indirect) utility. Note that all previous separability tests of which we are aware have tested for either homothetic or quasi-homothetic (homothetic in supernumerary quantities) separability, both of which are substantially stronger than separability (see, for example, Hancock 1987; and Serletis 1987). Also, neither homothetic nor quasi-homothetic separability is necessary for the existence of aggregates. A noteworthy exception and a potentially successful, new approach can be found in Blackorby, Schworm, and Fisher (1986), who test for separability in the production context without maintaining the homotheticity of the aggregator function. That approach, based upon the generalized Barnett model, has not yet been adapted to consumer-demand modelling because of the complications produced in the theory by nonhomotheticity — mainly problems with multistage budgeting and the loss of self-duality of separable structures between direct and indirect utility functions.

The tests we carry out for the weak-homothetic-separability conditions are based on the assumption that the translog functional form is a second-order approximation to an arbitrary utility function. This approach, suggested by Denny and Fuss (1977), provides a less restrictive test for separability than Berndt and Christensen's (1973a,b) framework, which is based on the maintained hypothesis that the translog specification is exact. Note, however, that as Barnett and Choi (1987) argue, the reliability of the various available tests for separability has never been determined (see their discussion of the deficiencies of the usual tests).

Following Serletis (1987), and since there are four variables at each stage of the multistage decision, we distinguish between three separability patterns: the separability of two variables from the other two variables; the symmetric separability of two variables from the other two variables; and the separability of three variables from the fourth. Overall, there are thirteen null hypotheses at each stage of the multistage decision. These hypotheses and the corresponding parametric restrictions are shown in the Appendix Table 9A.2.) For each null hypothesis, we express the independent parametric restrictions in terms of the free parameters of the model and calculate the Wald test statistic which is distributed as a chi-square with degrees of freedom equal to the number of independent parametric restrictions (see Serletis 1987 for more details). The results of the hypotheses tests are presented in Table 9.4.

TABLE 9.4

SEPARABILITY TESTS

Hypothesis	Degrees of Freedom	Wald Statistic			CV (1%)
		Stage 2	Stage 3	Stage 4	
1. [(1,2),3,4]	2	4.064	0.375	4.532	9.21
2. [(1,3),2,4]	2	4.173	4.173	6.450	9.21
3. [(1,4),2,3]	2	2.147	1.385	21.430	9.21
4. [(2,3),1,4]	2	2.372	8.002	10.992	9.21
5. [(2,4),1,3]	2	2.473	1.898	3.675	9.21
6. [(3,4),1,2]	2	1.298	12.472	3.470	9.21
7. [(1,2), (3,4)]	3	4.141	13.829	4.578	11.34
8. [(1,3), (2,4)]	3	4.231	19.295	7.833	11.34
9. [(1,4), (2,3)]	3	2.367	9.392	22.603	11.34
10. [(1,2,3), 4]	2	1.998	2.450	3.783	9.21
11. [(2,3,4), 1]	2	2.362	0.463	1.258	9.21
12. [(1,2,4), 3]	2	1.813	0.968	1.799	9.21
13. [(1,3,4), 2]	2	4.497	0.247	12.910	9.21

The results are remarkable and very rich in structural information. In the second stage, where Divisia M1 is treated as an elementary asset, all hypotheses of weak separability are accepted. This suggests that we cannot reject money measures broader than M1, but since the $[1, 2, 3, 4]$ group (which is Divisia M2) is not testable, we are left with a choice between a narrow and a broad aggregate. However, in the third and fourth stages, the results are not that conclusive. In the third stage, of the thirteen null hypotheses, three cannot be rejected (rows 6, 7, and 8). This implies that we cannot accept the conditions for the aggregation of large time deposits at thrifts and term RP's (row 6), nor the conditions for the further aggregation of Divisia M2, large time deposits at thrifts and at commercial banks, and term RP's (row 8). Also, regarding the separability of three variables from the fourth, the results indicate that, when money is measured as Divisia M2, the independent estimation of the three-argument–quantity-aggregator functions — $f_2^a(1,2,3)$, $f_2^b(1,2,4)$, and $f_2^c(1,3,4)$ — is possible. Alternatively, the values of these functions could be candidates for a definition of money suggested by this approach. In the fourth stage of the thirteen null hypotheses, four cannot be accepted (rows 3, 4, 9, and 13). Here, we cannot accept the hypothesis that Divisia M3 could be expanded to include savings bonds and short-term treasury securities. Also, the results indicate that when money is measured as Divisia M3, the independent estimation of the three-argument–quantity-aggregator functions — $f_3^a(1,2,3)$ and $f_3^b(1,2,4)$ — is possible.

Therefore, these econometric findings provide strong empirical support for monetary aggregates broader than M1, since M1, when treated as an elementary asset, can always be grouped together with other assets to form a broader money measure.[19] The results, however, provide no direct evidence regarding the appropriateness of the strong-recursive-separability assumptions implicit in the monetary-services utility function (9.4). Testing of these assumptions would require the estimation of a highly disaggregated demand system which could be econometrically intractable.[20]

9.5   Summary and Concluding Remarks

This chapter lays out an explicit theoretical framework for the demand for money; derives Divisia money-demand equations at different levels of aggregation, using the homothetic translog flexible functional form; and tests these equations on quarterly U.S. data for 1970i-1985i. The equations, after correcting for autocorrelation, fit quite well, and the empirical results, in addition to providing some information regarding money and "near-monies" substitutability, also provide interesting and useful informa-

---

[19]Even if the weak seprability conditions are rejected, aggregation might still be valid if the conditions for Hicksian aggregations are met. Investigation of the Hicksian aggregation conditions, however, is beyond the scope of this paper.

[20]For example, with η elementary assets, the homothetic translog has $\eta(\eta+3)/2$ parameters out of which $[\eta(\eta+1)-2]/2$ are free (that is, estimated directly). In the present application with $\eta = 27$, in the absence of any subaggregation, the number of free parameters would be 377.

tion regarding the appropriateness of the weak-separability (aggregation) assumptions underlying the different levels of monetary aggregation.

There is evidence that Divisia money is own-price inelastic and a gross complement to "near-monies" at the different aggregation levels. In terms of the Allen elasticities of substitution, Divisia M1 is revealed to be a net complement to "near monies," Divisia M2 is revealed to be a net substitute to "near monies," and Divisia M3 is revealed to be a net substitute to savings bonds and a net complement to short-term Treasury securities and to a Divisia index over bankers acceptances and commercial paper.

While most of the weak-separability hypotheses which are tested in this study cannot be rejected, this does not necessarily provide any valuable insight with regards to the "true" pattern of separability. Because of the high degree of aggregation, there has been little discussion of the problem of the choice of the grouping pattern to be imposed on the model. In particular, we start from a structure specified *a priori*, and we then use it to generate parameter estimates and tests of the validity of the weak separability restrictions. The test results for these *a priori* groupings do indicate that the weak-separability conditions cannot be rejected, especially at the low, M1 level of aggregation, thereby suggesting that the most popular definition of money, M1, can be expanded by adding in more of the quantity of financial intermediation. However, the sample is not exploited to find other, potentially more suitable groupings or perhaps the "optimal' grouping. This would require the estimation of a highly disaggregated demand system or perhaps, as Barnett and Choi (1987) suggest, newer, more sophisticated separability tests.

In this chapter we use homothetic utility functions throughout. While that assumption greatly simplifies the work and is desirable in a first attempt at using the theory fully, the assumption of homotheticity has strong implications for demand behavior, since it imposes unitary expenditure elasticities and expenditure shares that are independent of total expenditure. Furthermore, as Kohler (1983) proves, homotheticity restricts the Slutsky equation in ways that bias the own-price elasticity upwards. Weakening the homotheticity assumption is clearly an area for productive future research.

In this chapter little attention is paid to the dynamic structure of the models used, although the autoregressive error specification [equation (9.15)] may be accommodating a dynamic structure in the models which could be better represented by some other dynamic formulation. More recently, a number of demand studies focus attention on the development of dynamic generalizations of the traditional, static models, which would allow a test of the static models themselves as well as the theoretical restrictions and simplifications of demand theory. Anderson and Blundell (1982), for example, develop an unrestricted dynamic formulation to accommodate short-run disequilibrium situations by including lagged endogenous and exogenous variables as regressors. This approach to dynamic specification, although it stands in contrast to the theoretical approaches that maintain specific theories of dynamic adjustment, allows tests of the static specifications as well as the less dynamic specifications (that is, dynamic specifications representing particular underlying theories of short-run adjustment such as the autoregressive or partial-adjustment models). Consequently, the Anderson and Blundell approach is clearly an attractive feature on which to build.

9.6 Appendix

TABLE 9A.1

COMPONENTS OF THE MONETARY AGGREGATES

Component	Mnemonic	Asset Description
1	CUR	Currency and traveler checks
2	DDCON	Demand deposits held by consumers
3	DDBUS	Demand deposits held by businesses
4	OCD	Other checkable deposits
5	SNOWC	Super NOW accounts at commercial banks
6	SNOWT	Super NOW accounts at thrifts
7	ONRP	Overnight RP's
8	ONED	Overnight Eurodollars
9	MMMF	Money market mutual fund shares
10	MMDAC	MMDAs at commercial banks
11	MMDAT	MMDAs at thrifts
12	SDCB	Savings deposits at commercial banks
13	SDSL	Savings deposits at S&Ls
14	SDMSB	Savings deposits at mutual savings banks
15	SDCU	Savings deposits at credit unions
16	STDCB	Small time deposits and retail RP's at commercial banks
17	STDTH	Small time deposits at S&L's and MSB and retail RP's of thrifts
18	STDCU	Small time deposits at credit unions
19	LTDCB	Large time deposits at commercial banks
20	LTDTH	Large time deposits at thrifts
21	MMMFI	Institutional money market mutual funds
22	TRP	Term RP's at commercial banks and thrifts
23	TED	Term Eurodollars
24	SB	Savings bonds
25	STTS	Short-term Treasury securities
26	BA	Bankers acceptances
27	CP	Commercial paper

TABLE 9A.2

Hypothesis	Parametric Restrictions	No. of Independent Parametric Restrictions
$[(1,2),3,4]$	$\alpha_1/\alpha_2 = \beta_{13}/\beta_{23} = \beta_{14}/\beta_{24}$	2
$[(1,3),2,4]$	$\alpha_1/\alpha_3 = \beta_{12}/\beta_{23} = \beta_{14}\beta_{34}$	2
$[(1,4),2,3]$	$\alpha_1/\alpha_4 = \beta_{12}/\beta_{24} = \beta_{13}/\beta_{34}$	2
$[(2,3),1,4]$	$\alpha_2/\alpha_3 = \beta_{12}/\beta_{13} = \beta_{24}/\beta_{34}$	2
$[(2,4),1,2]$	$\alpha_2/\alpha_4 = \beta_{12}/\beta_{14} = \beta_{23}/\beta_{34}$	2
$[(3,4),1,2]$	$\alpha_3/\alpha_4 = \beta_{13}/\beta_{14} = \beta_{23}/\beta_{24}$	2
$[(1,2),(3,4)]$	$\alpha_1/\alpha_2 = \beta_{13}/\beta_{23} = \beta_{14}/\beta_{24}$ $\alpha_3/\alpha_4 = \beta_{13}/\beta_{14} = \beta_{23}/\beta_{24}$	3
$[(1,3),(2,4)]$	$\alpha_1/\alpha_3 = \beta_{12}/\beta_{23} = \beta_{14}/\beta_{34}$ $\alpha_2/\alpha_4 = \beta_{12}/\beta_{14} = \beta_{23}/\beta_{34}$	3
$[(1,4),(2,3)]$	$\alpha_1/\alpha_4 = \beta_{12}/\beta_{24} = \beta_{13}/\beta_{34}$ $\alpha_2/\alpha_3 = \beta_{12}/\beta_{13} = \beta_{24}/\beta_{34}$	3
$[(1,2,3),4]$	$\alpha_1\alpha_2 = \beta_{14}/\beta_{24}$ $\alpha_1/\alpha_3 = \beta_{14}/\beta_{34}$ $\alpha_2\alpha_3 = \beta_{24}/\beta_{34}$	2
$[(2,3,4),1]$	$\alpha_2/\alpha_3 = \beta_{12}/\beta_{13}$ $\alpha_2/\alpha_4 = \beta_{12}/\beta_{14}$ $\alpha_3/\alpha_4 = \beta_{13}/\beta_{14}$	2
$[(1,2,4),3]$	$\alpha_1/\alpha_2 = \beta_{13}/\beta_{23}$ $\alpha_1/\alpha_4 = \beta_{13}/\beta_{34}$ $\alpha_2/\alpha_4 = \beta_{23}/\beta_{34}$	2
$[(1,3,4),2]$	$\alpha_1/\alpha_3 = \beta_{12}/\beta_{23}$ $\alpha_1/\alpha_4 = \beta_{12}/\beta_{24}$ $\alpha_3/\alpha_4 = \beta_{23}/\beta_{24}$	2

Note: The derivation of the parametric restrictions is based on the apparatus developed by Denny and Fuss (1977). The parameters are those in the share equation, (9.14).

Chapter 10

Translog Flexible Functional Forms and Substitutability of Monetary Assets

Apostolos Serletis*

10.1 Introduction

The issue of substitutability/complementarity relationship of money and other monetary assets has attracted a great deal of attention recently in the literature. One reason for this concern is that the degree of substitutability among monetary assets has been used — explicitly or implicitly — to provide a rationale for the appropriate definition of money, which itself is an important problem in monetary theory, and it has been the focus of continuing controversy over the years.

Despite the volume of research undertaken, however, the results are still inconclusive and suggestive of a need for further empirical exploration. As Feige and Pearce (1977) put it, "the issue of substitutability between money and near-monies is likely to continue to be an important question for monetary economics just as it has been since the days of the currency-banking school controversy" (p. 465).

A number of recent works including Donovan (1978), Offenbacher (1979), Barnett (1981, 1983), Ewis and Fisher (1984, 1985), Serletis and Robb (1986), and Serletis (1987) have followed Chetty's (1969) innovative work and attempted to estimate the degree of substitutability among monetary assets using the demand-system approach, which views monetary assets as durable goods yielding a flow of nonobservable services that enter as arguments in aggregator functions to the demand for monetary assets. Those works were interesting and attractive; they included estimates of the degree of substitutability using some constrained flexible functional forms or unconstrained versions used to test for theoretical and functional form restrictions. Yet, Barnett (1983), Serletis and Robb (1986), and Serletis (1987) modeled the demand for aggregate monetary assets.

This approach, however, involves serious problems of estimation and interpretation. As Barnett and Lee (1985) and Diewert and Wales (1987) argued, one of the most important problems in estimating flexible functional forms is that most of the available flexible functional forms tend to violate the regularity conditions that are implied by economic theory, thereby generating noncredible elasticity estimates. For reference, consider the following from Barnett, Lee, and Wolfe (1985): "When originally proposed, those models were intended to be used only in those cases in which the specified utility function was found to be monotonically increasing and strictly quasi concave at *each* data point" (p. 3).

This chapter also takes a demand-system approach to the demand for monetary assets and attempts to establish the nature of the relationship between four assets [demand deposits, savings deposits at savings and loans institutions (S&L's), small time deposits at S&L's, and short-term treasury securities] using quarterly U.S. time-series data. This is achieved by estimating a sequence of nested demand systems: the *generalized translog* (GTL); the (BTL), *basic translog* a special case of the GTL; the *linear translog* (LTL), a homothetic special case of the GTL (or equivalently, a quasi-homothetic special case of the BTL); and the *homothetic translog* (HTL), a homothetic special case of the BTL.

Although the primary focus is on the estimation of price and substitution elasticities, there are two other features of the study that are important. The first is that the estimates of the degree of substitutability of monetary assets are based on the assumption that the aggregator function specifications are *flexible functional forms* — functional forms with enough free parameters to approximate to the second order an arbitrary-wide-continuously-differentiable function. [See Barnett (1983) for various formal definitions of the flexibility property.] The second feature is that demand system criteria are used to choose among the estimated translog forms. In particular, I perform tests of the nested structures, as well as tests on economic theory, to establish whether the parameter estimates are consistent with the utility-maximizing hypothesis underlying the models. I conclude, in the empirical part of the chapter, that the GTL satisfies the theoretical regularity conditions at each point of the data set, thereby generating empirically credible elasticity estimates. This is not a common result with translog specifications.

The plan of the chapter is as follows: Section 10.2 briefly outlines a general theoretical model. Section 10.3 is concerned with the specification of several translog indirect utility functions and the derivation of monetary asset demand equations. Details of data considerations are also provided. In Section 10.4, I spell out the stochastic specification and the method of estimation and discuss the results in terms of standard demand analysis. I conclude, in Section 10.5, with a discussion of the merits of the empirical findings and some comments and directions for future research.

10.2 The Theoretical Background

To investigate consumer monetary expenditure decisions in a utility-maximizing framework and to construct a demand system involving only the user costs, the quantities of monetary assets, and expenditure on the services of assets, I suppose an economy with identical individuals whose direct utility function is weakly separable (a direct tree) of the form

$$u = u(c, l, f(x)), \tag{10.1}$$

where c is a vector of the services of consumption goods , l is leisure time, and x is a vector of the services of monetary assets (assumed to be proportional to the stocks). The utility-tree structure (10.1) is treated as a maintained hypothesis in this chapter, although it implies the assumption that the demand for monetary services is independent of relative prices outside the monetary group.

Implicit in a utility-tree structure is a two-stage model of consumer behavior. In the first stage the consumer allocates his expenditure among broad categories, and then in the second stage he allocates expenditures within each category. This notion of two-stage optimization was investigated in the context of consumer theory by Strotz (1957, 1959) and Gorman (1959). The particular two-level structure that I would wish to utilize can be expressed by the following classical consumer problem:

$$\max_{x} f(x) \quad \text{subject to} \quad p'x = m, \tag{10.2}$$

in which $f(x)$, the monetary services aggregator function (quantity index), is assumed to satisfy the usual regularity conditions. The expenditure on the services of monetary assets is denoted by m, and p is a vector of monetary asset user costs, with the ith component given by

$$p_i = (R - r_i)/(1 + R), \qquad (10.3)$$

which denotes the discounted interest foregone by holding a dollar's worth of that asset. Here, R is the "benchmark" rate of interest and r_i is the market yield on the ith asset. The theoretical derivation of the user cost formula is by Barnett (1978).

By applying duality theory, a corresponding indirect aggregator function (price index) can then be derived, and all that remains in order to obtain a monetary asset demand system is to choose a specific functional form for the indirect aggregator function and apply Roy's identity. I take up this problem in the following section.

10.3   Demand System Specification and Data

10.3.1   Functional Forms

In recent years a number of empirical studies have made use of the flexible-functional-forms method to approximate aggregator functions. The advantage of this method is that the corresponding expenditure system will adequately approximate systems resulting from a broad class of aggregator functions. I decided to use the approximate translog specification in this analysis and estimate a sequence of four nested demand systems, the GTL, the BTL, the LTL, and the HTL. The GTL is a relatively new demand system, used by Pollak and Wales (1980) and Atrostic (1982).

Note, however, that as the translog is capable of approximating an arbitrary function only locally (at a point), a more constructive approach would be based on the use of flexible functional forms that possess global properties. Three such forms are the Fourier flexible functional form, the minflex Laurent generalized Leontief form, and the minflex Laurent translog flexible functional forms. The Fourier form uses the Fourier series expansion as the approximating mechanism (see Gallant 1981) and the Laurent minflex forms use the Laurent series expansion — a generalization of the Taylor series expansion, possessing a better-behaved remainder term — as the approximating mechanism (see Barnett 1985; Barnett and Lee 1985; Barnett, Lee, and Wolfe 1985).

The GTL flexible form of an indirect utility function may be written as

$$\ln V = \alpha_0 + \sum_i \alpha_i \ln \left[p_i / \left(m - \sum_k p_k \gamma_k \right) \right]$$

$$+ \frac{1}{2} \sum_i \sum_j \beta_{ij} \ln \left[p_i / \left(m - \sum_k p_k \gamma_k \right) \right]$$

$$\times \ln \left[p_j / \left(m - \sum_k p_k \gamma_k \right) \right], \tag{10.4}$$

with the symmetry restrictions, $\beta_{ij} = \beta_{ji}$, imposed. Applying Roy's identity allows us to derive the GTL model's share equations

$$s_i = \frac{p_i \gamma_i}{m} + \left[1 - \left(\sum_k p_k \gamma_k \right) / m \right]$$

$$\times \frac{\alpha_i + \sum_j \beta_{ij} \ln \left[p_j / (m - \sum_k p_k \gamma_k) \right]}{\sum_i \alpha_i + \sum_j \beta_{jM} \ln \left[p_j / (m - \sum_k p_k \gamma_k) \right]} + e_i, \tag{10.5}$$

for $i = 1, \ldots, n$, where s_i is the budget share of the ith asset, p_i is the user cost, m is the value of total expenditure on monetary assets, e_i is the random disturbance, and the α's, β's, and γ's are parameters to be estimated. The parameters (β_{ij}, β_{jM}) satisfy the restriction $\beta_{jM} = \sum_i \beta_{ji}$.

The BTL flexible form can be derived by imposing some restrictions on the GTL form, namely,

$$\gamma_i = 0 \quad \text{for all } i. \tag{10.6}$$

Applying restriction (10.6) to the GTL, we can derive the BTL model's share equations

$$s_i = \frac{\alpha_i + \sum_j \beta_{ij} \ln \left[p_j / m \right]}{\sum_i \alpha_i + \sum_j \beta_{jM} \ln \left[p_j / m \right]} + e_i, \quad i = 1, \ldots, n. \tag{10.7}$$

The LTL flexible form can be derived by imposing the restriction

$$\sum_i \beta_{ij} = 0 \quad \text{for all } j. \tag{10.8}$$

on the GTL. The LTL model's share equations are

$$s_i = \frac{p_i \gamma_i}{m} + \left[1 - \left(\sum_k p_k \gamma_k \right) / m \right]$$

$$\times \frac{\alpha_i + \sum_j \beta_{ij} \ln \left[p_j / (m - \sum_k p_k \gamma_k) \right]}{\sum_i \alpha_i} + e_i, \tag{10.9}$$

for $i = 1, \ldots, n$. This equation has linear Engel curves (income-consumption paths for fixed prices) but does not require them to pass through the origin.

Finally, the HTL flexible form can be derived either by imposing restrictions (10.6) and (10.8) on the GTL or by imposing restriction (10.8) on the BTL. The HTL model's share equation is

$$s_i = \frac{\alpha_i + \sum_j \beta_{ij} \ln [p_j/m]}{\sum_i \alpha_i} + e_i, \quad i = 1, \ldots, n. \qquad (10.10)$$

Equation (10.10) requires the Engel curves to pass through the origin.

Estimation of (10.5), (10.7), (10.9), or (10.10) requires some parameter normalization, as the share equations are homogeneous of degree 0 in the α's. I use the normalization

$$\sum_i \alpha_i = 1 \qquad (10.11)$$

for all budget-share systems.

10.3.2 Data

Time series data on interest rates and quantities of monetary assets employed in this chapter were used by Ewis and Fisher (1984, 1985) and derive entirely from the editorial office of the *Journal of Money, Credit, and Banking*. Basically, I deal with a portfolio of demand deposits (DD), savings deposits at S&L's (SDSL), small time deposits at S&L's (STDSL), and short-term treasury securities (STTS). As Ewis and Fisher (1984, 1985) reported, the data were monthly and converted to average quarterly data for the period 1969I-1979IV. The interest rate on DD is the implicit interest rate that was constructed by B. Klein and updated by Offenbacher (1979). User costs for the various monetary assets were computed according to the user-cost formula (10.3). All quantities were deflated by the Consumer Price Index (all commodities) and population (including overseas) to give per capita real monetary assets.

Prior to estimation, the prices were all scaled to 1.0 in 1969II. To ensure that the product of price and quantity series remained unchanged by the rescaling, the quantity series were adjusted accordingly by multiplying each one by the original base period value of the corresponding price series.

10.4 Econometric Results

In the previous section, I derived four distinct sets of budget-share equations, which for convenience of comparison are drawn together and presented in Table 10.1. Each set of budget share equations was estimated using an algorithm that generates full-information maximum likelihood (FIML) estimates under the assumed error structure. The errors are assumed to be additive, jointly normally distributed with zero means, and with constant but unknown variances and covariances. This distributional assumption on the errors is standard and is fundamental in the derivation of the FIML estimator. A multivariate logistic distribution might be a better assumption, but there is no algorithm that will generate FIML estimates under this assumption. Thus each set of budget share equations can be written as

$$s_t = f_t(x_t, \theta) + e_t. \tag{10.12}$$

Since demand theory provides that the budget shares sum to 1, it follows that the disturbance covariance matrix is singular. If autocorrelation in the disturbances is absent (as assumed here), Barten (1969) showed that FIML estimates of the parameters can be obtained by arbitrarily deleting an equation in such a system and that the estimation results are invariant with respect to the equation deleted. I initially estimated the model in (10.12). The computed equation-by-equation Durbin-Watson statistics were low, however, and this led me to believe that the disturbances were serially correlated. I, therefore, assumed a first-order autoregressive process such that

$$u_t = Ru_{t-1} + \varepsilon_t, \tag{10.13}$$

where $R = [R_{ij}]$ is a matrix of unknown parameters and ε_t is a nonautocorrelated vector disturbance term with constant covariance matrix. Then a result developed by Berndt and Savin (1975) was used. They showed that if one assumes no autocorrelation across equations (i.e., R is diagonal), the autocorrelation coefficients for each equation must be identical. Consequently this is what I have assumed, and by writing equation (10.12) for period $t-1$, multiplying by R, and substituting, I estimated stochastic budget share equations given by

$$s_t = f_t(x_t, \theta) - Rf(x_{t-1}, \theta) + Rs_{t-1} + \varepsilon_t. \tag{10.14}$$

For this work the equation for STTS is deleted. The parameter estimates of the deleted equation can be recovered from the restrictions imposed. To check invariance of maximum-likelihood parameter estimates with respect to the equation deleted, I estimated the models more than once, deleting a different equation each time.

All of the estimations were carried out with the TSP econometric package on a CDC 175 computer at the University of Calgary. The estimation results for the GTL [equation (10.5)], the BTL [equation (10.7)], the LTL [equation (10.9)], and the HTL [equation (10.10)] are presented in Table 10.2. Numbers in parenthesis are asymptotic standard errors and appear only in the first relevant place for only the free parameters (i.e., parameters that are estimated directly). With four assets, the GTL contains 17 free parameters; the BTL, like the LTL, contains 13 free parameters; and the HTL contains 9 free parameters (see Table 10.1).

In what follows, I choose among the estimated translog forms using demand system criteria and present the price and expenditure elasticities, as well as the elasticities of substitution.

10.4.1   The Functional-Form Tests

The results of the tests on functional form are given in Figure 10.1. The critical values (CV's) refer to the 1% level of significance, g stands for the number of restrictions, and LR represents the likelihood ratio statistic. Comparisons of the likelihood values and the likelihood ratio tests show that, although the GTL is a statistically insignificant improvement over the BTL ($\gamma_i = 0$ for all i), it is a significant generalization of both of its other nested specializations, the LTL ($\sum_i \beta_{ij} = 0$) and the HTL ($\sum_i \beta_{ij} = 0, \gamma_i = 0, \forall i$). Moreover, the BTL is a statistically significant improvement over the HTL ($\sum_i \beta_{ij} = 0$), but I cannot choose between the BTL and the LTL using likelihood ratio tests, since they are not nested hypotheses, although each is a special case of the GTL.

The results, therefore, indicate a decisive rejection of both homotheticity (linear Engel curves passing through the origin) and quasi-homotheticity (linear Engel curves not necessarily passing through the origin). As a consequence, my results decisively reject consistency of the two-stage optimization procedure, since such consistency rests on the assumption of either homothetically or quasi-homothetically separable preferences. Of course, the outcome of these tests might be influenced by the empirical modeling method. For example, no attention has been paid to the dynamic structure of the models. A particularly constructive approach would be to test for homotheticity and quasi-homotheticity after generalizing these models to allow interrelated dynamic feedback between current and past decisions. See, for example, Anderson and Blundell (1982).

10.4.2   The Regularity Tests

I now proceed to perform tests to establish whether the parameter estimates are consistent with the utility-maximizing hypothesis underlying the models. Following Christensen, Jorgenson, and Lau (1975), I restrict the parameters in (10.5), (10.7), (10.9), and (10.10), as part of the maintaine

TABLE 10.1

BUDGET SHARE EQUATIONS FOR THE GTL FORM AND ITS SPECIAL CASES

Model	Budget-share equations	Number of parameters		Restrictions used in estimation	Number of free parameters	
		General	Four assets		General	Four assets
GTL	$s_i = \frac{p_i\gamma_i}{m} + \left(1 - \frac{\sum_k p_k\gamma_k}{m}\right)$ $\times \frac{\alpha_i\left[\sum_j \beta_{ij}\ln\left[p_j/\left(m-\sum_k p_k\gamma_k\right)\right]\right]}{\sum \alpha_i + \sum_j \beta_{jm}\ln\left[p_j/\left(m-\sum_k p_k\gamma_k\right)\right]} + e_i$ $\beta_{ij} = \beta_{ji}$	$\eta(\eta+5)/2$	18	$\sum_i \alpha_i = 1$	$[\eta(\eta+5)-2]/2$	17
BTL	$s_i = \frac{\alpha_i + \sum_j \beta_{ij}\ln(p_j/m)}{\sum \alpha_i + \sum_j \beta_{jM}\ln(p_j/m)} + e_i$ $\beta_{ij} = \beta_{ji}$	$\eta(\eta+3)/2$	14	$\sum_i \alpha_i = 1$	$[\eta(\eta+3)-2]/2$	13
LTL	$s_i = \frac{p_i\gamma_i}{m} + \left(1 - \frac{\sum_k p_k\gamma_k}{m}\right)$ $\times \frac{\alpha_i + \sum_j \beta_{ij}\ln\left[p_j/\left(m-\sum_k p_k\gamma_k\right)\right]}{\sum \alpha_i} + e_i$ $\beta_{ij} = \beta_{ji}$	$\eta(\eta+5)/2$	18	$\sum_i \alpha_{ij} = 0$ $\sum_j \beta_{ij} = 0$	$[\eta(\eta+3)-2]/2$	13
HTL	$s_i = \frac{\alpha_i + \sum_j \beta_{ij}\ln(p_j/m)}{\sum \alpha_i} + e_i$ $\beta_{ij} - \beta_{ji}$	$\eta(\eta+3)/2$	14	$\sum_i \alpha_i = 1$ $\sum_j \beta_{ij} = 0$	$[\eta(\eta+1)-2]/2$	9

TABLE 10.2

PARAMETER ESTIMATES FOR THE GTL MODEL AND SPECIAL CASES

Asset i	γ_i	α_i	β_{i1}	β_{i2}	β_{i3}	β_{i4}	R
GTL model							
DD	-.121 (.150)	.204 (.140)	.208 (.107)	-.198 (.015)	-.531 (.039)	-.009 (.004)	.987 (.005)
SDSL	-.051 (.074)	.108 (.101)	-.198 (—)	.105 (.068)	.004 (.015)	-.008 (.002)	
STDSL	-.499 (.421)	.615 (.188)	-.531 (—)	.004 (—)	.269 (.104)	-.014 (.008)	
STTS	-.003 (.021)	.073 (—)	-.009 (—)	-.008 (—)	-.014 (—)	.025 (.016)	
BTL model							
DD		.080 (.328)	.288 (.052)	-.063 (.029)	-.075 (.034)	-.012 (.007)	.990 (.008)
SDSL		.045 (.233)	-.063 (—)	.168 (.021)	-.017 (.019)	-.014 (.006)	
STDSL		.779 (.485)	-.075 (—)	-.017 (—)	.165 (.040)	-.004 (.008)	
STTS		.096 (—)	-.012 (—)	-.014 (—)	-.004 (—)	.051 (.006)	
LTL model							
DD	.074 (.066)	.190 (.088)	.206 (.015)	-.073 (.015)	-.120 (.019)	-.013 (—)	.980 (.009)
SDSL	.027 (.062)	.126 (.112)	-.073 (—)	.138 (.032)	-.049 (.021)	-.016 (—)	
STDSL	-.170 (.151)	.620 (.166)	-.120 (—)	-.049 (—)	.176 (.021)	-.007 (—)	
STTS	.027 (.020)	.063 (—)	-.013 (—)	-.016 (—)	-.007 (—)	.036 (—)	
HTL model							
DD		.162 (.249)	.222 (.005)	-.097 (.006)	-.103 (.004)	-.022 (—)	.988 (.010)
SDSL		-.003 (.229)	-.097 (—)	.156 (.011)	-.041 (.007)	-.018 (—)	
STDSL		.724 (.439)	-.103 (—)	-.041 (—)	.155 (.007)	-.011 (—)	
STTS		.117 (—)	-.022 (—)	-.018 (—)	-.011 (—)	.051 (—)	

Note: A dash indicates that the parameter was derived from the restrictions imposed. The estimates shown incorporate the correction for serial correlation discussed previously.

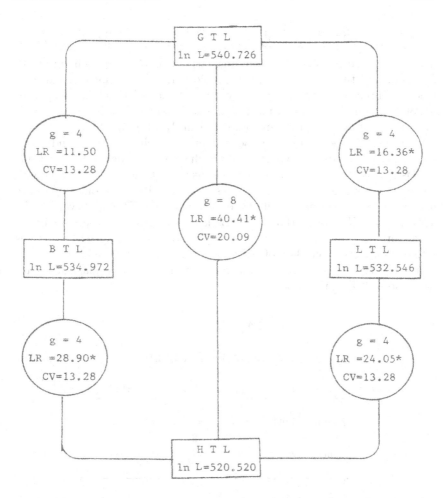

Figure 10.1: Tests on the Functional Form. An asterisk by the value of an LR indicates rejection at the 1% level.

hypothesis, to satisfy adding up and symmetry. I do test, however, at each data point, the theoretical restrictions that are not part of the maintained hypothesis — that is, nonnegativity, monotonicity, and the curvature conditions on the indirect utility function.

The nonnegativity restriction requires that the values of the fitted demand functions be nonnegative $(x_i \geq 0, \forall i)$, and it can easily be checked by direct computation of the values of the fitted budget shares. The monotonicity restriction requires that the indirect utility function be monotonically decreasing and it can also be checked by direct computation of the values of the gradient vector of the estimated indirect utility function. Finally, the curvature conditions require quasi-convexity of the indirect utility function, and they can be checked, provided the monotonicity conditions hold, by direct computation of the matrix of the Allen partial elasticities of substitution. This matrix must be negative semidefinite.

The results of the tests are presented in Table 10.3. Numbers in the table represent the number of observations in which the corresponding restrictions are satisfied. The striking conclusion to be derived from Table 10.3 is that all three theoretical restrictions are satisfied at all observations by the GTL, whereas the BTL satisfies monotonicity for about 74% of the observations and quasiconvexity for only about 40% of the observations. In addition, the LTL outperforms the BTL on the basis of monotonicity; it does more poorly, however, in terms of quasiconvexity — quasiconvexity is satisfied for only about 30% of the observations. Finally, the HTL satisfied monotonicity for about 41% of the observations and it is quasiconvex for only about 28% of the observations.

TABLE 10.3

REGULARITY-TEST RESULTS

Tests	GTL	BTL	LTL	HTL
Nonnegativity	43	43	43	43
Monotonicity	43	32	43	18
Quasiconvexity	43	17	13	12

10.4.3   The Elasticities

Having chosen GTL as a suitable maintained hypothesis, I now turn to interpret the estimated parameter values by computing the expenditure and price elasticities and the Allen elasticities of substitution. The expenditure and price-elasticity formulas are presented in Table 10.4. For a comparison, the elasticity formulas for the BTL, LTL, and HTL are also presented (and they are later used to calculate the elasticities). With any of the models, the elasticity of substitution between assets i and j, σ_{ij}, can be computed from the income elasticities and the price elasticities by using the Slutsky equation $\sigma_{ij} = \eta_i + \eta_{ij}/s_j$.

The elasticities, calculated at the mean of the data, are presented in Table 10.5, along with their standard errors. These standard errors were computed by linearizing the elasticity formulas around the estimated parameter values and then by using the standard formulas for the variance of linear functions of random variables. This was carried out in a somewhat automatic fashion by using the ANALYZ command in TSP. Such an approximation technique was recommended for translog aggregator functions by Toers (1980, 1982), and as Green, Hahn, and Rocke (1987) concluded, "it appears that demand analysts can have a certain amount of confidence in the asymptotic standard errors that are obtained from using Taylor series approximations" (p. 148).

It is interesting to note that the estimated elasticities are quite different across functional forms, thus supporting the likelihood ratio tests and the regularity tests of the two previous subsections. Given that we found the GTL form preferable, since it satisfies the important regularity conditions of demand theory at all of our sample points, the ensuing discussion concentrates on the GTL estimates only.

Two of the four GTL expenditure elasticities are significant at the 5% level and the other two at the 10% level. They suggest that all monetary assets, with the exemption of STTS, are luxury goods, with STDSL being more so; STTS are expenditure inelastic ($\eta_4 = .870$). One might be tempted to explain erroneously these findings by concluding that there are no economies of scale in money holdings. In this analysis, however, expenditure is defined as the sum of expenditures on individual monetary services and not as total spending. Therefore, no inference can be made as to whether a rise in total spending leads to a less-than-proportionate increase in the average holding of real money. The expenditure elasticity estimates for the BTL and the LTL are similar, but they are lower relative to the GTL. They are all, however, significant at the 1% level. Unit-expenditure elasticities occur in the HTL in which budget shares are unaffected by expenditure levels.

One of the four GTL-estimated own-price elasticities is significant at the 1% level and two are significant at the 5% level. They are all negative with the own-price elasticities for DD and (to a lesser extent) STDSL being particularly high. SDSL seems less sensitive to a change in its own price. Looking now at the cross-price elasticities, we see that most of them are significant at the 1% level and that, apart from η_{14}, η_{24}, and η_{34}, all are negative, suggesting that the assets are gross complements, although the effects are generally small. In contrast, the BTL, LTL, and HTL own-price elasticities are smaller than the GTL elasticities, and the cross-price elasticities indicate that *all* assets are gross complements. The latter is hard to believe and highlights the difference in estimates based on the different translog forms.

TABLE 10.4

Elasticity Formulas for the GTL Form and its Special Cases

Form	Expenditure elasticities	Own-price elasticities	Cross-price elasticities
GTL	$\eta_i = 1 + [-p_i\gamma_i/m + \lambda(\sum_k p_k\gamma_k)/$ $m - \sum_i\sum_j\beta_{ij}/\psi)/$ $m^* - \sum_j\beta_{ij}/\psi]/s_i$	$\eta_{ii} = -1 + [p_i\gamma_i(m^*-\lambda)\psi + m^*(m^*\beta_{ii}$ $+ p_i\gamma_i\sum_j\beta_{ij} - \lambda(m^*\sum_j\beta_{ij}$ $+ p_i\gamma_i\sum_i\sum_j\beta_{ij})]\div mm^* s_i\psi$	$\eta_{ij} = \Big[m^*\big(m^*\beta_{il} + p_i\gamma_{il}\sum_j\beta_{ij}\big)$ $-\lambda\big(m^*\sum_j\beta_{ij} + p_i\gamma_i$ $\times\big(\psi + \sum_i\sum_j\beta_{ij}\big)\Big]\div mm^* s_i\psi$
BTL	$\eta_i = 1 + \dfrac{-\sum_j\beta_{ij}/s_i + \sum_i\sum_j\beta_{ij}}{1+\sum_i\sum_j\beta_{ij}\ln(p_j/m)}$	$\eta_{ii} = -1 + \dfrac{\beta_{ii}/s_i - \sum_j\beta_{ij}}{1+\sum_i\sum_j\beta_{ij}\ln(p_j/m)}$	$\eta_{ij} = \dfrac{\beta_{ij}/s_i - \sum_i\beta_{ij}}{1+\sum_i\sum_j\beta_{IJ}\ln(p_J/m)}$
LTL	$\eta_i = 1 - p_i\gamma_i/s_i m + \sum_k p_k\gamma_k$ $\times\big(\alpha_i + \sum_j\beta_{ij}\ln p_j\big)/s_i m$	$\eta_{ii} = -1 + \beta_{ii}(1-\sum_k p_k\gamma_k/m)/$ $s_i + p_i\gamma_i\times\big(1-\alpha_i-\sum_j\beta_{ij}\ln p_j\big)/$ $s_i m$	$\eta_{ij} = \beta_{ij}\big(1-\sum_k p_k\gamma_k/m\big)/s_i$ $-p_i\gamma_i\big(\alpha_i + \sum_j\beta_{ij}\ln p_j\big)/s_i m$
HTL	$\eta_i = 1$	$\eta_{ii} = -1 + \beta_{ii}/s_i$	$\eta_{ij} = \beta_{ij}/s_i$

Note: The following expressions are used to simplify the GTL model's expressions for the elasticities: $m^* = m - \sum_k p_k\gamma_k$, $\lambda = ms_i - p_i\gamma_i$, and $\psi = -1 + \sum_i\sum_j\beta_{ij}\ln[p_j/(m - \sum_k p_k\gamma_k)]$. The elasticities are calculated directly from the budget-share equations using the following general formulas: $\eta_i = 1 + (\partial\ln s_i/\partial\ln m)(i = 1,\ldots,n)$, $\eta_{ii} = -1 + (\partial\ln s_i/\partial\ln p_i)(i = 1,\ldots,n)$, and $\eta_{ij} = (\partial\ln s_i/\partial\ln p_j)(i\neq j, ij = 1,\ldots,n)$.

TABLE 10.5

Elasticity and Substitution Terms

Asset i	Income elasticity	Price elasticities				Elasticities of substitution			
		η_{i1}	η_{i2}	η_{i3}	η_{i4}	σ_{i1}	σ_{i2}	σ_{i3}	σ_{i4}
GTL model estimates									
DD	$1.409^b(.639)$	$-1.510^b(.593)$	$-.040^a(.015)$	$-.113^b(.052)$	$.036^a(.011)$	$-1.680^a(.408)$	$1.248^c(.658)$	$.834^b(.337)$	$1.849^b(.865)$
SDSL	$1.353^c(.756)$	$-.888^a(.311)$	$-1.150^b(.581)$	$-.140^c(.050)$	$.156^c(.088)$		$-3.510^a(1.076)$	$.629^b(.294)$	$1.528^a(.352)$
STDSL	$3.729^c(1.907)$	$-.061^a(.004)$	$-.040^a(.009)$	$-1.343(.898)$	$.015(.027)$			$-3.350^c(2.001)$	$3.920^a(.921)$
STTS	$.878^b(.363)$	$-.041^b(.018)$	$-.019^a(.002)$	$-.060^b(.027)$	$-1.015^a(.350)$				$-10.721^a(3.560)$
BTL model estimates									
DD	$1.018^a(.061)$	$-.541^a(.015)$	$-.262^a(.023)$	$-.291^a(.037)$	$-.160^a(.008)$	$-.101^b(.041)$	$-.111(.073)$	$-.523^a(.143)$	$-.829^a(.123)$
SDSL	$.993^a(.065)$	$-.340^a(.040)$	$-.356^a(.067)$	$-.143^c(.066)$	$-.137^a(.021)$		$-.527^c(.284)$	$.210(.316)$	$-.547^b(.269)$
STDSL	$.941^a(.220)$	$-.468^a(.075)$	$-.158^a(.057)$	$-.193^c(.102)$	$-.089^b(.038)$			$-.081(.703)$	$-.111(.537)$
STTS	$1.072^a(.186)$	$-.163^b(.075)$	$-.181^a(.054)$	$-.078^c(.043)$	$-.427^a(.065)$				$-3.898^a(.786)$
LTL model estimates									
DD	$.957^a(.083)$	$-.548^a(.080)$	$-.149^a(.019)$	$-.229^a(.026)$	$-.030^a(.011)$	$-.164(.158)$	$.315(.238)$	$-.255^a(.099)$	$.620^b(.311)$
SDSL	$.995^a(.171)$	$-.311^a(.091)$	$-.411^b(.162)$	$-.200^a(.056)$	$-.066^a(.020)$		$-.753^a(.133)$	$-.081^a(.027)$	$.242^a(.099)$
STDSL	$1.027^a(.264)$	$-.638^a(.134)$	$-.262^a(.078)$	$-.086(.205)$	$-.035(.031)$			$.573(.458)$	$.613(.513)$
STTS	$.997^a(.231)$	$-.149(.105)$	$-.173^a(.065)$	$-.071(.124)$	$-.605^a(.215)$				$-5.905^a(1.076)$
HTL model estimates									
DD		$-.541^a(.010)$	$-.200^a(.012)$	$-.212^a(.009)$	$-.045^a(.007)$	$-.116^a(.021)$	$.153^a(.053)$	$-.113^b(.051)$	$.480^b(.082)$
SDSL		$-.412^a(.026)$	$-.334^a(.047)$	$-.176^a(.033)$	$-.076^a(.015)$		$-.432(.203)$	$.069(.175)$	$.124(.177)$
STDSL		$-.538^a(.024)$	$-.217^a(.041)$	$-.178^a(.039)$	$-.058^a(.032)$			$.062(.204)$	$.326(.375)$
STTS		$-.252^a(.039)$	$-.206^a(.041)$	$-.129(.718)$	$-.413^a(.079)$				$-3.721^a(.903)$

Notes: [a]Significant at the 1% level. [b]Significant at the 5% level. [c]Significant at the 10% level.

Finally, diagonal and upper off-diagonal Allen elasticities of substitution are reported, since these elasticities are symmetric. The striking result we obtain is that the GTL model's Allen elasticities of substitution are all positive, suggesting that the assets are significant net substitutes. Note especially the significant strong net substitutability between DD and STTS (σ_{14}) and (to a greater extent) STDSL and STTS (σ_{34}). This is particularly useful in view of the difficulties of arriving at some consistent conclusions regarding the establishment of an acceptable definition of money. The usefulness derives from the fact that the degree of substitutability among monetary assets has been used to provide — explicitly or implicitly — a rationale for the choice of assets to be included in a monetary aggregate. Our results concerning the somewhat strong substitutability among monetary assets suggest, although much work remains to be done, that broad definitions of money could be satisfactory policy targets. Note, however, that as there is no analytical framework capable of telling us how large the AES must be before the definition of money should be broadened, a more constructive approach would be to systematically test for the appropriateness of the weak separability conditions. [See Serletis (1987) for work along these lines.]

10.5   Conclusion

This chapter has investigated the substitutability/complementarity relationship among monetary assets by estimating the GTL demand system. This demand system can be estimated using straightforward nonlinear techniques and involves only four more parameters than the BTL it nests. Its principal attraction, however, is that in generalizing the BTL, LTL, and HTL, it allows separate tests for both homothetic and quasi-homothetic preferences and the BTL itself.

Using a standard modeling scenario, I estimated these models and performed tests on the nested structures as well as tests on economic theory to establish whether the parameter estimates are consistent with the utility-maximizing hypotheses underlying the models. My results yield two conclusions. First, judged by the likelihood ratio tests, both homotheticity and quasi-homotheticity are rejected, with the margin of rejection being smaller under the latter. The results thus indicate a decisive rejection of consistent two-stage optimization. Second, the GTL model does well; it satisfies the regularity conditions at each point of the data set, whereas the BTL, LTL, and HTL specifications satisfy some, but not all, properties of indirect utility functions.

In this chapter, I have not explicitly considered the basic source of disturbances in the share equations. The error terms may not be exactly normally distributed, in which case the multivariate normal would only serve as an approximation to the relevant underlying density. It is possible then that my results depend on this standard modeling scenario as well as on my other assumptions — exogenous prices and autoregressive error specification. If, however, my results hold for other modeling scenarios, the basic translog should be replaced as a standard flexible functional form by the generalized translog, and one should be wary of using the Strotz-Gorman two-stage optimization framework in modeling the demand for monetary assets, since consistency of such a two-stage optimization procedure rests on the assumption of either homothetically or quasi-homothetically separable preferences.

In this chapter little attention has been paid to the dynamic structure of the models used, although the autoregressive error specification [equation (10.14)] may be accommodating a dynamic structure in the models that could be better represented by some other dynamic formulation. More recently, a number of demand studies have focused attention on the development of dynamic generalizations of the traditional static models that allow a test of the static models themselves, as well as the theoretical restrictions and simplifications from demand theory. Anderson and Blundell (1982), for example, developed an unrestricted dynamic formulation to accommodate short-run disequilibrium situations by including lagged endogenous and exogenous variables as regressors. This approach to dynamic specification, although standing in contrast to the theoretical approaches that maintain specific theories of dynamic adjustment, allows tests of the static specifications as well as the less dynamic specifications (i.e., dynamic specifications representing particular underlying theories of short-run adjustment such as the autoregressive or partial-adjustment models). Consequently, the Anderson and Blundell (1982) approach is clearly an attractive feature on which to build.

I have estimated four demand systems generated by the translog indirect utility function. Clearly, alternative and perhaps more general and more robust specifications could be estimated. A particularly constructive approach would be based on the use of flexible functional forms that possess global properties. Three such forms are Gallant's Fourier flexible functional form [see Ewis and Fisher (1985) for an application with monetary data] and Barnett's minflex Laurent generalized Leontief and minflex Laurent translog flexible functional forms. Another possibility is the Barnett and Jonas (1983) Müntz-Szatz series model, which has not yet been applied with data.

Part 6

Dynamic Asset
Demand Systems

Overview of Part 6

Apostolos Serletis

The following table contains a brief summary of the contents of each chapter in Part 6 of the book. This part of the book is concerned with dynamic generalizations of the locally flexible demand systems, introduced in Part 5. In particular, we consider autocorrelation in money demand systems that may be caused by institutional constraints that prevent people from adjusting their asset holdings within one period.

Dynamic Monetary Asset Demand Systems

Chapter Number	Chapter Title	Contents
11	The Demand for Divisia Money in the United States: A Dynamic Flexible Demand System	Develops dynamic generalizations of the traditional static models in the spirit of error correction models.
12	Modeling the Demand for Consumption Goods and Liquid Assets	Develops microtheoretic dynamic generalizations of the traditional static models.

Chapter 11:

This chapter focuses on the development of dynamic generalizations of traditional static models. It applies the Anderson and Blundell (1982) approach and highlights the critical role played by the more general dynamic specifications in generalizing the less dynamic specifications and thereby allowing dynamic structure tests.

Chapter 12:

This chapter examines consumer expenditure decisions in a dynamic utility maximizing framework addressing the interdependence between the demand for liquid assets and consumption goods. The approach explicitly develops microtheoretic dynamic generalizations of the traditional static translog models, and it is shown that a version of the generalized dynamic translog fits the data best and that weak separability of liquid assets from consumption goods is supported by the data.

Chapter 11

The Demand for Divisia Money in the United States: A Dynamic Flexible Demand System

*Apostolos Serletis**

11.1 Introduction

The issue of money and other monetary assets substitutability/comple-mentarity relationship has attracted a great deal of attention recently in the literature. One reason for this concern is that the degree of substitutability among monetary assets has been used — explicitly or implicitly — to provide a rationale for the appropriate definition of money which, itself, is an important problem in monetary theory and it has been the focus of continuing controversy over the years.

A number of recent works including Donovan (1978), Barnett (1980, 1983), Ewis and Fisher (1984, 1985), Serletis and Robb (1986), and Serletis (1987, 1988) have followed Chetty's (1969) innovative work and attempted to estimate the degree of substitutability among monetary assets within a microtheoretical framework — utilizing the demand system approach — that views money as a durable good (or monetary assets as durable goods)

*Originally published in the *Journal of Money, Credit, and Banking* 23 (1991), 35-52. Reprinted with permission.

yielding a flow of nonobservable services which enter as arguments in aggregator functions.

Those works are interesting and attractive; they include estimates of the degree of substitutability using some constrained flexible functional forms or unconstrained versions used to test for theoretical and functional form restrictions. Yet Serletis (1987), in addition to modeling the demand for aggregate Divisia monetary assets, systematically tests for the appropriateness of the weak separability (aggregation) conditions using flexible functional form interpretations of the translog functional form.

However, all these studies except Barnett (1983) directly apply data to static models, implicitly assuming that the pattern of demand adjusts to change in exogenous variables instantaneously. No attention has been paid to the dynamic structure of the models used, although many studies report results with serially correlated residuals suggesting that the underlying models are dynamically misspecified.

More recently, a number of demand studies have focussed attention on the development of dynamic generalizations of the traditional static models that allow a test of the static model itself, as well as the theoretical restrictions and simplifications from demand theory. Anderson and Blundell (1982), for example, motivated from the lack of accord between the postulates of demand theory and empirical static demand functions estimated on time series data, develop an unrestricted dynamic formulation to accommodate short-run disequilibrium situations, by including lagged endogenous and exogenous variables as regressors.

The Anderson and Blundell approach to dynamic specification follows in the spirit of the error correction models and stands in contrast to the theoretical approaches that maintain specific theories of dynamic adjustment. It is, however, intuitively appealing as it seems that no theoretical approach is likely to deal with the actual dynamics of a demand system, which are likely to be a complicated amalgam of effects, including habit persistence, adjustment costs, the formation of expectations and misinterpretation of real price changes.

This chapter applies the Anderson and Blundell approach to the analysis of the demand for money and, in the spirit of Serletis (1987a), attempts to focus on the details of demand for services of money at different levels of aggregation consistent with the conventional hierarchical recursive nesting of monetary aggregates. This is achieved by conducting the analysis within a microtheoretical framework, making use of a number of theoretical advances in a set of related theories — index numbers, separability, duality, and expenditure systems — and by estimating a sequence of nested dynamic specifications and performing tests of the nested structures as well as on economic theory to establish the most restrictive dynamic specification acceptable to the data.

Another important contribution of this chapter is the systematic testing for the appropriateness of the weak separability (aggregation) conditions, at successive levels of aggregation, in a system of dynamic translog money demand functions, using the Denny and Fuss (1977) flexible functional form framework. All of the reported separability test results have been conducted using static models, although it seems that developing dynamic generalizations of the traditional static models would produce systematic improvements in the separability testing results.

The chapter is organized as follows. Section 11.2 presents a general theoretical model, elaborates on the specification of monetary services aggregator functions, and outlines the theory of consistent multistage optimization. Section 11.3 is concerned with the specification of a dynamic demand system, which aside from the dynamics is based on the indirect translog aggregator function. Details of data considerations and the problems of implementing the model empirically are discussed in section 11.4. The hypothesis tests are also outlined, and the empirical results are presented and discussed. Section 11.5 concludes the chapter.

11.2 Theoretical Foundations

The model is simple and is based on Barnett (1980) and Serletis (1987). The economy consists of identical individuals whose direct utility function is weakly separable (a direct tree) of the form

$$u = u(\boldsymbol{c}, l, f(\boldsymbol{x})) \tag{11.1}$$

where $\boldsymbol{c}$ is a vector of the services of consumption goods, l is leisure time, and $\boldsymbol{x}$ is a vector of the services of monetary assets (assumed to be proportional to the stocks).[1] The utility-tree structure (11.1) is treated as a maintained hypothesis in this chapter, although it implies the assumption that the demand for monetary services is independent of relative prices outside the monetary group.

It is assumed, in accordance with the Federal Reserve Board's a priori assignment of assets to monetary aggregates that the monetary services aggregator function, $f(\boldsymbol{x})$, has the homothetically strongly recursive separable

---

[1] According to the original definition of separability by Sono (1961) and Leontief (1947), an aggregator function $f(\cdot)$ is said to be weakly separable in (i, j) from k iff

$$\partial \left[(\partial f / \partial x_i) / (\partial f / \partial x_j) \right] / \partial x_k = 0, \quad i \neq j \neq k$$

where the expression in brackets refers to the marginal rate of substitution.

form[2]

$$f(x) = f_4(x^4, f_3(x^3, f_2(x^2, f_1(x^1))))$$ (11.2)

where the components of x^1 are those that are included in the Fed's M1 monetary aggregate, the components of x^2 are those of the Board's M2 aggregate net of x^1, the components of x^3 are those of the Board's M3 aggregate net of x^1 and x^2, and the components of x^4 are those of the Board's L aggregate net of x^1, x^2, and x^3.

Each aggregator function f_r $(r = 1, \ldots, 4)$, has two rather natural (mutually consistent) interpretations. On one hand it can be thought of as a (specific) category utility function; on the other hand, it may be interpreted as a subaggregate measure of monetary services. In the latter case, the aggregators f_r $(r = 1, \ldots, 4)$ are the Federal Reserve Board's functional monetary aggregates M1, M2, M3, and L, respectively. In particular, if Q_1 is the monetary aggregate for the components of M1, Q_2 for M2, Q_3 for M3, and Q_4 for L, then it follows that

$$Q_1 = f_1(x^1);$$ (11.3)

$$Q_2 = f_2(x^2, f_1(x^1)) = f_2(x^2, Q_1);$$ (11.4)

$$Q_3 = f_3(x^3, f_2(x^2, f_1(x^1))) = f_3(x^3, Q_2);$$ (11.5)

$$Q_4 = f_4(x^4, f_3(x^3, f_2(x^2, f_1(x^1)))) = f_4(x^4, Q_3).$$ (11.6)

In this study, the subaggregates Q_r $(r = 1, \ldots, 4)$, are constructed utilizing Diewert's (1976, 1978) and Barnett's (1980) pathbreaking contributions that provided a link between the functional and statistical approach to index numbers and between aggregation theory and monetary theory, respectively. Diewert defined the class of "superlative" index numbers, which approximate arbitrary exact aggregator functions up to a third-order remainder term, and Barnett, with his derivation of the user cost of monetary asset services, constructed Divisia monetary quantity indices which are elements of the superlative class and represent a theoretically meaningful alternative to the simple-summation aggregates.

Hence, the subaggregates Q_r $(r = 1, \ldots, 4)$ would be thought of as Divisia quantity indices corresponding to which there exist Divisia prices indices, P_r $(r = 1, \ldots, 4)$ Following Barnett (1983), these Divisia price indices are computed making use of Fisher's (1922) weak factor reversal test. The

---

[2]Again, according to the original definition of separability by Sono (1961) and Leontief (1947), the algebraic requirement of strong recursive separability is that

$$\partial\left[(\partial f/\partial x_i)/(\partial f/\partial x_j)\right]/\partial x_k = 0 \quad \forall i \in I_r, j \in I_s, k \in I_t, t > r, s.$$

Also, an aggregator function $f(\cdot)$ is homothetically separable if it is separable with homothetic subaggregator functions.

test states that the product of the values of the price and quantity indices should be equal to the ratio of total expenditure in the two periods.

To focus on the details of demand for services of money at different levels of aggregation a recursively decentralized decision-making process is assumed and is reflected in the solution to the optimization problems,

$$\max u(\boldsymbol{c}, l, Q_4) \quad \text{subject to} \quad \boldsymbol{qc} + wl + P_4 Q_4 = y \qquad (11.7)$$

and

$$\max f_r(\boldsymbol{x}^r, Q_{r-1}) \quad \text{subject to} \quad \boldsymbol{p}^r \boldsymbol{x}^r + P_{r-1} Q_{r-1} = P_r Q_r(\boldsymbol{x}^r, Q_r) \quad (11.8)$$

$(r = 4, 3, 2)$, where $\boldsymbol{q}$ is the vector of prices of $\boldsymbol{c}$; w is the price of leisure; P_r is the user cost aggregate corresponding to Divisia Q_r; y is total expenditure or full income.

Thus, the allocation of expenditure between the assets within the rth group and the $(r-1)$th monetary aggregate may be carried out optimally knowing only the prices within the rth group, the price index of the $(r-1)$th monetary aggregate, and the optimal expenditure on Q_r (being passed down recursively from the previous stage constrained maximization). This system of optimization problems reflects a sequential budgeting procedure, analogous to the two-stage budgeting procedure initially investigated, in the context of consumer theory, by Strotz (1957, 1959) and Gorman (1959).

Although the consumer is making his decentralization decisions from the top of the tree down, I will estimate conditional money demand models at successive levels of aggregation recursively, from the bottom up. Hence, the last stage of the consumer's multistage decision would be my first stage, and so on. This approach to the recursive estimation of utility trees has been developed by Barnett (1977) and Anderson (1977).

Instead of solving (11.7) and (11.8) to obtain Marshallian demand functions, one can apply Roy's identity to the corresponding indirect utility functions to derive utility maximizing demand functions. The indirect utility function approach is more appealing because it simplifies the estimation considerably, since it has prices exogenous in explaining consumer behavior. However, a structural property of the indirect utility function does not imply the same property on the direct utility function, and in order to implement a model of demand based on the indirect function that satisfies properties of the direct function, a correspondence between direct and indirect properties is needed.

Although nonhomothetic direct and indirect strongly recursive functions are independent structures, Blackorby *et al.* (1974) have shown that if the direct utility function is strongly recursive separable with homothetic aggregator functions (as assumed here) then the indirect utility function will have the same structure with respect to prices. The choice of the homothetic indirect translog function in the following section has been primarily motivated by these considerations.

11.3 Dynamic Demand System Specification

The demand systems used for estimation are derived by approximating the indirect aggregator functions, dual to the direct aggregator functions u and f_r $(r = 2, 3, 4)$, with the homothetic translog function:[3]

$$\ln \nu = \alpha_0 + \sum_i \alpha_i \ln \nu_i + \frac{1}{2} \sum_i \sum_j \beta_{ij} \ln \nu_i \ln \nu_j \qquad (11.9)$$

where ν_i is the expenditure normalized price of commodity i. By assuming symmetry and by applying Roy's identity, a set of linear share equations suitable for estimation purposes can be derived, namely,

$$w_i = \alpha_i + \sum_j \beta_{ij} \ln \nu_j + u_i, \quad i = 1, \ldots, n \qquad (11.10)$$

where w_i is the budget share of the ith asset, u_i is the random disturbance, and the α's an β's are parameters to be estimated. Equation (11.10) can be written in matrix form (for time t) as

$$w_t = \Pi v_t + u_t \qquad (11.11)$$

where w_t is an n vector of positive expenditure shares, v_t is an $(n + 1)$ vector of expenditure normalized prices with unity as the first element, Π is an $n \times (n + 1)$ matrix of preference parameters, and u_t is an n vector of random disturbances.

Since w_t satisfies the adding up (singularity) condition, we must have $i'\Pi = [1\ 0\ \ldots\ 0]$ and $i'u_t = 0$, for all t, where i is an appropriately dimensioned unit vector. Also, symmetry requires that $\beta_{ij} = \beta_{ji}$ and the imposition of these restrictions imposes the additional restriction of $\sum_j \beta_{ij} = 0$ for $i = 1, \ldots, n$. In all cases the system was estimated with these restrictions imposed.[4]

---

[3]As it was argued earlier the use of the homothetic translog would preserve the self duality of separable structures between indirect and direct aggregator functions. The restrictiveness, however, of the assumption of homotheticity should be kept in mind when the estimation results are analyzed.

[4]Of principal interest are the own- and cross-price elasticities [derived in a manner analogous to that in Ewis and Fisher (1984)], $\eta_{ii} = -1 + \beta_{ii}/w_i$ and $\eta_{ij} = \beta_{ij}/w_i$, as well as the elasticities of substitution [derived using the Slutsky equation], $\sigma_{ij} = 1 + \eta_{ij}/w_j$.

As mentioned in the introduction, most of the early studies tended to ignore dynamic aspects of the specification in (11.11), although the issue of dynamic adjustment has been considerably addressed in the "traditional" log-levels money demand specification by considering different, short-run dynamic adjustment processes. In particular, three fundamentally different, short-run dynamic adjustment processes have been considered in the traditional approach; the "real" adjustment specification (see Chow 1966), the "price" adjustment specification (see Gordon 1984), and the "nominal" adjustment specification (see Goldfeld 1973, 1976). Thornton (1985) provides an excellent summary of this approach.

Here, the dynamics are introduced by replacing the usual static assumption of instantaneous adjustment by a more general one that the static model holds only asymptotically. Under this assumption it is possible to specify the dynamic structure (data generation process) by a general stationary stochastic process. In particular, following Anderson and Blundell (1982), I replace w in (11.11) by a vector autoregressive process in w of order 1 and v by a vector autoregressive process in v of order 1. After some manipulation and consideration of the adding up restrictions (see Anderson and Blundell 1982, p. 1560-66), a general first-order dynamic model may be written as

$$\Delta w_t = D\Delta \bar{v}_t - A\left(w_{t-1}^n - \Pi^n v_{t-1}\right) + u_t \qquad (11.12)$$

where Δ represents the first difference operator, $\bar{v}$ refers to v with the first element excluded, superscript n on a matrix or a vector denotes the deletion of the nth row and D and A are appropriately dimensioned short-run coefficient matrices. Note that the adding-up restrictions associated with (11.11) require certain additional restrictions on the elements of D and A in (11.12). These imply that the column sums of D and A in (11.12) are all zero.

The advantage of estimating in the context of (11.12) is that equation (11.12) is the alternative hypothesis against which a number of hypotheses can be tested. For example, if $D = \Pi_1$, where Π_1 denotes Π with the first column corresponding to the intercept term deleted, equation (11.12) reduces to the static model with $AR(1)$ error term.[5] If $D = A\Pi_1$, equation (11.12) reduces to the partial adjustment model considered by Nadiri and Rosen (1969). Finally, if $D = \Pi_1$, and $A = I$, equation (11.12) reduces to the usual static model (11.11).

---

[5]This model was considered by Berndt and Savin (1975) and in the money demand literature by among others, Ewis and Fisher (1984, 1985), Serletis and Robb (1986), and Serletis (1987, 1988).

11.4 Econometric Results

Following conventional practice, it is assumed that the error terms in (11.12) are normally distributed with zero mean and constant covariance. This assumption and the fact that the dependent variables satisfy an adding-up condition (because this is a singular system) imply that the covariance matrix is also singular. To overcome this problem, one equation is dropped (see Barten 1969) and a FIML procedure is used. In this case any one equation may be deleted from the system and no additional parametric restrictions are implied. Here, the last equation was dropped at each stage of the multistage decision and the results were checked for global convergence by changing the initial conditions.

All the estimations are carried out with the TSP (Version 4.0) econometric package using the Davidson-Fletcher-Powell algorithm and U.S. time series data on three categories of goods. These data on goods consumption, leisure, and monetary assets are real per capita data for the period 1970:1 through 1985:1. The data for the three categories come from various sources.

The consumption of goods data come from the U.S. Department of Commerce (1986). The categories used here are purchases of durable goods, consumption of nondurable goods, and consumption of services. The implicit price deflator for each category of consumption has been taken from the same source. In calculating the one-period holding cost for a durable good, a 10 percent depreciation rate was used.

The monetary data come from official sources at the Federal Reserve Board. Serletis (1987a) provides a brief description of the data and the adjustments (that is, conversion to real per capita balances, the consolidation adjustment, and the "new goods problem") that were made to construct monetary aggregates consistent with the model used as well as with those computed by the Federal Reserve Board.

Finally, using the data on work and wages from the U.S. Department of Commerce (1983, 1983-1985), leisure time is assumed to be ninety-eight hours minus average hours worked per week during the quarter.[6] This number is then multiplied by fifty-two weeks to obtain an annualized quarterly figure for leisure time purchased. The wage rate is used as the opportunity cost of time.

The first objective is to establish a parsimonious but data-coherent dynamic representation of system (11.12). As Tables 11.1 and 11.2 indicate, the most unrestricted model admitted to the data, based upon a likelihood

---

[6] Available time, ninety-eight hours per week, is based on ten hours per day for fixed allocations of time such as eating and sleeping.

TABLE 11.1

TESTS ON THE DYNAMIC STRUCTURE

Model	Log Likelihood	Test	DF	χ^2	p-value
The demand for Divisia M1					
1. General	727.409				
2. Autoregressive	706.692	2 v 1	12	41.434	.000
3. Partial Adjustment	608.804	3 v 1	12	237.210	.000
4. Static	482.508	4 v 1	21	489.802	.000
		4 v 2	9	448.368	.000
		4 v 3	9	252.592	.000
The demand for Divisia M2					
1. General	498.295				
2. Autoregressive	472.499	2 v 1	12	51.592	.000
3. Partial Adjustment	421.945	3 v 1	12	152.700	.000
4. Static	300.019	4 v 1	21	396.552	.000
		4 v 2	9	344.960	.000
		4 v 3	9	243.862	.000
The demand for Divisia M3					
1. General	675.225				
2. Autoregressive	645.903	2 v 1	12	58.644	.000
3. Partial Adjustment	546.539	3 v 1	12	257.372	.000
4. Static	499.727	4 v 1	21	350.996	.000
		4 v 2	9	292.352	.000
		4 v 3	9	93.624	.000
The demand for Divisia L					
1. General	679.434				
2. Autoregressive	665.227	2 v 1	6	28.414	.000
3. Partial Adjustment	628.685	3 v 1	6	101.498	.000
4. Static	616.543	4 v 1	10	125.782	.000
		4 v 2	4	97.368	.000
		4 v 3	4	24.284	.000

ratio test, is the general model [equation (11.12)]. This model is a statistically significant improvement over each of the other models. Also, the autoregressive model and the partial adjustment model are each significant improvements over the static model, but we cannot choose between the autoregressive model and the partial adjustment model using likelihood ratio

TABLE 11.2

TESTS ON THE DYNAMIC STRUCTURE WITH SYMMETRY IMPOSED

Model	Log Likelihood	Test	DF	χ^2	p-value
The demand for Divisia M1					
1. General	721.490				
2. Autoregressive	700.385	2 v 1	12	42.210	.000
3. Partial Adjustment	595.692	3 v 1	12	251.596	.000
4. Static	447.511	4 v 1	21	547.958	.000
		4 v 2	9	505.748	.000
		4 v 3	9	296.362	.000
The demand for Divisia M2					
1. General	494.166				
2. Autoregressive	467.201	2 v 1	12	53.930	.000
3. Partial Adjustment	410.484	3 v 1	12	167.364	.000
4. Static	240.965	4 v 1	21	506.402	.000
		4 v 2	9	452.472	.000
		4 v 3	9	339.038	.000
The demand for Divisia M3					
1. General	669.375				
2. Autoregressive	617.537	2 v 1	12	103.676	.000
3. Partial Adjustment	515.713	3 v 1	12	307.324	.000
4. Static	437.134	4 v 1	21	464.482	.000
		4 v 2	9	360.806	.000
		4 v 3	9	157.158	.000
The demand for Divisia L					
1. General	677.220				
2. Autoregressive	643.589	2 v 1	6	67.262	.000
3. Partial Adjustment	580.901	3 v 1	6	192.639	.000
4. Static	556.931	4 v 1	10	240.578	.000
		4 v 2	4	173.316	.000
		4 v 3	4	47.940	.000

tests, since they are not nested hypotheses, although each model is a special case of the general model. Given these results the general model [equation (11.12)] is adopted as a suitable maintained hypothesis. With four (three) assets this model has thirty-six (eighteen) free parameters, whereas the autoregressive model has twenty-four (twelve) free parameters, the partial adjustment model, like the autoregressive model, has twenty-four (twelve) free parameters, and the static model has fifteen (eight) free parameters. Imposition of symmetry reduces the numbers of free parameters in each of the models by six (three) parameters.

Having chosen equation (11.12) as a suitable maintained hypothesis, tests based on economic theory may proceed. In fact only the symmetry restriction is tested and for a comparison, test results are also reported for the autoregressive model, the partial adjustment model, and the static model. The results of these tests are presented in Table 11.3. The striking conclusion to be derived from Table 11.3 is that the assumption of

TABLE 11.3

TESTS OF SYMMETRY

Model	Unrestricted Log Likelihood	Restricted Log Likelihood	DF	χ^2	p-value
The demand for Divisia M1					
1. General	727.409	721.490	6	11.838	.065
2. Autoregressive	706.692	700.385	6	12.614	.049
3. Partial Adjustment	608.804	595.692	6	26.224	.000
4. Static	482.508	447.511	6	69.994	.000
The demand for Divisia M2					
1. General	498.295	494.166	6	8.258	.219
2. Autoregressive	472.499	467.201	6	10.596	.101
3. Partial Adjustment	421.945	410.484	6	22.922	.000
4. Static	300.019	240.965	6	118.108	.000
The demand for Divisia M3					
1. General	675.225	669.375	6	11.700	.069
2. Autoregressive	645.903	617.537	6	56.732	.000
3. Partial Adjustment	546.539	515.713	6	61.652	.000
4. Static	499.727	437.134	6	125.186	.000
The demand for Divisia L					
1. General	679.434	677.220	3	4.428	.218
2. Autoregressive	665.227	643.589	3	43.276	.000
3. Partial Adjustment	628.685	580.901	3	95.568	.000
4. Static	616.543	556.931	3	119.224	.000

symmetry is not rejected by the data using the general dynamic model. This confirms the Anderson and Blundell (1982) findings regarding the dynamic specification and the symmetry tests and suggests that it would be worthwhile to reconsider negative test results on the theory of money demand within a dynamic framework.

Having chosen the general model [equation (11.12)] with symmetry imposed as a suitable maintained hypothesis, the estimated parameter values may now be interpreted by computing the price elasticities and the Allen elasticities of substitution. Tables 11.4 through 11.7 summarize the results. Table 11.4 pertains to the fourth stage of the consumer's multistage decision where the demand for Divisia M1 is modeled. Table 11.5 pertains to the third stage where the demand for Divisia M2 is modeled, Table 11.6 pertains to the second stage where the demand for Divisia M3 is modeled, and Table 11.7 pertains to the first stage where the demand for Divisia L is modeled.

The own- and cross-price elasticities and diagonal and upper off-diagonal Allen elasticities of substitution (the matrix of the Allen elasticities of substitution is symmetric), calculated at the mean of the data, are also presented in the said tables along with their standard errors. These standard errors were computed by linearizing the elasticities around the estimated parameter values and then using the standard formulas for the variance of linear functions of random variables. This was carried out in a somewhat automatic fashion by using the ANALYZ command in TSP.

For the case involving the demand for Divisia M1, it can be seen from Table 11.4 that the own- and cross-price elasticities reveal a pattern consistent with demand theory. All own-price elasticities are negative and the cross-price elasticities vary between positive and negative. The estimated elasticities of substitution, however, show quite a different pattern of substitution. All own elasticities of substitution are negative, while Divisia M1 is revealed to be a net substitute to small time deposits at commercial banks and a net complement to each of the two other assets. Also observe that savings deposits at S&Ls is a net substitute to small time deposits at commercial banks and a net complement to small time deposits at thrifts.

For the case involving the demand for Divisia M2, it can be seen from Table 11.5 that all own-price elasticities, with the exception of η_{44}, are negative while the cross-price elasticities vary between positive and negative. The own elasticities of substitution, however, are all negative and the cross elasticities of substitution apart from σ_{12} and σ_{23} are negative revealing a complementarity pattern.

TABLE 11.4

THE DEMAND FOR DIVISIA M1: PARAMETER ESTIMATES FOR THE
GENERAL SYMMETRIC MODEL, 1970:1–1985:1

Subscripts: (1) Divisia M1
             (2) Savings Deposits at Savings and Loans
             (3) Small Time Deposits at Commercial Banks
             (4) Small Time Deposits at Thrifts

Input i	α_i	β_{i1}	β_{i2}	β_{i3}	d_{i1}	d_{i2}	d_{i3}	d_{i4}	a_{i1}	a_{i2}	a_{i3}
(1)	.440**	−.071	.359	−.321	.197**	−.048**	−.109**	−.042	.070	−.214*	−.410*
	(.092)	(.336)	(.506)	(.303)	(.030)	(.015)	(.028)	(.025)	(.038)	(.098)	(.166)
(2)	.036		−.684	.452	−.112**	.147**	−.046**	−.000	.032	.047	.026
	(.135)		(.859)	(.510)	(.017)	(.009)	(.015)	(.013)	(.021)	(.050)	(.099)
(3)	.299**			−.175	−.053**	−.043**	.159**	−.055**	−.031	.136*	.269**
	(.081)			(.314)	(.017)	(.008)	(.016)	(.014)	(.021)	(.055)	(.094)

$DW_1 = 1.643$, $DW_2 = 1.895$, $DW_3 = 1.699$
Log of likelihood function = 721.490

ELASTICITY AND SUBSTITUTION TERMS

	Price Elasticities				Elasticities of Substitution			
Asset i	η_{i1}	η_{i2}	η_{i3}	η_{i4}	σ_{i1}	σ_{i2}	σ_{i3}	σ_{i4}
(1)	−1.154	.772	−.691	.073	−1.482	5.740	−2.604	1.406
	(.723)	(1.089)	(.651)	(.363)	(1.555)	(6.687)	(3.399)	(2.017)
(2)	2.204	−5.203	2.779	−.781		−30.932	15.500	−3.337
	(3.110)	(5.227)	(3.134)	(1.421)		(32.390)	(16.350)	(7.884)
(3)	−1.676	2.362	−1.917	.231			−9.001	2.283
	(1.581)	(2.664)	(1.638)	(.790)			(8.546)	(4.382)
(4)	.189	−.706	.246	−.728				−3.041
	(.938)	(1.283)	(.840)	(.639)				(3.546)

Note: Standard errors are in parentheses. Significant at the **1 percent level, *5 percent level.

TABLE 11.5

THE DEMAND FOR DIVISA M2: PARAMETER ESTIMATES FOR THE
GENERAL SYMMETRIC MODEL, 1970:4-1985:1

Subscripts: (1) Divisia M2
(2) Large Time Deposits at Commercial Banks
(3) Large Time Deposits at Thrifts
(4) Term RPs

Input i	α_i	β_{i1}	β_{i2}	β_{i3}	d_{i1}	d_{i2}	d_{i3}	d_{i4}	a_{i1}	a_{i2}	a_{i3}
(1)	.212*	.116**	.058	-.083	.117**	.006	-.057**	-.066**	.186**	-.268**	-.057
	(.084)	(.030)	(.031)	(.072)	(.020)	(.011)	(.009)	(.007)	(.057)	(.000)	(.033)
(2)	.093		-.130**	.152*	-.017	.020**	-.051**	-.035**	-.171**	.285**	.041
	(.083)		(.043)	(.076)	(.013)	(.007)	(.006)	(.005)	(.036)	(.044)	(.022)
(3)	.766			.189	-.060*	.078*	.088**	-.061**	.128	.104	.105*
	(.213)			(.201)	(.026)	(.014)	(.013)	(.010)	(.071)	(.076)	(.044)

$DW_1 = 1.663$, $DW_2 = 1.878$, $DW_3 = 1.758$
Log of likelihood function = 494.166

ELASTICITY AND SUBSTITUTION TERMS

	Price Elasticities				Elasticities of Substitution			
Asset i	η_{i1}	η_{i2}	η_{i3}	η_{i4}	σ_{i1}	σ_{i2}	σ_{i3}	σ_{i4}
(1)	-.388*	.306	-.442	-.476*	-1.045	3.148**	-.127	-.729
	(.158)	(.164)	(.383)	(.194)	(.835)	(1.150)	(.978)	(.704)
(2)	.407	-1.917**	1.067*	-.557*		-12.434**	3.723**	-1.022
	(.218)	(.031)	(.535)	(.226)		(2.113)	(1.360)	(.822)
(3)	-.213	.388*	-.517	-.657*			-.320	-1.384
	(.185)	(.195)	(.514)	(.309)			(1.313)	(1.122)
(4)	-.328*	-.288*	-9.34*	.551				-3.000
	(.133)	(.117)	(.439)	(.489)				(1.774)

Note: Standard errors are in parentheses. Significant at the **1 percent level, *5 percent level.

TABLE 11.6

THE DEMAND FOR DIVISIA M3: PARAMETER ESTIMATES FOR THE
GENERAL SYMMETRIC MODEL, 1970:1-1985:1

Subscripts: (1) Divisia M3
             (2) Savings Bonds
             (3) Short Term Treasury Securities
             (4) A Divisia Index over Bankers Acceptances and Commercial Paper

Input i	α_i	β_{i1}	β_{i2}	β_{i3}	d_{i1}	d_{i2}	d_{i3}	d_{i4}	a_{i1}	a_{i2}	a_{i3}
(1)	.346**	−.044	−.042	.135	.157**	−.015*	−.071**	−.081**	.276**	−.174**	.064
	(.048)	(.054)	(.052)	(.081)	(.013)	(.006)	(.007)	(.005)	(.061)	(.046)	(.055)
(2)	.100		−.014	.096	.078**	.041**	−.029**	−.054**	−.229**	.015	−.170**
	(.053)		(.058)	(.078)	(.011)	(.005)	(.006)	(.004)	(.054)	(.035)	(.052)
(3)	.308**			−.259	−.136**	.077	.127**	−.016**	.124	.182**	.209**
	(.069)			(.141)	(.017)	(.008)	(.009)	(.006)	(.077)	(.056)	(.068)

DW$_1$ = 1.776, DW$_2$ = 1.812, DW$_3$ = 1.456
Log of likelihood function = 669.375

ELASTICITY AND SUBSTITUTION TERMS

	Price Elasticities				Elasticities of Substitution			
Asset i	η_{i1}	η_{i2}	η_{i3}	η_{i4}	σ_{i1}	σ_{i2}	σ_{i3}	σ_{i4}
(1)	−1.115**	−.110	.353	−.127	−1.909**	.133	−2.514**	.500
	(.142)	(.137)	(.213)	(.103)	(.372)	(1.074)	(.913)	(.403)
(2)	−.332	−1.113*	.758	−.312		−7.736*	4.253	−.222
	(.412)	(.461)	(.617)	(.319)		(3.616)	(2.649)	(1.249)
(3)	.580	.414	−2.114**	.118			−8.063**	−1.464
	(.350)	(.337)	(.607)	(.294)			(2.605)	(1.148)
(4)	−.191	−.155	.108	−.760**				−1.972**
	(.154)	(.159)	(.267)	(.145)				(.566)

Note: Standard errors are in parentheses. Significant at the **1 percent level, *5 percent level.

TABLE 11.7

THE DEMAND FOR DIVISIA L: PARAMETER ESTIMATES
FOR THE GENERAL SYMMETRIC MODEL, 1970:1–1985:1

Subscripts: (1) Divisia L
              (2) Leisure
              (3) A Divisia Index over Durables, Nondurables, and Services

Input i	α_i	β_{i1}	β_{i2}	d_{i1}	d_{i2}	d_{i3}	a_{i1}	a_{i2}
(1)	−.007	.011	.117	.017**	−.023	−.029	−.019	.002
	(.083)	(.035)	(.190)	(0.005)	(.018)	(.020)	(.072)	(.008)
(2)	1.055		−1.753	−.0002	.041	−.128	−.005	.037
	(1.029)		(2.454)	(.002)	(1.053)	(−1.391)	(.052)	(.007)

$DW_1 = 2.802$, $DW_2 = 2.134$
Log of likelihood function = 677.220

ELASTICITY AND SUBSTITUTION TERMS

	Price Elasticities			Elasticities of Substitution		
Asset i	η_{i1}	η_{i2}	η_{i3}	σ_{i1}	σ_{i2}	σ_{i3}
(1)	−.407	6.072	−6.664	−20.052	21.690	−8.699
	(1.815)	(9.852)	(9.903)	(93.752)	(33.571)	(14.412)
(2)	.400	−6.974	5.574		−22.765	9.112
	(.649)	(8.362)	(7.849)		(28.492)	(11.423)
(3)	−.187	2.380	−3.193			−3.646
	(.279)	(3.352)	(3.157)			(4.595)

Note: Standard errors are in parentheses. Significant at the **1 percent level, *5 percent level.

For the case involving the demand for Divisia M3, it can be seen from Table 11.6 that the own-price elasticities are all negative with the own-price elasticity for Divisia M3 being particularly high. The cross-price elasticities vary between positive and negative. The own elasticities of substitution are all negative and the cross elasticities of substitution indicate that Divisia M3 should be considered a net complement for STTS and a net substitute for the other two assets. Also observe that savings bonds shows a strong substitutability with STTS.

It is interesting to note that the estimated elasticities are quite different from those reported in Serletis (1987a) on the same data, thus supporting the likelihood ratio tests presented above. Note that the present model [equation (11.12)], as compared with Serletis' (1987a) static model, goes some way to accommodate the dynamic nature of the underlying model generating the data, and gets nearer to generating empirically credible elasticity estimates.

Finally, for the case involving the demand for Divisia L, it can be seen from Table 11.7 that the own-price elasticities and the own elasticities of substitution are all negative — a pattern consistent with demand theory. Moreover, the cross-price elasticities as well ad the elasticities of substitution reveal that Divisia L is, as expected, a substitute to leisure and a complement to the consumption-of-goods Divisia index.

It is to be recalled that another objective of this chapter is to discover the structure of preferences over Divisia money and "near money," at successive levels of aggregation, in a system of dynamic translog money demand functions. Here, maintaining the assumption that the utility function (11.1) is weakly separable and that the monetary services utility function (11.2) is strongly recursive separable with homothetic aggregator functions, tests for the appropriateness of the weak separability conditions are performed at the fourth, third, and second stages of the multistage decision using the general model [equation (11.12)] with symmetry imposed. This is equivalent to testing for weak homothetic separability, which Barnett (1982, p. 696) calls the "Consistency Condition."

The tests carried out for the weak homothetic separability conditions are based on the assumption that the translog functional form is a second-order approximation to an arbitrary utility function (see Denny and Fuss 1977). It is to be noted, however, as Barnett and Choi (1989) argue, the reliability of the various available tests for separability has never been determined [see Barnett and Choi (1989) about the deficiencies of the usual tests].

Following Serletis (1987a), since there are four variables at each stage of the multistage decision, a distinction is made between three separability patterns: the separability of two variables from the other two variables; the symmetric separability of two variables from the other two variables;

and the separability of three variables from the fourth. Overall, there are thirteen null hypotheses at each stage of the multistage decision. For each null hypothesis, the independent parametric restrictions are expressed in terms of the free parameters of the model, and the Wald test statistic — distributed as a chi-square with degrees of freedom equal to the number of independent parametric restrictions — is calculated [see Serletis (1987a) for more details].

The results generated from these hypotheses tests are reported in columns 1, 2, and 3 of Table 11.8 for the fourth, third, and second stages of the consumer's multistage decision, respectively. In the fourth stage, where Divisia M1 is treated as an elementary asset, all hypotheses of weak separability are accepted. Also, in the third stage all hypotheses of weak separability cannot be rejected with the exception of the $[(3,4),1,2]$ an $[(1,2),(3,4)]$ types of weak separability. However, in the second stage the results are not that conclusive; of the thirteen null hypotheses, only seven cannot be rejected.

TABLE 11.8

SEPARABILITY TESTS

| | | | Wald Statistics | | |
	Hypothesis	DF	Stage 4	Stage 3	Stage 2
1.	$[(1,2),3,4]$	2	.856 (.651)	5.734 (.056)	2.187 (.335)
2.	$[(1,3),2,4]$	2	.914 (.633)	4.638 (.098)	4.135 (.126)
3.	$[(1,4),2,3]$	2	.716 (.699)	4.272 (.118)	6.777 (.033)
4.	$[(2,3),1,4]$	2	.668 (.716)	5.777 (.055)	6.563 (.037)
5.	$[(2,4),1,3]$	2	.867 (.648)	.201 (.904)	6.320 (.042)
6.	$[(3,4),1,2]$	2	.745 (.689)	7.084 (.028)	5.865 (.053)
7.	$[(1,2),(3,4)]$	3	1.023 (.795)	9.161 (.027)	10.524 (.014)
8.	$[(1,3),(2,4)]$	3	.915 (.821)	2.514 (.472)	7.354 (.061)
9.	$[(1,4),(2,3)]$	3	1.011 (.798)	5.653 (.129)	14.514 (.002)
10.	$[(1,2,3),4]$	2	.255 (.880)	3.122 (.209)	.748 (.687)
11.	$[(2,3,4),1]$	2	.664 (.717)	3.607 (.164)	6.250 (.043)
12.	$[(1,2,4),3]$	2	.852 (.653)	4.846 (.088)	.699 (.705)
13.	$[(1,3,4),2]$	2	.959 (.619)	3.120 (.210)	5.867 (.053)

Note: p-values are in parentheses.

It is interesting to note that the separability test results generally support those in Serletis (1987a), especially in the fourth and third stages of the consumer's multistage decision. However, these results provide no evidence regarding the appropriateness of the strong recursive separability assumptions implicit in the monetary services utility function (11.2). Testing these assumptions would require the estimation of a highly disaggregated demand system.

11.5 Conclusion

The results presented in this chapter have important implications. They highlight the critical role played by the more general dynamic specification in generalizing the less dynamic specifications and thereby allowing dynamic structure tests. They also suggest that static specifications or dynamic specifications representing particular underlying theories of short-run adjustment such as the simple autoregressive or partial adjustment models may be restrictive since they are unlikely to provide reasonable explanations of time series data.

This chapter has used a homothetic demand system generated by the translog indirect utility function. While the homotheticity assumption greatly simplified the work and is desirable in a first attempt at using the theory fully, it has strong implications for demand behavior, since it imposes unitary expenditure elasticities and expenditure shares that are independent of total expenditure. Weakening the homotheticity assumption and dealing with the complications produced in the theory by nonhomotheticity (problems with multistage budgeting, and the loss of self duality of separable structures between indirect and direct utility functions) is an area for potentially productive future research.

Also, alternative and perhaps more general and more robust specifications could be estimated. A particularly constructive approach would be based on the use of flexible functional forms that possess global properties. Three such forms are Gallant's (1981) Fourier flexible functional form [see Ewis and Fisher (1985) for an application with monetary data] and Barnett's Minflex Laurent generalized Leontief and Minflex Laurent translog flexible functional forms (see Barnett and Lee 1985). Another possibility is the Asymptotically Ideal Model (see Barnett and Yue 1988) which is derived from the Müntz-Szatz series expansion (see Barnett and Jonas 1983), when estimated seminonparametrically.

Chapter 12

Modeling the Demand for Consumption Goods and Liquid Assets

*Apostolos Serletis**

12.1 Introduction

In recent years the issue of money and other monetary assets substitutability/complementarity relationship has attracted a great deal of attention in the literature. In particular, a number of recent works follow Chetty's (1969) innovative work and attempt to estimate the degree of substitutability among monetary assets within a microtheoretical framework — utilizing the demand system approach — that views money as a durable good (or monetary assets as durable goods) yielding a flow of non-observable services which enter as arguments in aggregator functions.[1]

However, all of these studies, except Barnett (1983) and Serletis (1991), implicitly assume that the representative individual's utility function is weakly separable (implying a utility tree) in the liquid assets group from consumption goods. This separability assumption implies that liquid asset demands are independent of relative prices outside the monetary group and, therefore, ignores the complicated interdependencies between liquid assets

*Originally published in the *Journal of Macroeconomics,* 13 (1991), 435-457. Reprinted with permission.
[1]See, for example, Donovan (1978), Barnett (1980, 1983), Ewis and Fisher (1984, 1985), Serletis and Robb (1986), and Serletis (1987a, 1988, 1991).

and consumption goods. Moreover, all of these studies (except Barnett 1983 and Serletis 1991) directly apply data to static models, implicitly assuming maximization of a static utility function. No attention has been paid to the dynamic structure of the models used, although recently a number of demand studies have focused attention on the development of dynamic generalizations of the traditional static models.[2]

Motivated by these considerations, and in order to investigate consumer expenditure decisions in a utility-maximizing framework that takes into account the interdependencies between liquid assets and consumption goods, this chapter develops microtheoretic dynamic generalizations of the traditional static models that allow a test of the static models themselves, as well as the theoretical restrictions and simplifications from demand theory. This is accomplished by appealing to the habit "hysteresis" theory and assuming that consumers' current preferences depend on their past consumption pattern so that lagged variables will influence current demand. In particular, I estimate a sequence of nested dynamic and static demand systems: the dynamic and static "generalized translog" (GTL), the dynamic and static "basic translog" (BTL), the dynamic and static "linear translog" (LTL), and the dynamic and static "homothetic translog" (HTL).

The specification of translog aggregator functions allows us to also test for the consumption goods and monetary assets separability assumed in almost all money demand studies. Here, I systematically test for the appropriateness of the weak homothetic and quasi-homothetic (homothetic in supernumerary quantities) separability conditions to provide some valuable insight with regard to the structure of preferences over consumption goods and monetary assets — the traditional money-nonmoney dichotomization. Moreover, these tests are carried out in a dynamic demand system. All previous separability tests of which I am aware, with the exemption of Serletis (1991), have been conducted using static models, although it seems that developing dynamic generalizations of the traditional static models would produce systematic improvements in the separability testing results.

The rest of the chapter is organized as follows. In the next section there is a discussion of the subaggregates approach to modeling the demand for consumption goods and liquid assets and a discussion of the price of liquid assets. Section 12.3 is concerned with the development of a general dynamic theoretical model. Section 12.4 is concerned with the specification of several

---

[2]Anderson and Blundell (1982), for example, develop an unrestericted dynamic formulation to accommodate short-run disequilibrium situations, by including lagged endogenous and exogenous variables as regressors. This approach to dynamic specification, adopted in the money demand literature by Serletis (1991), stands in contrast to the theoretical approaches that maintain specific theories of dynamic adjustment such as the concept of habit formation considered in this chapter.

dynamic translog indirect utility functions and the derivation of dynamic and static budget share systems to be used in the subsequent analysis. Section 12.5 discusses empirical implementation of the translog models, and Section 12.6 presents the results in terms of standard demand analysis. Section 12.7 provides a summary and statement of conclusions.

12.2 Aggregation and Subutility Functions

The approach in this chapter focuses explicit attention on the fact that consumption consists of a relatively large number of assets and goods with their corresponding prices and that aggregation is necessary to reduce the number of parameters to be estimated in an econometric model of consumer behavior. The analysis based on such a model has to start therefore with subaggregates and price indices for these subaggregates and has to be carried out in a microtheoretically consistent framework.

Let $\underline{z} = (z_1, \ldots, z_n)$ be a vector of the services of consumption goods and monetary assets (assumed to be proportional to the stocks). Assume that these services enter as arguments in the representative individual's utility function

$$u = u(\underline{z}),$$

where u is twice-differentiable and quasi-concave in $\underline{z}$.

The consumer is assumed to maximize $u(\cdot)$ over $\underline{z}$ subject to the budget constraint

$$\underline{\pi}'\underline{z} = m,$$

where $\underline{\pi}$ is a vector (with the prime indicating a row vector) of prices of consumption goods and monetary assets, and m denotes total expenditure available to the decision maker. The price of the ith monetary asset is given (as in Barnett 1978) by

$$\pi_i = (R - r_i) / (1 + R),$$

where R is the highest rate of interest ("benchmark" rate) and r_i is the own rate of return on the ith asset. Hence, the expenditure on monetary services is the interest foregone by not holding the "benchmark" asset.

As the number of consumption goods and monetary assets is large, the estimation of a highly disaggregated demand system encompassing this many variables is econometrically intractable, because of computational difficulties in the large parameter space. The number of variables is reduced by assuming weak homothetic separability and using Divisia subaggregate indices. It is therefore assumed that $u(\cdot)$ is weakly homothetically separable (implying a utility tree) of the form[3]

$$u = u\left[u_1(\underline{z}^1), u_2(\underline{z}^2), u_3(\underline{z}^3)\right],$$

where the vector $\underline{z}$ has been partitioned into category vectors $\underline{z} = (\underline{z}^1, \underline{z}^2, \underline{z}^3)$, the first of which consists of the services of consumption goods, the second of the services of M1, and the third of the services of all monetary assets other than those that are included in M1. Utility therefore depends on the Divisia subaggregates as branches of the utility tree.

12.3   Direct and Indirect Utility Functions under Habit Formation and "Supernumerary" Quantities

Let $\underline{y}$ be the three-dimensional current-period subaggregate quantity vector (derived in the previous section), $\underline{p}$ the corresponding subaggregate price vector, and let γ be a three-dimensional vector of subaggregate "committed" quantities. The dynamics are incorporated by assuming that the representative individual has the following dynamic direct utility function with time-varying preferences:

$$U = U(\underline{x}; \underline{s}, t); \tag{12.1}$$

where $\underline{x} = (\underline{y} - \gamma)$ is the three-dimensional subaggregate "supernumerary" quantity vector, $\underline{s}$ is a vector of state variables representing levels of habits of the corresponding subaggregate "supernumerary" quantities, and t is time. Suppose function U is twice differentiable in $(\underline{x}, \underline{s}, t)$ and increasing and strictly quasi-concave in $\underline{x}$.

As in the Stone-Geary system, the consumer purchases first the minimum required quantities and expends $\underline{p}'\gamma$. He is left with the "supernumerary" expenditure, namely, $m - \underline{p}'\gamma$. Therefore, at each time, given the state of habits, the consumer maximizes utility subject to the budget constraint

$$\underline{p}'\underline{x} = m - \underline{p}'\gamma. \tag{12.2}$$

Necessary conditions for an interior optimum consist of (12.2) and

$$\partial U/\partial \underline{x} - \lambda \underline{p} = 0, \tag{12.3}$$

---

[3]A (direct) utility function $u(\cdot)$ is said to be weakly separable in the goods i and j from k, if $\partial\left[(\partial u/\partial z_i)/(\partial u/\partial z_j)\right]/\partial z_k = 0$, $\forall i,j \in I_r$, $k \notin I_r$. Also, $u(\cdot)$ is homothetically separable if it is separable with homothetic subaggregtor functions.

where λ is the Lagrange multiplier. The system (12.2) and (12.3) can be solved to give the dynamic Marshallian demand functions

$$\underline{x}^* = \underline{x}^* \left[\underline{p}/ \left(m - \underline{p}'\underline{\gamma} \right) ; \underline{s}, t \right] . \tag{12.4}$$

Substituting solution (12.4) into the objective function in (12.1) yields the maximum attainable utility given prices $\underline{p}$ and "supernumerary" expenditure $m - \underline{p}'\underline{\gamma}$, that is, the indirect utility function

$$V \left[\underline{p}/ \left(m - \underline{p}'\underline{\gamma} \right) ; \underline{s}, t \right] = \max_{\underline{x}} U \left(\underline{x}; s, t \right) \tag{12.5}$$

subject to

$$\underline{p}'\underline{x} = m - \underline{p}'\underline{\gamma},$$

where V is strictly decreasing and convex in $\underline{p}/ \left(m - \underline{p}'\underline{\gamma} \right)$. Note that the state variables and time play a passive role in the dual transformation relations and do not influence the theorems on duality.

Instead of solving (12.2) and (12.3) to obtain (12.4), one can apply Roy's identity to the dynamic indirect utility function to derive utility maximizing demand functions. Given the state of habits, the two approaches (the dynamic direct utility approach in the commodity space and the dynamic indirect utility approach in the price space) are dual characterizations of the same preference structure.

I now turn to a specific form of the habit formation variables, s_i, and assume (see Boyer 1983)

$$s_{it} = x_{i,t-1} \quad (i = 1, \ldots, n) . \tag{12.6}$$

That is, the level of habits for each subaggregate "supernumerary" quantity is given by the consumption of this quantity in the previous period, but consumption in the more distant past does not influence current preferences and demand.[4]

---

[4]For the purpose of this chapter, I consider only the previous period consumption vector in the habit formation process. A higher order habit formation process may be required to capture the underlying dynamic process. This can be accomplished by assuming (see Pollak 1970 and Boyer 1983) that

$$s_{it} = \theta \sum_{k=1}^{\infty} (1 - \theta)^{k-1} x_{i,t-k}, \quad 0 < \theta \leq 1,$$

which reduces to (12.6) when $\theta = 1$.

12.4   Demand System Specification

In recent years a number of empirical studies have made use of the flexible
functional forms method to approximate unknown aggregator functions.
The advantage of this method is that the corresponding expenditure system will approximate systems resulting from a broad class of aggregator
functions.

This chapter uses the translog flexible functional form and estimates a
sequence of eight (possible) nested demand systems: the dynamic and static
"generalized translog" (GTL); the dynamic and static "basic translog"
(BTL), a special case of the GTL; the dynamic and static "linear translog"
(LTL), a homothetic special case of the GTL (or equivalently, a quasi-
homothetic special case of the BTL); and the dynamic and static "homothetic translog" (HTL), a homothetic special case of the BTL. The objective
is to establish the most restrictive (dynamic) specification acceptable to the
data.

Although the translog is the most commonly used flexible functional
form and is capable of approximating an arbitrary function locally (at a
point), one perhaps could use flexible functional forms that possess global
properties. Three such forms are the Fourier flexible functional form and
the Minflex Laurent generalized Leontief and Minflex Laurent translog flexible functional forms. The Fourier form uses the Fourier series expansion as
the approximating mechanism (see Gallant 1981), and the Laurent Minflex
forms use the Laurent series expansion, a generalization of the Taylor series
expansion, possessing a better behaved remainder term, as the approximating mechanism (see Barnett and Lee 1985).

The GTL flexible functional form of the dynamic indirect utility function (12.5) may be written as

$$\ell n V = a_0 + \underline{a}' \ell n \underline{q} + (\underline{a}^s) \, \ell n \underline{s} + a_t t$$

$$+ \frac{1}{2} \left[\ln \underline{q}, \ln \underline{s}, t \right] \begin{bmatrix} B & C & \underline{b} \\ C' & B^s & \underline{c} \\ \underline{b}' & \underline{c}' & \beta_{tt} \end{bmatrix} \begin{bmatrix} \ln \underline{q} \\ \ln \underline{s} \\ t \end{bmatrix} ; \qquad (12.7)$$

where $\underline{a} = (a_1, \ldots, a_n)$, $\underline{\gamma} = (\gamma_1, \ldots, \gamma_n)$, $\underline{q} = \underline{p}/(m - \sum_k p_k \gamma_k)$, $\underline{a}^s = (a_1^s, \ldots, a_n^s)$, $\underline{b} = (b_{1t}, \ldots, b_{nt})$, $\underline{c} = (c_{1t}, \ldots, c_{nt})$, $B = [\beta_{ij}]$, $B^s = [\beta_{ij}^s]$, and $C = [C_{ij}]$ are, respectively, vectors and matrices of unknown parameters.[5] The vector of state variables is $\underline{s}$, and time is t, a catchall for changes
in the distribution of income, the introduction of new products and changes
of preferences over time.

---

[5]These parameters can be identified with the values of the first- and second-order
partial derivatives of the dynamic indirect utility function (12.7) at the point of approximation.

Applying the logarithmic form of Roy's identity,

$$w_i = -\left(\partial \ell n V/\partial \ell n p_i\right)/\left(\partial \ell n V/\partial \ell n m\right) \quad i = 1, \ldots, n, \qquad (12.8)$$

allows us to derive the dynamic GTL model's share equations (see Pollak and Wales 1980)

$$w_i = p_i \gamma_i/m + \left[\sum_k p_k \gamma_k/m\right] A_i/D + u_i, \quad \text{for} \quad i = 1, \ldots, n, \qquad (12.9)$$

where

$$A_i = a_i + \sum_j \beta_{ij} \ell n q_j + \sum_j c_{ij} \ell n s_j + b_{it} t;$$

and

$$D = \sum_k a_k + \sum_j \beta_{jM} \ell n q_j + \sum_j c_{jM} \ell n s_j + b_{Mt} t,$$

where $b_{jM} = \sum_i \beta_{ji}$, $c_{jM} = \sum_i c_{ji}$, and $b_{Mt} = \sum_k b_{kt}$. The normalization $\sum_k a_k = 1$ is required for estimation as the share equations are homogeneous of degree zero in the as. Also, note that $D = \sum A_i$ and that the parameters in B^s and $\underline{c}$ and the parameters a_t and β_{tt} have no effect on the budget shares and cannot be identified by econometric estimation.

Following conventional practice, it is assumed that the stochastic errors, u_i, in (12.9) are additive, jointly normally distributed with zero mean and with constant but unknown variances and covariances. This distributional assumption on the errors is standard and is fundamental in the derivation of the full information maximum likelihood (FIML) estimator.

The advantage of estimating in the context of (12.9) is that equation (12.9) is the alternative hypothesis against which a number of null hypotheses can be tested. For example, the static GTL can be derived by imposing the restriction $C = 0$ on equation (12.9). Also the dynamic and static BTL can be derived by imposing the restrictions $\underline{\gamma} = 0$ and $C = 0$ and $\underline{\gamma} = 0$, respectively, on equation (12.9). These models and some further alternatives are drawn together and presented, along with their budget shares, in Table 12.1.

12.5 Estimation and Testing

The models in Table 12.1 were estimated with the equality and symmetry restrictions imposed (see, for example, Christensen, Jorgenson, and Lau

1975) using quarterly data observations provided in Fayyad (1986). The data consist of time series on, and prices of food and two blocks of monetary assets for the period 1969:i-1985:i. Together the two blocks of monetary assets, M1 and ABM1, comprise the 27 assets that the Fed currently recognizes as potential sources of monetary services in the U.S. economy. The quantity and price data which correspond to these subaggregates were generated using Divisia indices of the quantities and prices of their respective components.

As Fayyad reports, the data reflect the revisions introduced by Farr and Johnson (1985). A brief description of the monetary data (used to construct the two blocks of monetary assets, M1 and ABM1) is presented in the Appendix. See Fayyad (1986, chap. 4), however, for a more detailed description of the data and the adjustments (that is, conversion to real per capita balances and the "new goods problem") that were made to construct subaggregates consistent with the model used.[6]

Each set of budget share equations was estimated using an algorithm which generates FIML estimates under the assumed error structure. Since the budget shares sum to one, one equation was dropped in estimation (see Barten 1969), and the results were checked for global convergence by estimating the model more than once, changing the initial conditions each time. Also, the number of parameters in each of the models was reduced by assuming that the underlying indirect utility function is groupwise homogeneous in $\underline{s}$. This implies the additional restriction $c_{jM} = 0$, for all j.

12.6 Empirical Results

The first objective is to test the null hypotheses in Table 12.1 against the alternative hypothesis, equation (12.9) to establish the most restrictive specification acceptable to the data. Likelihood ratio test results are presented in Table 12.2. Clearly, the static models are all decisively rejected in favor of their dynamic counterparts. In fact, the dynamic GTL is a statistically significant improvement over each of the other dynamic and static models. Moreover, the dynamic BTL and LTL are each significant improvements over the dynamic HTL. I cannot, however, choose between the dynamic BTL and the dynamic LTL since they are not nested hypotheses, although each model is a special case of the dynamic GTL.

---

[6]It should also be noted that Fayyad reports quarterly time series on, and prices of, food, nondurables, services, and the two bloks of monetary assets. Only the data on three of these five goods (food and the two blocks of monetary assets) are used here to avoid the computational difficulties in the large parameter space. The introduction of dynamics already creates enough problems.

TABLE 12.1

ALTERNATIVE DYNAMIC AND STATIC MODELS

Basic Equation: Equation (12.9)

Model	Restrictions on Basic Equation (12.9)	Budget-Share Equations
Static GTL	$C = 0$	$w_i = p_i\gamma_i/m + \left[1 - \left(\sum_k p_k\gamma_k\right)/m\right]\dfrac{a_i + \sum_j \beta_{ij}\ell n q_j + b_{it}t}{\sum_k a_k + \sum_j \beta_{jM}\ell n q_j + b_{Mt}t} + u_i.$
Dynamic BTL	$\underline{\gamma} = 0$	$w_i = \dfrac{a_i + \sum_j \beta_{ij}\ell n(p_j/m) + \sum_j c_{ij}\ell n s_j + b_{it}t}{\sum_k a_k + \sum_j \beta_{jM}\ell n(p_j/m) + \sum_j c_{jM}\ell n s_j + b_{Mt}t} + u_i.$
Static BTL	$C = 0$ $\underline{\gamma} = 0$	$w_i = \dfrac{a_i + \sum_j \beta_{ij}\ell n(p_j/m) + b_{it}t}{\sum_k a_k + \sum_j \beta_{jM}\ell n(p_j/m) + b_{Mt}t} + u_i.$
Dynamic LTL	$\beta_{jM} = 0$, all j $c_{jM} = 0$, all j $b_{Mt} = 0$	$w_i = p_i\gamma_i/m + \left[1 - \left(\sum_k p_k\gamma_k\right)/m\right]\dfrac{a_i + \sum_j \beta_{ij}\ell n q_j + \sum_j c_{ij}\ell n s_j + b_{it}t}{\sum_k a_k} + u_i.$
Static LTL	$C = 0$ $\beta_{jM} = 0$, all j $b_{Mt} = 0$	$w_i = p_i\gamma_i/m + \left[1 - \left(\sum_k p_k\gamma_k\right)/m\right]\dfrac{a_i + \sum_j \beta_{ij}\ell n q_j + b_{it}t}{\sum_k a_k} + u_i.$
Dynamic HTL	$\underline{\gamma} = 0$ $\beta_{jm} = 0$, all j $c_{jM} = 0$, all j $b_{jM} = 0$	$w_i = \dfrac{a_i + \sum_j \beta_{ij}\ell n(p_j/m) + \sum_j c_{ij}\ell n s_j + b_{it}t}{\sum_k a_k} + u_i.$
Static HTL	$C = 0$ $\underline{\gamma} = 0$, all j $\beta_{jM} = 0$ $b_{Mt} = 0$	$w_i = \dfrac{a_i + \sum_j \beta_{ij}(p_j/m) + b_{it}t}{\sum_k a_k} + u_i.$

TABLE 12.2

TESTS ON THE DYNAMIC AND STATIC STRUCTURES

Model	Log Likelihood	Test	χ^2	DF	p-value
1. Dynamic GTL	606.519				
2. Dynamic BTL	558.892	2 v 1	95.265*	3	0.000
3. Dynamic LTL	591.512	3 v 1	30.014*	4	0.000
4. Dynamic HTL	542.007	4 v 1	129.024*	7	0.000
		4 v 2	33.770*	4	0.000
		4 v 3	99.010*	3	0.000
5. Static GTL	589.843	5 v 1	33.352*	6	0.000
6. Static BTL	517.150	6 v 1	178.738*	9	0.000
		6 v 2	83.484*	6	0.000
		6 v 5	145.386*	3	0.000
7. Static LTL	554.688	7 v 1	103.662*	10	0.000
		7 v 3	73.648*	6	0.000
		7 v 5	70.310*	4	0.000
8. Static HTL	509.557	8 v 1	193.924*	13	0.000
		8 v 2	98.670*	10	0.000
		8 v 3	163.910*	9	0.000
		8 v 4	64.900*	6	0.000
		8 v 5	160.572*	7	0.000
		8 v 6	15.186*	4	0.000
		8 v 7	90.262*	3	0.000

Notes: The test statistic is twice the difference between the log likelihood in the unrestricted model and that with the null hypothesis imposed, and is distributed χ^2 with degrees of freedom equal to the number of independent parametric restrictions. An * by the value of a test statistic indicates rejection at the 1% level.

Given these results the dynamic GTL [equation (12.9)] has been adopted as a suitable maintained hypothesis. The estimated coefficients from the dynamic GTL are presented in Table 12.3.[7] To judge the validity of these coefficient estimates, the expenditure and price elasticities and the Allen

---

[7]Note that with three inputs, the dynamic GTL has 20 free parameters (that is, parameters that are estimated directly). The remaining parameters can be recovered from the restrictions imposed.

TABLE 12.3

PARAMETER ESTIMATES FOR THE DYNAMIC GTL

Input i	γ_i	a_i	β_{i1}	β_{i2}	β_{iM}	β_{it}	c_{i1}	c_{i2}	c_{i3}	β_{mt}
(1)	0.249	−0.264	0.617*	0.107*	0.958*	−0.009*	0.127*	−0.079*	0.026*	−0.013*
	(0.976)	(−0.56)	(3.85)	(7.17)	(5.02)	(−4.67)	(3.06)	(−4.58)	(3.08)	(−4.19)
(2)	0.007*	0.336		0.019*	0.153*	−0.001*	−0.034	0.026*	−0.010*	
	(4.54)	(1.98)		(4.01)	(6.94)	(−4.97)	(−2.21)	(3.94)	(−2.90)	
(3)	−0.008*				0.347*					
	(−3.15)				(7.33)					

DW$_1$ = 0.906, DW$_2$ = 0.910, Log of likelihood Function = 606.519

	Income	Price Elasticities			Elasticities of Substitution		
Asset i	Elasticity	η_{i1}	η_{i2}	η_{i3}	σ_{i1}	σ_{i2}	σ_{i3}
(1)	0.529*	−0.935*	−0.447*	−0.448*	−0.729*	−4.972*	−2.038*
	(8.94)	(−60.36)	(−4.36)	(−4.30)	(−14.38)	(−3.87)	(−3.28)
(2)	0.753*	−0.006*	−0.999*	−0.008*		−11.531*	0.706*
	(6.50)	(−4.40)	(−55.89)	(−5.23)		(−99.16)	(6.19)
(3)	1.063*	−0.041*	−0.043*	−1.001*			−4.662*
	(8.44)	(−4.96)	(−5.41)	(−29.45)			(−37.23)

Notes: Numbers in parentheses are t-statistics. An * denotes significance at the 1% level.

Subscripts: (1) Food; (2) M1; and (3) AMB1.

elasticities of substitution, calculated at the mean of the data, are also presented along with their standard errors. The standard errors were computed by linearizing the elasticity formulas around the estimated parameter values and then by using the standard formulas for the variance of linear functions of random variables.

The income (expenditure) elasticities from the indirect dynamic GTL were calculated as

$$\eta_i = 1 + \partial \ell n w_i / \partial \ell n m$$

$$= 1 + \left[-p_i \gamma_i / m - \beta_{iM} / D \right.$$

$$\left. + \lambda \left(\sum_k p_k \gamma_k / m + \sum \beta_{jM} / D \right) \right] w_i, \qquad (12.10)$$

the own-price elasticities as

$$\eta_{ii} = -1 + \partial \ell n w_i / \partial \ell p_i$$

$$= -1 + [p_i \gamma_i (m^* - \lambda) D + m^* (m^* \beta_{ii} + p_i \gamma_i \beta_{iM})$$

$$- \lambda (m^* \beta_{iM} + p_i \gamma_i \sum \beta_{jM})] / m m^* w_i D, \qquad (12.11)$$

and the cross-price elasticities

$$\eta_{i\ell} = \partial \ell n w_i / \partial \ell n p_\ell$$

$$= \left\{ m^* (m^* \beta_{i\ell} + p_\ell \gamma_\ell \beta_{iM}) \right.$$

$$\left. - \lambda \left[m^* \beta_{\ell M} + p_\ell \gamma_\ell \left(D + \sum_j \beta_{jM} \right) \right] \right\} / m m^* w_i D, \qquad (12.12)$$

where $m^* = m - \sum p_k \gamma_k$ and $\lambda = m w_i - p_i \gamma_i$. The elasticity of substitution between assets i and j was computed from the income elasticities and the price elasticities by using the Slutsky equation, $\sigma_{ij} = \eta_i + \eta_{ij}/w_j$.

Turning to the elasticity estimates in Table 11.3, it is interesting to note that all estimated elasticities are significant at the 1% level and that they reveal a pattern consistent with demand theory. In particular, the income elasticities are all positive ($n_i > 0$) with Divisia ABM1 being a "luxury good" ($n_3 = 1.063$). The own-price elasticities are negative ($n_{ii} < 0$) with the own-price elasticity for (Divisia) ABM1 being particularly high ($n_{33} = -1.001$). Looking now at the cross-price elasticities, we see that all are negative ($n_{ij} < 0$), suggesting that (Divisia) food, M1, and ABM1 are gross complements. Finally, diagonal and upper off-diagonal elasticities of substitution are also reported. The own elasticities of substitution are all negative $(\sigma_{ii} < 0)$, and (Divisia) food is revealed to be a net complement to each of the (Divisia) monetary subaggregates. (Divisia) M1 is revealed to be a net substitute to (Divisia) ABM1.

Another objective of this chapter is to discover the structure of preferences by testing for weak separability using the Denny and Fuss (1977) flexible functional form framework. As Barnett and Choi (1989) put it:

> "The practical importance of separability results from three facts: a) separability provides the fundamental linkage between aggregation over goods and the maximization principles in economic theory; b) separability provides the theoretical basis for partitioning the economy's structure into sectors; and c) separability provides a theoretical hypothesis, which can produce powerful parameter restrictions, permitting great simplification in estimation of large demand systems."

It is to be noted that a test for separability of the indirect utility function cannot be used to test for separability of the direct utility function unless it is a test for either homothetic or quasihomothetic separability (see, for example, Lau 1969). Therefore, since I am interested in testing separability hypotheses on the direct utility function and since the flexible functional forms that I consider are approximations to the indirect utility function, I consider only the homothetic and quasi-homothetic cases to assure the existence of a separable dual structure between the approximated indirect and unknown direct utility functions.

Following Denny and Fuss (1977), and since there are three variables, there are three null hypotheses. These hypotheses and the corresponding (local) separability restrictions are shown in Table 12.4. For each null hypothesis, I express the weak separability conditions in terms of the free parameters of the model, and calculate the Wald test statistic which is distributed asymptotically as a chi-square with degrees of freedom equal to the number of independent parametric restrictions. The Wald test statistic is asymptotically equivalent to the likelihood-ratio test statistic but the Wald test (unlike the likelihood-ratio test) does not require the numerical minimization of both constrained and unconstrained models. The tests cannot reject both weak homothetic and quasi-homothetic separability assumed virtually in all money demand studies since Chetty (1969) without benefits of results provided by the present chapter.

As it was argued earlier, weak separability provides, among other things, the theoretical basis for partitioning the economy's structure into sectors. This means that, in the present context, one could now move further down the utility tree and formulate submodels for the allocation of the category expenditures. This can be accomplished by assuming a two-stage optimization procedure, investigated in the context of consumer theory by Strotz (1957, 1959) and Gorman (1959). It refers to a sequential expenditure allocation, where in the first stage the consumer allocates his expenditure among then in the second stage he allocates expenditure within each category. The second stage of this two-stage decision is beyond the scope of this chapter.

TABLE 12.4

TEST STATISTICS FOR THE
APPROXIMATE WEAK SEPRABILITY RESTRICTIONS

Null		Test Statistic	
Hypothesis	Restrictions	Dynamic HTL	Dynamic LTL
Weak Separability			
$[(1,2),3]$	$\alpha_1/\alpha_2 = \beta_{13}/\beta_{23}$	2.738 (0.097)	2.766 (0.096)
$[(1,3),2]$	$\alpha_1/\alpha_3 = \beta_{12}/\beta_{23}$	0.270 (0.603)	1.876 (0.170)
$[(2,3),1]$	$\alpha_2/\alpha_3 = \beta_{12}/\beta_{13}$	6.190 (0.012)	6.386 (0.011)

Notes: Numbers in parentheses are p-values. See notes to Table 12.2.
Subscripts: (1) Food; (2) M1; and (3) AMB1.

The separability tests carried out here cannot be conclusive but rather should be viewed as a first step toward shedding some light on the problem of modeling the demand for monetary services independently of nonmonetary goods. Further research is clearly needed in this area. In particular, more attention should be paid to the choice of variables and aggregation. By having food be the only consumption good, it has been implicitly assumed that the demand for food is separable from the demands for all other consumption goods. Moreover, as Barnett and Choi (1989) argue, in examining the capability of flexible functional forms in providing correct inferences about separability, these models are not well suited for testing for weak separability, although they perform well at producing other inferences. They conclude that newer, more sophisticated approaches to testing for separability are needed.

12.7   Conclusion

This chapter has laid out an explicit theoretical framework to the demand for money and has derived money demand functions using the generalized translog flexible functional form. It has also investigated the substitutability/complementarity and weak (homothetic and quasi-homothetic) separability relationships between Divisia money and consumption goods by paying explicit attention to the dynamic structure of the model. The dynamics have been incorporated assuming that the utility function has as arguments both the current and the previous consumption vectors.

It has been argued that the dynamic generalized translog model — being a statistically significant improvement over the other models considered — comes nearer to generating empirically credible elasticity estimates and to producing systematic improvements in the separability testing results. This has been attributed to misspecifications of the dynamic structure (data generation process) of the less dynamic specifications considered. The results have important implications. They highlight the critical role played by the more general dynamic specifications in generalizing the less dynamic specifications and thereby allowing dynamic structure tests. They suggest that static specifications may be restrictive, since they may not be reasonable explanations of time series data.

This chapter has estimated demand systems generated by the family of translog flexible functional forms. As it was mentioned earlier, alternative and perhaps more general and more robust specifications could be estimated. A particularly constructive approach would be based on the use of flexible functional forms that possess global properties. Three such forms are Gallant's (1981) Fourier flexible functional form (see Ewis and Fisher 1985 for an application with monetary data) and Barnett's Minflex Laurent generalized Leontief and Minflex Laurent translog flexible functional forms (see Barnett and Lee 1985 and Barnett, Lee, and Wolfe 1985, 1987). Another possibility is the Asymptotically Ideal Model (see Barnett and Yue 1989) which is derived from the Müntz-Szatz series expansion (see Barnett and Jonas 1983), when estimated seminonparametrically.

APPENDIX TABLE 12A.1

A TAXONOMY OF MONETARY ASSETS AND INTEREST RATE SERIES

Monetary Aggregate	Component	Mnemonic	Asset Description	Own Rate
M1	1	CUR	Currency and traveler checks	Zero
	2	DDCON	Demand deposits held by consumers	Zero
	3	DDBUS	Demand deposits held by businesses	1-2 month CP rate×(1-maximum marginal reserve requirement on demand deposits)
	4	OCD	Other checkable deposits	The Regulation Q ceiling rate
	5	SNOWC	Super NOW accounts at commercial banks	A monthly average obtained from the Fed's "Monthly Survey of Selected Deposits and Other Accounts"
	6	SNOWT	Super NOW accounts at thrifts	A monthly average obtained from the Fed's "Monthly Survey of Selected Deposits and Other Accounts"
	7	ONRP	Overnight RPs	A monthly average of dealer rates on RPs converted to an effective monthly yield and annualized[a]
	8	ONED	Overnight Eurodollars	A monthly average of daily overnight rates converted to an effective monthly yield and annualized (using the same method as for ONRP)
	9	MMMF	Money market mutual fund shares	Donoghue's average of money market mutual fund yields
	10	MMDAC	MMDAs at commercial banks	Fed survey
	11	MMDAT	MMDAs at thrifts	Fed survey

APPENDIX TABLE 12A.1 CONT'D

Monetary Aggregate	Component	Mnemonic	Asset Description	Own Rate
	12	SDCB	Savings deposits to commercial banks	Fed's monthly model series RSAV
	13	SDSL	Savings deposits at S&Ls	Ceiling rate
	14	SDMSB	Savings deposits at mutual savings banks	Ceiling rate
	15	SDCU	Savings deposits at credit unions	Ceiling rate
	16	STDCB	Small time deposits and retail RPs at commercial banks	Fed's monthly model series FITZ
	17	STDTH	Small time deposits at S&Ls and MSB and retail RPs of thrifts	Rate on STDCB + 0.25
M2	18	STDCU	Small time deposits at credit unions	Yield curve-adjusted ceiling rates[b]
	19	LTDCB	Large time deposits at commercial banks	Maximum of (yield-curve adjusted, to one month) 1, 3 and 6-month CD rates
	20	LTDTH	Large time deposits at thrifts	Rate on LTDCB - 0.1
	21	MMMFI	Institutional money market mutual funds	Donoghue's average of money market fund yields
	22	TRP	Term RPs at commercial banks and thrifts	Federal Fund Rate - 0.25
	23	TED	Term Eurodollars	Prior to Jan. 1971, the yield-curve adjusted (to one month) 3-month Eurodollar rate. After Jan. 1971, the 7-day, 1, 3, and 6-month rates are yield-curve adjusted to one month and the rate is set equal to the maximum of these adjusted rates.

APPENDIX TABLE 12A.1 CONT'D

Monetary Aggregate	Component	Mnemonic	Asset Description	Own Rate
	24	SB	Savings bonds	Maximum savings bonds yield ×365/360
	25	STTS	Short-term Treasury securities	Investment yield of a one-month U.S. Treasury bill
	26	BA	Bankers acceptances	Investment (yield-curve adjusted) yield of the 3-month BA rate
L	27	CP	Commercial paper	Discount rates on CP of maturities of 5-14 days, 15-29 days, 1-2 months, 2-3 months and 3-6 months are converted to an investment yield basis. These yields are then yield-curve adjusted[c] and the CP rate is set equal to the maximum of these adjusted yields.

Note: For more details, see Fayyad (1986, Chap. 4) from which this table draws.

[a] Letting x represent the monthly average of dealer rates on RPs, the rate on ONRPs was then calculated as $\{12*100*[(1+x/36000)^{30}-1]\}$.

[b] The ceiling rates are: Prior to 79:vii: 7.75, 79:vii-79:xi: Max of $\{7.75, (4\text{yr. C.M.-1})\}$; 79:xii-80:vi: Max of $\{7.75, \min(12, [2\frac{1}{2}\text{yr. C.M. -0.5}])\}$; 80:vi: Max of $\{9.50, \min[12, (2\frac{1}{2}\text{yr. C.M.-0.5})]\}$.

[c] The yields are yield-curve adjusted assuming average maturities of 0.33, 0.67, 1.5, 2.5 and 4 months.

Part 7

Empirical Comparisons

Overview of Part 7

Apostolos Serletis

The following table contains a brief summary of the contents of each chapter in Part 7 of the book. In this part of the book, we pay explicit attention to the theoretical regularity conditions of neoclassical microeconomic theory and to globally flexible semi-nonparametric functional forms, such as the Fourier and the Asymptotically Ideal Model (AIM).

Empirical Comparison of Demand Systems

Chapter Number	Chapter Title	Contents
13	An Empirical Comparison of Flexible Demand System Functional Forms	Estimates eight frequently used flexible functional forms and provides a comparison.
14	Semi-Nonparametric Estimates of the Demand for Money in the United States	This chapter represents the last 'word'on the subject.

Chapter 13:

This chapter compares the performance of eight frequently used flexible forms that are either (1) locally flexible, (2) 'effectively globally regular', or (3) asymptotically globally flexible. Results show that the functions with global properties generally perform better, particularly those models having asymptotic properties.

Chapter 14:

This chapter focuses on the demand for money in the United States in the context of two globally flexible functional forms — the Fourier and the Asymptotically Ideal Model (AIM) — estimated subject to full regularity, using methods suggested over 20 years ago by Gallant and Golub (1984). It concludes the book by arguing that the inter-related problems of monetary aggregation and money demand will be successfully investigated only in the context of globally flexible functional forms that satisfy regularity globally.

Chapter 13

An Empirical Comparison of Flexible Demand System Functional Forms

*Douglas Fisher, Adrian R. Fleissig, and Apostolos Serletis**

13.1   Introduction

This chapter presents an empirical comparison and evaluation of the effectiveness of some well-known flexible functional forms on U.S. aggregate consumption data. There are two main purposes to our investigations. First and foremost, we want to investigate the differences among eight flexible functional forms as they perform on an interesting data set (the quarterly U.S. aggregate consumption data for the period 1960:1 to 1991:4). Second, we re interested in what the better-performing flexible forms have to say about aggregate consumption in the United States. That is, while our first task provides the main focus on the chapter, we try not to lose sight of the fact that this activity has a purpose, which is to find the best possible way to model U.S. consumption behavior.

The flexible functional forms examined are either parametric or semi-nonparametric. We want to emphasize that while the seminonoparametric forms generally have more desirable asymptotic properties than the parametric functions, it does not follow that one is to be preferred to the other

*Originally published in the *Journal of Applied Econometrics*, 16, (2001), 59-80. Reprinted with permission.

on particular data sets (such as the U.S. aggregate consumption data). To
effect such a comparison, we propose a variety of criteria, drawing on the literature of course, and using data that have been prefiltered to be consistent
with a well-behaved aggregate utility function over much of the sample.[1]
The empirical problem, then, is to use the different functional forms to
approximate the underlying indirect utility function for these data. The
relative satisfaction of the regularity conditions for the aggregate consumer
is what we will seek, although we will also look at expenditure responses
over a range of expenditures, study the results of forecasting exercises, and
examine the estimates of the elasticities of substitution to see if they are
consistent with economic theory.

The plan of this chapter is as follows. In section 13.2 we briefly sketch
the theory behind our approach; our purpose here is to explain how our
choices of flexible functional form fit into the theoretical literature and to try
to explain why one form might be expected to perform better than another.
Section 13.3 explains the specific characteristics of each of the eight flexible
functional forms. The data set, and how it was constructed, is described
in Section 13.4. The empirical part of the chapter begins, in Section 13.5,
with a comparison of the performance of the eight flexible functional forms
on the quarterly U.S. data, elasticities of substitution (in Section 13.6), and
out-of-sample forecasts (in Section 13.7). Our brief conclusions appear in
Section 13.8.

13.2   The Demand Systems Approach

The demand-systems approach provides an effective method to impose and
test neoclassical restrictions on individual behavior; specifically the monotonicity and curvature restrictions.[2] A functional form is selected to approximate the indirect utility or cost function and then the corresponding
demand or share equations are derived using Roy's identity or Shephard's
lemma.   There are, however, many functional forms that can be used.
These flexible functional forms differ in their specific parameterization and
approximation properties which are now briefly discussed.

Among the most popular of the earliest *locally flexible* functional forms
are the generalized Leontief, translog, and Almost Ideal Model (AIDS)
specifications. These locally flexible functional forms initially showed some
promise but they have some troublesome limitations. For example, Caves

---

[1] We are referring here to the use of the NONPAR procedure of Varian (1982, 1983),
itself an application of the Generalized Axiom of Revealed Preference.

[2] The monotonicity restriction requires that the values of fitted demand be non-
negative. The curvature condition requires quasi-convexity of the indiret utility function.

and Christensen (1980), Barnett and Lee (1985) and Barnett *et al.* (1985) show that the regularity regions of local flexible functional forms can be relatively small. Furthermore, the Monte Carlo analyses of Guilkey and Lovell (1980) and Guilkey *et al.* (1983) find that the generalized Leontief and the translog fail to provide a satisfactory approximation to the true data-generating process for the moderate and even large elasticities of substitution that often arise in applications. Another troublesome result is that the translog can classify goods as complements when they are actually substitutes. Finally, an important reason for the failure of these locally flexible forms is that they can only provide a local approximation to the true data-generating function at a single point in a delta neighborhood of an unknown and often small size.

These problems led to the development of locally flexible functional forms that have larger regularity regions and higher rank models that can better approximate non-linear Engel curves. Cooper and McLaren (1996) discuss functions that have larger regularity regions that include all data points in the domain, as well as real expenditures, calculated from any combination of prices and nominal expenditures, exceeding the minimum value in the sample. Examples of these functions include the Laurent models introduced by Barnett (1983, 1985), Barnett and Lee (1985) and Barnett *et al.* (1985, 1987) and the General Exponential Form (GEF) of Cooper and McLaren (1996). The rank of a demand system, as discussed in Lewbel (1987a,b, 1990, 1991), has implications for aggregation and the non-linearity of Engel curves. Higher rank models, such as the Quadratic Almost Ideal Demand System (QUAIDS) of Banks *et al.* (1997) which is rank 3, can approximate more nonlinear Engel curves often found in empirical analysis. They note that at sufficiently high expenditure levels, a QUAIDS budget share may violate the zero-to-one range. Nonetheless, it appears as though the regular region is considerably larger than the locally flexible forms and thus we classify the QUAIDS model as effectively globally regular. While these models provide a better approximation over the initial flexible forms, they may not be asymptotically regular and may fail to provide an effective approximation of the derivatives — and hence the curvature of the true data-generating function.

Seminonparametric (SNP) functions can provide an asymptotically global approximation for complex economic relationships.[3] These SNP functions provide global approximations to the true data generating process and its partial derivatives. By *global approximation* we mean that the flexible functional form is capable, in the limit, of approximating the unknown underlying generating function at all points and thus of producing

---

[3]Elbadawi, *et al.* (1983) define a seminonparametric function as a truncated series expansion that is dense in a Sobolev norm.

arbitrarily accurate elasticities at all points. Two such SNP functions are the Fourier flexible functional form (FFF) and the Asymptotically Ideal Model (AIM).

13.3   Eight Flexible Functional Forms

We now provide a theoretical comparison of the eight different functional forms just mentioned by grouping them into three sets that have broadly similar characteristics. These sets are (1) locally flexible forms, (2) effectively globally regular forms, and (3) asymptotically globally flexible. We selected these eight forms, even though there are many other possibilities,[4] because they provide a representation of the three groups of functional forms that are in the widest use in such studies.

13.3.1   Locally Flexible Functional Forms

The Generalized Leontief (GL) Model

The GL function, due to Diewert (1971), can be written as follows:

$$h(v) = \alpha + \sum_{i=1}^{n} \alpha_i v_i^{1/2} + \frac{1}{2} \sum_{i=1}^{n} \sum_{j=1}^{n} \beta_{ij} v_i^{1/2} v_j^{1/2} \qquad (13.1)$$

where v_i is the expenditure normalized price for good i. A sufficient condition for global regularity is that $\beta_{ij} > 0$, $\alpha_i > 0$ for all i and j. Caves and Christensen (1980) have shown that the GL has satisfactory local properties when preferences are nearly homothetic and substitution is low, implying that the GL can approximate Leontief preferences well. However, when preferences are not homothetic and substitution increases, they show that the GL has a rather small regularity region. Symmetry ($\beta_{ij} = \beta_{ji}$) and adding up ($\sum \alpha_i = 1$) restrictions (for $i = 1, \ldots, n$) are imposed in estimation.

The Basic Translog (BTL) Model

The BTL introduced by Christensen *et al.* (1975) approximates the reciprocal of the indirect utility function using a second-order Taylor series

---

[4]Lewbel (1987b, 1990, 1991, 1995) classifies functional forms in terms of fractional demand systems, full rank demand systems, and Engel curve approximation. He speculates that the asymptotically global models should obtain asymptotic consistency while still maintaining integrability.

expansion:

$$\ln h(v) = \alpha_0 + \sum_{i=1}^{n} \alpha_i \ln v_i + \frac{1}{2} \sum_{i=1}^{n} \sum_{j=1}^{n} \beta_{ij} \ln v_i \ln v_j. \qquad (13.2)$$

Symmetry, adding up, and homogeneity require that $\beta_{ij} = \beta_{ji}$ and $\sum \alpha_i = 1$ restrictions (for $i = 1, \dots, n$) are imposed in estimation.[5] Guilkey *et al.* (1983) show that the translog is globally regular if and only if preferences are Cobb-Douglas, meaning that the translog performs well if substitution between all commodities is close to unity. They show that the regularity properties deteriorate rapidly when substitution diverges from unity.

The Almost Ideal Demand System (AIDS)

The AIDS model of Deaton and Muellbauer (1980) is a widely used flexible demand specification obtained from the following PIGLOG (price-independent generalized logarithmic) expenditure function:

$$\ln C(U, p) = \alpha_0 + \sum_{i=1}^{n} \alpha_i \ln p_i$$

$$+ \frac{1}{2} \sum_{i=1}^{n} \sum_{j=1}^{n} \gamma_{ij} \ln p_i \ln p_j + U^* \beta_0 \prod_{k=1}^{n} p_k^{\beta_k} \qquad (13.3)$$

where C is the minimum level of expenditure that is necessary to achieve utility level U^* at given prices. The demand equations in budget share form appear as follows:

$$s_i = \alpha_i + \sum_{j=1}^{n} \gamma_{ij} \ln p_j + \beta_i \ln \left(\frac{m}{p} \right) \qquad (i = 1, \dots, n). \qquad (13.4)$$

Here P is a translog price index defined by

$$\ln P = \alpha_0 + \sum_{k=1}^{n} \alpha_k \ln p_k + \frac{1}{2} \sum_{j=1}^{n} \sum_{k=1}^{n} \gamma_{jk} \ln p_j \ln p_k.$$

Adding up, symmetry, and homogeneity restrictions require that $\sum \alpha_i = 1$, $\sum \gamma_{ij} = 0$, $\sum \beta_i = 0$, and $\gamma_{ij} = \gamma_{ji}$ for $i, j = 1, \dots, n$. Since the estimation

---

[5]The BTL is a special case of the Generalized Translog (GTL) due to Pollak and Wales (1980). See Serletis (1988) for a comparison of various translog flexible forms.

of the AIDS model is difficult using the translog price index, Stone's price
index P^* is often used instead of P, where

$$\ln P^* = \sum_{k=1}^{n} w_k \ln p_k \quad w_k = \frac{p_k X_k}{m}$$

are budget shares. Results from Pashardes (1993), Buse (1994), and Alston *et al.* (1994) show that using the Stone index approximation can
severely bias the results. Therefore, our empirical work uses a procedure
recommended by Pashardes (1993),[6] and does not use the Stone index approximation. However, even in this case, the approximation performance
of the AIDS model may still be poor because it is a locally flexible form
and may have a relatively small regularity region.[7]

As argued earlier, models such as the GL, BTL, and AIDS are locally
flexible but may have a relatively small regular region.

13.3.2   Effectively Globally Regular Functional Forms

A partial solution to the problem just discussed has recently been provided
by Barnett (1983), Banks *et al.* (1997), Cooper and McLaren (1996), and
others. These authors, as discussed above, developed locally flexible functional forms with larger theoretical regularity regions that are capable of
approximating more general Engel curves. These functions are labeled by
Cooper and McLaren as "effectively globally regular".

The Full Laurent Model

Barnett (1983), Barnett and Lee (1985), and Barnett, Lee, and Wolfe (1985,
1987) developed functional forms that employ the Laurent series expansion
as the approximating mechanism. The full Laurent model,[8] defined by

---

[6]We multiply the translog price index by $\ln(p_{it})$, add α_0 to both sides, and then sum
over i to get the following expression:

$$\ln P = \frac{\left(\alpha_0 + \frac{1}{2} \sum_{i=1}^{n} \sum_{j=1}^{n} \gamma_{ij} \ln p_i \ln p_j - \ln m \sum_{i=1}^{n} B_i \ln p_i \right)}{\left(1 - \sum_{i=1}^{n} B_i \ln p_i \right)}.$$

We then set α_0 equal to the minimum of $\ln(m)$. The AIDS model is then estimated,
conditioned on the value for α_0, using the Stone index with the parameter estimates as
starting values. This iterative procedure is repeated until the AIDS model converges;
this is assured since a quadratic equation is minimized at each step.

[7]Ramajo (1994), using the Laurent series expansion, and Chalfant (1987), using
Fourier series, show how to increase the regularity region of the AIDS model considerably.

[8]Two other flexible forms based on Laurent series expansions are the Minflex Laurent
Generalized Leontief and the Minflex Laurent translog (see Barnett, 1983; Barnett and
Lee, 1985; Barnett *et al.* (1985, 1987)).

Barnett (1983), is based on the (second-order) Laurent reciprocal indirect utility function of

$$h(v) = \alpha_0 + 2 \sum_{i=1}^{n} (\alpha_i w_i - b_i w_i^{-1})$$

$$+ \sum_{i=1}^{n} \sum_{j=1}^{n} (\alpha_{ij} w_i w_j - b_{ij} w_i^{-1} w_j^{-1}) \tag{13.5}$$

where $w_i = v_i^{1/2}$. The share equations (see Barnett, 1983) are homogeneous of degree zero in the parameters and require an arbitrary normalization.

Quadratic AIDS (QUAIDS)

Since Engel curves for U.S. consumption data appear to be more nonlinear than the rank two AIDS and translog models, Banks *et al.* (1997) develop a rank three demand system extension of the AIDS model, the Quadratic AIDS model. The indirect utility function for the QUAIDS model is

$$\log V(p,m) = \left(\frac{b(p)}{\log \frac{m}{a(p)}} - \lambda(p) \right)^{-1} \tag{13.6}$$

where $a(p) = \alpha_0 + \sum \alpha_a \log(p_a) + \sum \sum \gamma_{ar} \log(p_a) \log(p_r)$, $log(b(p)) = \sum \beta_a \log(p_a)$, and $\log(\lambda(p)) = \sum a_g \log(p_g)$. The corresponding share equations are:

$$w_s = \alpha_s + \sum_r \gamma_{sr} \log p_r + \beta_s \log \frac{m}{a(p)} + \gamma_s \frac{\left(\log \frac{m}{a(p)} \right)^2}{b(p)}. \tag{13.7}$$

The constraints $\{ \sum_s \alpha_s = 1, \sum_s B_s = 0, \sum_s \gamma_{sr} = 0, \sum_r \gamma_{sr} = 0, \sum_s \gamma_s = 0 \}$ are imposed so that the estimated demands satisfy the budget constraint and are homogeneous of degree 0 in prices and total expenditure.

The General Exponential Form (GEF)

Another flexible form that increases the range of Engel curves responses is the General Exponential Form (GEF) of Cooper and McLaren (1996) that has the utility function of $U(c,P) = (c - kP1)/P2$. The price indices $P1$ and $P2$ are defined as CES:

$$Pk(p) = \left[\sum \beta k_i p_i^{\rho k} \right]^{1/\rho k} \qquad \sum_i \beta k_i = 1 \qquad k = 1, 2. \tag{13.8}$$

The share equations are

$$w_{it} = EP1_i(1 - Z_t) + EP2_i Z_t + u_{it} \quad \text{where} \quad EPk_i = \frac{\partial \ln pk}{\partial \ln p_i} \quad (13.9)$$

where Z is calculated from equation 13.7 of Cooper and McLaren (1996). Conditions for effective global regularity for the systematic part of the share equations over the region $c > kP1$ require $\beta \kappa_i \geq 0$, $pk \leq 1$, $0 \leq \eta \geq 1$, $\mu \geq -1$ for $i = 1, \ldots, n$, and $k = 1, 2$.

13.3.3   Globally Flexible Functional Forms

As already pointed out, the functional forms considered so far are capable of approximating an arbitrary function locally at a single point in a delta neighborhood of an often small but unknown size. A more general approach to approximating the true data-generating function is to use functional forms that have global properties. The idea behind these seminonparametric (SNP) functions is to expand the order of the series expansion, as the sample size increases, until the SNP function converges asymptotically to the true data-generating process and therefore to the true elasticities of substitution. Two such functional forms in general use are the Fourier flexible functional form and the Asymptotically Ideal Model (AIM). Monte Carlo studies of Fleissig *et al.* (1997), Terrell (1995) and Chalfant and Gallant (1985) show that the regularity region of the AIM and Fourier is much larger than that of the GL and BTL.

The Fourier Model

A way to obtain global flexibility — and gain some generality at the same time — is to estimate a demand system based on the classical Fourier sine/cosine series expansion of the reciprocal of the indirect utility function. Following Gallant (1981), the Fourier flexible form approximation of the indirect utility function may be written as

$$h_k(v) = u_0 + b'v + \frac{1}{2}v'Cv$$

$$+ \sum_{\alpha=1}^{A} \left(u_{0\alpha} + 2\sum_{j=1}^{J} [u_{j\alpha} \cos(jk'_\alpha v) - w_{j\alpha} \sin(jk'_\alpha v)] \right) \quad (13.10)$$

in which $C = -\sum_{\alpha=1}^{A} u_{0\alpha} k_\alpha k'_\alpha$ and v is a vector of the expenditure normalized prices. Here k_α is called a 'multi-index' and b, u, and w are the parameters to be estimated. The parameters are homogeneous of degree zero and the normalization $\sum b_i = 1$ is imposed. The empirical problem is to choose A and J to determine the length and degree of the approximation.

The Asymptotically Ideal Model (AIM)

Using Gallant's (1981) framework, Barnett and Jonas (1983) and Barnett and Yue (1988) developed the globally flexible AIM from the Müntz-Szatz series expansion of

$$h_k(v) = \alpha_0 + \sum_{k=1}^{K} \sum_{i=1}^{n} a_{ik} v_i^{\lambda(k)}$$

$$+ \sum_{k=1}^{K} \sum_{m=1}^{K} \left(\sum_{i=1}^{n} \sum_{j=1}^{n} a_{ijkl} v_i^{\lambda(k)} v_j^{\lambda(m)} \right) + \cdots \qquad (13.11)$$

Here $i \neq j$, $j \neq h$, $i \neq h$, $\lambda(k) = 2^{-k}$ for $k = 1, \ldots, \infty$ are the exponent set and $a_{ik}, a_{ijkl}, \ldots$ are the parameters to be estimated. As in the Fourier model, the order of the Müntz-Szatz series expansion is determined empirically.[9]

13.4 The U.S. Consumption Data

We use the quarterly private consumption expenditure data set constructed by Fleissig *et al.* (2000). This data set covers the period from 1960:1 to 1991:4 and is constructed using all of the disaggregated series from the U.S. private consumption expenditure accounts. Prices and expenditure of nondurables and services are from the *National Income and Product Accounts* (NIPA). Since proper prices for durables are not available in the official statistics, the user cost of durables is calculated using Diewert's (1974) formula. Also, quarterly stock series for durables are constructed by extending the Campbell and Mankiw (1990) approach. All series are converted into per-capita terms using total population (see Fleissig *et al.* 2000, for more details).

Fleissig *et al.* tested the hypothesis that this data set has been generated by a utility-maximizing agent. In particular, they used Varian's NONPAR program and showed that the consumption data are usually inconsistent with the Generalized Axiom of Revealed Preference (GARP).[10] They found, however, two subsamples over which there are no violations of GARP. These are 1960:1-1980:4 and 1981:4-1991:4. The aggregate consumption model is

---

[9]For $K = 1$, the AIM is identically equal to the GL. Barnett and Yue (1988) provide an example of the share equations for $K > 1$.

[10]NONPAR does a linear programming exercise to find if the data satisfy GARP and reports any violations. A violation occurs when a consumption bundle is revealed 'not preferred' in one period but then is bought in another period even though the bundle that was previously revealed preferred is a feasible choice.

therefore consistent with the data over each of the two subsamples but not over the entire sample used in this chapter. This suggests that we might expect no violations of the regularity conditions over each subsample but might encounter some violations when the entire data set is used.[11]

As this data set involves many categories of consumption, the estimation of a highly disaggregated demand system encompassing this many variables is econometrically intractable. This is especially important for SNP functions, since these functions can become very parameter intensive. Following Fleissig *et al.* (2000), we reduce the number of variables by constructing three subaggregates using Divisia aggregation methods. The Divisia index is used because Diewert (1976, 1978) shows that it is a superlative index that gives a second-order approximation to any arbitrary unknown aggregator function. The three subaggregates are motor vehicles, other durables, and nondurables and services (combined).

The data set warrants further discussion. A recent finding in the econometrics literature is that estimation and hypothesis testing critically depend on the integration and cointegration properties of the variables. In the context of linear demand systems, for example, Ng (1995) and Attfield (1997) test the null hypothesis of homogeneity (with respect to prices and nominal income) and show that this cannot be rejected once the time series properties of the data are imposed in estimation. They both use the AIDS model whose share equations are linear in the variables; this implies that testing for linear cointegration (in the spirit of Engle and Granger, 1987), and constructing a linear form of the error-correction model, is appropriate. In addition, Lewbel (1996) finds some evidence of non-stationarity for NIPA data using a similar approach. In our case, however, all models except the AIDS have share equations that are nonlinear. As Granger (1995) points out, nonlinear modelling of nonstationary variables is a new, complicated, and largely undeveloped area. We generally ignore this issue in this chapter, keeping in mind that this is an area for future research. Nonetheless, as a proxy for non-stationarity we report unit root tests on the residuals for the estimated equations.

Some other limitations of the data set used concern the quality and definition of the NIPA data recently discussed by Wilcox (1992) and Slesnick (1998). There is also a difference between purchases and the use of durables. We approximate the use of durables by using the user cost of durables and by assuming service flows are proportional to the stock of durables (as calculated by Fleissig *et al.*, 2000). In addition, aggregate data have relatively less income variation than household data.

---

[11]We note that for Varian's test the data are likely to pass GARP when income grows over the sample, which occurs for most of the data set. Clearly, the effectively globally regular functions are designed to accommodate such income growth.

Lastly, Lewbel (1996) provides a new rationalization for aggregation across goods. He finds that the empirical assumptions regarding price movements of a group of NIPA goods appear to hold for a generalized composite commodity aggregation but are inconsistent with some assumptions of separable utility. Taking the results of Lewbel (1996) and ours together (we show separability), even though the data sets differ, we would argue that in our case the aggregation bias across goods may be relatively small.

13.5 Econometric Results

In the previous section, we have introduced eight systems of budget-share equations. McElroy (1987) shows that in estimation additive errors are preferable to multiplicative errors, so that we can write each system of budget share equations as $s_t = f(v_t, \theta) + e_t$. Further, since the budget shares sum to unity the disturbance covariance matrix is singular. Barten (1969) shows that the Maximum Likelihood estimates can be obtained by dropping any equation. All estimation is performed in International TSP 4.2 using the nonlinear LSQ procedure.

In our initial tests the computed equation-by-equation Durbin-Watson statistics were low, suggesting significant positive serial correlation. We therefore assume a first-order autoregressive process (AR(1)) such that $e_t = \rho e_{t-1} + \varepsilon_t$ where $\rho = [\rho_{ij}]$ is a matrix of unknown parameters and ε_t is a nonautocorrelated vector disturbance term with constant covariance matrix.[12] The autocorrelation could be due to the effects of omitted dynamics (see e.g. Pollak and Wales, 1992), nonstationarity of prices (Lewbel, 1996), or the result of income effects that arise from aggregation across individual consumers (Stoker, 1986). As a proxy for possible omitted dynamics, demographic shifts, and deterministic nonstationarity, all models were estimated both without and with a time trend.

In our empirical work we have chosen to present two subperiods of the data, 1960:1-1991:4 (the entire period) and 1960:1-1980:4. The latter period was chosen because, as discussed above, the underlying data were consistent with the General Axiom of Revealed Preference (GARP) for this subperiod. The second GARP-consistent period, 1981:4-1991:4, was judged to be too short for effective estimation to be possible. Note that all estimation includes an AR(1) correction, as already discussed, with symmetry, homogeneity and adding-up imposed.[13]

---

[12] Following Berndt and Savin (1975), we assume that there is no autocorrelation across equations (i.e. assume that ρ is diagonal). As they point out, the autocorrelation coefficients for each equation must be identical for results to be invariant to which equation is deleted in the estimation.

[13] The actual coefficients produced by the various models, while interesting to special-

Before trying to compare these models, it is useful to look at unit root tests on the residuals from all of the models estimated. We use two alternative unit root testing procedures, to deal with anomalies that arise when the data are not very informative about whether or not there is a unit root. In particular Table 13.1 reports p-values [based on the response surface estimates given by MacKinnon (1994)] for the augmented Dickey-Fuller (ADF) test (see Dickey and Fuller, 1981), and the nonparametric, $Z(t_\alpha)$ test of Phillips (1987) and Phillips and Perron (1988).

For the ADF test, the optimal lag length is taken to be the order selected by the Akaike Information Criterion (AIC) plus 2 — see Pantula *et al.* (1994) for details regarding the advantages of this rule for choosing the number of augmenting lags. The $Z(t_\alpha)$ test is done with the same Dickey-Fuller regression variables, using no augmenting lags. Based on the p-values for the ADF and $Z(t_\alpha)$ unit root tests, the null hypothesis of a unit root is generally rejected for both sets of residuals.

Interpreting the results from estimating a system of nonlinear equations is complicated when residuals appear to be stationary and when an AR(1) correction term is included. When estimating a linear system of equations, if the residuals are stationary, then the demand equations may be cointegrated. To obtain precise parameter estimates of the cointegrating vector when the variables are linear, Attfield (1997) and Ng (1995) suggest using the DOLS method of Stock and Watson (1995) or the FMOLS approach of Phillips (1995). Since these methods cannot be applied to a nonlinear system of equations, we cannot modify the estimation procedure to adjust for the potential estimation bias in our tests. In addition, for a linear system of equations, if the AR(1) correction provides an approximation to first differencing the data, then the equations are misspecified unless an error-correction term is also included. Since the unit root tests have low power in distinguishing between a unit root and a near unit root, and our systems of equations are nonlinear, we cannot determine if they are misspecified or not. While any of our inferences based on the residuals may be reliable since the residuals appear stationary, estimates of the standard errors for the parameters and forecasts may be imprecise. However, since the asymptotically flexible forms give a global approximation to the data function at all data points, the potential bias of the standard errors for these functions may be relatively small.

---

ists, are of no particular value in our comparisons of the models. Tables of these results are available from any of the authors. We do note, though, that each of the functional forms fits reasonably well.

TABLE 13.1

UNIT ROOT TESTS 1950:1-1980:4[a]

	No time trend						Time trend					
	Eqn (13.1)		Eqn (13.2)		Eqn (13.3)		Eqn (13.1)		Eqn (13.2)		Eqn (13.3)	
	ADF	$Z(t_\alpha)$	ADF	$Z(t_\alpha)$	ADF	$Z(t_\alpha)$	ADF	$Z(t_\alpha)$	ADF	$Z(t_\alpha)$	ADF	$Z(t_\alpha)$
GL	0.000	0.000	0.000	0.000	0.230	0.000	0.000	0.000	0.000	0.000	0.230	0.000
BTL	0.001	0.000	0.000	0.000	0.000	0.000	0.000	0.000	0.000	0.000	0.004	0.000
AIDS	0.000	0.000	0.000	0.000	0.000	0.000	0.000	0.000	0.000	0.000	0.999	0.689
LAUR	0.000	0.000	0.000	0.000	0.000	0.000	0.000	0.000	0.000	0.000	0.000	0.000
QUAID	0.000	0.000	0.000	0.000	0.000	0.000	0.000	0.000	0.000	0.000	0.999	0.877
GED	0.383	0.000	0.373	0.000	0.000	0.000	0.000	0.000	0.000	0.000	0.000	0.000
AIM	0.044	0.000	0.072	0.000	0.000	0.000	0.000	0.000	0.000	0.000	0.001	0.000
FFF	0.000	0.000	0.000	0.000	0.000	0.000	0.000	0.000	0.000	0.000	0.014	0.000

Note: [a]p-values for the null hypothesis of a unit root ADF (Augmented Dickey-Fuller) and $Z(t_\alpha)$(Phillips-Perron test).

There is a tradeoff between estimating a system of linear or nonlinear equations. If the data-generating function is nonlinear, and this appears to be the case for our data set, then estimates from a linear approximation may be biased. If the variables are cointegrated then results from our nonlinear models may be imprecise. Future research estimating nonlinear models with data that may be nonstationary may consider bootstrapping or a Monte Carlo simulation, but such an investigation goes well beyond the scope of the present chapter.

To begin the process of comparison, Table 13.2 reports performance statistics for all the functional forms. We test for autocorrelation using the Lagrange multiplier test because lagged endogenous variables are used. To perform the Lagrange multiplier test, the residuals from each share equation are regressed on the exogenous variables (expenditure normalized prices) and the lagged residuals from the ith share equation $\hat{e}_{it} = \sum_{j=1}^{4} \gamma_j v_j + \sum_{j=1}^{p} \rho_i \hat{e}_{it-j}$. The Lagrange multiplier test is distributed as Chi-square with p degrees of freedom. Failing to reject the null, $H_0 : \rho_1 = \rho_2 = \cdots = \rho_p = 0$, indicates no autocorrelation. Four lagged values are included since quarterly data are used; this gives a Chi-square test-statistic of 9.49 at the 5% level. The Lagrange multiplier statistics (shown as LM* in the table) indicate little or no serial correlation for the GEF, QUAIDS and both globally flexible forms. There is still some evidence of serial correlation for the other functional forms. The adjusted R^2 calculations are generally high for all functional forms and thus provide little information in distinguishing between specifications; similarly, the mean square error (MSE) is always very small in all of these tests.

No matter what degree of flexibility one adopts, there exists the possibility that regularity conditions will be rejected, implying rejection of the theory and/or the data, other things being equal. This is especially likely with local approximations since the frequency of such violations is likely to rise away from the point of approximation, but less likely for either the effectively globally flexible forms or the globally flexible forms. Even so, the more flexible functional forms are not immune to this problem for, after all, the data are bearing a heavy load of assumption no matter what technique is employed. In addition to data problems, violations of regularity can be attributed to factors such as omitted demographics, aggregation bias, and misspecified dynamics.

Following Christensen *et al.* (1975), we have restricted the parameters of the estimated equations, as part of the maintained hypothesis, to satisfy adding-up, homogeneity, and symmetry. But we can test for the satisfaction of the theoretical restrictions that are not part of the maintained

TABLE 13.2

PERFORMANCE STATISTICS

LOCALLY FLEXIBLE FORMS

| | No time trend | | | | | | Time trend | | | | | |
| | 1960:1-1991:4 | | | 1960:1-1980:4 | | | 1960:1-1991:4 | | | 1960:1-1980:4 | | |
	Adj R^2	LM^a	MSE	Adj R^2	LM^a	MSE	Adj R^2	LM^a	MSE	Adj R^2	LM^a	MSE
GL Eqn (1)	0.952	24.301	0.000065	0.953	17.516	0.000080	0.996	13.319	0.000005	0.998	9.158	0.000003
GL Eqn (2)	0.970	17.424	0.000188	0.967	13.899	0.000250	0.996	10.717	0.000004	0.998	9.545	0.000003
GL Eqn (3)	0.931	24.284	0.000188	0.935	16.358	0.000250	0.993	6.749	0.000001	0.994	4.803	0.000001
BTL Eqn (1)	0.998	21.676	0.000004	0.998	9.630	0.000003	0.998	30.198	0.000003	0.998	29.661	0.000003
BTL Eqn (2)	0.998	3.354	0.000002	0.998	2.132	0.000002	0.999	15.169	0.000002	0.999	12.201	0.000002
BTL Eqn (3)	0.983	29.272	0.000003	0.978	11.034	0.000004	0.985	29.351	0.000003	0.982	8.391	0.000004
AIDS Eqn (1)	0.998	4.420	0.000003	0.998	7.503	0.000003	0.997	6.737	0.000003	0.998	4.531	0.000003
AIDS Eqn (2)	0.993	10.556	0.000010	0.994	11.126	0.000010	0.994	8.292	0.000008	0.994	15.181	0.000006
AIDS Eqn (3)	0.958	29.212	0.000014	0.952	35.484	0.000012	0.957	19.497	0.000015	0.950	25.443	0.000035

TABLE 13.2 CONT'D

PERFORMANCE STATISTICS

EFFECTIVELY GLOBALLY REGULAR FORMS

	No time trend						Time trend					
	1960:1-1991:4			1960:1-1980:4			1960:1-1991:4			1960:1-1980:4		
	Adj R^2	LM^a	MSE	Adj R^2	LM^a	MSE	Adj R^2	LM^a	MSE	Adj R^2	LM^a	MSE
Laur Eqn (1)	0.999	13.394	0.000002	0.999	13.612	0.000001	0.999	13.944	0.000003	0.999	8.110	0.000002
Laur Eqn (2)	0.999	13.656	0.000001	0.999	20.844	0.000001	0.999	9.808	0.000001	0.999	5.748	0.9×10^{-6}
Laur Eqn (3)	0.990	40.731	0.000001	0.998	20.195	0.000001	0.998	35.771	0.3×10^{-6}	0.998	15.967	0.3×10^{-6}
QUAIDS Eqn (1)	0.997	9.541	0.000003	0.997	11.376	0.000003	0.998	9.323	0.000003	0.980	7.144	0.000003
QUAIDS Eqn (2)	0.993	23.520	0.000002	0.991	25.186	0.000002	0.997	18.175	0.000002	0.979	9.325	0.000002
QUAIDS Eqn (3)	0.954	6.873	0.000001	0.955	6.727	0.000001	0.976	65.753	0.000023	0.964	25.404	0.000170
GEF Eqn (1)	0.989	10.477	0.000002	0.995	9.654	0.000001	0.994	11.357	0.000001	0.997	7.1574	0.000001
GEF Eqn (2)	0.997	9.514	0.000042	0.998	7.564	0.000004	0.998	8.235	0.000022	0.999	5.664	0.000003
GEF Eqn (3)	0.987	16.591	0.000034	0.996	14.351	0.000003	0.998	12.241	0.000018	0.998	9.276	0.000001

TABLE 13.2 CONT'D

PERFORMANCE STATISTICS

ASYMPTOTICALLY GLOBALLY FLEXIBLE FORMS

| | No time trend | | | | | | Time trend | | | | | |
| | 1960:1-1991:4 | | | 1960:1-1980:4 | | | 1960:1-1991:4 | | | 1960:1-1980:4 | | |
	Adj R^2	LM^a	MSE	Adj R^2	LM^a	MSE	Adj R^2	LM^a	MSE	Adj R^2	LM^a	MSE
AIM Eqn (1)	0.999	6.255	0.0000004	0.999	5.788	0.8×10^{-7}	0.999	9.996	0.000001	0.999	3.079	0.000001
AIM Eqn (2)	0.999	16.392	0.0000002	0.999	16.601	0.5×10^{-9}	0.999	8.024	0.000005	0.999	7.744	0.6×10^{-7}
AIM Eqn (3)	0.995	13.131	0.0000542	0.999	5.421	0.7×10^{-9}	0.998	33.949	0.3×10^{-6}	0.999	8.197	0.2×10^{-7}
FFF Eqn (1)	0.999	13.547	0.0002653	0.999	8.070	0.0001795	0.998	9.176	0.000340	0.998	7.840	0.000025
FFF Eqn (2)	0.999	20.269	0.0001210	0.999	10.910	0.0000859	0.999	8.787	0.000138	0.999	6.645	0.000009
FFF Eqn (3)	0.997	22.711	0.0000007	0.998	9.113	0.0000003	0.996	23.509	0.8×10^{-6}	0.998	10.239	0.4×10^{-6}

Notes: ^{a}Lagrange multiplier test for autocorrelation

Equation (1) is for motor vehicles.

Equation (2) is the aggregate of other durables

Equation (3) is the aggregate of nondurables and services.

hypothesis at each point. These restrictions are nonnegativity, monotonicity, and the curvature conditions on the indirect utility functions.[14] There are no violations of the nonnegativity and monotonicity restrictions for all functional forms so the only regularity tests reported in Table 13.3 are the results of the quasi-convexity tests.

Table 13.3 shows the percentage of violations over the data space for each of the models. As is readily apparent, all functional forms have the same or fewer violations over the GARP consistent period than over the total period. This is the expected result. Furthermore, the BTL, AIDS and Laurent models have relatively more violations of concavity than the GL, GEF, QUAIDS, AIM, and Fourier models.[15] For all samples and whether a time trend is included or not, the GEF and QUAIDS models always had no violations of concavity. Recall that the regular region for these models grows as income grows, which probably occurred over much of the sample even though GARP is rejected over the entire sample. Thus, for this data set, the GEF and QUAIDS models find the data consistent with rational consumer behavior even though the data failed the GARP test. On net, on the basis of this table, it appears that the QUAIDS, GEF, AIM and Fourier are the better models.

In our tests, we use standard information criteria for comparing the models. Table 13.3 (Part B) reports the Akaike Information Criterion (AIC) and Bayesian-Schwarz Information Criterion (SIC) for these tests. These information criteria, for which a low value is desirable, show that the GEF is the clear winner but that the differences among the models often are small. This is an important result because then one might be more likely to prefer the effectively global forms over the AIM and FFF since the latter are more parameter intensive than the other functions.[16]

Next we provide a simple way of comparing how the eight functional forms measure income responses by examining how the models fit the three smallest and largest values over the estimated sample (1960-80); this

---

[14]Nonnegativity requires that the values of the fitted demand functions be nonnegative $(x_i \geq 0, \forall i)$. Monotonicity requires that the indirect utility function be monotonically decreasing and this can be checked by direct computation of the values of the gradient vector of the estimated indirect utility function. Finally, the curvature conditions require quasi-convexity of the indirect utility function; these can be checked, provided the monotonicity conditions hold, by direct computation from the utility function.

[15]Fisher (1992) also found some violations of quasi-convexity using monetary data and the Fourier Flexible Form.

[16]Theoretical results imply that both the AIM and Fourier will approximate the true data-generating function asymptotically, but the results can be different in small samples. On the other hand, the effectively globally regular GEF and QUAIDS specifications are not asymptotically globally regular so that both asymptotic and small sample results may differ.

TABLE 13.3

EIGHT FLEXIBLE FUNCTIONAL FORMS COMPARED

A. Quasi-convexity tests — percentage of violations

	No time trend		Time trend	
	1960:1-1991:4	1960:1-1980:4	1960:1-1991:4	1960:1-1980:4
GL	0.08	0.06	0.09	0.06
BTL	0.16	0.13	0.18	0.15
AIDS	0.18	0.14	0.20	0.22
Full Laurent	0.27	0.16	0.25	0.18
QUAIDS	0.00	0.00	0.00	0.00
GEF	0.00	0.00	0.00	0.00
AIM	0.04	0.00	0.05	0.00
Fourier	0.12	0.05	0.08	0.04

B. Information criteria

	No time trend				Time trend			
	1960:1-1991:4		1960:1-1980:4		1960:1-1991:4		1960:1-1980:4	
	AIC	SIC	AIC	SIC	AIC	SIC	AIC	SIC
GL	1042.8	1042.9	668.1	668.3	1290.8	1290.9	862.3	862.5
BTL	1294.1	1294.3	839.5	839.7	1314.6	1314.8	860.6	861.0
AIDS	1209.3	1209.5	776.5	776.7	1213.3	1213.5	778.2	778.4
LAUR	1478.5	1478.6	978.5	978.8	1510.0	1510.1	994.1	994.3
QUA	1205.4	1205.6	836.9	837.0	1314.3	1314.4	803.6	803.7
GEF	994.6	993.8	789.4	788.5	948.2	948.0	778.2	777.6
AIM	1481.8	1482.4	967.6	968.4	1545.5	1546.1	989.9	990.6
FFF	1429.5	1429.9	957.7	958.2	1386.5	1386.9	900.8	901.3

appear in Table 13.4.   We test to see if the fitted value is statistically significantly different from the realized value for the Wald statistic using the delta method. Adopting the 5% level of significance, we are looking for large p-values as evidence in favor of a particular specification. Accordingly, for the 36 'observations' in the table (taking 'time' and 'non-time' as separate tests), we have 23/36 instances in which the QUAIDS model successfully fits the extreme observations. This was the best performance, but the two other effectively global models (the Laurent and the GEF) did almost as well, as did the AIM model. We are not surprised at the performance of the QUAIDS model, since this rank 3 model was designed to deal with nonlinear Engel curves.

The final issue, for our data set, is how to choose among the GEF, QUAIDS and the two global models, the AIM and the Fourier. A method of comparing the informational content of the parameter estimates is to look at the behavior of the output of the models in the form of the elasticities of substitution; we will do this in Section 13.6.   Here we are looking for inconsistencies in the pattern of elasticities from one model to the next. Our final way of comparison, discussed in Section 13.7, is through out-of-sample forecasts.

13.6   Morishima Elasticities of Substitution

Although the Allen elasticity of substitution (AES) has been used widely to study substitution behavior and structural instability, Blackorby and Russell (1981, 1989) have shown that the AES is quantitatively and qualitatively ambiguous. In fact, when there are more than two variables, the Morishima elasticity of substitution is a generally better measure of the substitution elasticity.[17] The Morishma elasticity of substitution, σ_{ij}^m, is defined (Blackorby and Russell 1981, 1989) as follows:

$$\sigma_{ij}^m = s_i(\sigma_{ij}^a - \sigma_{ji}^a).$$

It categorizes goods as complements $\left(\sigma_{ij}^m < 0\right)$ if an increase in the price of j causes x_i/x_j to decrease. If $\sigma_{ij}^m > 0$, goods are Morishima substitutes.

---

[17]The AES between goods i an j, σ_{ij}^a, is traditionally computed from the cost function as

$$\sigma_{ij}^a = \frac{C(u, P)C_{ij}(u, P)}{c_i(u, P)c_j(u, P)}.$$

It categorizes goods as complements if an increase in the price of good j causes a decreased consumption of good i ($\sigma_{ij}^a < 0$). If $\sigma_{ij}^a > 0$, goods are Allen substitutes.

TABLE 13.4

P-VALUES FOR THREE SMALLEST AND LARGEST EXPENDITURES

		1961:1			Smallest 1961:2			1962:1		
		sh1	sh2	sh3	sh1	sh2	sh3	sh1	sh2	sh3
GL	No time	0.104	0.000	0.000	0.000	0.000	0.000	0.343	0.320	0.299
GL	time	0.990	0.003	0.000	0.926	0.027	0.015	0.166	0.000	0.000
BTL	No time	0.216	0.000	0.000	0.000	0.000	0.000	0.084	0.000	0.000
BTL	time	0.000	0.000	0.000	0.898	0.000	0.000	0.044	0.504	0.196
AIDS	No time	0.418	0.000	0.000	0.573	0.000	0.000	0.059	0.014	0.000
AIDS	time	0.752	0.000	0.022	0.013	0.000	0.000	0.968	0.473	0.000
LAUR	No time	0.988	0.223	0.084	0.329	0.031	0.428	0.692	0.003	0.000
LAUR	time	0.521	0.830	0.065	0.549	0.409	0.893	0.801	0.211	0.003
QUAIDS	No time	0.885	0.432	0.112	0.111	0.432	0.253	0.832	0.005	0.003
QUAIDS	time	0.886	0.568	0.213	0.349	0.123	0.451	0.933	0.007	0.015
GEF	No time	0.362	0.254	0.524	0.135	0.432	0.563	0.002	0.000	0.023
GEF	time	0.521	0.830	0.065	0.549	0.409	0.893	0.801	0.211	0.003
FFF	No time	0.934	0.414	0.419	0.082	0.361	0.056	0.188	0.000	0.005
FFF	time	0.011	0.000	0.223	0.000	0.000	0.014	0.006	0.000	0.027
AIM	No time	0.061	0.031	0.657	0.101	0.084	0.478	0.005	0.000	0.780
AIM	time	0.208	0.134	0.682	0.134	0.120	0.345	0.001	0.000	0.203

TABLE 13.4 CONT'D

| | | Largest | | | | | | | | |
| | | 1980:4 | | | 1980:1 | | | 1980:2 | | |
		sh1	sh2	sh3	sh1	sh2	sh3	sh1	sh2	sh3
GL	No time	0.000	0.000	0.000	0.043	0.000	0.001	0.000	0.000	0.000
GL	time	0.000	0.000	0.000	0.019	0.026	0.000	0.000	0.000	0.809
BTL	No time	0.000	0.000	0.000	0.001	0.000	0.902	0.325	0.989	0.546
BTL	time	0.000	0.000	0.008	0.317	0.000	0.035	0.549	0.612	0.380
AIDS	No time	0.000	0.001	0.000	0.000	0.556	0.000	0.938	0.802	0.876
AIDS	time	0.000	0.006	0.000	0.000	0.396	0.000	0.801	0.550	0.000
LAUR	No time	0.000	0.000	0.358	0.000	0.245	0.000	0.965	0.002	0.000
LAUR	time	0.000	0.000	0.000	0.002	0.002	0.021	0.849	0.850	0.894
QUAIDS	No time	0.000	0.005	0.032	0.000	0.643	0.003	0.966	0.533	0.333
QUAIDS	time	0.000	0.012	0.000	0.059	0.444	0.041	0.941	0.125	0.414
GEF	No time	0.000	0.000	0.124	0.000	0.108	0.003	0.086	0.005	0.000
GEF	time	0.000	0.000	0.000	0.009	0.071	0.022	0.051	0.631	0.000
FFF	No time	0.000	0.000	0.016	0.000	0.001	0.000	0.062	0.000	0.000
FFF	time	0.000	0.000	0.000	0.000	0.068	0.000	0.000	0.934	0.000
AIM	No time	0.000	0.000	0.035	0.001	0.262	0.000	0.814	0.216	0.006
AIM	time	0.000	0.000	0.000	0.005	0.022	0.003	0.114	0.462	0.009

Notes: The null is rejected at the 5% level for values less than 0.05. sh1 = share of motor vehicles, sh2 = other durables aggregate, sh3 = aggregate of nondurables and services.

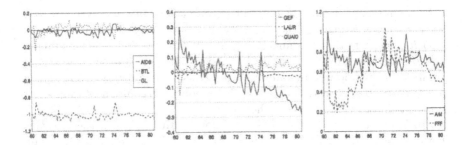

Figure 13.1: Morishima elasticities for motor vehicles and other durables (price of motor vehicles varying).

We are interested, in this chapter, in the relations among three types of consumption goods. To this point it has not been possible to dig into the economic questions, but with a measure of the elasticity of substitution, this is now possible. The types of goods we are working with are (1) motor vehicles, (2) other durables, and (3) nondurables and services. We would expect each of these broad categories to be a substitute for each of the others and we might expect the substitution to be stronger between 1 and 2 than between, say 1 and 3. In what follows, then, we will try to balance our interest in model comparison with the underlying economics.

The Morishima elasticities between motor vehicles (1) and other durables (2) for all eight models excluding a time trend are displayed in Figure 13.1. Note that this is the Morishima elasticity calculated by varying the price of motor vehicles.[18]

Here the asymptotically globally flexible AIM and Fourier models show elasticities in the range between 0.25 and 1, while the other four (local) approximations show lower substitution, with the basic translog model showing complementarity (around -1.0). All the remaining flexile models have a number of cases in which complementarity is exhibited. We believe these results show how model-specific results can be in this literature. Of course, consumer theory does not rule out complementarity, so we can hardly claim that the results for the Fourier or AIM model are correct. Nevertheless, most researchers expect substitution rather than complementarity for such broad aggregates. It is also noteworthy in figure 13.1 that the two asymptotically globally flexible models show considerably more variation in the elasticities of substitution. Again this is a result that appears to be model-specific. While we have no *a priori* view as to what is appropriate here,

---

[18]In table 13.5 below, we discuss the precision of the estimates by displaying the percentage of statistically significant elasticities.

it is worth emphasizing that obtaining greater flexibility with models that are capable of estimating the elasticity to an arbitrary degree of accuracy *globally*, suggests that the underlying utility surfaces are in fact nonlinear and perhaps highly so. This might suggest that studies of aggregate consumption would do well to maintain this level of disaggregation, since weak and/or variable substitution elasticities among the components make for poorly behaved aggregates, on the whole.

In figure 13.2 we pursue these questions with respect to the relations between other durables (2) and nondurables and services (3). Our main interest is in investigating what are likely to be the strongest links in the chain, and we anticipate somewhat lower substitution in this case. This appears to be true for the AIM and Fourier models, both of which show lower substitution than in Figure 13.1. For the other models, the results are ambiguous, on the whole. Figure 13.2, further, again shows that the globally functional forms (the AIM and Fourier models) show positive elasticities (substitution) and typically greater variability of the Morishima parameter (we are varying the price of 'other durables' in this experiment). It is noticeable, in fact, that all of the series show a 'cyclical' pattern, much of which seems related to cyclical activity in the U.S. economy. We hypothesize that business cycle turning points produce relatively large changes in user costs that, in turn, interact with the highly nonlinear utility function of the aggregate consumer. The asymptotically globally flexible functional forms seem more adept at picking up this behavior than the local functions studied here. While this is merely an interpretation, it is worth emphasizing that the QUAIDS, GEF, and AIM specifications exhibited *no* failures of the regularity conditions at any points in the data (and the Fourier failed 6% of the time), and that this data set passed the tests for conformity with

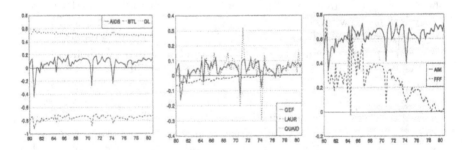

Figure 13.2: Morishima elasticities for other durables and nondurables (price of non-durables varying).

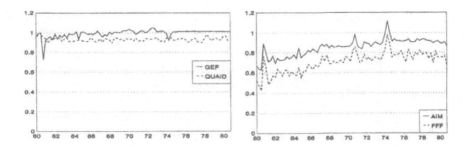

Figure 13.3: Expenditure elasticities for nondurables.

the General Axiom of Revealed Preference and weak separability. Notice, finally that the basic translog model continues to exhibit complementarity between these two commodity bundles.

Pursing the topic of the expenditure elasticities we first look at those for nondurables in Figure 13.3. We concentrate on expenditure elasticities from the GEF, QUAIDS, AIM and Fourier flexible forms since these appear to be the functions that give the best approximations on these data. These expenditure elasticities, calculated without a time trend, range from 0.4 to 1.1 with the AIM and Fourier estimates, for the most part, slightly smaller estimates. We have no firm priors about these elasticities, although we find the fact that the estimated expenditure elasticities are often less than unity for nondurables a reasonable finding. We note that the two globally flexible functions show rising expenditure elasticities through the 1960s, while the two effectively global functions tested do not. We suspect the rising elasticities are possibly correct, as per capita incomes rose considerably during this period.

Finally, Figure 13.4 is used to analyze the affect of including a time trend and shows the expenditure elasticities for the AIM and Fourier functions. It is apparent that including a time trend lowers estimates of expenditure elasticities and may even produce considerably less variability in the substitution elasticities. It also removes the upwards drift in the AIM model, but not in the Fourier. It is worth noting that in all these graphs there are sharp spikes at the start of the recession of 1973-5.

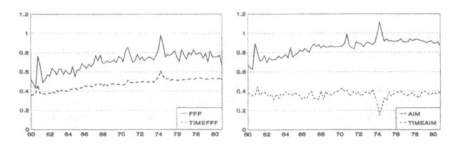

Figure 13.4: Expenditure elasticities and the effect of time trend.

13.7 Forecast Results

A final way to evaluate contrasting models of the same phenomenon is to compare their out-of-sample forecasting performance. It appears as though the two asymptotically globally flexible models provide the best approximations for the data used in this chapter, but it is common among such studies to find that simpler methods sometimes forecast as well as more complicated methods. Of course, our main interest is in comparing the effectively global and the asymptotically global specifications but, as will be readily apparent, we cannot make a clear case. There are actually numerous ways to compare the forecasting capabilities of econometric models. We follow Mathews and Diamantopoulos (1994) who suggest four measures based on an extensive evaluation of many methods for evaluating forecasts. They propose using the following metrics: the average absolute percentage error, root mean square error, mean absolute error, and R-square. All eight functional forms were used to predict the shares for 1, 2 and 3 years ahead starting at 1981:1, using the AR(1) correction. That is, the eight functional forms were estimated over the period 1960:1-1980:4 and forecasted to 1983:4 for one-, two-, and three-period intervals. The results are displayed in Table 13.5, aggregated for each year in the forecasts.

While this is not a complete tabulation, it covers the best forecasting results for the eight models. Our selection criterion was to use the best two results in each category and then to include in the table those functions that dominated in this comparison. In Part A of the table, the GL, AIM, and Fourier produced an overwhelming percentage of the best results (11/12 for line 1, for example). When the time trend was included, the Laurent replaced the GL; the AIM and Fourier still came in well (and the three again produced 11/12 best results for line 1). In Part B, the Laurent, AIM, and Fourier dominated, whether the time trend was included

TABLE 13.5
EVALUATING FORECASTS

(A) No time			Mean Absolute Error			Root Mean Square Error	
trend	Year	share1	share2	share3	share1	share2	share3
GL	1	0.000032	0.000024	0.000015	0.000206	0.000156	0.000090
	2	0.000079	0.000049	0.000037	0.000348	0.000213	0.000182
	3	0.000115	0.000068	0.000054	0.000423	0.000246	0.000217
AIM	1	0.000063	0.000044	0.000031	0.000309	0.000230	0.000154
	2	0.000133	0.000088	0.000059	0.000464	0.000309	0.000234
	3	0.000206	0.000133	0.000087	0.000585	0.000376	0.000277
FFF	1	0.000045	0.000058	0.000031	0.000230	0.000290	0.000167
	2	0.000106	0.000100	0.000076	0.000381	0.000365	0.000299
	3	0.000150	0.000139	0.000099	0.000450	0.000411	0.000323

Time			share1	share2	share3	share1	share2	share3
trend	Year							
LAUR	1		0.000041	0.000025	0.000019	0.000212	0.00162	0.000097
	2		0.000085	0.000049	0.000079	0.000295	0.000210	0.000309
	3		0.000148	0.000068	0.000129	0.000412	0.000236	0.000394
AIM	1		0.000083	0.000055	0.000027	0.000402	0.000276	0.000128
	2		0.000162	0.000124	0.000063	0.000559	0.000455	0.000212
	3		0.000207	0.000162	0.000092	0.000604	0.000490	0.000252
FFF	1		0.000035	0.000040	0.000028	0.000168	0.000188	0.000175
	2		0.000078	0.000085	0.000040	0.000261	0.000280	0.000186
	3		0.000106	0.000104	0.000052	0.000298	0.000297	0.000196

TABLE 13.5 CONT'D

(B) No time	trend	Year	Average Absolute Percentage Error			Adjusted R-Squared		
			share1	share2	share3	share1	share2	share3
	LAUR	1	0.003487	0.003002	0.001259	0.998597	0.999426	0.997227
		2	0.004235	0.002722	0.001908	0.998829	0.999723	0.989396
		3	0.004042	0.002416	0.001937	0.999217	0.999787	0.993006
	AIM2	1	0.004123	0.002585	0.001923	0.998233	0.999561	0.986208
		2	0.004419	0.002609	0.001814	0.998667	0.999771	0.990851
		3	0.004443	0.002688	0.001787	0.998953	0.999798	0.993725
	FFF	1	0.002928	0.003470	0.001912	0.998633	0.999235	0.998173
		2	0.003502	0.002965	0.002338	0.998775	0.999575	0.984512
		3	0.003225	0.002807	0.002043	0.999158	0.999624	0.989942

Time	trend	Year		share2	share3	share1	share2	share3
			share1	share2	share3	share1	share2	share3
	LAUR	1	0.002730	0.001528	0.001234	0.998720	0.998947	0.999306
		2	0.002834	0.001468	0.002450	0.999279	0.999467	0.994677
		3	0.003193	0.001382	0.002666	0.999446	0.999333	0.995759
	AIM	1	0.005478	0.003323	0.001691	0.997326	0.998673	0.991954
		2	0.005370	0.0033693	0.001938	0.998615	0.998949	0.997053
		3	0.004454	0.003276	0.001895	0.998168	0.998319	0.997633
	FFF	1	0.002310	0.002390	0.001784	0.999379	0.999960	0.991722
		2	0.002592	0.002539	0.001252	0.999480	0.999962	0.995693
		3	0.002282	0.002112	0.001081	0.999555	0.999741	0.996174

TABLE 13.6

P-VALUES FOR ONE-TO-FOUR-QUARTERS-AHEAD FORECASTS[a]

No time trend

	GL			BTL			AIDS		
Year	sh1	sh2	sh3	sh1	sh2	sh3	sh1	sh2	sh3
81.1	0.000	0.000	0.000	0.000	0.045	0.529	0.709	0.000	0.000
81.2	0.000	0.921	0.016	0.000	0.000	0.195	0.000	0.046	0.107
81.3	0.000	0.000	0.000	0.000	0.001	0.067	0.000	0.000	0.777
81.4	0.007	0.194	0.378	0.000	0.000	0.000	0.000	0.080	0.026

	LAUR			QUAIDS			GEF		
Year	sh1	sh2	sh3	sh1	sh2	sh3	sh1	sh2	sh3
81.1	0.170	0.736	0.017	0.000	0.180	0.001	0.000	0.007	0.000
81.2	0.000	0.000	0.058	0.000	0.000	0.071	0.000	0.000	0.001
81.3	0.149	0.000	0.002	0.040	0.000	0.000	0.003	0.001	0.008
81.4	0.001	0.000	0.569	0.000	0.000	0.000	0.000	0.000	0.000

	FFF				AIM		
Year	sh1	sh2	sh3		sh1	sh2	sh3
81.1	0.002	0.180	0.001		0.055	0.927	0.000
81.2	0.000	0.000	0.131		0.000	0.000	0.001
81.3	0.444	0.000	0.000		0.136	0.001	0.018
81.4	0.000	0.000	0.000		0.000	0.000	0.010

Time trend

	GL			BTL			AIDS		
Year	sh1	sh2	sh3	sh1	sh2	sh3	sh1	sh2	sh3
81.1	0.000	0.001	0.000	0.944	0.161	0.237	0.194	0.000	0.000
81.2	0.000	0.000	0.147	0.000	0.001	0.000	0.000	0.001	0.000
81.3	0.000	0.000	0.003	0.000	0.000	0.378	0.000	0.000	0.000
81.4	0.000	0.000	0.231	0.000	0.016	0.000	0.000	0.001	0.000

	LAUR			QUAIDS			GEF		
Year	sh1	sh2	sh3	sh1	sh2	sh3	sh1	sh2	sh3
81.1	0.211	0.045	0.539	0.000	0.000	0.000	0.000	0.001	0.025
81.2	0.001	0.006	0.000	0.000	0.000	0.055	0.000	0.000	0.000
81.3	0.415	0.921	0.071	0.044	0.000	0.000	0.202	0.103	0.065
81.4	0.471	0.958	0.071	0.000	0.000	0.000	0.000	0.006	0.000

	FFF				AIM		
Year	sh1	sh2	sh3		sh1	sh2	sh3
81.1	0.001	0.002	0.000		0.000	0.001	0.013
81.2	0.000	0.000	0.436		0.000	0.000	0.000
81.3	0.017	0.000	0.000		0.137	0.202	0.174
81.4	0.000	0.000	0.000		0.000	0.006	0.000

[a]The null is rejected at the 5% level for values less than 0.05

Note: sh1 = share of motor vehicles, sh2 = other durables aggregate, sh3 = aggregate of nondurables and services

or not. Inescapably, the globally flexible AIM and Fourier dominate in these comparisons, with the effectively global Laurent not far behind.

To test if the forecasted value is statistically different from the realized value, we calculate p-values for the Wald statistic using the delta method. At the 5% level of significance, all models without a time trend fail to accept the null at over 50% of the quarters with the worst case of the GEF rejecting the null for all shares in all quarters. The results are similar for the models once a time trend is included but the Laurent model does particularly well (Table 13.6). Overall, no flexible form appears to be statistically better than the others in this list.

13.8   Conclusions

This chapter evaluates and compares three types of flexible functional forms — locally flexible, effectively globally regular, and asymptotically globally flexible — in terms of violations of regularity conditions, information criteria, performance in the tails of the expenditure space, substitution elasticities, and forecasts. All models are estimated using U.S. aggregate consumption data that itself was found to be consistent with a well behaved utility function over much of the sample. As we shall explain in our summary, the global models, especially the QUAIDS, FFF, and AIM seem to have dominated on these tests.

The breakdown of the tests is as follows. All the models fit the data well, but a preference should be expressed for the more parametrically parsimonious functions; these are the GL and the AIDS models. Over the GARP consistent data set, quasi-concavity tests indicated that the QUAIDS, GEF, AIM, FFF, and GL did the best, with and without the time trend. The SIC and AIC tests favored the GL, AIDS, GEF, and QUAIDS models, with the GEF doing the best. The Laurent, GEF, and particularly the QUAIDS model fit the extreme levels of expenditures best; the AIM model also did well in this test. Looking at substitution elasticities, we found those from the globally flexible AIM and FFF most plausible, with the GL least plausible. Finally, more support was obtained for the forecasting performance of the AIM, FFF, and Laurent models, although the GL was best in one category.

Across all tests, three specifications seem to stand out. These are the QUAIDS, FFF, and AIM models, the first being effectively global and the latter two being asymptotically global. The GEF model (also an effectively global specification) also did well on most tests. If nothing else, the importance of employing a globally regular model is convincingly demonstrated in this chapter. We cannot say whether this should be achieved 'effectively' or 'asymptotically' on the evidence, but if one worries about parametric parsimony, then the effectively global methods (QUAIDS and GEF) might be preferable.

A particularly interesting result in this chapter is that the LAURENT, QUAIDS, GEF and the globally flexible functions generally find that motor vehicles, other consumer durables, and nondurables generally are substitutes for each other. Finding substitution is a result most researchers expect. In addition, in the better-fitting models we found sharp-changes in these elasticities around recession periods (and occasionally at other times), results which if correct call into question the use of constant elasticity of substitution methods. The advantages of the global models are relatively greater when utility surfaces are highly nonlinear, when user costs fluctuate considerably (over time). Their relatively good performance compared to the local flexible forms in the period tested suggest that these observations have some merit. We conclude that the AIM model, closely followed by the Fourier, provides the most satisfactory results.

Finally, we note that the low income variation and the relatively large price variation often found in aggregate data may favor employing functional forms that allow for more price flexibility (such as the AIM and Fourier). Aggregate data may also bias results toward functions having simple Engel curves and/or low rank although our results show no evidence of this. In contrast, functions having more income flexibility relative to price flexibility may be preferred when using household-level data, such as the QUAIDS and GEF models. We think future research should examine how flexible forms perform using household-level data, particularly when there are many variables and a relatively small sample which may limit the use of the asymptotically globally flexible forms. Developing an asymptotically globally flexible QUAIDS or GEF model by adding Fourier series or a Müntz-Szatz expansion is another useful direction for future work.

Chapter 14

Semi-Nonparametric Estimates of the Demand for Money in the United States

*Apostolos Serletis and Asghar Shahmoradi**

14.1   Introduction

For many years the literature on monetary asset demand systems employed globally regular generating functions such as the Cobb-Douglas or the Constant Elasticity of Substitution (CES) utility functions — see, for example Chetty (1969). These forms had the advantage of conforming to the neoclassical conditions for constrained consumer maximization. However, when Uzawa (1962) proved that one cannot simultaneously obtain arbitrary estimates of elasticities of substitution and have a CES specification, the approach ran into a dead end.

To overcome that problem flexible functional forms that provide local approximations to the demand functions were then used. Specifically, a popular local approximation to the indirect utility function was achieved by a translog specification. In this way duality theory would provide access to all the implications of aggregate integrability at least at a point. On

*Originally published in *Macroeconomic Dynamics*, 9 (2005), 542–559. Reprinted with permission.

the demand for money, Offenbacher (1979) was the first to employ a flexible functional form (the translog) in this manner. As noted, these models can attain arbitrary elasticities at a single point and according to Barnett, Geweke, and Wolfe (1991), do so at a high degree; as a consequence they have revolutionized microeconometrics by providing access to all of neoclassical microeconomic theory in econometric applications.

However, although locally flexible functional forms provide arbitrary elasticity estimates at the point of approximation, they gain this precision at the expense of giving up global regularity. There is also evidence that these models fail to meet the regularity conditions for consumer maximization in large regions. Barnett (1983, 1985), Barnett and Lee (1985) and Barnett, Lee, and Wolfe (1985, 1987) provided a partial solution to this problem by proposing the minflex Laurent model that is locally flexible and regular over a large region but is still not globally regular. But the problem persisted that the flexibility was achieved only at a single point. An innovation in this respect are the semi-nonparametric flexible functional forms that possess global flexibility and in which asymptotic inferences are, potentially, free from any specification error.

Semi-nonparametric functions can provide an asymptotically global approximation to complex economic relationships. These functions provide global approximations to the true data generating process and its partial derivatives. By global approximation, we mean that the flexible functional form is capable, in the limit, of approximating the unknown underlying generating function at all points and thus of producing arbitrarily accurate elasticities at all data points. Two such semi-nonparametric functions are the Fourierflexible functional form, introduced by Gallant (1981), and the Asymptotically Ideal Model (AIM), introduced by Barnett and Jonas (1983) and employed and explained in Barnett and Yue (1988) — see also Fisher and Fleissig (1997), Fisher, Fleissig, and Serletis (2001), Fleissig and Serletis (2002), Fleissig and Swofford (1996, 1997), and Drake, Fleissig, and Swofford (2003) for some interesting applications.

This chapter focuses on the demand for money in the United States in the context of these two globally flexible functional forms — the Fourier and the Asymptotically Ideal Model. We compare these two models in terms of violations of the regularity conditions for consumer maximization and also provide a policy perspective, using (for the first time) parameter estimates that are consistent with global regularity, in that a very strong case can be made for abandoning the simple sum approach to monetary aggregation, on the basis of the low elasticities of substitution among the components of the popular M2 aggregate of money. We believe that much of the older literature that investigates the substitutability/complementarity relation between monetary assets in the context of demand systems does not impose full regularity (as we do in this chapter) and hence has to be disregarded.

The chapter is organized as follows. Section 14.2 briefly sketches out the neoclassical monetary problem while Section 14.3 discusses monetary aggregation and measurement matters and uses the Divisia index to aggregate monetary assets. In Sections 14.5-9 we estimate the models, assess the results in terms of their consistency with optimizing behavior, and explore the economic significance of the results. The final section concludes the chapter.

14.2   The Demand for Monetary Services

We assume a weakly separable monetary utility function, so that the representative money holder faces the following problem

$$\max_{x} f(x) \quad \text{subject to} \quad p'x = m,$$

where $x = (x_1, x_2, \cdots, x_8)$ is the vector of monetary asset quantities described in Table 14.1; $p = (p_1, p_2, \cdots, p_8)$ is the corresponding vector of monetary asset user costs; and m is the expenditure on the services of monetary assets.

TABLE 14.1

MONETARY ASSETS/COMPONENTS

1   Currency + Travelers checks
2   Demand deposits
3   Other checkable deposits at commercial banks including Super Now accounts
4   Other checkable deposits at thrift institutions including Super Now accounts

5   Savings deposits at commercial banks including money market deposit accounts
6   Savings deposits at thrift institutions including money market deposit accounts

7   Small denomination time deposits at commercial banks
8   Small denomination time deposits at thrift institutions

Source: Anderson, Jones, and Nesmith (1997, p. 61).

Because the economic agent involved in this study is the household, it is important to work with data that reflect this composite agent's selection of monetary services. In practice, the assets in the official M2 definition of money are appropriate, but we have excluded the rapidly growing retail money market mutual funds, as does much of the empirical literature, mainly because satisfactory monetary aggregates cannot be obtained using this asset most probably because the household employs this particular asset for its savings properties and not for its monetary services.

Moreover, because the flexible functional forms are parameter intensive we rationalize the estimation to a small set of monetary asset demand equations by imposing the following separable structure of preferences

$$f(\boldsymbol{x}) = f\left(f_1\left(x_1, x_2, x_3, x_4\right), \; f_2\left(x_5, x_6\right), \; f_3\left(x_7, x_8\right)\right)$$

where the subaggregator functions f_i $(i = 1, 2, 3)$ provide subaggregate measures of monetary services. Here the subaggregates will be thought of as Divisia quantity indexes that can allow for less than perfect substitutability among the relevant monetary components.

As already noted, the main reason for employing subaggregates, rather than studying all eight items, is that our models are very parameter intensive. We have separated the group of assets into three collections based on empirical pre-testing. The pre-testing, for which there is a large literature [see Barnett, Fisher, and Serletis (1992)] is based on the NONPAR GARP procedure of Varian (1982, 1983). The specific collection used here is very much like that reported in the literature.

14.3 The Data

The Federal Reserve Bank of St. Louis, in its Monetary Services Index project, provides monetary quantities as well as user costs, for the eight items listed in Table 14.1 (and many others, up through the L definition of money in the Federal Reserve's lexicon). For our empirical work we require per capita real data and to that end we have divided each measure of monetary services by the U.S. CPI (for all items) and total U.S. population. That data are quarterly from 1970:1 to 2003:2 (a total of 134 observations). The calculation of the user costs, which are the appropriate prices for monetary services, is explained in several online publications of the Federal Reserve Bank of St. Louis or in Barnett, Fisher, and Serletis (1992), Barnett and Serletis (2000), and Serletis (2001).

In order to provide the three subaggregates shown in Table 14.1, we employ a Divisia quantity index, defined (in discrete time) as

$$\log M_t - \log M_{t-1} = \sum_{j=1}^{n} s_{jt}^* (\log x_{jt} - \log x_{j,t-1})$$

According to which the growth rate of the subaggregate is the weighted average of the growth rates of the component quantities, with the Divisia weights being defined as the expenditure shares averaged over the two periods of the change, $s_{jt}^* = (1/2)(s_{jt} + s_{j,t-1})$ for $j = 1, ..., n$, where $s_{jt} = \pi_{jt} x_{jt} / \sum \pi_{kt} x_{kt}$ is the expenditure share of asset j during period t, and π_{jt} is the user cost of asset j. What this does, up to a third order remainder term, is preserve the microeconomic characteristics of the underlying monetary assets.

The collection of assets, then are as follows: Subaggregate A is composed of currency, travelers checks and other checkable deposits including Super NOW accounts issued by commercial banks and thrifts (series 1 to 4 in Table 14.1). Subaggregate B is composed of savings deposits issued by commercial banks and thrifts (series 5 and 6) and subaggregate C is composed of small time deposits issued by commercial banks and thrifts (series 7 and 8). Finally, Divisia user cost indexes are calculated by applying Fisher's (1922) weak factor reversal test.

14.4   The Fourier and AIM Models

Our objective is to estimate a system of demand equations derived from an indirect utility function. The most important advantage of using the indirect utility approach is that prices enter as exogenous variables in the estimation process and the demand system is easily derived by applying Roy's identity.

In this section we will briefly present the basic properties of two models that we plan to use in our empirical work. As we have already indicated, the models are the Fourier and the AIM. While there is some comparison implied in our presentation in this section, our purpose is basically to make clear the properties of the models that we will work with.

14.4.1 The Fourier

We follow the procedure explained in Gallant (1981) for expanding the indirect utility function using the Fourier series

$$h(\boldsymbol{v}) = u_0 + \boldsymbol{b}'\boldsymbol{v} + \frac{1}{2}\boldsymbol{v}'\boldsymbol{C}\boldsymbol{v}$$

$$+ \sum_{\alpha=1}^{A}\left(u_{0\alpha} + 2\sum_{j=1}^{J}\left[u_{j\alpha}\cos(j\boldsymbol{k}'_\alpha\boldsymbol{v}) - w_{j\alpha}\sin(j\boldsymbol{k}'_\alpha\boldsymbol{v})\right]\right) \qquad (14.1)$$

in which

$$\boldsymbol{C} = -\sum_{\alpha=1}^{A} u_{0\alpha}\boldsymbol{k}_\alpha\boldsymbol{k}'_\alpha$$

where $\boldsymbol{v}$ denotes income normalized prices ($=\boldsymbol{p}/m$), $\boldsymbol{k}_\alpha$ is a multi-index — an n-vector with integer components — and u_0, $\{b\}$, $\{u\}$, and $\{w\}$ are parameters to be estimated. As Gallant (1981) shows, the length of a multi-index, denoted as $|\boldsymbol{k}_\alpha|^* = \sum_{i=1}^{n}|k_{i\alpha}|$, reduces the complexity of the notation required to denote high-order partial differentiation and multivariate Fourier series expansions.[1] The parameters A (the number of terms) and J (the degree of the approximation) determine the degree of the Fourier polynomials.[2]

By applying Roy's modified identity,

$$s_i(\boldsymbol{v}) = \frac{v_i\left(\partial h(\boldsymbol{v})/\partial v_i\right)}{\boldsymbol{v}'\left(\partial h(\boldsymbol{v})/\partial v_i\right)}, \qquad (14.2)$$

---

[1] For example, with $n = 3$ in (14.1), the multi-index $\lambda' = (5, 2, 7)$, generates the 14th order partial derivative, as follows

$$D^\lambda h(\boldsymbol{v}) = \frac{\partial^{|\lambda|^*}}{\partial v_1^{\lambda_1}\partial v_2^{\lambda_2}\partial v_3^{\lambda_3}}h(\boldsymbol{v}) = \frac{\partial^{14}}{\partial v_1^5\partial v_2^2\partial v_3^7}h(\boldsymbol{v}),$$

see Gallant (1981) for more details.

[2] The Fourier flexible functional form has the ability of achieving close approximation in Sobolev norm which confers nonparametric properties on the functional form. This is the reason the Fourier flexible form is considered to be a semi-nonparametric functional form.

to (14.1), we obtain the Fourier demand system

$$
s_i = \cfrac{v_i b_i - \displaystyle\sum_{\alpha=1}^{A} \left(u_{0\alpha} \boldsymbol{v}' \boldsymbol{k}_\alpha + 2 \displaystyle\sum_{j=1}^{J} j \left[u_{j\alpha} \sin(j\boldsymbol{k}'_\alpha \boldsymbol{v}) + w_{j\alpha} \cos(j\boldsymbol{k}'_\alpha \boldsymbol{v}) \right] \right) k_{i\alpha} v_i}{\boldsymbol{b}' \boldsymbol{v} - \displaystyle\sum_{\alpha=1}^{A} \left(u_{0\alpha} \boldsymbol{v}' \boldsymbol{k}_\alpha + 2 \displaystyle\sum_{j=1}^{J} j \left[u_{j\alpha} \sin(j\boldsymbol{k}'_\alpha \boldsymbol{v}) + w_{j\alpha} \cos(j\boldsymbol{k}'_\alpha \boldsymbol{v}) \right] \right) \boldsymbol{k}'_\alpha \boldsymbol{v}},
$$

$$(14.3)$$

for $i = 1, 2, 3$ monetary assets — the time subscript t has been suppressed.

Eastwood and Gallant (1991) show that Fourier functions produce consistent and asymptotically normal parameter estimates when the number of parameters to be estimated equals the number of effective observations raised to the power of $2/3$ — this result follows from Huber (1981) and is similar to optimal bandwidth results in many non-parametric models. In our case, with $n = 3$ and $T = 134$, the number of effective observations is $268\ (= 2 \times 134)$ — since we estimate $(n-1)$ share equations — and we should therefore estimate (approximately) $41\ (= 268^{2/3})$ parameters. As we impose the normalization $b_n = \sum_{i=1}^{n-1} b_i$, the Fourier demand system has $(n-1)\ b$, $A\ u_{0\alpha}$, $AJ\ u_{j\alpha}$, and $AJ\ w_{j\alpha}$ parameters to be estimated, for a total of $(n-1) + A(1+2J)$ free parameters. By setting $(n-1) + A(1+2J)$ equal to 41, in this application we choose the values of A and J to be 13 and 1, respectively. This also determines the elementary multi-indexes used in this chapter, as shown in Table 14.2.

As a Fourier series is a periodic function in its arguments but the indirect utility function is not, the scaling of the data is also important. In empirical applications, to avoid the approximation from diverging from the true indirect utility function the data should be rescaled so that the income normalized prices lie on $0 \le v_i \le 2\pi$. The income normalized prices $v_i\ (i = 1, \cdots, n)$ are typically rescaled as follows $v_i \times [(2\pi - \varepsilon)/\max\{v_i : i = 1, \cdots, n\}]$, with $(2\pi - \varepsilon)$ set equal to 6, as in Gallant (1982). In our case, however, the income normalized prices $v_i\ (i = 1, \cdots, n)$ are already between 0 and 2π, so we performed no such rescaling.

TABLE 14.2

ELEMENTARY MULTI-INDEXES $\{k\}_{\alpha=1}^{13}$

α	1	2	3	4	5	6	7	8	9	10	11	12	13
v_1	1	0	0	1	1	0	1	0	0	1	1	2	2
v_2	0	1	0	1	0	1	1	1	2	2	0	1	0
v_3	0	0	1	0	1	1	1	2	1	0	2	0	1
$|k_\alpha|^*$	1	1	1	2	2	2	3	3	3	3	3	3	3

14.4.2 The AIM

Following Barnett and Yue (1988), the reciprocal indirect utility function for the asymptotically ideal model of first order approximation for $n = 3$ (our problem in hand) is

$$h(v) = a_0 + \sum_{k=1}^{K} \sum_{i=1}^{3} a_{ik} v_i^{\lambda(k)} + \sum_{k=1}^{K} \sum_{m=1}^{K} \left[\sum_{i=1}^{3} \sum_{j=1}^{3} a_{ijkm} v_i^{\lambda(k)} v_j^{\lambda(m)} \right]$$

$$+ \sum_{k=1}^{K} \sum_{m=1}^{K} \sum_{g=1}^{K} \left[\sum_{i=1}^{3} \sum_{j=1}^{3} \sum_{h=1}^{3} a_{ijhkmg} v_i^{\lambda(k)} v_j^{\lambda(m)} v_h^{\lambda(g)} \right] \qquad (14.4)$$

where $\lambda(z) = 2^{-z}$ for $z = \{k, m, g\}$ is the exponent set and a_{ik}, a_{ijkm}, and a_{ijhkmg}, for all $i, j, h = 1, 2, 3$, are the parameters to be estimated. The number of parameters is reduced by deleting the diagonal elements of the parameter arrays so that $i \neq j$, $j \neq h$ and $i \neq h$. This does not alter the span of the model's approximation.

To avoid the extensive multiple subscripting in the coefficients a_{ijhkmg}, we follow Barnett and Yue (1988), and reparameterize by stacking the coefficients as they appear in (14.4) into a single vector of parameters,

$\mathbf{b} = (b_0, \cdots, b_{26})'$ containing the 27 coefficients in (14.4), as follows

$$h(\boldsymbol{v}) = b_0 + b_1 v_1^{1/2} + b_2 v_2^{1/2} + b_3 v_3^{1/2} + b_4 v_1^{1/4} + b_5 v_2^{1/4} + b_6 v_3^{1/4} + b_7 v_1^{1/2} v_2^{1/2}$$

$$+ b_8 v_1^{1/2} v_2^{1/4} + b_9 v_1^{1/4} v_2^{1/2} + b_{10} v_1^{1/4} v_2^{1/4} + b_{11} v_1^{1/2} v_3^{1/2} + b_{12} v_1^{1/2} v_3^{1/4}$$

$$+ b_{13} v_1^{1/4} v_3^{1/2} + b_{14} v_1^{1/4} v_3^{1/4} + b_{15} v_2^{1/2} v_3^{1/2} + b_{16} v_2^{1/2} v_3^{1/4} + b_{17} v_2^{1/4} v_3^{1/2}$$

$$+ b_{18} v_2^{1/4} v_3^{1/4} + b_{19} v_1^{1/2} v_2^{1/2} v_3^{1/2} + b_{20} v_1^{1/4} v_2^{1/2} v_3^{1/2} + b_{21} v_1^{1/2} v_2^{1/4} v_3^{1/2}$$

$$+ b_{22} v_1^{1/2} v_2^{1/2} v_3^{1/4} + b_{23} v_1^{1/2} v_2^{1/4} v_3^{1/4} + b_{24} v_1^{1/4} v_2^{1/2} v_3^{1/4}$$

$$+ b_{25} v_1^{1/4} v_2^{1/4} v_3^{1/2} + b_{26} v_1^{1/4} v_2^{1/4} v_3^{1/4} \tag{14.5}$$

Applying the modified version of Roy's identity, (14.2), to (14.5) we obtain the AIM demand system,

$$s_1 = \Big(2b_1 v_1^{\frac{1}{2}} + b_2 v_1^{\frac{1}{4}} + 2b_7 v_1^{\frac{1}{2}} v_2^{\frac{1}{2}} + 2b_8 v_1^{\frac{1}{2}} v_2^{\frac{1}{4}} + b_9 v_1^{\frac{1}{4}} v_2^{\frac{1}{2}} + b_{10} v_1^{\frac{1}{4}} v_2^{\frac{1}{4}} + 2b_{11} v_1^{\frac{1}{2}} v_3^{\frac{1}{2}}$$

$$+ 2b_{12} v_1^{\frac{1}{2}} v_3^{\frac{1}{4}} + b_{13} v_1^{\frac{1}{4}} v_3^{\frac{1}{2}} + b_{14} v_1^{\frac{1}{4}} v_3^{\frac{1}{4}} + 2b_{19} v_1^{\frac{1}{2}} v_2^{\frac{1}{2}} v_3^{\frac{1}{2}} + b_{20} v_1^{\frac{1}{4}} v_2^{\frac{1}{2}} v_3^{\frac{1}{2}}$$

$$+ 2b_{21} v_1^{\frac{1}{2}} v_2^{\frac{1}{4}} v_3^{\frac{1}{2}} + + 2b_{22} v_1^{\frac{1}{2}} v_2^{\frac{1}{2}} v_3^{\frac{1}{4}} 2b_{23} v_1^{\frac{1}{2}} v_2^{\frac{1}{4}} v_3^{\frac{1}{4}} + b_{24} v_1^{\frac{1}{4}} v_2^{\frac{1}{2}} v_3^{\frac{1}{4}}$$

$$+ b_{25} v_1^{\frac{1}{4}} v_2^{\frac{1}{4}} v_3^{\frac{1}{2}} + b_{26} v_1^{\frac{1}{4}} v_2^{\frac{1}{4}} v_3^{\frac{1}{4}} \Big) / D \tag{14.6}$$

$$s_2 = \Big(2b_3 v_2^{\frac{1}{2}} + b_4 v_2^{\frac{1}{4}} + 2b_7 v_1^{\frac{1}{2}} v_2^{\frac{1}{2}} + b_8 v_1^{\frac{1}{2}} v_2^{\frac{1}{4}} + 2b_9 v_1^{\frac{1}{4}} v_2^{\frac{1}{2}} + b_{10} v_1^{\frac{1}{4}} v_2^{\frac{1}{4}} + 2b_{15} v_2^{\frac{1}{2}} v_3^{\frac{1}{2}}$$

$$+ 2b_{16} v_2^{\frac{1}{2}} v_3^{\frac{1}{4}} + b_{17} v_2^{\frac{1}{4}} v_3^{\frac{1}{2}} + b_{18} v_2^{\frac{1}{4}} v_3^{\frac{1}{4}} + 2b_{19} v_1^{\frac{1}{2}} v_2^{\frac{1}{2}} v_3^{\frac{1}{2}} + 2b_{20} v_1^{\frac{1}{4}} v_2^{\frac{1}{2}} v_3^{\frac{1}{2}}$$

$$+ b_{21} v_1^{\frac{1}{2}} v_2^{\frac{1}{4}} v_3^{\frac{1}{2}} + 2b_{22} v_1^{\frac{1}{2}} v_2^{\frac{1}{2}} v_3^{\frac{1}{4}} + b_{23} v_1^{\frac{1}{2}} v_2^{\frac{1}{4}} v_3^{\frac{1}{4}} + 2b_{24} v_1^{\frac{1}{4}} v_2^{\frac{1}{2}} v_3^{\frac{1}{4}}$$

$$+ b_{25} v_1^{\frac{1}{4}} v_2^{\frac{1}{4}} v_3^{\frac{1}{2}} + b_{26} v_1^{\frac{1}{4}} v_2^{\frac{1}{4}} v_3^{\frac{1}{4}} \Big) / D \tag{14.7}$$

$$s_3 = \Big(2b_5 v_3^{\frac{1}{2}} + b_6 v_4^{\frac{1}{4}} + 2b_{11} v_1^{\frac{1}{2}} v_3^{\frac{1}{2}} + b_{12} v_1^{\frac{1}{2}} v_3^{\frac{1}{4}} + 2b_{13} v_1^{\frac{1}{4}} v_3^{\frac{1}{2}} + b_{14} v_1^{\frac{1}{4}} v_2^{\frac{1}{4}}$$

$$+ 2b_{15} v_1^{\frac{1}{2}} v_3^{\frac{1}{2}} + b_{16} v_2^{\frac{1}{2}} v_3^{\frac{1}{4}} + 2b_{17} v_2^{\frac{1}{4}} v_3^{\frac{1}{2}} + b_{18} v_2^{\frac{1}{4}} v_3^{\frac{1}{4}} + 2b_{19} v_1^{\frac{1}{2}} v_2^{\frac{1}{2}} v_3^{\frac{1}{2}}$$

$$+ 2b_{20} v_1^{\frac{1}{4}} v_2^{\frac{1}{2}} v_3^{\frac{1}{2}} + 2b_{21} v_1^{\frac{1}{2}} v_2^{\frac{1}{4}} v_3^{\frac{1}{2}} + b_{22} v_1^{\frac{1}{2}} v_2^{\frac{1}{2}} v_3^{\frac{1}{4}} + b_{23} v_1^{\frac{1}{2}} v_2^{\frac{1}{4}} v_3^{\frac{1}{4}}$$

$$+ b_{24} v_1^{\frac{1}{4}} v_2^{\frac{1}{2}} v_3^{\frac{1}{4}} + 2b_{25} v_1^{\frac{1}{4}} v_2^{\frac{1}{4}} v_3^{\frac{1}{2}} + b_{26} v_1^{\frac{1}{4}} v_2^{\frac{1}{4}} v_3^{\frac{1}{4}} \Big) / D \tag{14.8}$$

where D is the sum of the numerators in equations (14.6), (14.7), and (14.8).

14.5 Computational Considerations

Demand systems (14.3) and (14.6)-(14.8) can be written as

$$s_t = \psi(v_t, \boldsymbol{\theta}) + \epsilon_t \tag{14.9}$$

with an error term appended. In (14.9), $\boldsymbol{s} = (s_1, \cdots, s_n)'$, $\boldsymbol{\psi}(\boldsymbol{v}, \boldsymbol{\theta}) = (\psi_1(\boldsymbol{v}, \boldsymbol{\theta}), \cdots, \psi_n(\boldsymbol{v}, \boldsymbol{\theta}))'$, and $\psi_i(\boldsymbol{v}, \boldsymbol{\theta})$ is given by the right-hand side of each of (14.3) and (14.6)-(14.8).

As Gallant and Golub (1984, p. 298) put it,

> "all statistical estimation procedures that are commonly used in econometric research can be formulated as an optimization problem of the following type [Burguete, Gallant and Souza (1982)]:
>
> $$\widehat{\boldsymbol{\theta}} \text{ minimizes } \varphi(\boldsymbol{\theta}) \text{ over } \Theta$$
>
> with $\varphi(\boldsymbol{\theta})$ twice continuously differentiable in $\boldsymbol{\theta}$."

In this chapter, we follow Gallant and Golub (1984) and use Zellner's (1962) seemingly unrelated regression method to estimate $\boldsymbol{\theta}$. Hence, $\varphi(\boldsymbol{\theta})$ has the form

$$\varphi(\boldsymbol{\theta}) = \frac{1}{T}\epsilon_t'\epsilon_t = \frac{1}{T}\sum_{t=1}^{T}\left[s_t - \psi(v_t, \boldsymbol{\theta})\right]' \widehat{\boldsymbol{\Sigma}}^{-1}\left[s_t - \psi(v_t, \boldsymbol{\theta})\right] \tag{14.10}$$

where T is the number of observations and $\widehat{\boldsymbol{\Sigma}}$ is an estimate of the variance-covariance matrix of (14.9). In minimizing (14.10), we use the TOM-LAB/NPSOL tool box with MATLAB — see http://tomlab.biz/products/npsol. NPSOL uses a sequential quadratic programming algorithm and is suitable for both unconstrained and constrained optimization of smooth (that is, at least twice-continuously differentiable) nonlinear functions.

As results in nonlinear optimization are sensitive to the initial parameter values, to achieve global convergence, we randomly generated 500 sets of initial parameter values and chose the starting θ that led to the lowest value of the objective function. The parameter estimates that minimize the objective function are reported in the first column of Tables 14.3 and 14.4 for the Fourier and AIM, respectively. As in Gallant (1981) and Barnett and Yue (1988) we do not have access to asymptotic standard errors that can be supported by statistical theory. We also report the number of positivity, monotonicity, and curvature violations, since the usefulness of flexible functional forms depends on whether they satisfy these theoretical regularity conditions. The regularity conditions are checked as follows:

- Positivity is checked by direct computation of the values of the estimated budget shares, $\widehat{\boldsymbol{s}}_t$. It is satisfied if $\widehat{\boldsymbol{s}}_t \geq 0$, for all t.

- Monotonicity is checked by choosing a normalization on the indirect utility function so as to make $h(\boldsymbol{p}, m)$ decreasing in its arguments and by direct computation of the values of the first gradient vector of the estimated indirect utility function. It is satisfied if $\widehat{h}_{\boldsymbol{p}}(\boldsymbol{p}, m) < 0$ and $\widehat{h}_m(\boldsymbol{p}, m) > 0$ or, equivalently, if $\nabla\widehat{h}(\boldsymbol{v}) < 0$, where $\nabla\widehat{h}(\boldsymbol{v}) = (\partial/\partial\boldsymbol{v})\widehat{h}(\boldsymbol{v})$.

- Curvature requires that the Slutsky matrix be negative semidefinite and is checked by performing a Cholesky factorization of that matrix and checking whether the Cholesky values are nonpositive [since a matrix is negative semidefinite if its Cholesky factors are nonpositive — see Lau (1978, Theorem 3.2)]. Curvature can also be checked by examining the Allen elasticities of substitution matrix provided that the monotonicity condition holds. It requires that this matrix be negative semidefinite.

The results of the regularity tests for each model are presented in the last three rows of each of Tables 14.3 and 14.4. The numbers in the tables represent the number of times the regularity conditions are violated. For both models, the positivity and monotonicity conditions are satisfied at every data point whereas the curvature condition is violated at 108 data points with the Fourier and at every data point with the AIM. As Barnett (2002, p. 199) put it in his *Journal of Econometrics* Fellow's opinion chapter, without satisfaction of all three theoretical regularity conditions

> "the second-order conditions for optimizing behavior fail, and duality theory fails. The resulting first-order conditions, demand functions, and supply functions become invalid."

TABLE 14.3

FOURIER PARAMETER ESTIMATES

Parameter	Unconstrained estimates	Curvature constrained estimates at 1970:3	at every data point
b_1	9.8827	8.5167	16.9159
b_2	−9.9711	−4.0648	−1.0983
u_{01}	−0.0696	2.2966	−1.4401
u_{02}	−5.6783	9.9527	1.1614
u_{03}	−9.9572	−9.1946	7.1087
u_{04}	−1.5888	−3.8524	−3.9854
u_{05}	−5.0808	4.1590	0.1090
u_{06}	3.2362	−7.3311	15.0890
u_{07}	7.1422	6.0079	−11.5471
u_{08}	−9.9668	−9.4677	−4.5413
u_{09}	0.5889	−0.4065	−8.8838
u_{010}	1.0631	−7.6313	−7.4249
u_{011}	3.2555	1.4469	12.2196
u_{012}	−3.5331	6.1231	−11.7106
u_{013}	9.9695	−4.1753	−4.1391
u_1	6.4092	−6.7076	5.6165
u_2	−9.9992	8.0034	−1.3177
u_3	−9.9190	−9.9272	3.5608
u_4	6.9514	9.9793	−3.5899
u_5	3.8301	6.0373	5.1845
u_6	8.9304	7.5087	−1.7951
u_7	−9.5384	−4.1124	−5.5275
u_8	−1.4891	2.9607	−3.9751
u_9	1.8537	−0.1595	1.3432
u_{10}	−0.8674	−1.4024	−2.4942
u_{11}	3.2000	0.2988	−3.9673
u_{12}	0.5853	−0.3216	−1.6734
u_{13}	−4.2998	−0.7962	3.6057
w_1	−9.8585	−0.9393	12.6244
w_2	−0.7191	−1.6648	2.3662
w_3	4.7892	3.9253	−2.4496
w_4	−0.6886	−5.3475	31.6423
w_5	2.4978	2.2708	27.2746
w_6	−1.0254	1.9781	12.2804
w_7	4.7737	4.9621	44.9271
w_8	−1.6789	−4.7961	13.3554
w_9	−1.7263	−0.5501	−3.9293
w_{10}	1.5112	2.0612	5.1504
w_{11}	−6.7651	−3.1831	−9.4060
w_{12}	−3.4348	−0.5506	−4.4091
w_{13}	9.7170	2.2052	−7.4667
$S(\widehat{\theta})$	0.1453	0.1497	0.2255
Positivity violations	0	0	0
Monotonicity violations	0	0	0
Curvature violations	108	107	0

Note: Sample period, quarterly data 1970:1-2003:2 ($T = 134$).

TABLE 14.4

AIM(2) PARAMETER ESTIMATES

Parameter	Unconstrained estimates	Curvature constrained estimates at 1970:3	at every data point
b_1	29.5875	11.1562	−6.9260
b_2	−9.2315	−13.5795	−1.9350
b_4	41.7477	48.3525	−2.9772
b_5	−23.1435	−4.2921	−14.1856
b_6	24.1658	19.6995	−4.4322
b_7	−24.4985	9.8734	−3.3260
b_8	−47.7210	−44.9723	−11.1158
b_9	48.0046	47.4123	14.8184
b_{10}	20.6273	−19.9689	2.4160
b_{11}	47.7143	−7.6556	−12.3775
b_{12}	−43.9928	−4.9000	12.8131
b_{13}	−49.9942	−45.2815	−10.8964
b_{14}	13.4080	25.4421	4.4255
b_{15}	1.6750	15.8453	3.5688
b_{16}	−49.8608	−23.2905	−13.1646
b_{17}	49.9930	5.1945	−4.1361
b_{18}	49.3032	26.7168	5.0354
b_{19}	2.2844	15.6453	−7.4257
b_{20}	−38.7443	−44.4347	2.6264
b_{21}	2.8921	44.4650	13.9129
b_{22}	30.3519	−10.1999	−0.7214
b_{23}	−18.8956	−32.9601	1.9801
b_{24}	39.0944	6.1177	5.7279
b_{25}	−4.9706	0.6263	−7.0509
b_{26}	−29.1445	14.0451	5.6272
$S(\widehat{\boldsymbol{\theta}})$	0.1905	0.1977	0.2360
Positivity violations	0	0	0
Monotonicity violations	0	0	0
Curvature violations	134	109	0

Note: Sample period, quarterly data 1970:1-2003:2 $(T = 134)$.

14.6 Imposing Curvature Restrictions

The indirect utility function should be a quasi-convex function in income normalized prices, v_i $(i = 1, \cdots, n)$ — as already noted, this is the curvature condition. Gallant and Golub (1984), following Diewert, Avriel, and Zang (1977), argue that a necessary and sufficient condition for quasi-convexity of $h(v, \theta)$ is

$$g(v, \theta) = \min_{z} \left\{ z' \nabla^2 h(v, \theta) z : z' \nabla h(v, \theta) = 0, z'z = 1 \right\} \qquad (14.11)$$

where $\nabla h(v, \theta) = (\partial/\partial v) h(v, \theta)$ and $\nabla^2 h(v, \theta) = (\partial^2/\partial v \partial v') h(v, \theta)$, and $g(v, \theta)$ is non-negative (that is, zero or positive) when the quasi-convexity (curvature) constraint is satisfied and negative when it is violated. $g(v, \theta)$ is refered to as the 'constraint indicator.' Hence, as in Gallant and Golub (1984), we impose quasi-convexity by modifying the optimization problem as follows

$$\text{minimize } \varphi(\theta) \text{ subject to } \min_{v \in \Omega} g(v, \theta) \geq 0,$$

where Ω is a finite set with the finite number of elements v_i $(i = 1, \cdots, n)$. Curvature can be imposed at some representative point in the data (that is, locally), over a region of data points, or at every data point in the sample (that is, globally).

Let us briefly describe in more detail the Gallant and Golub (1984) method for imposing curvature restrictions on flexible functional forms. Define a real symmetric $n \times n$ matrix $\mathbf{A} = \nabla^2 h(v, \theta)$ — note that this is the Hessian matrix of the indirect utility function, $h(v, \theta)$ — and an $n \times 1$ vector $\alpha = \nabla h(v, \theta)$ as the gradient vector of $h(v, \theta)$. The curvature condition (14.11) can be written as

$$g(v, \theta) = \min_{z} \left\{ z' \mathbf{A} z : z'\alpha = 0, z'z = 1 \right\}$$

The next step is to partition α as $\alpha = (\alpha_1, \alpha'_{(2)})'$, where α_1 is the first element of α and $\alpha_{(2)}$ is an $(n-1) \times 1$ vector of the remaining elements of α, and construct an $n \times 1$ vector u

$$u = \begin{pmatrix} \alpha_1 - \|\alpha\| \\ \alpha_{(2)} \end{pmatrix}$$

where $\|\alpha\|$ is the norm of α, defined as $\|\alpha\| = \left(\sum_{i=1}^{n} \alpha_i^2 \right)^{1/2}$. With this notation we define the following

$$\gamma = -\frac{1}{2}u'u$$
$$\omega = -\gamma^{-1}Au$$
$$\Phi = \left(\gamma^{-2}u'Au\right)$$
$$\phi = (\Phi/2)u - \omega$$

where γ is a scalar, Φ is an $n \times n$ matrix, and ω and ϕ are $n \times 1$ vectors. The next and final step is to form an $n \times n$ matrix K as follows

$$K = A + u\phi' + \phi u'$$

Let's delete the first row and column of K and rename the $n - 1$ by $n - 1$ thereby obtained matrix as K_{22}. A necessary and sufficient condition for curvature (or equivalently for the indicator function (14.11) to be non-negative) is that K_{22} should be a positive semidefinite matrix. In this chapter, we use the 'chol' command in MATLAB to perform a Cholesky factorization of the K_{22} matrix and construct an indicator of whether K_{22} is positive semidefinite (this indicator is zero when K_{22} is positive semidefinite and a positive integer otherwise). Hence, we run a constrained optimization subject to the constraint that K_{22} is positive semidefinite (in which case curvature is satisfied). As already noted, we can evaluate K_{22} at a single data point, over a region of data points, or at every data point in the sample.

Using NPSOL we performed the computations and report the results in the second and third columns of Tables 14.3 and 14.4 — the second column shows the results when the quasi-convexity constraint is imposed locally (in 1970:3) and the third column shows the results when the constraint is imposed at every data point in the sample. Clearly, the effect of imposing the quasi-convexity constraint locally is negligible, as the number of curvature violations drops from 108 to 107 with the Fourier and from 134 to 109 with the AIM. Note also that the imposition of local curvature does not induce violations of monotonicity for both the Fourier and AIM that satisfy monotonicity (at all observations) when the local curvature condition is not imposed.

However, imposing the constraint at every data point (again using NPSOL), we obtain the results reported in the last column of each of Tables 14.3 and 14.4. Imposition of the quasi-convexity constraint globally has a significant impact on both models, as we obtain parameter estimates that are consistent with all three theoretical regularity restrictions (positivity, monotonicity, and curvature) at every data point in the sample. In this regard, Barnett and Pasupathy (2003, p. 151) argue that "imposing curvature without monotonicity, while perhaps to be preferred to the prior common practice of imposing neither, is not adequate without at least reporting data points at which violations of monotonicity occur. Monotonicity is too important to be ignored."

In our case, the imposition of curvature globally does not produce spurious violations of monotonicity, thereby assuring true theoretical regularity. Hence, in what follows we discuss the income and price elasticities as well as the elasticities of substitution based on the Fourier and AIM models which (with our data set) satisfy both the neoclassical monotonicity and curvature conditions. We believe that much of the older literature in this area does not impose full regularity — i.e., both monotonicity and curvature — and hence has to be disregarded.

14.7   Income and Price Elasticities

In the demand systems approach to estimation of economic relationships, the primary interest, especially in policy analysis, is in how the arguments of the underlying functions affect the quantities demanded. This is conventionally and completely expressed in terms of income and price elasticities and in elasticities of substitution. These elasticities can be calculated directly from the estimated budget share equations by writing the left-hand side as

$$x_i = \frac{s_i m}{p_i}, \quad i = 1, \ldots, n.$$

In particular, the income elasticities, η_{im}, can be calculated as

$$\eta_{im} = \frac{m}{s_i} \frac{\partial s_i}{\partial m} + 1, \quad i = 1, \ldots, n,$$

and the uncompensated (Cournot) price elasticities, η_{ij}, as

$$\eta_{ij} = \frac{p_j}{s_i} \frac{\partial s_i}{\partial p_j} - \delta_{ij}, \quad i, j = 1, \ldots, n,$$

where $\delta_{ij} = 0$ for $i \neq j$ and 1 otherwise. If $\eta_{ij} > 0$ the assets are gross substitutes, if $\eta_{ij} < 0$ they are gross complements, and if $\eta_{ij} = 0$ they are independent.

We begin be presenting the income elasticities in Part A of Table 14.5, evaluated at the mean of the data, for the three subaggregates and the two models.[3] η_{Am}, η_{Bm}, and η_{Cm} are all positive (suggesting that assets A, B, and C are all normal goods) which is consistent with economic theory. However, there are differences between the models. For example, time deposits have an income elasticity greater than one in the Fourier model but an income elasticity of 0.115 in the AIM model. In Table 14.5 we also show the own- and cross-price elasticities for the three assets. The own-price elasticities are all negative (as predicted by the theory) except for η_{CC} which is positive with the Fourier. For the cross-price elasticities, economic theory does not predict any signs, but we note that most of the off-diagonal terms are negative, indicating that the assets taken as a whole, are gross complements.

14.8 Elasticities of Substitution

From the point of view of monetary policy, the measurement of the elasticities of substitution among the three monetary assets is of prime importance. As we have already pointed out, the currently popular simple sum approach to monetary aggregation requires, in effect, that the elasticities of substitution be very high among the components of, especially, the aggregate M2. By 'very high' we mean infinite, of course, but since the policy literature has not addressed the question of how high such an estimate should be to warrant a simple sum calculation from a practical standpoint, all we can do is report our results.

There are currently two methods employed for calculating the partial elasticity of substitution between two variables, the Allen and the Morishima. Following Serletis (2001), the Allen partial elasticity of substitution between two liquid assets i and j, σ_{ij}^a, can be calculated as

$$\sigma_{ij}^a = \eta_{im} + \frac{\eta_{ij}}{s_j}.$$

The Allen elasticity of substitution is the traditional measure and has been employed to measure substitution behavior and structural instability in a variety of contexts. However, when there are more than two goods the Allen elasticity may be uninformative. For two assets the relationship is unambiguous — the assets must be substitutes. When there are more than two assets the relationship becomes complex and depends on things like the direction taken towards the point of approximation. In that case the Morishima elasticity of substitution is the correct measure of substitution

---

[3]All elasticities in this paper have been acquired using numerical differentiation to produce the values of $\partial s_i/\partial m$ and $\partial s_i/\partial p_j$ for $i, j = 1, 2, 3$.

elasticity

$$\sigma_{ij}^m = s_i \left(\sigma_{ji}^a - \sigma_{ii}^a\right),$$

where s_i is the share of asset i in the consumer's budget. Notice that the Morishima elasticity looks at the impact on the ratio of two goods (x_i/x_j). Assets will be Morishima complements (substitutes) if an increase in the price of j causes x_i/x_j to decrease (increase).

Table 14.6 shows estimates of both the Allen and Morishima elasticities, evaluated at the means of the data. For Part A, we expect the three diagonal terms, representing the Allen own-elasticities of substitution for the three assets to be negative. This expectation is clearly achieved. However, because the Allen elasticity of substitution produces ambiguous results off-diagonal, we will use the Morishima elasticity of substitution to investigate the substitutability/complementarity relation between assets. Based on the asymmetrical Morishima elasticities of substitution — the correct measures of substitution — as documented in Part B of Table 14.6, the assets are Morishima substitutes with only one of these elasticities being negative. Moreover, all Morishima elasticities of substitution are less than unity, irrespective of the model used.

This clearly indicates difficulties for a simple-sum based monetary policy and helps explain why recent attempts to target and control the money supply (simple sum M2) have been abandoned in favor of interest rate procedures.

14.9   On Confidence Intervals

The elasticities are parametric functions, $\sigma(\theta)$, and a parametric bootstrap could be used, as in Gallant and Golub (1984), to compute standard errors or confidence intervals for the estimates reported in Tables 14.5 and 14.6. This involves the use of Monte Carlo methods to obtain a reliable estimate of the sampling distribution of $\sigma(\theta)$ by generating a large enough sample from the distribution of the constrained estimator — see also Anderson and Thursby (1986) for similar Monte Carlo experiments in the case of translog demand models. At each Monte Carlo trial, however, we need to search over a wide range of starting values of θ, using TOMLAB/NPSOL (as discussed in Section 14.5), to achieve global convergence.

In particular, as already mentioned in Section 14.5, for each Monte Carlo trial we need to randomly generate 500 sets of initial parameter values and choose the starting θ that leads to the lowest value of the objective function. In terms of cost, with 134 observations and the models used in this chapter, it takes on average 2.5 minutes of CPU time on a Pentium 4 PC per random draw of initial parameter values. This amounts to over 20 hours of CPU time for each Monte Carlo trial. If we were to use 250 Monte Carlo trials, as in Gallant and Golub (1984), it will take over 5,000 hours of CPU time to obtain bootstrap standard errors! This is not affordable at present, unless we use a smaller number of sets of initial parameter values at each Monte Carlo trial. We are against such an approach, however, because it will likely lead to the non-optimization of the objective function in some (if not all) of the Monte Carlo trials and consequently to extremely wide confidence intervals.

14.10   Conclusions

We have investigated the demand for money in the United States in the context of two semi-nonparametric flexible functional forms — the Fourier and the AIM. We have argued that inferences based on flexible functional forms are virtually worthless unless all three theoretical regularity conditions (of positivity, monotonicity, and curvature) are satisfied, since violations of regularity violate the maintained hypothesis and invalidate the duality theory that produces the estimated model. We have also argue that unless regularity is attained by luck, flexible functional forms should always be estimated subject to regularity.

As Barnett and Pasupathy (2003, p. 136) put it

> "an earlier practice with 'flexible functional forms' was to impose neither monotonicity nor curvature, but check those conditions at each data point *ex post*. Experience in that tradition has suggested that when violations of regularity occur, they are much more likely to occur through violations of curvature conditions than through violations of monotonicity conditions. Based on those results, the more recent approach of imposing curvature alone seems constructive and reasonable. But once curvature is imposed without the imposition of monotonicity, the earlier observation may no longer apply."

We have shown that (with our data set) imposition of global curvature in the Fourier and AIM models, using methods suggested over 20 years ago by Gallant and Golub (1984), does not produce spurious violations of monotonicity, thereby assuring true regularity — i.e., both monotonicity and curvature.

We have also indicated throughout this chapter that a primary concern was to show how our results affect the formulation of monetary policy.

As we have noted, considerable research has indicated that the simple-sum approach to monetary aggregation, in the face of cyclically fluctuating incomes and interest rates (and hence user costs), cannot be the best that can be achieved. Our study corroborates the existence of these phenomena and hence concurs with the general preference for the use of chain-linked monetary aggregates based on, for example, the Divisia index. A second consideration that favors such an approach, again corroborated in our study, is that the elasticities of substitution among the monetary assets (in the popular M2 aggregate) are consistently and believably below unity. The simple sum approach is invalid in such a case, because the method requires that the monetary components of the aggregates be perfect substitutes. The Divisia method of aggregation again solves this problem.

TABLE 14.5

INCOME AND PRICE ELASTICITIES AT THE MEAN

Subaggregate i		A. Income elasticities η_{im}	B. Price elasticities		
			η_{iA}	η_{iB}	η_{iC}
(A)	Fourier	0.999	-0.490	-0.338	-0.197
	AIM	0.988	-0.551	-0.225	-0.211
(B)	Fourier	0.998	-0.860	-0.686	0.454
	AIM	1.821	-0.750	-0.751	-0.322
(C)	Fourier	1.004	0.173	0.153	0.245
	AIM	0.115	0.025	0.130	-0.270

Note: Sample period, quarterly data 1970:1-2003:2 ($T = 134$).

        Chapter 14. A Semi-Nonparametric Approach

TABLE 14.6

ALLEN AND MORISHIMA ELASTICITIES OF
SUBSTITUTION AT THE MEAN

Subaggregate i		A. Allen elasticities			B. Morishima elasticities		
		σ_{iA}	σ_{iB}	σ_{iC}	σ_{iA}^m	σ_{iB}^m	σ_{iC}^m
(A)	Fourier	-0.196	-0.122	0.315		0.030	0.209
	AIM	-0.212	0.190	0.170		0.185	0.176
(B)	Fourier		-1.278	-0.574	0.348		-0.218
	AIM		-0.833	0.575	0.289		0.427
(C)	Fourier			-0.150	0.047	0.203	
	AIM			-0.934	0.285	0.363	

Note: Sample period, quarterly data 1970:1-2003:2 ($T = 134$).

Consolidated References

[1] Akaike, H. "Statistical Predictor Identification." *Annals of the Institute of Statistical Mathematics* 21 (1969a), 203-217.

[2] Akaike, H. "Fitting Autoregressions for Prediction." *Annals of the Institute of Statistical Mathematics* 21 (1969b), 243-247.

[3] Alston, J., K.A. Foster, and R. Green. "Estimating Elasticities with the Linear Approximate Ideal Demand System: Some Monte Carlo Results." *Review of Economics and Statistics* 76 (1994), 351-356.

[4] Andrews, D.W.K. "Power in Econometric Applications." *Econometrica* 57 (1989), 1059-1090.

[5] Anderson, G.J. and R.W. Blundell. "Estimation and Hypothesis Testing in Dynamic Singular Equation Systems." *Econometrica* 50 (1982), 1559-71.

[6] Anderson, R.G. and J.G. Thursby. "Confidence Intervals for Elasticity Estimators in Translog Models." *Review of Economics and Statistics* 68 (1986), 647-656.

[7] Anderson, R.G., B.E. Jones, and T.D. Nesmith. "Monetary Aggregation Theory and Statistical Index Numbers." Federal Reserve Bank of St. Louis *Review* 79 (1997a), 31-51.

[8] Anderson, R.G., B.E. Jones, and T.D. Nesmith. "Building New Monetary Services Indexes: Concepts, Data and Methods." Federal Reserve Bank of St. Louis *Review* 79 (1997b), 53-82.

[9] Anderson, R.W. "Perfect Price Aggregation and Empirical Demand Analysis." *Econometrica* 47 (1979), 1209-30.

[10] Atrostic, B.K. "The Demand for Leisure and Nonpecuniary Job Characteristics." *American Economic Review* 72 (1982), 428-440.

[11] Attfield, C.L.F. "Estimating a Cointegrating Demand System." *European Economic Review* 41 (1997), 61-73.

[12] Backus, D.K. and P.J. Kehoe. "International Evidence on the Historical Properties of Business Cycles." *American Economic Review* 82 (1992), 864-88.

[13] Bailey, M.J. "The Welfare Cost of Inflationary Finance." *Journal of Political Economy* 64 (1956), 93-110.

[14] Bali, T.G. "U.S. Money Demand and the Welfare Cost of Inflation in a Currency-Deposit Model." *Journal of Economics and Business* 52 (2000), 233-258.

[15] Banks J., R. Blundell, and A. Lewbel "Quadratic Engel Curves and Consumer Demand." *Review of Economics and Statistics* 79 (1997), 527-539.

[16] Barnett, W.A. "Recursive Subaggregation and a Generalized Hypocycloidal Demand Model." *Econometrica* 45 (1977), 1117-36.

[17] Barnett, W.A. "The User Cost of Money." *Economics Letters* 1 (1978), 145-149.

[18] Barnett, W.A. "Economic Monetary Aggregates: An Application of Aggregation and Index Number Theory." *Journal of Econometrics* 14 (1980), 11-48.

[19] Barnett, W.A. *Consumer Demand and Labor Supply: Goods, Monetary Assetes, and Time.* Amsterdam: North-Holland (1981).

[20] Barnett, W.A. "The Optimal Level of Monetary Aggregation." *Journal of Money, Credit, and Banking* 14 (1982), 687-710.

[21] Barnett, W.A. "New Indices of Money Supply and the Flexible Laurent Demand System." *Journal of Business and Economic Statistics* 1 (1983), 7-23.

[22] Barnett, W.A. "The Minflex Laurent Translog Functional Form." *Journal of Econometrics* 30 (1985), 33-44.

[23] Barnett, W.A. "The Microeconomic Theory of Monetary Aggregation." In *New Approaches to Monetary Economics*, edited by W.A. Barnett and K. Singleton. Cambridge: Cambridge University Press (1987), pp. 115-168.

[24] Barnett, W.A. "Developments in Monetary Aggregation Theory." *Journal of Policy Modelling* 12 (1990), 205-257.

[25] Barnett, W.A. "A Reply to Julio J. Rotemberg." In *Monetary Policy on the Seventy-Fifth Anniversary of the Federal Reserve System*, edited by M.T. Belongia. Deventer: Kluwer (1991), pp. 232-243.

[26] Barnett, W.A. "Tastes and Technology: Curvature is not Sufficient for Regularity." *Journal of Econometrics* 108 (2002), 199-202.

[27] Barnett, W.A. and J. Binner (eds). *Functional Structure and Approximation in Econometrics.* Elsevier, Amsterdam (2004).

[28] Barnett, W.A. and P. Chen. "The Aggregation-Theoretic Monetary Aggregates are Chaotic and have Strange Attractors: An Econometric Application of Mathematical Chaos." In *Dynamic Econometric Modeling* (Proceedings of the Third International Symposium in Economic Theory and Econometrics), edited by W.A. Barnett, E. Berndt, and H. White. Cambridge: Cambridge University Press (1988), pp. 199-246.

[29] Barnett, W.A. and S. Choi. "A Monte Carlo Study of Tests of Blockwise Weak Spearability." *Journal of Business and Economic Statistics* 7 (1989), 363-377.

[30] Barnett, W.A. and M.J. Hinich. "Empirical Chaotic Dynamics in Economics." *Annals of Operations Research* 37 (1993), 1-15.

[31] Barnett, W.A. and A. Jonas. "The Müntz-Szatz Demand System: An Application of a Globally Well-Behaved Series Expansion." *Economics Letters* 11 (1983), 337-42.

[32] Barnett, W.A. and Y.W. Lee. "The Global Properties of the Minflex Laurent, Generalized Leontief, and Translog Flexible Functional Forms." *Econometrica* 53 (1985), 1421-37.

[33] Barnett, W.A. and M. Pasupathy. "Regularity of the Generalized Quadratic Production Model: A Counterexample." *Econometric Reviews* 22 (2003), 135-154.

[34] Barnett, W.A. and P.A. Samuelson (eds). *Inside the Economist's Mind: The History of Modern Economic Thought, as Explained by Those Who Produce It.* Boston, Blackwell Publishing (2006).

[35] Barnett, W.A. and A. Serletis. *The Theory of Monetary Aggregation.* Contributions to Economic Analysis 245. Amsterdam: North-Holland (2000).

[36] Barnett, W.A. and P. Yue. "Semi-nonparametric Estimation of the Asymptotically Ideal Model: The AIM Demand System." In *Advances in Econometrics* (vol. 7), edited by G. Rhodes and T.B. Fomby. Greenwich, CT: JAI Press (1988), pp. 229-251.

[37] Barnett, W.A., D. Fisher, and A. Serletis. "Consumer Theory and the Demand for Money." *Journal of Economic Literature* 30 (1992), 2086-2119.

[38] Barnett, W.A., J. Geweke, and M. Wolfe. "Semi-nonparametric Bayesian Estimation of the Asymptotically Ideal Production Model." *Journal of Econometrics* 49 (1991), 5-50.

[39] Barnett, W.A., Y.W. Lee, and M.D. Wolfe. "The Three-Dimensional Global Properties of the Minflex Laurent, Generalized Leontief, and Translog Flexible Functional Forms." *Journal of Econometrics* 30 (1985), 3-31.

[40] Barnett, W.A., Y.W. Lee, and M.D. Wolfe. "The Global Properties of the Two Minflex Laurent Flexible Functional Forms." *Journal of Econometrics* 36 (1987), 281-98.

[41] Barnett, W.A., E.K. Offenbacher, and P.A. Spindt. "New Concepts of Aggregated Money." *Journal of Finance* 36 (1981), 497-505.

[42] Barnett, W.A., E.K. Offenbacher, and P.A. Spindt. "The New Divisia Monetary Aggregates." *Journal of Political Economy* 92 (1984), 1049-85.

[43] Barnett, W.A., P.A. Spindt, and E.K. Offenbacher. "Empirical Comparisons of Divisia and Simple Sum Monetary Aggregates." Conference Paper No. 122, National Bureau of Economic Research, Cambridge, MA, 1981.

[44] Barnett, W.A., B. Jones, M. Kirova, T. Nesmith, and M. Pasupathy. "The Nonlinear Skeletons in the Closet." In M. Belongia and J. Binner (eds.), *Money, Measurement, and Computation*, Palgrave (2005).

[45] Barnett, W.A., A.R. Gallant, M.J. Hinich, J.A. Jungeilges, D.T. Kaplan, and M.J. Jensen. "Robustness of Nonlinearity and Chaos Tests to Measurement Error, Inference Method, and Sample Size." *Journal of Economic Behavior and Organization* 27 (1995), 301-320.

[46] Barnett, W.A., A.R. Gallant, M.J. Hinich, J.A. Jungeilges, D.T. Kaplan, and M.J. Jensen. "A Single-Blind Controlled Competition Among Tests for Nonlinearity and Chaos." *Journal of Econometrics* 82 (1997), 157-192.

[47] Barten, A.P. "Maximum Likelihood Estimation of a Complete System of Demand Equations." *European Economic Review* 1 (1969), 7-73.

[48] Baxter, M. and R.G. King. "Approximate Band-Pass Filters for Economic Time Series." NBER Working Paper No. 5052 (1995).

[49] Belongia, M.T. "Measurement Matters: Recent Results from Monetary Economics Re-examined." *Journal of Political Economy* 104 (1996), 1065-83.

[50] Berndt, E.R. and L.R. Christensen. "The Specification of Technology in U.S. Manufacturing." Working Paper No. 18, Bureau of Labor Statistics, Washington, D.C. (1973a).

[51] Berndt, E.R. and L.R. Christensen. "The Internal Structure of Functional Relationships: Separability, Substitution and Aggregation." *Review of Economic Studies* 60 (1973b), 403-10.

[52] Berndt, E.R. and E. Savin. "Estimation and Hypothesis Testing in Singular Equation Systems with Autoregressive Disturbances." *Econometrica* 43 (1975), 937-57.

[53] Blackorby, C. and R.R. Russell. "The Morishima Elasticity of Substitution, Symmetry, Constancy, Separability, and its Relationship to the Hicks and Allen Elasticities." *Review of Economic Studies* 48 (1981), 147-158.

[54] Blackorby, C. and R.R. Russell "Will the Real Elasticity of Substitution Please Stand Up? A Comparison of the Allen/Uzawa and Morishima Elasticities." *American Economic Review* 79 (1989), 882-888.

[55] Blackorby, C., D. Nissen, D. Primont, and R.R. Russell. "Recursively Decentralized Decision Making." *Econometrica* 42 (1974), 487-96.

[56] Blackorby, C., D. Primont, and R.R. Russell. "Budgeting, Decentralization, and Aggregation." *Annals of Economic and Social Measurement* 4/1 (1975), 23-44.

[57] Blackorby, C., D. Primont, and R.R. Russell. *Duality, Separability and Functional Structure.* New York: Elsevier North-Holland, (1978).

[58] Blackorby, C., W. Schworm, and T. Fisher. "Testing for the Existence of Input Aggregates in an Economy Production Function." University of British Columbia, Mimeo (1986).

[59] Boyer, M. "Rational Demand and Expenditure Patterns under Habit Formation." *Journal of Economic Theory* 31 (1983), 27-53.

[60] Brock, W.A. "Money and Growth: The Case of Long Run Perfect Foresight." *International Economic Review* 15 (1974), 750-777.

[61] Brock, W.A. and C.L. Sayers. "Is the Business Cycle Characterized by Deterministic Chaos"? *Journal of Monetary Economics* 22 (1988), 71-90.

[62] Brock, W.A., W.D. Dechert, and J. Scheinkman. "A Test for Independence Based on the Correlation Dimension." Discussion paper, University of Wisconsin-Madison, Dept. of Economics, 1987.

[63] Burguete, J.F., A.R. Gallant, and G. Souza. "On Unification of the Asymptotic Theory of Nonlinear Econometric Models." *Econometric Reviews* 1 (1982), 151-190.

[64] Burns, A. and W.C. Mitchell. *Measuring Business Cycles.* NBER (1946).

[65] Buse, A. "Evaluating the Linearized Almost Ideal Demand System." *American Journal of Agricultural Economics* 76 (1994), 781-793.

[66] Cagan, P. "The Monetary Dynamics of Hyperinflation." In *Studies in the Quantity Theory of Money*, edited by Milton Friedman. Chicago: The University of Chicago Press (1956).

[67] Campbell, J. and N.G. Mankiw. "Permanent Income, Current Income, and Consumption." *Journal of Business and Economic Statistics* 8 (1990), 265-269.

[68] Caves, D. and L. Christensen. "Global Properties of Flexible Functional Forms." *American Economic Review* 70 (1980), 422-432.

[69] Chadha, B. and E. Prasad. "Are Prices Countercyclical? Evidence from the G7." *Journal of Monetary Economics* 34 (1994), 239-57.

[70] Chalfant, J.A. "A Globally Flexible Almost Ideal System." *Journal of Business and Economic Statistics* 5 (1987), 233-242.

[71] Chalfant, J.A. and A.R. Gallant. "Estimating Substitution Elasticities with the Fourier Costs Function: Some Monte Carlo Results." *Journal of Econometrics* 28 (1985), 205-222.

[72] Chetty, V.K. "On Measuring the Nearness of Near-Moneys." *American Economic Review* 59 (1969), 270-281.

[73] Chow, G.C. "On the Long-Run and Short-Run Demand for Money." *Journal of Political Economy* 74 (1966), 111-31.

[74] Christensen, L.R., D.W. Jorgenson, and L.J. Lau. "Transcendental Logarithmic Utility Functions." *American Economics Review* 65 (1975), 367-83.

[75] Christiano, L.J. "Money and the U.S. Economy in the 1980s: A Break from the Past?" Federal Reserve Bank of Minneapolis *Quarterly Review* 10 (1986), 2-13.

[76] Christiano, L.J. "Searching for a Break in GNP." *Journal of Business and Economic Statistics* 10 (1992), 237-250.

[77] Cockerline, J. and J. Murray. "Superlative Monetary Aggregation: Some Preliminary Results." Unpublished mimeograph, Bank of Canada, File No. 105-7-4, 1981.

[78] Cogley, T. and J.M. Nason. "Effects of the Hodrick-Prescott Filter on Trend and Difference Stationary Time Series: Implications for Business Cycle Research." *Journal of Economic Dynamics and Control* 19 (1995), 253-78.

[79] Cooley, T.F. and L.E. Ohanian. "The Cyclical Behavior of Prices." *Journal of Monetary Economics* 28 (1991), 25-60.

[80] Cooper, R.J. and K.R. McLaren. "A System of Demand Equations Satisfying Effectively Global Regularity Conditions." *Review of Economics and Statistics* 78 (1996), 359-364.

[81] Deaton, A. and J. Muellbauer. "An Almost Ideal Demand System." *American Economic Review* 70 (1980), 312-326.

[82] DeCoster, G.P. and D.W. Mitchell. "Nonlinear Monetary Dynamics." *Journal of Business and Economic Statistics* 9 (1991), 455-462.

[83] DeCoster, G.P. and D.W. Mitchell. "A Reply." *Journal of Business and Economic Statistics* 12 (1994), 136-137.

[84] Deneckere, R. and S. Pelikan. "Competitive Chaos." *Journal of Economic Theory* 40 (1986), 13-25.

[85] Denny, M. and M. Fuss. "The Use of Approximation Analysis to Test for Separability and the Existence of Consistent Aggregates." *American Economic Review* 67 (1977), 404–19.

[86] Dickey, D.A. and W.A. Fuller. "Distribution for the Estimators for Autoregressive Time Series With a Unit Root." *Journal of the American Statistical Association* 74 (1979), 427-431.

[87] Dickey, D.A. and W.A. Fuller. "Likelihood Ratio Statistics for Autoregressive Time Series with a Unit Root." *Econometrica* 49 (1981), 1057-72.

[88] Diewert, W.E. "An Application of the Shephard Duality Theorem: a Generalized Leontief Production Function." *Journal of Political Economy* 79 (1971), 481-507.

[89] Diewert, W.E. "Applications of Duality Theory." In *Frontiers of Quantitative Economics* II, edited by M. Intriligator and D. Kendrick. Amsterdam: North-Holland (1974), pp.106-171.

[90] Diewert, W.E. "Exact and Superlative Index Numbers." *Journal of Econometrics* 4 (1976), 115-146.

[91] Diewert, W.E. "Superlative Index Numbers and Consistency in Aggregation." *Econometrica* 46 (1978), 883-900.

[92] Diewert, W.E. "Aggregation Problems in the Measurement of Capital." In *The Measurement of Capital,* edited by D. Usher. Chicago: University of Chicago Press (1980), pp. 433-528.

[93] Diewert, W.E. and T.J. Wales. "Flexible Functional Forms and Global Curvature Conditions." *Econometrica* 55 (1987), 43-68.

[94] Diewert, W.E., M. Avriel, and I. Zang. "Nine Kinds of Quasiconcavity and Concavity." *Journal of Economic Theory* 25 (1977), 397-420.

[95] Donovan, D.J. "Modelling the Demand for Liquid Assets: An Application to Canada." International Monetary Fund *Staff Papers* 25 (1978), 676-704.

[96] Drake, L.M., A.R. Fleissig, and J.L. Swofford. "A Seminonparametric Approach to the Demand for U.K. Monetary Assets." *Economica* 70 (2003), 99-120.

[97] Eastwood, B. "Asymptotic Normality and Consistency of Seminonparametric Regression Estimators Using an Upwards F-test Truncation Rule." *Journal of Econometrics* 57 (1991), 307-340.

[98] Eastwood, B.J. and A.R. Gallant. "Adaptive Rules for Seminonparametric Estimators that Achieve Asymptotic Normality." *Econometric Theory* 7 (1991), 307-340.

[99] Eckmann, J.P., and D. Ruelle. "Ergodic Theory of Strange Attractors." *Reviews of Modern Physics* 57 (1985), 617-656.

[100] Elbadawi, I.A., A.R. Gallant, and G. Sousa. "An Elasticity Can Be Estimated Consistently Without a Prior Knowledge of Functional Form." *Econometrica* 51 (1983), 1731-1752.

[101] Ellner, S., D.W. Nychka, and A.R. Gallant. "LENNS, a Program to Estimate the Dominant Lyapunov Exponent of Noisy Nonlinear Systems from Time Series Data." Institute of Statistics Mimeo Series 2235 (BMA Series 39), North Carolina State University, Statistics Dept. 1992.

[102] Engle, R.F. and C.W.J. Granger. "Cointegration and Error Correction: Representation, Estimation and Testing." *Econometrica* 55 (1987), 251-276.

[103] Evans, G.W. and S. Honkapohja. "An Interview of Thomas Sargent," *Macroeconomic Dynamics* 4 (2005). Reprinted in: Barnett, William A. and Paul A. Samuelson (eds.), *Inside the Economist's Mind: The History of Modern Economic Thought, as Explained by Those Who Produce It*, Boston, Blackwell Publishing (2006).

[104] Ewis, N.A. and D. Fisher. "The Translog Utility Function and the Demand for Money in the United States." *Journal of Money, Credit, and Banking* 16 (1984), 34-52.

[105] Ewis, N.A. and D. Fisher. "Toward a Consistent Estimate of the Substitutability between Money and Newar Monies: An Application of the Fourier Flexible Form." *Journal of Macroecononomics* 7 (1985), 151-74.

[106] Farr, H.T. and D. Johnson. "Revisions in the Monetary Services (Divisia) Indexes of Monetary Aggregates." Board of Governors of the Federal Reserve System, Mimeo (1985).

[107] Fayyad, S.K. "Monetary Asset Componenet Grouping and Aggregation: An Inquiry into the Definition of Money." Ph.D. dissertation, University of Texas at Austin (1986).

[108] Feige, E.L. and D.K. Pearce. "The Substitutability of Money and Near Monies: A Survey of the Time Series Evidence." *Journal of Economic Literature* 15 (1977), 439-69.

[109] Fiorito, R. and T. Kollintzas. "Stylized Facts of Business Cycles in the G7 from a Real Business Cycles Perspective." *European Economic Review* 38 (1994), 235-69.

[110] Fisher, D. "Money-Demand Variability: A Demand-Systems Approach." *Journal of Business and Economic Statistics* 10 (1992), 143-152.

[111] Fisher, D. and A.R. Fleissig. "Monetary Aggregation and the Demand for Assets." *Journal of Money, Credit, and Banking* 29 (1997), 458-475.

[112] Fisher, D. and A. Serletis. "Velocity and the Growth of Money in the United States, 1970-1985." *Journal of Macroeconomics* 11 (1989), 323-332.

[113] Fisher, D., A.R. Fleissig, and A. Serletis. "An Empirical Comparison of Flexible Demand System Functional Forms." *Journal of Applied Econometrics* 16 (2001), 59-80.

[114] Fisher, I. *The Making of Index Numbers: A Study of Their Varieties, Tests, and Reliability.* Boston: Houghton Mifflin (1922).

[115] Fisher, M. and J. Seater. "Long-Run Neutrality and Superneutrality in an ARIMA Framework." *American Economic Review* 83 (1993), 402-415.

[116] Fleissig, A.R. and A. Serletis. "Semi-Nonparametric Estimates of Substitution for Canadian Monetary Assets." *Canadian Journal of Economics* 35 (2002), 78-91.

[117] Fleissig, A.R. and J.L. Swofford. "A Dynamic Asymptotically Ideal Model of Money Demand." *Journal of Monetary Economics* 37 (1996), 371-380.

[118] Fleissig, A.R. and J.L. Swofford. "Dynamic Asymptotically Ideal Models and Finite Approximation." *Journal of Business and Economic Statistics* 15 (1997), 482-492.

[119] Fleissig, A.R., A.R. Hall, and J.J. Seater. "GARP, Separability, and the Representative Agent." *Macroeconomic Dynamics* 4 (2000), 324-342.

[120] Fleissig, A.R., T. Kastens, and D. Terrell. "Semi-nonparametric Estimates of Substitution Elasticities." *Economics Letters* 54 (1997), 209-219.

[121] Frank, M.Z. and T. Stengos. "Some Evidence Concerning Macroeconomic Chaos." *Journal of Monetary Economics* 22 (1988), 423-438.

[122] Frank, M.Z. and T. Stengos. "Measuring the Strangeness of Gold and Silver Rates of Return." *Review of Economic Studies* 56 (1989), 553-567.

[123] Friedman, B.M. "Lessons on Monetary Policy ¿From the 1980s." *Journal of Economic Perspectives* 2 (1988), 51-72.

[124] Friedman, M. "The Quantity Theory of Money — a Restatement." In *Studies of the Quantity Theory of Money*, edited by M. Friedman. Chicago: University of Chicago Press (1956), pp. 3-21.

[125] Friedman, M. *The Optimum Quantity of Money and Other Essays.* Chicago: University of Chicago Press (1969).

[126] Fuller, W.A. *Introduction to Statistical Time Series.* New York: John Wiley (1976).

[127] Fuss, M.A. "The Demand for Energy in Canadian Manufacturing." *Journal of Econometrics* 5 (1977), 89-116.

[128] Gallant, A.R. "On the Bias in Flexible Functional Forms and an Essentially Unbiased Form: The Fourier Flexible Form." *Journal of Econometrics* 15 (1981), 211-245.

[129] Gallant, A.R. "Unbiased Determination of Production Technologies." *Journal of Econometrics* 20 (1982), 285-323.

[130] Gallant, A.R. and G.H. Golub. "Imposing Curvature Restrictions on Flexible Functional Forms." *Journal of Econometrics* 26 (1984), 295-321.

[131] Gallant, A.R. and H. White. "On Learning the Derivatives of an Unknown Mapping with Multilayer Feedforward Networks." *Neural Networks* 5 (1992), 129-138.

[132] Gavin, W.T. and F.E. Kydland. "Endogenous Money Supply and the Business Cycle." Discussion Paper 95-010A, Federal Reserve Bank of St. Louis (July 1995).

[133] Gencay, R. and W.D. Dechert. "An Algorithm for the n-Lyapunov Exponents of an n-Dimensional Unknown Dynamical System." *Physica D* 59 (1992), 142-157.

[134] Goldfeld, S.M. "The Demand for Money Revisited." *Brookings Papers on Economic Activity* (1973), 577-638.

[135] Goldfeld, S.M. "The Case of the Missing Money." *Brookings Papers on Economic Activity* (1976), 683-730.

[136] Goodfriend, M. "Interest Rate Smoothing and Price Level Trend-Stationarity." *Journal of Monetary Economics* 19 (1987), 335-348.

[137] Gordon, R.J. "The Short-Run Demand for Money: A Reconsideration." *Journal of Money, Credit, and Banking* 16 (1984), 403-34.

[138] Gorman, W.M. "Separable Utility and Aggregation." *Econometrica* 27 (1959), 469-81.

[139] Gorman, W.M. "On a Class of Preference Fields." *Metroeconomica* 13 (1961), 53-6.

[140] Gould, J. and C. Nelson. "The Stochastic Structure of the Velocity of Money." *American Economic Review* 64 (1974), 405-418.

[141] Granger, C.W.J. "Investigating Causal Relations by Econometric Models and Cross-Spectral Methods." *Econometrica* 37 (1969), 424-438.

[142] Granger, C.W.J. "Modelling Nonlinear Relationships Between Extended-Memory Variables." *Econometrica* 63 (1995), 265-279.

[143] Granger, C.W.J. and P. Newbold. "Spurious Regressions in Econometrics." *Journal of Econometrics* 2 (1974), 111-120.

[144] Green, R., D. Rocke, and W. Hahn. "Standard Errors for Elasticities: A Comparison of Bootstrap and Asymptotic Standard Errors." *Journal of Business and Economic Statistics* 5 (1987), 145-149.

[145] Guilkey, D. and C. Lovell. "On the Flexibility of the Translog Approximation." *International Economic Review* 21 (1980), 137-147.

[146] Guilkey, D., C. Lovell, and C. Sickles. "A Ccomparison of the Performance of Three Flexible Functional Forms." *International Economic Review* 24 (1983), 591-616.

[147] Hall, T.E. "Price Cyclicality in the Natural Rate — Nominal Demand Shock Model." *Journal of Macroeconomics* 17 (1995), 257-72.

[148] Hall, T.E. and N.R. Noble. "Velocity and the Variability of Money Growth: Evidence From Granger-Causality Tests." *Journal of Money, Credit, and Banking* 44 (1987), 112-116.

[149] Hancock, D. "Aggregation of Monetary Goods: A Production Model." In *New Approaches to Monetary Economics*, edited by W.A. Barnett and K. Singleton. Cambridge: Cambridge University Press (1987).

[150] Haraf, W.S. "Monetary Velocity and Monetary Rules." *Cato Journal* 6 (1986), 642-662.

[151] Hinich, M.J. "Testing for Gaussianity and Linearity of a Stationary Time Series." *Journal of Time Series Analysis* 3 (1982), 169-176.

[152] Heckman, James J. "Interview with James J. Heckman." *The Region*, Federal Reserve Bank of Minneapolis (June, 2005).

[153] Hsiao, C. "Autoregressive Modeling of Canadian Money and Income Data." *Journal of the American Statistical Association* 74 (1979a), 553-560.

[154] Hsiao, C. "Causality Tests in Econometrics." *Journal of Economic Dynamics and Control* 1 (1979b), 321-346.

[155] Hsiao, C. "Autoregressive Modeling and Money-Income Causality Detection." *Journal of Monetary Economics* 7 (1981), 85-106.

[156] Hsieh, D.A. "Chaos and Nonlinear Dynamics: Application to Financial Markets." *Journal of Finance* 46 (1991), 1839-1877.

[157] Huber, P.J. *Robust Statistics*. New York: Wiley (1981).

[158] Johansen, S. "Statistical Analysis of Cointegrated Vectors." *Journal of Economic Dynamics and Control* 12 (1988), 231-254.

[159] Judd, J.P. and B. Motley. "The Great Velocity Decline of 1982-83: A Comparative Analysis of M1 and M2." Federal Reserve Bank of San Francisco *Economic Review* (1984), 56-74.

[160] Kang, H. "The Effects of Detrending in Granger Causality Tests." *Journal of Business and Economic Statistics* 3 (1985), 344-349.

[161] Keynes, John Maynard. *The General Theory of Employment, Interest, and Money*, New York, Harcourt, Brace & World, Inc. (1936).

[162] Kifer, Y. *Ergodic Theory of Random Transformations*. Basel: Birkhauser (1986).

[163] King, R.G. and S.T. Rebelo. "Low Frequency Filtering and Real Business Cycles." *Journal of Economic Dynamics and Control* 17 (1993), 207-31.

[164] King, R.G. and M. Watson. "Testing Long-Run Neutrality." Federal Reserve Bank of Richmond *Economic Quarterly* 83 (1997), 69-101.

[165] Kohler, D.F. "The Bias in Price Elasticity Estimates Under Homothetic Separability: Implications for Analysis of Peak-Load Electricity Pricing." *Journal of Business and Economic Statistics* 1 (1983), 202-10.

[166] Koopmans, T. "Measurement Without Theory." *Review of Economics and Statistics* 29 (1947), 161-72.

[167] Koustas, Z. and A. Serletis. "On the Fisher Effect." *Journal of Monetary Economics* 44 (1999), 105-30.

[168] Koustas, Z. and A. Serletis. "Monetary Aggregation and the Neutrality of Money." *Economic Inquiry* 39 (2001), 124-138.

[169] Kwiatkowski, D., P.C.B. Phillips, P. Schmidt, and Y. Shin. "Testing the Null Hypothesis of Stationarity against the Alternative of a Unit Root.' *Journal of Econometrics* 54 (1992), 159-78.

[170] Kydland, F.E. and E.C. Prescott. "Business Cycles: Real Facts and a Monetary Myth." Federal Reserve Bank of Minneapolis *Quarterly Review* (Spring 1990), 3-18.

[171] Kydland, F.E. and E.C. Prescott. "Time to Build and Aggregate Fluctuations." *Econometrica* 50 (1982), 1345-70.

[172] Lau, L.J. "Duality and the Structure of Utility Functions." *Journal of Economic Theory* 1 (1969), 374-96.

[173] Lau, L.J. "Testing and Imposing Monotonicity, Convexity, and Quasi-Convexity Constraints." In *Production Economics: A Dual Approach to Theory and Applications* (vol. 1), edited by M. Fuss and D. McFadden. Amsterdam: North Holland (1978), pp. 409-453.

[174] Leontief, W.W. "Introduction to a Theory of the Internal Structure of Functional Relationship." *Econometrica* 15 (1947), 361-73.

[175] Lewbel, A. "Characaterizing Some Gorman-Engel Curves." *Econometrica* 55 (1987a), 1451-1459.

[176] Lewbel, A. "Fractional Demand Systems." *Journal of Econometrics* 36 (1987b), 311-337.

[177] Lewbel, A. "Full Rank Demand Systems." *International Economic Review* 31 (1990), 289-300.

[178] Lewbel, A. "The Rank of Demand Systems: Theory and Nonparametric Estimation." *Econometrica* 59 (1991), 711-730.

[179] Lewbel, A. "Utility Functions and Global Regularity of Fractional Demand Systems." *International Economic Review* 36 (1995), 943-961.

[180] Lewbel, A. "Aggregation Without Separability: a Generalized Composite Commodity Theorem." *American Economic Review* 86 (1996), 524-543.

[181] Ljung, G.M. and G.E.P. Box. "On a Measure of Lack of Fit in Time Series Models." *Biometrica* 65 (1978), 297-303.

[182] Lucas, R.E. Jr. "Expectations and the Neutrality of Money." *Journal of Economic Theory* 4 (1972), 103-24.

[183] Lucas, R.E. Jr. "Nobel Lecture: Monetary Neutrality." *Journal of Political Economy* 104 (1996), 661-82.

[184] Lucas, R.E. Jr. "Understanding Business Cycles." In *Stabilization of the Domestic and International Economy* (vol. 5), edited by K. Brunner and A.H. Meltzer. Carnegie-Rochester Conference Series on Public Policy (1997), pp. 7-29.

[185] Lucas, R.E. Jr. "Inflation and Welfare." *Econometrica* 68 (2000), 247-274.

[186] MacKinnon, J.G. "Approximate Asymptotic Distribution Functions for Unit-Root and Cointegration Tests." *Journal of Business and Economic Statistics* 12 (1994), 167-176.

[187] Mankiw, N.G. "Real Business Cycles: A New Keynesian Perspective." *Journal of Economic Perspectives* 3 (1989), 79-90.

[188] Manser, M.E. "Elasticities of Demand for Food: An Analysis Using Non-Additive Utility Functions Allowing for Habit Formation." *Southern Economic Journal* 43 (1976), 879-91.

[189] Marty, A.L. "The Welfare Cost of Inflation: A Critique of Bailey and Lucas." Federal Reserve Bank of St. Louis *Review* 81 (1999), 41-46.

[190] Mathews, B.P. and A. Diamantopoulos. "Towards a Taxonomy of Forecast Error Measures." *Journal of Forecasting* 13 (1994), 409-416.

[191] McCaffrey, D.F., S. Ellner, A.R. Gallant, and D.W. Nychka. "Estimating the Lyapunov Exponent of a Chaotic System with Nonparametric Regression." *Journal of the American Statistical Association* 87 (1992), 682-695.

[192] McCallum, B.T. and M. Goodfriend. "Demand for Money: Theoretical Studies." In *The New Palgrave: A Dictionary of Economics*, edited by J. Eatwell, M. Milgate, and P. Newman. London: Macmillan (1987), pp. 775-781.

[193] McElroy, M.B. "Additive General Error Models for Production, Costs, and Derived Demand or Share Systems." *Journal of Political Economy* 95 (1987), 737-757.

[194] Muscatelli, V.A. and F. Spinelli. "The Long-Run Stability of the Demand for Money: Italy 1861-1996." *Journal of Monetary Economics* 45 (2000), 717-739.

[195] Nadiri, I.I. and S. Rosen. "Interrelated Factor Demand Funcctions." *American Economic Reivew* 59 (1969), 457-71.

[196] Nelson, C.R. and H. Kang. "Pitfalls in the Use of Time as an Explanatory Variable in Regression." *Journal of Business and Economic Statistics* 2 (1984), 73-82.

[197] Nelson, C.R. and C.I. Plosser. "Trends and Random Walks in Macroeconomic Time Series: Some Evidence and Implications." *Journal of Monetary Economics* 10 (1982), 139-162.

[198] Newey, W.K. and K.D. West. "A Simple, Positive Semi-Definite, Heteroskedasticity and Autocorrelation Consistent Covariance Matrix." *Econometrica* 55 (1987), 703-8.

[199] Newey, W.K. and K.D. West. "Automatic Lag Selection in Covariance Matrix Estimation." *Review of Economic Studies* 61 (1994), 631-654.

[200] Ng, S. "Testing for Homogeneity in Demand Systems When the Regressors are Nonstationary." *Journal of Applied Econometrics* 10 (1995), 147-163.

[201] Nychka, D.W., S. Ellner, A.R. Gallant, and D. McCaffrey. "Finding Chaos in Noisy Systems." *Journal of the Royal Statistical Society* B 54 (1992), 399-426.

[202] Offenbacher, E.K. *The Substitution of Monetary Assets.* Ph.D. Dissertation, University of Chicago (1979).

[203] Pantula, S.G., G. Gonzalez-Farias, and W. Fuller. "A Comparison of Unit-Root Test Criteria." *Journal of Business and Economic Statistics* 12 (1994), 449-459.

[204] Pashardes, P. "Bias in Estimating the Almost Ideal Demand System with the Stone Index Approximation." *Economic Journal* 103 (1993), 908-915.

[205] Perron, P. "The Great Crash, the Oil Price Shock, and the Unit Root Hypothesis." *Econometerica* 57 (1989), 1361-1401.

[206] Pesaran, M.H, Y. Shin, and R.J. Smith. "Bounds Testing Approaches to the Analysis of Level Relationships." *Journal of Applied Econometrics* 16 (2001), 289-326.

[207] Phillips, P.C.B. "Time Series Regression with a Unit Root." *Econometrica* 55 (1987), 277-301.

[208] Phillips, P.C.B. "Fully Modified Least Squares and Vector Autoregression." *Econometrica* 62 (1995), 1023-1078.

[209] Phillips, P.C.B. and P. Perron. "Testing for a Unit Root in Time Series Regression." *Biometrica* 75 (1987), 335-346.

[210] Pollak, R.A. "Habit Formation and Dynamic Demand Functions." *Journal of Political Economy* 78 (1970), 745-63.

[211] Pollak, R.A. and T.J. Wales. "Comparison of the Quadratic Expenditure System and Translog Demand System with Alternative Specifications of Demographic Effects." *Econometrica* 48 (1980), 595-615.

[212] Pollak, R.A. and T.J. Wales. *Demand System Specification and Estimation.* Oxford University Press: New York (1992).

[213] Priestley, M.B. *Spectral Analysis and Time Series.* New York: Academic Press (1981).

[214] Prescott, E.C. "Theory Ahead of Business Cycle Measurement." Federal Reserve Bank of Minneapolis *Quarterly Review* 10 (1986), 9-22.

[215] Prescott, E.C. "Commentary [on King and Wolman, "Inflation Targeting in a St. Louis Model of the 21st Century"]." Federal Reserve Bank of St. Louis *Review* 78 (1996), 112-115.

[216] Pudney, S.E. "An Empirical Method of Approximating the Separable Structure of Consumer Preferences." *Review of Economic Studies* (1981), 561-77.

[217] Ramajo, J. "Curvature Restrictions on Flexible Functional Forms: An Application of the Minflex Almost Ideal Demand System to the Pattern of Spanish Demand." *Journal of Business and Economic Statistics* 4 (1994), 431-436.

[218] Ramsey, J.B. and P. Rothman. "Comment on 'Nonlinear Monetary Dynamics' by DeCoster and Mitchell." *Journal of Business and Economic Statistics* 12 (1994), 135-136.

[219] Ramsey, J.B., C.L. Sayers, and P. Rothman. "The Statistical Properties of Dimension Calculations using Small Data Sets: Some Economic Applications." *International Economic Review* 31 (1988), 991-1020.

[220] Rotemberg, J.J. "Commentary: Monetary Aggregates and Their Uses." In *Monetary Policy on the 75th Anniversary of the Federal Reserve System*, edited by M.T. Belongia. Deventer: Kluwer (1991), pp. 223-231.

[221] Rotemberg, J.J., J.C. Driscoll, and J.M. Poterba. "Money, Output and Prices: Evidence from a New Monetary Aggregate." *Journal of Business and Economic Statistics* 13 (1995), 67-83.

[222] Samuelson, Paul A. "Reflections on How Biographies of Individual Scholars Can Relate to a Science's Biography." In: W.A. Barnett and P.A. Samuelson (eds.). *Inside the Economist's Mind: The History of Modern Economic Thought, as Explained by Those Who Produce It*, Boston, Blackwell Publishing (2006).

[223] Santoni, G.J. "Changes in Wealth and the Velocity of Money." Federal Reserve Bank of St. Louis *Review* 67 (1987), 16-26.

[224] Scheinkman, J.A. and B. LeBaron. "Nonlinear Dynamics and GNP Data." In *Economic Complexity: Chaos, Sunspots, Bubbles and Nonlinearity, Proceedings of the Fourth International Symposium in Economic Theory and Econometrics*, edited by W.A.Barnett, J. Geweke, and K. Shell. Cambridge, U.K.: Cambridge University Press (1989a), pp. 213-231.

[225] Scheinkman, J.A. and B. LeBaron. "Nonlinear Dynamics and Stock Returns." *Journal of Business* 62 (1989b), 311-337.

[226] Schwartz, G. "Estimating the Dimension of a Model." *The Annals of Statistics* 6 (1978), 461-464.

[227] Serletis, A. "The Demand for Divisia M_1, M_2, and M_3 in the United States." *Journal of Macroeconomics* 9 (1987a), 567-91.

[228] Serletis, A. "Monetary Asset Separability Tests." In *New Approaches to Monetary Economics*, edited by W.A. Barnett and K. Singleton. Cambridge: Cambridge University Press (1987b).

[229] Serletis, A. "Translog Flexible Functional Forms and Substitutability of Monetary Assets." *Journal of Business and Economic Statistics* 6 (1988), 59-67.

[230] Serletis, A. "The Demand for Divisia M1, M2, and M3 in the United States: A Dynamic Flexible Demand System." *Journal of Money, Credit, and Banking* 23 (1991), 35-52.

[231] Serletis, A. "Random Walks, Breaking Trend Functions, and the Chaotic Structure of the Velocity of Money." *Journal of Business and Economic Statistics* 13 (1995), 453-458.

[232] Serletis, A. *The Demand for Money: Theoretical and Empirical Approaches*. Amsterdam: Kluwer (2001).

[233] Serletis, A. and Z. Koustas. "International Evidence on the Neutrality of Money." *Journal of Money, Credit, and Banking* 30 (1998), 1-25.

[234] Serletis, A. and Z. Koustas. "Monetary Aggregation and the Neutrality of Money." *Economic Inquiry* 39 (2001), 124-138.

[235] Serletis, A. and A.L. Robb. "Divisia Aggregation and Substitutability Among Monetary Assets." *Journal of Money, Credit, and Banking* 18 (1986), 430-46.

[236] Serletis, A. and K. Yavari. "The Welfare Cost of Inflation in Canada and the United States." *Economics Letters* 84 (2004), 199-204.

[237] Serletis, A. and K. Yavari. "The Welfare Cost of Inflation in Italy." *Applied Economics Letters* 12 (2005), 165-168.

[238] Sidrauski, M. "Rational Choice and Patterns of Growth in a Monetary Economy." *American Economic Review* 57 (1967), 534-544.

[239] Sims, C.A. "Money, Income and Causality. *American Economic Review* 62 (1972), 540-552.

[240] Slesnik, D.T. "Are Our Data Relevant to the Theory? The Case of Aggregate Consumption." *Journal of Business and Economic Statistics* 16 (1998), 52-61.

[241] Smith, R.T. "The Cyclical Behavior of Prices." *Journal of Money, Credit, and Banking* 24 (1992), 413-30.

[242] Sono, M. "The Effect of Price Changes on the Demand and Supply of Separable Goods." *International Economic Review* 2 (1961), 239-71.

[243] Spindt, P. A. "Money Is What Money Does: Monetary Aggregation and the Equation of Exchange." *Journal of the Political Economy* 93 (1985), 175-204.

[244] Stock, J.H. and M.W. Watson. "A Simple Estimator of Cointegrating Vectors in Higher Order Integrated Systems." *Econometrica* 61 (1995), 783-820.

[245] Stoker, T.M. "Simple Tests of Distributional Effects on Macroeconomic Equations." *Journal of Political Economy* 94 (1986), 763-795.

[246] Strotz, R.H. "The Empirical Implications of a Utility Tree." *Econometrica* 25 (1957), 169-80.

[247] Strotz, R.H. "The Utility Tree — A Correction and Further Appraisal." *Econometrica* 27 (1959), 482-88.

[248] Swofford, J.L. and G. Whitney. "Nonparametric Tests of Utility Maximization and Weak Separability for Consumption, Leisure and Money." *Review of Economics and Statistics* 69 (1987), 458-464.

[249] Swofford, J.L. and G. Whitney. "A Comparison of Nonparametric Tests of Weak Separability for Annual and Quarterly Data on Consumption, Leisure, and Money." *Journal of Business and Economic Statistics* 6 (1988), 241-246.

[250] Swofford, J.L. and G. Whitney. "A Revealed Preference Test for Weakly Separable Utility Maximization with Incomplete Adjustment." *Journal of Econometrics* 60 (1994), 235-49.

[251] Tatom, J.A. "Was the 1982 Velocity Decline Unusual?" Federal Reserve Bank of St. Louis *Review* 67 (1983), 5-15.

[252] Taylor, H. "What Has Happened to M1?" Federal Reserve Bank of Philadelphia *Business Review* (1986), 3-14.

[253] Terrell, D. "Flexbility and Regularity Properties of the Asymptotically Ideal Production Model." *Econometric Reviews* 14 (1995), 1-17.

[254] Thornton, D.L. "Money Demand Dynamics: Some New Evidence." Federal Reserve Bank of St. Louis *Review* 67 (1985), 14-23.

[255] Thornton, D.L. and D.S. Batten. "Lag-Length Selection and Tests of Granger Causality Between Money and Income." *Journal of Money, Credit, and Banking* 17 (1985), 164–178.

[256] Thornton, D.L. and P. Yue. "An Extended Series of Divisia Monetary Aggregates." Federal Reserve Bank of St. Louis *Review* 74 (1992), 35-52.

[257] Tiao, G.C. and G.E.P. Box. "Modeling Multiple Time Series With Application." *Journal of the American Statistical Association* 75 (1981), 602-616.

[258] Toers, A.L. "Approximate Variance Formulas for the Elasticities of Substitution Obtained From Tanslog Production Functions." *Economics Letters* 5 (1980), 155-160.

[259] Toers, A.L. "Approximate Variance Formulas for the Elasticities of Substitution Obtained From Translog Cost Functions." *Economics Letters* 10 (1982), 107-113.

[260] U.S. Department of Commerce. (1983), Business Statistics 1982, a Supplement to the *Survey of Current Business* (23rd ed.), Washington, D.C.: U.S. Government Printing Office.

[261] U.S. Department of Commerce. *Survey of Current Business*, various issues, (1983-1985) , Washington, D.C.: U.S. Government Printing Office.

[262] U.S. Department of Commerce. *Survey of Current Business*, Vol. 66, No. 9, (1986), Washington, D.C.: U.S. Government Printing Office.

[263] Uzawa, H. "Production Functions with Constant Elasticities of Substitution." *Review of Economic Studies* 29 (1962), 291-299.

[264] Varian, H.R. "The Nonparametric Approach to Demand Analysis." *Econometrica* 50 (1982), 945-973.

[265] Varian, H.R. "Nonparametric Tests of Consumer Behavior." *Review of Economic Studies* 50 (1983), 99-110.

[266] Vartia, Y.O. "Relative Changes and Economic Indices." Licensiate Thesis in Statistics, University of Helsinki (1974).

[267] Walsh, C.E. "In Defense of Base Drift." *American Economic Review* 76 (1986), 692-700.

[268] Wasserfallen, W. "Non-Stationarities in Macro-Economic Time Series — Further Evidence and Implications." *Canadian Journal of Economics* 15 (1986), 498-510.

[269] Wilcox, D.W. "The Construction of U.S. Consumption Data: Some Facts and Their Implications for Empirical Work." *American Economic Review* 82 (1992), 922-941.

[270] Wolf, A., B. Swift, J. Swinney, and J. Vastano. "Determining Lyapunov Exponents from a Time Series." *Physica D* 16 (1985), 285-317.

[271] Zellner, A. "An Efficient Method of Estimating Seemingly Unrelated Regressions and Tests for Aggregation Bias." *Journal of the American Statistical Association* 57 (1962), 348-368.

[272] Zivot, E. and D.W.K. Andrews. "Further Evidence on the Great Crash, the Oil Price Shock, and the Unit Root Hypothesis." *Journal of Business and Economic Statistics* 10 (1992), 251-270.

Subject Index

adding-up, 177
ADF test, 75, 258
aggregation theory, 18
aggregator functions, 14, 171, 191
    homothetic, 224
    specifications, 171
Akaike Information Criterion (AIC), 33
Allen elasticities of substitution, 177, 179, 204, 219, 266, 294
Almost Ideal Demand System (AIDS), 248, 251
Asymptotically Ideal Model (AIM), 226, 250, 254, 255, 285

Bank of Canada, 159
basic translog (BTL), 190, 250
Bayesian Information Criterion (BIC), 127, 138, 140
benchmark asset, 29
benchmark rate, 150, 160
breaking trend functions, 119
budgeting, 13
business cycle myths, 48
business cycles, 47

Canada Savings Bonds, 155
causality, 61, 71
    F-test, 61
    Granger-Sims test, 62, 70
    money and income, 66
    statistical issues, 62
    VARMA models, 71
CE index, 20
chaos, 120
chaos tests, 135
    Barnett *et al.*, 124
    empirical results, 127, 142, 143

GARCH (1,1) model, 128
Gencay and Dechert, 125
LENNS program, 126
Nychka *et al.*, 125
Wolf *et al.*, 125
chaotic dynamics, 124
Cholesky factorization, 288
Cobb-Douglas function, 15, 278
cointegration tests, 78
commercial paper rate, 50
confidence intervals, 295
Consistency Condition, 224
Constant Elasticity of Substitution (CES), 278
Consumer Price Index, 50, 159
consumption goods, 149, 169, 191, 215
Credit Unions and Caisses Populaires, 155
cross-price elasticities, 154, 163, 219, 238
curvature, 160, 288

Davidson-Fletcher-Powell algorithm, 215
decentralization, 13
definition of money, 6
demand systems, 37, 190, 248
    Almost Ideal Demand System (AIDS), 248, 251
    Asymptotically Ideal Model (AIM), 255, 285
    basic translog (BTL), 190, 250
    budget share equations, 234
    dynamic adjustment, 209
    dynamic specification, 209, 213
    econometric considerations, 177
    estimation and testing, 233
    Fourier, 226, 232, 254, 284

Full Laurent, 252
functional-form tests, 196
General Exponential Form (GEF),
    249, 253
generalized Barnett, 182
generalized Leontief (GL), 248,
    250
generalized translog (GTL),
    190
homothetic translog (HTL),
    152, 177, 190, 213
linear translog (LTL), 152, 190
minflex Laurent generalized
    Leontief, 192, 205, 226,
    232
minflex Laurent translog, 192,
    205, 226, 232
Quadratic Almost Ideal De-
    mand System (QUAIDS),
    249, 253
quasi-homothetic translog, 160
regularity tests, 196
separability tests, 240
stochastic specification, 153
demand-systems approach, 168
Dickey-Fuller unit root tests, 58
difference-stationary (DS) processes,
    58
distance function, 39
Divisia index, 17, 39, 50, 60, 74,
    133, 185, 241, 256
Divisia second moments, 41
dominant Lyapunov exponent, 125,
    138
duality, 174, 209
durable goods, 215
dynamic adjustment, 209, 214
dynamic demand systems
    autoregressive, 216
    budget share equations, 234
    dynamic GTL, 233
    estimation and testing, 233

Fourier, 226, 232
    minflex Laurent generalized
        Leontief, 226, 232
    minflex Laurent translog, 226,
        232
    partial adjustment, 216
    separability tests, 240
dynamic programming, 101
dynamic specification, 209

elasticities, 154, 200
    Allen elasticities of substitu-
        tion, 177, 179, 204, 219
    cross-price, 154, 163
    income, 154, 163
    Morishima elasticities of sub-
        stitution, 266
    own-price, 154, 163
elasticities of substitution, 162, 294
    Allen, 177, 179, 219
    Allen
    confidence intervals, 295
    Morishima, 266
Engel curves, 40, 196
expenditure elasticities, 163

F-test, 61
factor reversal test, 211
Federal Reserve Economic Database
    (FRED), 74, 103, 134
FIML estimator, 160, 195
Fisher Ideal index, 17, 61
Fisher's factor reversal test, 18
Fisher's system of tests, 17
flexible functional forms, 28, 190,
    226, 239, 250, 278, 296
    Almost Ideal Demand System
        (AIDS), 248, 251
    Asymptotically Ideal Model
        (AIM), 255, 285
    basic translog (BTL), 250
    dynamic GTL, 233

Fourier, 31, 226, 232, 254, 279
Full Laurent, 252
General Exponential Form (GEF), 249, 253
generalized Leontief, 28, 248, 250
generalized translog (GTL), 190
homothetic translog (HTL), 190, 213
linear translog (LTL), 190
minflex Laurent generalized Leontief, 31, 192, 205, 226, 232
minflex Laurent translog, 31, 192, 205, 226, 232
Quadratic Almost Ideal Demand System (QUAIDS), 249, 253
regularity tests, 196, 288
translog, 15, 28, 182, 248
Fourier demand system, 31, 250, 254, 284
Fourier series expansion, 232, 283
FPE-lag structure, 67
free parameters, 218
full income, 212
Full Laurent Model, 252
functional forms, 192
    Almost Ideal Demand System (AIDS), 248, 251
    Asymptotically Ideal Model (AIM), 255, 285
    basic translog (BTL), 190, 250
    Cobb-Douglas, 15, 278
    Constant Elasticity of Substitution (CES), 278
    dynamic GTL, 233
    Fourier, 226, 232, 254, 279
    Full Laurent, 252
    General Exponential Form (GEF), 249, 253

    generalized Leontief, 248, 250
    generalized translog (GTL), 190
    homothetic translog (HTL), 190, 213
    linear translog (LTL), 190
    minflex Laurent generalized Leontief, 192, 205, 226, 232
    minflex Laurent translog, 192, 205, 226, 232
    Quadratic Almost Ideal Demand System (QUAIDS), 249, 253
    regularity tests, 196
    translog, 182, 248
functional-form tests, 196

GARCH (1,1) model, 128, 139
General Exponential Form (GEF), 249, 253
Generalized Axiom of Revealed Preference (GARP), 255
generalized Barnett model, 182
generalized Gorman polar form, 151
generalized Leontief, 28, 248, 250
generalized translog (GTL), 190
global approximations, 249
    Asymptotically Ideal Model (AIM), 250
    Fourier, 250
global curvature, 296
globally flexible functional forms, 254
    Asymptotically Ideal Model (AIM), 255, 285
    curvature, 288
    econometric results, 257
    forecast results, 272
    Fourier, 254, 279
    monotonicity, 288

Morishima elasticities of sub-
        stitution, 266
    regularity tests, 288
globally regular functional forms,
        252
    econometric results, 257
    forecast results, 272
    Full Laurent, 252
    General Exponential Form (GEF),
        253
    Morishima elasticities of sub-
        stitution, 266
    Quadratic Almost Ideal De-
        mand System (QUAIDS),
        253
Gorman polar forms, 151
Granger causality, 70
Granger-Sims test, 62

habit formation, 230
Hicksian aggregation, 11
homothetic translog (HTL), 177,
        190, 213
homothetic utility functions, 185
homotheticity, 166
HP filter, 49

implicit interest rate, 194
imposing curvature restrictions, 291
income elasticities, 154
income normalized prices, 284
index number theory, 16, 18, 148
indirect aggregator function, 27
indirect utility function, 193
    basic translog (BTL), 190
    dynamic, 231
    Fourier, 283
    generalized translog (GTL),
        190
    homothetic translog (HTL),
        190
    linear translog (LTL), 190

translog, 30
inflation, 97
integrability conditions, 160
intertemporal optimization, 13, 37

Jacobian matrix, 127

KPSS tests, 77

Lagrange multiplier, 231
Lagrange multiplier test, 260
Laspeyres index, 16
Laurent series expansion, 31, 192,
        232
leisure time, 149, 169, 191
LENNS program, 126
likelihood-ratio test, 162, 239
linear translog (LTL), 190
liquid assets, 227
logistic distribution, 127
long-horizon regressions, 105
long-run derivative, 105
long-run neutrality, 72
luxury goods, 163
Lyapunov exponent, 125, 135

Malmquist index, 39
marginal rate of substitution, 25
Marshallian demand functions, 150,
        212
maximum-likelihood estimates, 177
minflex Laurent generalized Leon-
        tief, 31, 205, 226
minflex Laurent translog, 31, 205,
        226
missing money puzzle, 42
monetary aggregation, 16, 97
    CE index, 20
    Divisia index, 39, 60, 74, 133,
        256
    Divisia second moments, 41
    Divisiaindex, 17
    Fisher Ideal index, 17, 61

MQ index, 19
simple-sum index, 7
user cost, 133
monetary subaggregates, 239
money demand function, 99
double-log, 100
semi-log, 100
money, prices, and income, 66
monotonicity, 160, 288
Morishima complements, 295
Morishima substitutes, 266
MQ index, 19
multistage optimization framework,
168, 212
multivariate logistic distribution,
195
Müntz-Szatz series expansion, 226

near-bank liabilities, 155
near-monies, 173, 185
neoclassical consumer problem, 14
nested like assets, 168, 174
neural network models, 127, 135
neutrality of money
long-run, 72
neutrality tests, 78, 83–85
superneutrality tests, 72, 86–
93
new goods problem, 176, 215
nominal stylized facts, 47
commercial paper rate, 50
consumer price index, 50
Divisia aggregates, 50
HP filter, 49
simple-sum aggregates, 50
Treasury bill rate, 50
nondurable goods, 215
nonlinear functions, 16, 43
nonlinear optimization, 287
NONPAR procedure, 27, 255
normal goods, 163
normalized prices, 213

own-price elasticities, 154, 163, 219,
238

Paasche price index, 16
partial adjustment model, 205, 214
positivity, 160, 288
prediction, 121
preference structure, 170
price aggregation, 13

Quadratic Almost Ideal Demand
System (QUAIDS), 249,
253
quasi-homothetic separability, 182
quasi-homothetic translog, 160
quasi-homotheticity, 166
Quebec Savings Banks, 155

random walks, 119
rational expectations, 37
recursive multistage decentralization, 172
regularity conditions
curvature, 160, 288
monotonicity, 160, 288
positivity, 160, 288
regularity tests, 196, 288
rental prices, 12
risk aversion, 38
Roy's Identity, 29, 175, 212, 233

semi-nonparametric functions, 249,
279
Asymptotically Ideal Model
(AIM), 250, 285
computational considerations,
287
curvature, 288
econometric results, 257
forecast results, 272
Fourier, 250, 279
monotonicity, 288
Morishima elasticities, 266

regularity tests, 288
separability, 209
separability tests, 182, 210, 240
series expansions
    Fourier, 232
    Laurent, 232
    Taylor, 232
services of monetary assets, 149
Sidrauski model, 102
simple-sum index, 7, 50
Slutsky equation, 175, 238
Slutsky matrix, 288
St. Louis Equation, 33
stationarity-inducing transformations, 53
statistical indices
    and Fisher's system of tests, 17
    CE, 20
    Divisia, 17, 39
    Fisher Ideal, 17
    Laspeyres, 16
    Malmquist, 39
    MQ, 19
    Paasche, 16
    superlative, 173
statistical issues, 62
Stone index approximation, 252
substitutability, 147
subutility functions, 229
superlative indices, 173
superneutrality, 72
supernumerary quantities, 182

Taylor series expansion, 31, 192, 232
translog, 28
translog demand systems, 190
    basic translog (BTL), 190
    econometric results, 194
    functional-form tests, 196

generalized translog (GTL), 190
homothetic translog (HTL), 152, 190, 213
linear translog (LTL), 190
regularity tests, 196
translog flexible functional forms, 15, 30, 182, 189, 248
Treasury bill rate, 50
trend-stationary (TS) processes, 58
Trust and Mortgage Loan (TMLs) Companies, 155
two-stage budgeting, 172, 212
two-stage optimization, 13, 148, 149, 169, 191

uncertainty, 37
unit root tests, 104
    ADF, 75, 104, 258
    KPSS, 77
    Perron, 121, 258
    weighted symmetric (WS), 104
    Zivot and Andrews, 122
user cost, 12, 29, 60, 74, 133
utility tree, 174, 227, 230

VARMA models, 71

wage rate, 215
weak factor reversal test, 159
weak homothetic separability, 182
weak separability, 13, 25, 40, 150, 167, 209, 210, 239
welfare cost of inflation, 98, 102, 103, 108, 109
    and income taxation, 103
    compensating variation approach, 101
    consumer surplus approach, 100
    empirical evidence, 107
    money demand function, 99
    Sidrauski model, 102

Author Index

Akaike, H., 33
Alston, J., 252
Anderson, G.J., 37, 185, 205, 209, 214
Anderson, R.G., 73, 74, 103, 131, 132, 134, 196, 295
Anderson, R.W., 151
Andrews, D.W.K., 106, 107, 114, 120–124
Atrostic, B.K., 192
Attfield, C.L.F., 256, 258
Avriel, M., 291

Backus, D.K., 48, 53
Bailey, M.J., 98, 100
Banks, J., 249, 252, 253
Barnett, W.A., 12, 19, 20, 30, 31, 33, 38, 39, 41, 48, 50, 73, 74, 93, 99, 103, 121, 124, 131–134, 141, 148, 159, 165–169, 171, 172, 182, 185, 190, 192, 205, 208–212, 224, 226–228, 232, 239–241, 249, 252, 253, 255, 279, 281, 285, 287, 288, 292, 296
Barten, A.P., 153, 177, 195, 215, 234, 257
Baxter, M., 53, 54
Belongia, M.T., 33, 48, 50
Berndt, E.R., 153, 177, 182, 195
Blackorby, C., 175, 182, 212, 266
Blundell, R.W., 37, 185, 196, 205, 209, 214, 249, 252, 253
Box, G.E.P., 128, 139
Boyer, M., 231
Brock, W.A., 101, 124, 125, 135
Brunner, K., 12
Burguete, J.R., 287

Burns, A., 47
Buse, A., 252

Cagan, P., 33, 98
Campbell, J., 255
Caves, D., 249, 250
Chadha, B., 48, 53
Chalfant, J.A., 33, 254
Chen, P., 124, 131, 132, 141
Chetty, V.K., 190, 208, 227, 239, 278
Choi, S., 182, 185, 224, 239, 240
Chow, G.C., 214
Christensen, L.R., 28, 149, 182, 196, 233, 249, 250, 260
Christiano, L.J., 33, 120–122
Cockerline, J., 155
Cogley, T., 53
Cooley, T.F., 48, 53
Cooper, R.J., 249, 252–254

Dechert, W.D., 124, 125, 127
DeCoster, G.P., 124, 131
Denny, M., 169, 182, 210, 224, 239
Diamantopoulos, A., 272
Dickey, D.A., 75, 104, 120, 258
Diewert, W.E., 18, 28, 39, 74, 131, 133, 148, 168, 172, 176, 190, 211, 250, 256, 291
Donovan, D.J., 19, 168, 190, 208
Drake, L.M., 279
Driscoll, J.C., 20, 74, 131, 133

Eastwood, B.J., 284
Eckmann, J.P., 125
Ellner, S., 120, 121, 124–129, 132, 135–138, 140
Engle, R.F., 54, 78, 104, 256

Ewis, N.A., 168, 190, 194, 205, 208, 226, 241

Farr, H.T., 176, 234
Fayyad, S.K., 234
Feige, E.L., 147, 189
Fiorito, R., 49
Fisher, D., 33, 35, 48, 74, 93, 119, 121, 168, 190, 194, 205, 208, 226, 241, 279, 281
Fisher, I., 16, 43, 159, 211
Fisher, M., 72, 75, 99, 105, 106, 114
Fisher, T., 182
Fleissig, A.R., 93, 254–256, 279
Foster, K.A., 252
Frank, M.Z., 124
Friedman, B.M., 50, 119
Friedman, M., 3, 7, 9, 33, 100
Fuller, W.A., 75, 104, 120, 258
Fuss, M., 169, 182, 210, 224, 239

Gallant, A.R., 31, 35, 120, 121, 124–129, 132, 135–138, 140, 141, 192, 226, 241, 254, 279, 283, 284, 287, 291, 295, 296
Gavin, W.T., 48
Gencay, R., 125, 127
Geweke, J., 279
Goldfeld, S.M., 4, 29, 42, 214
Golub, G.H., 287, 291, 295, 296
Gonzalez-Farias, G., 75, 104, 258
Goodfriend, M., 88, 103
Gordon, R.J., 214
Gorman, W.M., 13, 40, 149, 151, 168, 191, 212, 240
Gould, J., 120
Granger, C.W.J., 54, 78, 104, 256
Green, R., 201, 252
Guilkey, D., 249, 251

Hahn, W., 201

Hall, A.R., 255, 256
Hall, T.E., 48, 119
Hancock, D., 41, 182
Haraf, W.S., 120
Hicks, J.R., 11
Hinich, M.J., 41, 124, 141
Hsieh, D.A., 124, 127
Huber, P.J., 284

Jensen, M.J., 141
Johnson, D., 176, 234
Jonas, A., 205, 226, 241, 255, 279
Jones, B.E., 73, 74, 103, 131, 132, 134
Jorgenson, D.W., 28, 149, 196, 233, 250, 260
Judd, J.P., 3, 4, 119
Jungeilges, J.A., 141

Kaplan, D.T., 141
Kastens, T., 254
Kehoe, P.J., 48, 53
Kifer, Y., 125
King, R.G., 53, 54, 72, 73, 75, 78, 79, 83, 85, 91
Kohler, D.F., 185
Kollintzas, T., 49
Koopmans, T., 47
Koustas, Z., 54, 72, 103
Kydland, F.E., 47, 48, 50, 53, 54

Lau, L.J., 28, 149, 196, 233, 239, 250, 260, 288
LeBaron, B., 124
Lee, Y.W., 30, 31, 190, 192, 226, 232, 241, 249, 252, 279
Leontief, W.W., 13
Lewbel, A., 249, 252, 253, 257
Ljung, G.M., 128, 139
Lovell, C., 249, 251
Lucas, R.E., Jr., 47, 72, 98–104, 108

MacKinnon, J.G., 75, 79, 80, 104, 258
Mankiw, N.G., 48, 255
Marty, A.L., 114
Mathews, B.P., 272
McCaffrey, D.F., 120, 121, 124–129, 132, 135–138, 140
McCallum, B.T., 103
McElroy, M.B., 257
McLaren, K.R., 249, 252–254
Meltzer, A.H., 12
Mitchell, W.C., 47, 124, 131
Motley, B., 119
Murray, J., 155
Muscatelli, V.A., 99

Nadiri, I.I., 214
Nason, J.M., 53
Nelson, C.R., 120, 121, 128
Nesmith, T.D., 73, 74, 103, 131, 132, 134
Newbold, P., 104
Newey, W.K., 107
Ng, S., 256, 258
Niehans, J., 5
Nissen, D., 175, 212
Noble, N.R., 119
Nychka, D.W., 120, 121, 124–129, 132, 135–138, 140

Offenbacher, E.K., 33, 50, 165, 167, 168, 171, 190, 194, 279
Ohanian, L.E., 48, 53

Pantula, S.G., 75, 104, 258
Pashardes, P., 252
Pasupathy, M., 292, 296
Patinkin, D., 11
Pearce, D.K., 147, 189
Perron, P., 104, 120–122, 258
Phillips, P.C.B., 76, 77, 104, 258
Plosser, C.I., 120, 121, 128
Pollak, R.A., 192, 233, 257

Poterba, J.M., 20, 74, 131, 133
Prasad, E., 48, 53
Prescott, E.C., 47–50, 53, 54, 107
Primont, D., 175, 212

Ramsey, J.B., 124, 132
Rebelo, S.T., 53
Robb, A.L., 168, 190, 208
Rocke, D., 201
Roper, D., 19
Rosen, S., 214
Rotemberg, J.J., 20, 74, 99, 103, 131, 133, 134
Rothman, P., 124, 132
Ruelle, D., 125
Russell, R.R., 175, 212, 266

Santoni, G.J., 119
Savin, E., 153, 177, 195
Sayers, C.L., 124, 125, 132, 135
Scadding, J., 3, 4
Scheinkman, J.A., 124
Schmidt, P., 76, 77
Schwartz, A.J., 7, 9
Schwartz, G., 127, 138
Schworm, W., 182
Seater, J.J., 72, 75, 99, 105, 106, 114, 255, 256
Serletis, A., 33, 37, 41, 48, 54, 72, 74, 93, 98, 99, 103, 119, 121, 132, 141, 168, 169, 182, 183, 190, 204, 208–210, 215, 224, 225, 227, 228, 279, 281, 294
Shin, Y., 76, 77
Sickles, C., 249, 251
Sidrauski, M., 101, 108
Slesnick, D.T., 256
Smith, R.T., 48
Sono, M., 13
Souza, G., 287
Spindt, P.A., 19, 33, 50, 165, 167, 171

Spinelli, F., 99
Stengos, T., 124
Stock, J.H., 258
Stoker, T.M., 257
Strotz, R.H., 13, 149, 168, 191, 212, 240
Swift, B., 125, 135
Swinney, J., 125, 135
Swofford, J.L., 93, 279

Tatom, J.A., 119
Taylor, H., 119
Terrell, D., 254
Thornton, D.L., 47, 48, 121, 214
Thursby, J.G., 295
Tobin, J., 5
Toers, A.L., 201
Turnovsky, S., 19

U.S. Department of Commerce, 215
Uzawa, H., 278

Varian, H.R., 26, 30, 281
Vastano, J., 125, 135

Wales, T.J., 190, 192, 233, 257
Walsh, C.E., 120
Watson, M.W., 72, 73, 75, 78, 79, 83, 85, 91, 258
Weber, W.E., 41
West, K.D., 107
White, H., 127, 138
Whitney, G., 93
Wilcox, D.W., 256
Wolf, A., 125, 135
Wolfe, M.D., 31, 190, 192, 241, 249, 252, 279

Yavari, K., 98, 99
Yue, P., 47, 48, 121, 226, 241, 255, 279, 285, 287

Zang, I., 291
Zellner, A., 287
Zivot, E., 120–124